Field Manual for

Christian
Apologetics

Dr. John M. Oakes

Field Manual for Christian Apologetics

ipi

Field Manual for Christian Apologetics

© 2011 by Dr. John M. Oakes and Illumination Publishers

All rights are reserved. No part of this book may be duplicated, copied, translated, reproduced or stored mechanically, digitally, or electronically without specific, written permission of the author and publisher.

Printed in the United States of America

ISBN: 978-0-9817373-1-7

Unless otherwise indicated, all Scripture references are from the Holy Bible, New International Version, copyright 1973, 1978, 1984 by the International Bible Society. Used by permission of Zondervan Bible Publishers.

Cover and Book design: Toney C. Mulhollan

John M. Oakes is a professor of chemistry at Grossmont College. John became a Christian while attending graduate school in 1978. John earned a Ph.D. in chemical physics in 1984 from the University of Colorado. That same year he married his wife Jan. They have three children and reside in San Diego, California. John also serves as president of the Apologetics Research Society. His other books include: *Is There A God?*, *From Shadow to Reality*, *Reasons for Belief*, *Daniel: Prophet to the Nations* and *That You May Believe*.

Illumination Publishers International
www.ipibooks.com
6010 Pinecreek Ridge Court
Spring, Texas 77379-2513

Dedication

I would like to dedicate this handbook to my friend of thirty years, Foster Stanback. Without his vision and support the web site www.Evidenceforchristianity.org would not exist and the questions and answers included in this volume would not have been written. Thank you so much Foster for your love, encouragement, friendship, support and partnership in our common passion, which is helping to build up people's faith in Jesus Christ and in the Word of God.

—John Oakes

Table of Contents

Chapter One
Reliability of the Biblical Text • 11

Chapter Two
Archaeology, History and the Bible • 69

Chapter Three
Supposed Inconsistencies in the Bible • 95

Chapter Four
The Resurrection of Jesus • 129

Chapter Five
Biblical Prophecy • 139

Chapter Six
The Book of Daniel • 159

Chapter Seven
Science and the Bible • 173

Chapter Eight
Evolution • 215

Table of Contents

Chapter Nine
The Genesis Flood • 225

Chapter Ten
Miracles • 235

Chapter Eleven
The Relationship between Christianity and Other Religions • 241

Chapter Twelve
General Apologetics • 297

Chapter Thirteen
Philosophical/Theological Questions • 311

Chapter Fourteen
The Da Vinci Code and Related Topics • 325

Chapter Fifteen
The History of Christianity • 333

Chapter Sixteen
General Biblical Questions • 351

Introduction

Always be prepared to give an answer. This could be called a biblical rallying cry—a motto of the Christian apologist—and it's found in 1 Peter 3:15-16:

> *"Always be prepared to give an answer to everyone who asks you to give the reason for the hope that you have. But do this with gentleness and respect, keeping a clear conscience, so that those who speak maliciously against your good behavior in Christ may be ashamed of their slander."*

The context of this passage is found in 1 Peter. The book was written to people who were experiencing persecution and suffering for doing good. Those who followed Jesus were being admonished to be prepared to give an answer to the questions which the world was throwing at them (and I would add, to the questions they threw at themselves). Not just any answer would do. God's people, both then and now, are admonished to give respectful, reasoned answers so that they can maintain a clear conscience before God and their hearers; and, ultimately, so their hearers can come into a saved relationship with God. According to *Webster's Dictionary*, apologetics is "the branch of theology which defends Christian doctrine on the grounds of reason." The passage above is a call for followers of Jesus to be apologists. This book is intended to help believers toward that goal.

I became a Christian more than 30 years ago while a graduate student in chemical physics at the University of Colorado. Because of a personal inclination, and also because of a natural tendency for scientists to be viewed that way, I became sort of an "answer man" for young believers around me almost from the beginning. At about the same time, I was inspired to pursue Christian apologetics by the work of one of my heroes, John Clayton. About 15 years later, I began work on my first book, *Is There a God?* When I was asked to run a Christian apologetics website in 1999, one of the first things I began to do was to accept questions from visitors to the site and provide them with answers. The questions and answers included in this book are culled from the hundreds which have come to the site **www.EvidenceForChristianity.org** in the past several years as well as ones that have been addressed directly to me. Some of these questions come from skeptics, others from believers who have nagging doubts. In each case, I have tried to look at all sides of these questions. I certainly am not providing "the only answer." Sometimes I give what I believe is the correct answer; but sometimes I provide food for thought and leave it up to the reader to inquire and search for more data. In editing the questions for this book, I have tried to retain the feel of the immediacy of the original question and answer, mainly correcting grammar and incorrect statements.

I have used the title *Field Manual for Christian Apologetics* because this book covers such a broad area of apologetic topics and it will hopefully serve as a useful tool for believers who want to engage their own doubts and provide answers to a culture that is inquiring about God.

John Oakes, PhD
San Diego, June 2011

Note:
In the answers throughout the text, my book *Reasons for Belief: A Handbook of Christian Evidences* is abbreviated as **RFB**; the book *Is There A God? Questions of Science and the Bible* as **ITAG**; *Daniel, Prophet to the Nations* as **Daniel**; and *From Shadow to Reality* as **FSTR**. My website, *www.EvidenceForChristianity.org* is referred to as **EFC**.

Also note that all quoted biblical scripture will be in italic.

Chapter One

Reliability of the Biblical Text

QUESTION:
 I have increasingly heard the argument that many of the sayings of Jesus (the Lord's Prayer, for example) had already been recorded in earlier writings by other people. Those who make this argument suggest that Jesus simply borrowed them. Is this true?

ANSWER:
 In order to answer this question thoroughly, I would need specific examples. Without any specifics, let me at least take a stab at the question in general. There will always be those who see it as their personal mission to try to undermine belief in Jesus as the Son of God. People try to claim that he sinned. The problem is that there is no record of him sinning. People try to claim that the apostles made up the stories of Jesus' miracles. The problem with arguments like these is that there is no evidence to support the claim that he did not work miracles, but plenty that he did (see **EFC** ch. 2). When theologians run out of possible attacks on the deity of Jesus, it is not surprising that they try to attack him by claiming that nothing he said was original, and that he was simply echoing those who came before him.
 I am sure that a few of the things which Jesus said had already been said by someone before him. Jesus is famous for saying *"It is more blessed to give than to receive"* (Acts 20:35). Surely, Jesus was

not the first to notice this proverbial truth, nor the first to teach it to his followers. Another truism used by Jesus, but surely not original to him is *"A man reaps what he sows"* (Galatians 6:7). Besides, Jesus often consciously quoted from the Old Testament. It is likely that Jesus also used well-known sayings of the Jews of his day to illustrate his teachings, and perhaps the proverbs of neighboring Greek and Persian culture in his teaching as well. If historians of other cultures find such parallels in the sayings of Jesus and those who came before him, that alone will do nothing to discredit either the teachings of Jesus or the veracity of the New Testament writers. However, there are definitely many sayings of Jesus which will prove to be unique: For example: *"Can any of you prove me guilty of sin?"* (John 8:46), or *"I and the Father are one"* (John 10:30) and *"I am the way, the truth and the life. No one comes to the Father except through me"* (John 14:6). The fact that a careful researcher can scan ancient documents and find statements which are somewhat similar to things said by Jesus does not mean that he stole his sayings, and it certainly does not prove that he is not the Son of God. The question is not whether Jesus ever (quoted a previous person without giving credit. The question is whether he was who he claimed he was. If Jesus is *"The Resurrection and the Life"* (John 11:25), what difference would it make if some of his sayings had been said by someone else before him? This attack on Jesus is a smoke-screen, plain and simple.

As to whether or not the Lord's Prayer was a quote by Jesus, verbatim from someone before him, I would have to say that I am very skeptical of this claim, unless someone could show me evidence. My guess is that someone found one particular phrase in the Lord's Prayer recorded elsewhere, rather than the entire prayer. However, even if it were partially true, it does not take away from the fact that Jesus is the Son of God, the Resurrection and the Life, the Bread of Life, the Way, the Truth and the Life and so forth. He proved his right to make these claims by doing things such as raising Lazarus from the dead, feeding the five thousand and calming a great storm (see **RFB** ch. 1). Even if it were true that some famous sayings of Jesus were actually quotes from others before him, I fail to see why this would detract from his deity.

QUESTION:

Everyone knows the story of Noah and his ark. The Epic of Gilgamesh is the one of the earliest written stories ever discovered. This epic describes how Gilgamesh took two of each animal plus his family into an ark to avoid a worldwide flood sent by the angry gods.

The story was written down between the years of 2750 and 2500 BC. It was most likely passed by word of mouth before it was written. My question is this: Is the story of Noah a stolen or borrowed myth?

ANSWER:

In the end, it will be difficult to prove the case either way. It seems undeniable that the Genesis account and the Gilgamesh Epic are similar. Details in both accounts such as the Noah figure sending out birds to know when it would be safe to leave the ark point to this. The question is who borrowed from whom, or are they separate accounts of one actual event? What we should do is ask, "What is the most reasonable explanation?" When I read the Gilgamesh Epic's version of the flood, I detect obvious elements of mythology, but not so with the Genesis account. Based on the massive (and I believe incontrovertible) evidence that the Bible is the inspired word of God, I believe that the flood actually happened and that the story recorded in Genesis is an accurate account of the events surrounding the flood. The fact is that almost every ancient civilization had a story of a great catastrophic flood. In fact, the stories are so widespread and general, it creates the impression that these accounts are the cultural records of some sort of actual event in the distant past. If this is true, there are two possibilities: Either the Epic of Gilgamesh borrows from the same genuine record as the writer of Genesis, or it is a separate but garbled mythologized account by the Sumerians/Akkadians of the actual events. I believe the second choice is more likely the correct one.

One might argue that this is circular reasoning. The skeptic might point out that I am assuming that the Bible is the inspired word of God in order to prove that it is the inspired word of God. That is not the case. I am simply pointing out that the evidence for the Bible being a reliable account of past history is overwhelming if one compares it to myths such as the Gilgamesh Epic. This known reliability predisposes me to believing the biblical account is closer to the actual events. Many scholars have analyzed both stories in attempts to prove which might have been derived from the other. I believe the case is inconclusive and one must reach their own conclusions. However, given the solid evidence that the Bible is inspired by God, and given the fact that there is no reason at all to believe that the Gilgamesh Epic is inspired by any type of god at all, I would go with the biblical account. You, of course, must reach your own conclusions.

QUESTION:
What are the Dead Sea Scrolls and why are they important?

ANSWER:
The Dead Sea Scrolls are a collection of a large number of manuscripts which were found in a series of caves in the general area around the ruins of the desert community of Qumran. Qumran was a settlement in the steep and arid hills at the northwest end of the Dead Sea. Although there is some argument from scholars, most believe that Qumran was a community of Essenes, an ascetic sect of Jews who were waiting for the Messiah and who had rejected the priesthood in Jerusalem. It has been proposed that, due to the upheavals at the time of the destruction of Jerusalem in AD 70, these manuscripts were carried to a number of caves in the general area of Qumran so that they would not be destroyed, and they were eventually abandoned there.

The Dead Sea documents include a number of complete scrolls on vellum, as well as many fragments and even some manuscripts on copper and other materials. They contain many of the writings of the Essenes and other Jewish sects, including a number of apocalyptic and theological treatises. Most significantly for Christians, the scrolls include a number of fragments and even some complete scrolls of Old Testament books. This is particularly significant to the case for the accuracy of the current Hebrew text because, before the discovery of the Dead Sea Scrolls, the oldest known manuscript of the Old Testament in Hebrew was the Cairo Codex of AD 895. The oldest complete manuscript in Hebrew was the Leningrad Codex from the eleventh century.

The Dead Sea Scrolls have been dated by experts from about 250 BC to around AD 50. This discovery moved the oldest manuscripts of the Old Testament back over one thousand years, spanning as much as two-thirds of the time from when some of the books were written and the oldest previously available manuscript. So why is this so important? In general, the Dead Sea Scrolls are very similar to the Masoretic Text, which is the oldest previously available text. This version of the Jewish Bible was assembled by the Masoretes, a group of dedicated Hebrew scholars in the second half of the first millennium. In most cases in which the Dead Sea manuscripts differ from the Masoretic Text, they bear similarity to the Septuagint, a Greek translation of the Old Testament which was completed in the third and second centuries BC.

The significance of the Dead Sea Scrolls is that they provide strong support for the belief that our present text of the Hebrew Old Testament is very similar to the original writings. The text of the Old Testament had been copied again and again over the centuries, and scribes inevitably make copying errors. We find such minor changes from the time of the Dead Sea Scrolls to the Masoretic Text one thousand years later, but the changes are quite minor. It is also possible for those copying the manuscripts to make changes on purpose, but we see very little evidence for this. The Dead Sea Scrolls demonstrate what we thought we knew already, which is that the Jews were fanatically careful in their work of preserving the Jewish Bible, giving us even greater confidence that we have available to us the very words of God. (For further study, see **EFC** ch. 6).

QUESTION:

Are segments of the Old Testament plagiarized from the Zoroastrian scriptures?

ANSWER:

Quite simply, no! Many unsubstantiated theories are thrown about by scholars, looking for a controversial idea on which to build their reputation. This is one of these attractive but unfounded ideas. Zoroastrianism is a pseudo-monotheistic religion which includes fire worship. Its theology is in fact dualistic. This means that it is based on a belief that the universe is in a battle between more or less equal forces of good and evil. The *Zend Avesta* is the principle scripture of Zoroastrianism. The religion was founded by Zarathustra in present-day Persia. Zarathustra was probably a real person who lived in about the seventh century BC. The traditional dates for Zarathustra (Greek: Zoroaster) are 628-551 BC. The *Zend Avesta* is supposed to be the philosophy and sayings of Zarathustra, although parts of the document may derive from earlier writings, and some was written as late as the first century BC. The Gathas are part of the Avesta. These are poems supposedly composed by Zarathustra. The history of the text of the *Zend Avesta* is difficult to follow, as the scriptures of Zoroastrianism were collected gradually over many centuries, taking its final form under Sassanid emperor Shapur II (AD 309-379).

There are a few problems with the theory that Judaism is derived from Zoroastriansim. First, the theology of the two religions is in diametric opposition. Judaism is avowedly non-dualistic in its concept of God. Second, Judaism's roots go back farther than Zoroastrianism. Most of the Old Testament was written before Zoroaster lived. It is not logical to think that the Jews borrowed their theology and teachings from a person who was born after Moses, David, Solomon and Isaiah died. There is another important reason to reject the idea that the Old Testament writers plagiarized the writers of the Zend Avesta. I have looked at some of the so-called parallels in the teaching and find them not to be convincing. It is a simple matter to scan the entire scripture of two religions and to find ideas which are similar at face value. Finding parallel sayings or teachings does not prove one borrowed from the other. Logically, if anyone borrowed from anyone, Zarathustra borrowed from Moses. However, if we look at the history of Zoroastrianism, it is more likely that its theology was borrowed from nascent Hindu theology, not from the Jews. The parallels between early Hindu and Zoroastrian thought and language are obvious, as scholars have shown.

To summarize, the idea that Judaism derives its theology from Zoroastrianism is attractive for those who make it their goal to undermine Christianity. However, common sense, as well as the evidence, tells us that this is simply not the case.

QUESTION:

Who were the books of the New Testament written by and what was the relationship of these writers to Jesus?

ANSWER:

In some cases, it is hard to establish with certainty who wrote each individual book of the New Testament. Many of the letters of Paul were "signed" by him, making it fairly certain he was the author. But even this is not absolute proof. The early church fathers settled on a consensus of the authors for almost all the New Testament books by the second century. How authoritative these designations are is debatable, but given that we have this based on the testimony of people who were only a couple of generations removed from the original writers, their testimony is fairly strong. I would encourage you to do your own research on the arguments for the authorship of individual books. Most any commentary will supply the details. Below is a list of the traditionally accepted authors of the New Testament books:

Matthew	The apostle Matthew
Mark	John Mark, friend of Peter, companion of Paul on his first missionary journey
Luke	Luke, doctor, amateur historian and traveling companion with Paul

John	The apostle John
Acts	Luke, the author of Luke
Romans-Philemon	The apostle Paul
Hebrews	Unknown
James	James, the brother of Jesus
1, 2 Peter	The apostle Peter
1, 2, 3 John	The apostle John
Jude	Jude, the brother of Jesus
Revelation	The apostle John

The author of Hebrews is the most hotly debated. Even the early church debated the identity of the author of Hebrews. Bottom line, we do not know who wrote this book. You should be very skeptical of anyone who identifies the author of Hebrews with confidence. The authorship of 1, 2, 3 John, 2 Peter, Jude and, to some extent, Revelation are considered controversial by some. There is some debate on the authorship of the other books, but most conservative scholars accept that the author identified above is likely the actual writer of these books.

All the authors mentioned above knew Jesus personally, with the exception of Luke. The writer of Acts and Luke was a Gentile who came into contact with Christianity through the missionary work of Paul. Luke was a very careful historian who apparently interviewed eyewitnesses to the events.

To the believer, the most important question is not who wrote the book but whether it was inspired by God. For myself personally, I trust in the faithfulness of God and in his wisdom to use the consensus of the early church fathers to preserve his scriptures in a form which he approved, inspired, and preserved.

QUESTION:

I am presently taking a Comparative Religion course on the New Testament and have been struggling with some of the themes that have surfaced so far. Our course text is *The New Testament: A Historical Introduction to Early Christian Writings* by Bart Ehrman. This author argues that the Book of Acts presents varying accounts of the conversion of Paul. In chapter 9, Paul's companions heard a voice but saw no one, while in chapter 22, he claims that they saw the light but did not hear the voice. Ehrman also finds contradictions in whether the bystanders stood up (ch. 9) or fell down (ch. 26), or whether Paul got instructions from Ananias or Jesus directly, without going to Damascus. Ehrman also finds contradiction between Acts and Galatians with regard to Paul's meeting with the apostles in Jerusalem. He relies heavily on quoting out of context and in citing "scholarly opinion" which he doesn't bother to delineate. Unfortunately, my professor relies on similar tactics. I believe such "scholarly opinions" are very biased, but he raises questions I cannot adequately answer. In addition, my professor argues that the Pastoral Epistles, 1 and 2 Timothy and Titus are pseudonymous letters; in other words, that Paul did not write them. He even questions whether Paul wrote Ephesians, Colossians and 2 Thessalonians based on writing style, which seems dubious since we have only a limited sample of Paul's writings. What do you say about this debate? How certain can we be that Paul wrote these books? And what about the words of Jesus, which seem for sure inspired, versus narratives about the birth of Jesus. What basis do we have for assuming all of these are "breathed by God?" The argument that one writer calls another Bible writer inspired (2 Peter 3:15-16) seems weak to me. I want to be able to separate what I believe by faith from what I believe because of the evidence. Can you help me here?

ANSWER:

It sounds like you have a good handle on the specifics. Most of these supposed contradictions are very easily worked out if one simply considers how both accounts might be justified. For example, when Paul went to Jerusalem as described in Acts 9, he visited Peter and James, but not the other apostles, which explains Paul's statement that he did not meet with the apostles until fourteen years later. Similarly, the accounts of the vision on the road to Damascus do not contradict, but give complementary information. These supposed proofs that the Bible is full of mistakes fall on their face as soon as one gives reasonable benefit of the doubt to the Bible writers. I try to listen carefully to each criticism of the Bible, as I do not want to be a hypocrite when I critique the opponents of Christianity. However, each of the supposed contradictions you mentioned from Ehrman is explained quite easily by common sense.

Really, it is the big picture which is most important, and that is what you bring up in your interesting question. How do we really know every single word of the New (or for that matter, the Old) Testament is inspired? The answer is that it is obvious that we will never be able to prove (sufficient for a court of law) that every single word in the Bible is inspired by God. I can provide general evidence, for example, from prophecy fulfillment and from type/antitype fulfillment (see **FSTR**). I can make the logical argument that Jesus proved who he is by his miracles and his resurrection, which lends general credence to the inspiration of the gospels, and by implication to those whom he clearly chose as his spokesmen. However, when it comes down to the details, it is clear that I will not be able to prove, first of all, that Paul even wrote Philemon, and second, that verse seventeen of Philemon is inspired. How could one ever prove that Psalms 94, verse eight, is inspired? Anyone who expects such proof is making a logically unreasonable request. Those who are unwilling to accept that the Bible is inspired by God choose to ignore all the obvious evidence for inspiration, trying to find some little detail that we cannot explain. Believers will never be able to explain every possible question, but the critics miss the main point. What does the evidence tell us, on balance?

The quality and quantity of information we need to support faith in God's word is sufficient evidence to make convincing the general conclusion that the documents as a whole are inspired, or at least that the greater part of the documents show evidence of inspiration. We need evidence that certain specific passages and sections of the Bible have marks of inspiration. We certainly have that, and in abundance. My book *Reasons For Belief* lists literally hundreds of examples of marks of inspiration in the Bible.

Once one has a sufficient volume of supportive evidence, one can either consider moving into the realm of reasonable faith, in which the Bible is given the benefit of the doubt, or one can put oneself into an insoluble position of demanding proof that there is not one mistake—proof that every word, specifically, is inspired. This is, and always will be, beyond possibility, and it is foolish for anyone to move in that direction (although that is exactly what the skeptics do).

As a scientist, I am very skeptical of unfalsifiable claims. The claim that the Bible is full of mistakes is unfalsifiable. Believers will never be able to prove the critic's claims of biblical error as absolutely wrong. All the Bible critic has to do is keep moving around. Every time you show another supposed inconsistency or myth or historical error to not be a problem, they simply move along to the next one. Unfalsifiable claims are not useful for making reasonable arguments. What the critics need is something like the resurrection, except in reverse—a clear example supporting their claim; and the simple fact is that they do not have one. What any reasonable person must do is decide at what point it becomes reasonable to move into the category of beginning to give the Bible the benefit of the doubt. Personally, I reached that place a long time ago. I am guessing you have as well. Once one gets to this place, it is no longer necessary to answer every question raised by these people, at least not for the sake of your own faith.

So, at some point, I or anyone else can conclude that the basic case is made. I now assume that God's hand was behind the writing and the putting together of the Bible. It simply does not matter to me who wrote Hebrews. So what? Whether Paul or an apostle, or whether Timothy or someone else wrote it, it is in the Bible because God, by his will, influenced what ended up in the New Testament. How do I know that? I am confident for literally thousands of reasons. This is not blind faith at all. To use an analogy, I know from sufficient experience with the grapes in my yard that purple grapes are sweet and green grapes are sour. I have done enough experiments that, although I cannot absolutely state as fact that all green grapes are sour, I can say with confidence, even without eating that one green grape on the table over there, that it is sour. Does this mean that I am no longer thinking? Does this mean that I am closed-minded? No, it means that I am doing what is reasonable. I have sufficient experience to no longer need to do the experiment. It is the same with the Bible for me. I have sufficient evidence that I have earned the intellectual right to assume that Psalm 94 is inspired by the weight of the general evidence.

Now, let me get to the specifics. Are 1 and 2 Timothy and Titus *pseudepigraphic* (falsely attributed to Paul)? I have looked at the evidence and will admit that the case that Paul wrote these books is not sufficient to call this a slam dunk. Okay. So what? I believe they are written by Paul because of the context of the writings themselves. It is not inconceivable that someone took the genuine ideas of Paul and created this book to reflect those ideas. I doubt it very much, but I cannot prove this claim wrong. The question is whether they are inspired or not. I say they are. I have read actual pseudepigraphic books (*The Epistle of Barnabus, The Gospel of Thomas*), and the nature and quality of these writings compared to the two letters of Timothy is striking. I also agree with your line of reasoning about the difference in style of Paul's writing not proving anything. Letters written fifteen years apart for very different reasons can vary greatly in style and vocabulary. Regarding the books of *Philemon* or *Jude*, the content of the letters themselves is so limited that it is hard for me to say with a clear conscience that they show unmistakable marks of inspiration. But God has already made his case as far as I am concerned with the other books. The evidence is sufficient for me to move on to faith. I suggest you be willing to do the same—not blindly, but with your eyes open.

QUESTION:

Do you know how things were published in the first/second century? Were things actually "published" and put into a library of some sort? When scholars say that the gospels were written in the 70s, 80s and 90s, does it mean people read them in the 70s, 80s and 90s? I mean, is it possible that they were just written then, but not shown to people until much later?

ANSWER:

Things were not "published" in the modern sense in the first and second century. To publish implies to create a significant number of identical copies of an original version of a printed work. In the first centuries AD, the only way to obtain copies of a book was to make them by hand, one at a time. As you might imagine this was a painstaking process, to say the least. For this reason, most books only existed in dozens or hundreds of copies, even if they were influential and important works.

We know that the gospels and epistles were written in the first century AD. This is true because of the number of early church fathers who quoted them as early as AD 95 [A*uthor's note: more specific facts to back up this claim will be found in other questions and answers in this book*]. Paul was quite specific to say that his works were written to be distributed among the churches, as were Luke and other New Testament writers. You can assume that, for those books which the church believed to have apostolic authority, multiple copies were created very soon after they were originally penned. So the answer to your question is "no." It is not possible that some of these books lay around unread for many years. If this had happened, they would never have ended up in the New Testament canon. We do not have a detailed history of the spread of the New Testament books, but we do know that, by the early second century AD, there were copies of the four gospels and most or all of the letters were being circulated widely among the churches; so by then, there were certainly hundreds of copies of the original in circulation. It would not be accurate to describe these books as being published in the modern sense, but we know that they were distributed widely. Evidence for the wide distribution of copies of the New Testament books is found in the fact that we have many times more ancient manuscripts of the biblical text than any other ancient work.

QUESTION:

I have read claims that the church really shaped the Bible for their own purposes. That is implied by *The Da Vinci Code*. Some of the people I've talked to don't believe in Jesus because they don't think the Bible is legitimate, but that Jesus was just a teacher and that the church turned him into a god. I have read that the church didn't decide what went in and what didn't, because the authority of the books came from God and not from the church. However, I completely understand people's skepticism since technically the church did decide what went into the Bible and what didn't. My question was this: I've read short arguments on how the church didn't decide—they simply recognized what belonged and what didn't. These arguments have been pretty limited and didn't address opposing viewpoints. I was wondering if the opposing viewpoint that the later church chose the Bible has any evidence. How do they prove that the later church tampered with the Bible?

ANSWER:

I get the impression that when you were a younger Christian, you pretty much accepted the idea that the Bible is from God without questioning the evidence in support of that belief. This is a common trait among believers. Believing in Jesus and in the Bible by a simple faith is fine for a new believer, but I have discovered that, as we mature, it is important to ask hard questions about the evidence underlying our faith. It is not unspiritual to ask why we should believe that the New Testament is truly from God. This is the spirit of the Bereans, as found in Acts 17:10-12. An unreasoned faith is a faith in danger of attack from those who do not accept the truth of the Bible.

Having finished my little sermon, let me get back to your question. Apparently, you have heard that "the church didn't decide what went in and what didn't because the authority of the books came from God and not from the church." Those who say such things sound spiritual and are probably very sincere, but this is simply not true. The fact is that the books of the New Testament were chosen by consensus of the early church. Of course, Bible believers accept that God had his hand both in the writing of these books and in the selection of the books. However, it is clear that God used human beings in this process. If God managed to get the books he wanted into the New Testament, then he used imperfect human beings to accomplish that work. The same can be said for the Old Testament.

By coincidence, I just finished writing an article on the claims of Dan Brown in *The Da Vinci Code*. He is certainly not alone in claiming that the church in the early fourth century changed the

Bible to agree with the doctrines which were emerging at that time. I am including the article below, including my response to this claim. Let me give you the extremely short version now. The canon (or rule) of New Testament books was chosen by consensus of the church based on apostolic authority. A number of early church fathers' writings give us insight into the process. The books which were eventually chosen for inclusion were the ones which all (or virtually all) the church leaders agreed were either written by the original apostles or were clearly given an apostolic stamp of approval. We know from early church writings that the presently accepted canon was assembled in nearly its final form in the second century AD. From the writings of very early church fathers such as Polycarp, Ignatius and Clement of Rome, we know that the letters of Paul and the four Gospels were circulating as a group already in the late first century. However, it wasn't until the second century that a relatively fixed canon was established. Even in the second century, there was some argument about a couple of books, specifically second and third John, Hebrews, second Peter and Revelation. By about the end of the second century, this discussion amongst the church "fathers" was more or less settled. It is worth noting that there were a small number of other books which were considered as worthy of reading in the churches, but not apostolic. These included the *Epistle of Barnabas* and the *Didache*.

    Now, about the claims that the church leaders in the fourth century, especially around the time of Constantine, changed the Bible or excluded books which they did not like—these claims are completely false. There is not a shred of evidence that books were changed, added or deleted from the canon at the council of Nicaea or by any other group at this time. The churches at the time would have vehemently opposed any attempt to change the canon which had already been fixed for well over one hundred years. We have tens of thousands of quotes from the New Testament by early church fathers in the second and third century. If the New Testament had been added to or altered, this fact would be made obvious by comparison to the quotes of the early church fathers.

    You ask "what is the complete opposing view?" of the canon. The fact is that the opposing view does not have any evidence. For example, they cannot point to quotes from Gnostic writings such as the *Gospel of Thomas* by early church writers. They have no evidence at all, either from manuscripts of the accepted books or from quotations from the New Testament prior to the Council of Nicaea that any of the New Testament books were removed, added or altered by Constantine or anyone else. All they can do is try to cast doubt on the existing canon. These people mention a number of other non-canonical books such as the *Gospel of Thomas* or the recently published *Gospel of Judas*. Such books were indeed written in the second and third century, and even later. Most of these are Gnostic writings. They are obviously from heretical groups who were trying to create an alternative gospel. There is absolutely no evidence at all that the *Gospel of Thomas* or any of the Gnostic apocryphal books were ever considered to be apostolic—even by the Gnostics! The Gnostics never included their own fake "gospels" in their lists of inspired books as far as we know.

The writers you refer to try to confuse the issue by mentioning additional books which were used in the early church, such as the *Didache* or the *Epistle of Barnabas*. I encourage you to read these books. You can find them in any collection of the writings of the early church fathers. The earliest of these writings do not contain anything heretical or much in the way of major new doctrines. However, when you read these books, you will see immediately that they are of lesser quality than the New Testament books. You will see why they were not accepted into the canon. Bottom line, there is no evidence supporting the alternative canon hypothesis. The only "evidence" is to try to create doubt in the currently accepted canon.

The following is an article concerning *The Da Vinci Code* I wrote, which may be helpful.

The Da Vinci Code: A Review

Dan Brown's book, *The Da Vinci Code*, has been by far the best selling book in the past few years. Its only recent rival has been the Harry Potter series. Recently a blockbuster movie based on the book was produced. What is the attraction of the book, and why has it raised so much religious controversy? This review is intended to answer these questions.

Let me start with an extremely brief summary of my take on this book.

1. Great book to read

2. Fairly good amount of research behind the book

3. Extremely poor scholarship underlying the premises of the book

Bottom line, this is a very entertaining fictional book. It is one of the more enjoyable books I have read in the past few years. I believe the attraction of the book comes from its combination of excellent writing, gripping suspense, a smart premise and an intelligent writing style that does not go over the head of the average reader. The book has all the ingredients for a good read: a love interest, a titillating controversy and a not-very-subtle slap at some established authorities we sometimes love to hate. The book is loaded with interesting historical background, giving the reader the sense that he or she is learning something while being entertained. Add to this the fact that the book appeals to our sense of pride that we know things better than the religious establishment and you have a very popular book.

Underlying all this is the controversial premise of the book. Dan Brown begins his book by the usual disclaimer, "All characters and events in this book are fictitious, and any resemblance to actual persons, living or dead, is purely coincidental." This is a book of fiction, but one gets the distinct impression when reading it that several of the characters are speaking for Brown, and that he has a definite religious/historical agenda lying unsubtly in the background of the novel. Let me summarize the basic premise of the book—ideas which the author expects the reader to take at least with some seriousness.

1. Jesus Christ was secretly married to Mary Magdalene and had children by her. Jesus' and Mary's descendants are still alive today. The "Holy Grail" is the hidden, metaphorical truth that Jesus has living descendants through his sexual union with Mary.

2. The early church was very heterogeneous. Most did not believe Jesus was deity. Many included worship of the holy feminine. It was the work of Constantine, through the Council of Nicea in AD 325, which created the version of Christianity that we accept today.

3. There exists a secret society known as the Priory of Sion which has guarded and protected the secret about Mary Magdalene and her royal bloodline for one thousand years.

4. There is also a conservative Roman Catholic brotherhood known as the Opus Dei which conspires to suppress and cover up the scandalous truth that Jesus Christ was married to Mary Magdalene.

There is no escaping the fact that Brown is trying to convince the audience of the legitimacy of these premises. In the book, he stages a one-way debate with Bible believers. In this debate, the believer is assumed to be wrong by their silence, even though Brown does not let them speak. This manipulative way to make a point can be very deceiving to the average reader.

Let us look at the premises of the book in the light of historical fact and the evidence Brown uses. First of all, Brown makes the bold claim that the early church did not believe that Jesus Christ was God. According to Brown, it was the first Christian emperor, Constantine, who, in the fourth century AD, created the myth of the deity of Christ. Brown claims that, under the sway of Constantine, the bishops assembled at the council of Nicaea (AD 325) radically altered the New Testament so that they could claim godhood for Jesus Christ.

This charge is absolutely unsubstantiated by the evidence. The fact is that the council of Nicaea did not even consider changing the contents of the New Testament canon. Although this council of bishops did confirm the canon, the reality is that they were only agreeing with a list of books which had been accepted by virtually all Christians for over one hundred years. Even if they had wanted to change the New Testament, they could not have done so, as there were thousands of manuscripts already in circulation. It has been estimated that over ninety percent of the New Testament can be reproduced from quotations of the church fathers in the first two centuries of the church—long before the reign of Constantine. The charge that Constantine somehow altered the New Testament is completely without support. Anyone who makes this charge is either ignorant of the evidence or is purposefully ignoring the facts in order to deceive his or her audience. I assume that the latter is the case with Dan Brown.

As already stated, Brown claims that before Nicea, most Christians did not believe in the deity of Christ. He implies that the deity of Christ was debated at the council and it was the interference of Constantine which won the day for the deity of Christ. This, too, is a gross distortion of the facts. All the parties at this council believed in the deity of Christ. The council was called to settle the question of Arianism. Arius had argued that Jesus was divine, but that his deity was imparted to him by the Father—that Jesus was created. This heretical teaching was denounced by the bishops who assembled at Nicea. Even a cursory study of the early church writers will prove that the mainstream church considered the deity of Jesus a settled matter. Many New Testament passages to that effect explain this fact (John 8:56-59, 10:25-33; Colossians 1:15-20; Titus 2:15; and many more).

Brown repeatedly mentions that there were many competing gospels other than the four accepted ones: Matthew, Mark, Luke and John. To quote p. 231, "More than eighty gospels were considered for the New Testament and yet only a relative few were chosen for inclusion—Matthew, Mark, Luke and John." For an author who claims his book is based on facts, this statement is downright irresponsible. First of all, it is true that there were a number of apocryphal books composed in the second and third centuries. These books were written by heretical groups, especially the Gnostics. The most famous of these is the *Gospel of Thomas*. Where Brown gets the number eighty is not clear. There may very well have been eighty Gnostic apocryphal letters produced, but only a few of them could rightly be considered as gospels (stories of Jesus' life). There is absolutely no credible evidence that the Christian church considered any of these for inclusion in the biblical canon. A telling fact is that Marcion, one of the most important Gnostic leaders, did not include any of these alternative books in his canon. Apparently, even he did not have the nerve to try to impute apostolic authority to the *Gospel of Thomas* or any of the other documents to which Brown alludes.

Brown makes a statement concerning the *Nag Hammadi*, a collection of apocryphal books found in the desert in Egypt (p. 245 of his book). He says they "are a more accurate reflection of the original gospels than the canonically received gospels." It is hard to know how to respond to such an outrageous claim. What Brown fails to do is give a single piece of evidence that any of these books were ever considered by the early church for inclusion in the New Testament. The early church fathers quoted the canonical gospels freely, but never quoted authoritatively from any of the apocryphal writings Brown prefers. The Gnostics had an incorrect, heretical view of Jesus, but even they considered him deity! What they questioned was whether he had occupied a physical body. Given that Brown proposes that Jesus had children, he would not agree with the Gnostics on this claim! Yet he has the nerve to imply that these "gospels" support his thesis.

Anyone who would like to can read the "Gospels" of Thomas, Philip or Mary. These documents contain fantastic stories of Jesus working miracles as a baby and many supposed sayings of Jesus which are radically inconsistent with the Jesus we find in the canonical gospels. *The Gospel of Thomas* was written, probably in Egypt, around AD 150. Anyone reading this book can discover the difference in quality when compared to the four canonical gospels. One thing we can know for sure is that Thomas did not write this book.

Brown makes a number of other equally unsubstantiated claims, but probably the most outrageous is that Jesus had sexual relations with Mary Magdalene which led to her giving birth to a son. He claims the "Holy Grail" which Christian mystics searched for the past two thousand years was actually the secret that Mary Magdalene had a son. Brown quotes from the *"Gospel of Phillip"* on page 246 of his book: "And the companion of the Savior is Mary Magdalene. Christ loved her more than all the disciples and used to kiss her often on her mouth. The rest of the disciples were offended by it and expressed disapproval. They said to him, 'Why do you love her more than all of us.'" The Gospel of Phillip is not really a gospel (life of Jesus) at all. It is also an obvious Gnostic writing with no connection to the gospel story. In addition, only the first part of this quote actually comes from the book. The best I can tell, Brown made up the rest of the quote.

In order for us to accept that Jesus secretly married Mary Magdalene, we will be required to believe that the apostles were responsible for a massive cover-up of this scandal. According to Brown, the early church worshipped the mother goddess. It was only the later Catholic Church which suppressed the worship of the "holy feminine" and removed all reference to this from the New Testament. To quote Brown (p. 238), "The Grail (i.e. the secret about Mary Magdalene) is literally the ancient symbol for womanhood, and the Holy Grail represents the sacred feminine and the goddess, which has never been lost, but was virtually eliminated by the Church." And here's another quote from Brown (p. 407): "My dear, the Church has two thousand years of experience pressuring those who threaten to unveil its lies. Since the days of Constantine, the Church has successfully hidden the truth about Mary Magdalene and Jesus." Again, what Brown fails to do is produce even a single shred of evidence of this change in teaching at the time of Constantine. In fact, he does not produce a single piece of evidence that this liaison between Jesus and Mary happened at all. The reason is that there is no such evidence.

One of Brown's techniques by which he tries to lend credence to his outrageous claims is to supply just enough truth to make his conclusions sound credible. For example, Brown makes the truthful charge that the Roman Catholic Church cast unfair aspersions against the character of Mary Magdalene. The Roman church from the time of Pope Gregory in the 500s AD charged Mary with being a prostitute (albeit a reformed one). They claimed that she was the sinful woman in Luke 7 who wiped Jesus' feet with her tears and her hair. The problem with this claim is that it is not supported biblically. It appears that Mary of Magdala was a well-to-do supporter of Jesus' ministry. She certainly was not a former woman of the streets. What motivated Gregory's false charge against Mary is not clear. What we can be sure of is that it was not done in order to cover up for the truth that she had a secret relationship with Jesus, as Brown implies.

Similarly, Brown sprinkles factual information about the Knights Templar, a militant order of monks who served the Roman church from the 11th century onward, as well as some factual data about Opus Dei. This group is a semi-underground conservative lay movement within Catholicism founded in the 1930s. He also provides some information about the Priory of Sion, a shadowy and secretive sect of Catholic Christianity founded in 1956. Brown falsely implies that the group has existed in secret since AD 1099. The fact is, however, that the Priory is the creation of the imagination of a French writer. He also claims that Leonardo Da Vinci, Boticelli, Robert Boyle, Isaac Newton and other very influential people were involved in the cover-up of the "truth" about Mary Magdalene as former heads of the Priory of Sion. What he fails to do, of course, is provide any evidence at all that these groups played the roles he assigns to them. In his interesting plot, the Templars hid the evidence of Mary having an illicit relationship with Jesus, and the Priory of Sion hid the actual descendants of Mary and Jesus as well as the truth about the Holy Grail. Brown has Opus Dei involved in a murderous plot to steal the secret of the Grail so they can bury it once and for all. If there is any actual data supporting these contentions, this author is not aware of it.

What should be the Christian response to the book or to the movie? It is probably true that some people will be given a distorted view of Jesus and the Bible from the movie. This, of course, is tragic. However, what we can do is be an antidote to the lies. How often do our friends talk about Jesus at the office or the work site? If we will do our homework, we will have a great opportunity to share about the volume of evidence supporting the accuracy of the New Testament text. Maybe the interest sparked in the movie can motivate a friend to go to church. Believers who have a reactionary response will come across as holier-than-thou and are not likely to engage non-believers in fruitful conversation. Perhaps some of them will. It is not my place to say what God can or will do. However, I suggest we take the whole business in stride and use the great opportunity afforded us to share our faith in the real Jesus—the one found in the canonical Gospels.

—John Oakes, PhD

QUESTION:

Have you seen the manuscript *The Gospel of Judas?* I saw a reference to it in the news. It appears to me that this book is a pile of trash which portrays Judas as a great man, when nothing could be further from the truth. Why is it that people value these books, and why do they even exist? I have also heard a reference to a book of Thomas. What are these books and what was it that set the first four books of the New Testament apart from these?

ANSWER:

Recently, I wrote an article on the *Gospel of Judas*. I am including it below. With regard to the book of Thomas, it is actually called the *Gospel of Thomas*. This book is definitely real. Fragments of the *Gospel of Thomas* were found in Oxyrhyncus in Egypt in 1897 and 1903. A full text of this book in the Coptic language was found in 1945 as part of the *Nag Hamadi* Library. The original Thomas was a Gnostic composition in Greek, composed around AD 150 (more on the Gnostics below). Clearly, this work was not written by Thomas or by anyone who knew Thomas.

The *Gospel of Thomas* is made up of 114 supposed sayings of Jesus, some of which are recognizable from the canonical gospels. However, it has many sayings attributed to Jesus which make no sense at all. Here's one example: "Jesus said, 'Lucky is the lion that the human will eat, so that the lion becomes human. And foul is the human that the lion will eat, and the lion still will become human'" (GT 7). Another passage which seems to make no sense is this one: "Mary said to Jesus, 'What are your disciples like?' He said, 'They are like little children living in a field that is not theirs. When the owners of the field come, they will say, 'Give us back our field.' They take off their clothes in front of them in order to give it back to them, and they return their field to them'" (GT 21). In this case, what seems like nonsense actually makes sense if one understands that this is a Gnostic gospel. The reference to removing one's clothes is not about walking around nude. It is about removing the body which clothes us (to paraphrase the *Gospel of Judas*). This is an oblique reference to shedding our gross, physical body in order to occupy a higher, spiritual body. Here we have Gnosticism revealed.

Another passage from Thomas which has rather obvious Gnostic influence is in GT 22: "They said to him, 'Then shall we enter the kingdom as babies?' Jesus said to them, 'When you make the two into one, and when you make the inner like the outer and the outer like the inner, and the upper like the lower, and when you make male and female into a single one, so that the male will not be male nor the female be female, when you make eyes in place of an eye, a hand in place of a hand, a foot in place of a foot, an image in place of an image, then you will enter [the kingdom].'" A rather disturbing "saying" of Jesus is this one, found in GT 114: "Simon Peter said to them, 'Make Mary leave us, for females don't deserve life.' Jesus said, 'Look, I will guide her to make her male, so that she too may become a living spirit resembling you males. For every female who makes herself male will enter the kingdom of Heaven.'" This is in dramatic opposition to the kind of respect that Jesus showed to the women who followed him.

Those who try to support the claim that the *Gospel of Thomas* is in the same league with the canonical gospels clearly have some explaining to do. Many of the problems with Thomas are mirrored in the recently translated *Gospel of Judas*. Below is the article I wrote on the *Gospel of Judas*.

Judas: Another Gospel?

"The secret account of the revelation that Jesus spoke in conversation with Judas Iscariot." These words begin a startling new discovery, announced to the world in April of this year. First, there was *The Da Vinci Code*; now there is the *Gospel of Judas*. It seems like when it rains it pours.

On the face of it, the apostle who betrayed Jesus is an unlikely candidate for writing an inspired account of the life of Jesus, especially if we consider that he killed himself the day Jesus died. When did he write this book? If we are to believe the *National Geographic* article which announced the translation of the *Gospel of Judas* from the Coptic language, this is one of a number of equally valid traditions about the life and teachings of Jesus Christ. If this is true, then it will radically change our concept of the relationship between Jesus and the disciples. In the newly discovered "gospel," Judas is the closest of all the apostles to Jesus. He is the one who received a special, deeper knowledge of the Kingdom of God from Jesus. Is the manuscript a legitimate ancient copy of the *Gospel of Judas*? What is the basic message of this "gospel?" What is its relevance to Christianity and to the accepted canon of scripture? Does it throw any new light on the canonical gospels? Let us consider these questions.

Is the Gospel of Judas a Legitimate Document?

Perhaps some of us hope that this whole thing will turn out to be a hoax. Like it or not, the Gospel of Judas is very much real, and the manuscript uncovered in the desert in Egypt 1970s is certainly not a forgery. After its discovery, the 26-page manuscript (actually, part of a longer, 66-page codex which includes other Gnostic writings) languished untranslated for over two decades in the collections of various dealers in antiquities because its owners did not realize its significance. The codex is made of very fragile papyrus and it had deteriorated significantly in the nearly 30 years since its recovery. Although the original *Gospel of Judas* was almost certainly in Greek, this manuscript is written in Coptic. This was the local language of Egypt in the early centuries AD. Coptic script is very closely related to Greek writing. Finally, in 2000, the Coptic language scholar, Rodolphe Kasser, got a hold of this papyrus. He must have been shocked to realize he had in his hand a copy of the long lost and long reviled *Gospel of Judas*.

It is important to note that the existence of this "gospel" has been known to scholars for centuries. Although no manuscript of the letter was discovered until this century, the early church father, Irenaeus, mentioned the book in around AD 180. He quoted from it in his polemic treatise *Against Heresies*. Irenaeus fiercely denounced the message of Judas for its Gnostic underpinning, calling it a "fictitious history." From Irenaeus' reference, scholars have guessed that this apocryphal letter was written somewhere around AD 150-170. The original was in Greek, so the manuscript discovered in Egypt is a translation. Its authenticity had been confirmed, both by the composition of the ink used and by Carbon-14 dating, which places the papyrus between AD 220 and 340.

What Is the Message of the Letter?

The controversy over the *Gospel of Judas* manuscript does not stem from a debate over its authenticity. It is the message and the events portrayed in the letter which has generated a lot of heat. We should bear in mind, however, that although we have a lot of new information about this letter, the general thrust of its content was already known from the comments of Irenaeus.

Let us consider the content of this very controversial manuscript. First of all, it is important to note that it is not really a gospel, if we allow the four canonical gospels to define the term. It is not a biography of Jesus. It does not include the passion events, and it does not show him healing people or preaching to the people. It does not provide any sort of chronological picture of the life and ministry of Jesus Christ. This letter is only about 3,200 words long, which makes it equivalent to three or four chapters of material from one of the canonical gospels. The document contains a number of very obtuse allegorical/philosophical statements which are obviously a reflection, not of genuine events from the life of Jesus, but of Gnostic philosophical speculation (more on Gnosticism below).

The reader should bear in mind that the *Gospel of Judas* is just one of several known Gnostic pseudo-gospels. Others include the *Gospel of Thomas, the Gospel of Mary, the Secret Book of John, the Gospel of Phillip* and more. These books are considered pseudepigraphal, which means that the author is clearly not the person after whom the book is named. No scholar claims that Mary wrote the gospel of Mary or that Thomas wrote the Gospel of Thomas. The same can be said for the Gospel of Judas. Whatever its source, it certainly was not written by, or even influenced by, Judas.

If the *National Geographic* sponsors of the translation are to be believed (see the May, 2006 volume of *National Geographic*), the historical reliability of Matthew and John are more or less on par with this book. The National Geographic authors claim that the Ebionites, the Marcionites, the Gnostics and the mainstream of Christianity—the one which eventually won out—are equally Christian. Their picture of Christianity in the first three centuries is one of a fluid religion with no clear "correct" teaching or story of Jesus. We will see that this view does not hold up to good scholarship.

Let us consider some of the "historical" events portrayed in this document. When we do so, we will soon see that the content of the Gospel of Judas is nothing short of bizarre by comparison to the accepted gospels. There are a few passages in Judas which are vaguely familiar. Jesus tells his followers not to sow seed on rock and expect to harvest the fruit, reminiscent of Matthew 13:5. He also describes coming from a place which *"no eye has ever seen and no thought of the heart has ever comprehended"*

(1 Corinthians 2:9). Beyond a small number of familiar allusions, the book veers dramatically from the four gospels. In the book, Jesus heaps contempt on the apostles. He often laughs at them for their ignorance of the deeper mysteries. The disciples tell Jesus of a vision of the temple with twelve priests before an altar accepting gifts. The priests sacrifice their wives and children, engage in homosexual acts and commit other heinous sins. Jesus tells the apostles that the priests in the vision are symbols of the apostles themselves (and by implication, the Jews): "Those you have seen receiving the offerings at the altar—that is who you are. That is the God you serve." (*Gospel of Judas*, p. 38) For those not familiar with Gnosticism, this may seem strange. However, if we understand that the Gnostics, including the writer of the Gospel of Judas, considered the God of the Old Testament to be an evil God, then this passage makes sense.[2] Another passage in Judas confirms this Gnostic perspective: "The cattle you have seen brought for sacrifice are the many people you lead astray" (Gospel of Judas, p. 39).

Most of the last half of the Judas letter puts a confusing treatise on Gnostic cosmology into the mouth of Jesus: "Come, that I may teach you about [secrets] no person [has] ever seen. For there exists a great and boundless realm, whose extent no generation of angels has seen" (GJ, p. 47). The secret cosmology which Jesus reveals to his closest apostle, Judas, includes 72 luminaries, or perhaps it is 360, or perhaps it is 12. That is unclear. There are twelve aeons (see below on Gnosticism) and six heavens for each of the aeons to dwell in, along with five firmaments for each of the 72 heavens. Unfamiliar characters in this cosmology (except to the initiates of Gnosticism, of course) include Nebro Yaldabaoth, Saklas, Galila, Yobel and Adonaios. Jesus is also known as Seth, and he is one of the five rulers over the underworld.

The key line of the entire gospel is found near the end: "But you [i.e. Judas] will exceed all of them. For you will sacrifice the man that clothes me" (GJ, p. 56). The Judas letter writer has Jesus praising Judas as the greatest of all the apostles. Why? Because he betrayed him to the Jewish leaders for execution. Believe it or not, as we will see below, this statement actually makes sense if one follows Gnostic philosophy. The bizarre content of the Gospel of Judas begs the question: Is it reasonable to believe that these are the actual words of Jesus?

Who Are the Gnostics?

"For you will sacrifice the man that clothes me." If he had not given himself away before this, the writer of Judas makes it clear what his philosophical perspective is when he put these words into the mouth of Jesus. This is a clear statement of the Gnostic idea. It is not possible to understand

the origin or message of the *Gospel of Judas* without some background in the Gnosticism of the first, second and third centuries AD. Let us consider the nature of Gnostic Christianity.

It is important to bear in mind that Gnostics who called themselves Christians in the early centuries AD had a broad range of beliefs. The teaching of the orthodox Christian church varied somewhat, but the church's doctrines and organization was fairly consistent. That was definitely not the case with the Gnostics. It is also important to recognize that the source of Gnostic teaching was not Christianity. From their writings, we can observe that the teachings of the Gnostics were based principally in the Mystery religions (such as the cults of Dionysius and Osiris), Near Eastern Dualism (such as Zoroastrianism and Mithraism) as well as neo-Platonist philosophy as exemplified by the teaching of Plotinus. At the risk of oversimplifying, Gnostic practice was based on the Mystery religions, its theology was based on dualistic religion, its philosophy was based on Platonism or later on neo-Platonism and its story (its myth) was based on Christianity. When scholars study the Gnostic writings, such as the *Gospel of Thomas*, and, in particular, when we study the *Gospel of Judas*, it is fair to describe these "gospels" as Gnostic religion dressed up to look like Christianity. As an example of this, the Nag Hamadi, a library of Gnostic writings found in Egypt in the 1940s, contains two similar books. One of them, The Book of Eugnostos the Blessed," is a Greek neo-Platonist speculation. Another of them, known as the "Sophia of Jesus Christ," has virtually the identical material, except that the words of Greek philosophical speculation in Eugnostos are put into the mouth of Jesus Christ in the latter work. Clearly, Greek philosophy has been given a "Christian" veneer.

The cultic practice underlying Gnosticism finds its roots in the Mystery religions which pervaded the Roman Empire at that time. The Greek mystery religion was the cult of Dionysius. The equivalent in Egypt was the cult of Osiris. The Mysteries were ritualistic/symbolic rites which led the initiates into an ever-deeper knowledge of "God." The practitioners were sworn to secrecy with regard to these rites. Followers of the Mystery cults were given successively deeper knowledge of the meaning of the cultic practices. This is the source of the word Gnostic, which comes from the Greek *gnosis*, or knowledge. We do not know a lot about the actual mystery rites because of the enforced secrecy, but hints from Greek writers give us some glimpses into the Baccanalia—the chief festival of the Dionysius cult. This days-long festival included sexual activity, alcohol and other inducements which produced an ecstatic religious experience for the participants.

The influence of the Mystery religions on the *Gospel of Judas* is obvious. The Judas letter has Jesus saying to Judas, "[Come] that I may teach you about [secrets] no person [has] ever seen. For there exists a great and boundless realm, whose extent no generations of angels has seen" (GJ, p. 47). In the Judas account, Jesus is a sort of personal spiritual guru, with Judas as his closest student. Jesus says to Judas, "step away from the others and I shall tell you the mysteries of the kingdom" (GJ, p. 39). The question to be asked is this: Which is more likely; that the writer of the *Gospel of Judas* was influenced by the actual relationship between Jesus and Judas, or that he was influenced by the Mystery religions?

The theology of the *Gospel of Judas* is at least in part explained by influence from the many dualistic religions common in the Near East at that time. Most familiar to modern readers is Zoroastrianism, because a small remnant of this religion lives on today, mostly in India. The religion finds its roots in present-day Iran. Zoroastrianism, Manichaeism and Mithraism all find their beginnings in Persia or the Eastern Roman Empire. Of course, these groups had beliefs which varied, but their chief relevant quality for us is found in the belief that the world is in a more or less equal battle between the forces of good and evil. The god of good and the god of evil are in battle over us earth-bound souls. Dualism finds its influence in Gnosticism and in the *Gospel of Judas*. The Gnostics believed that Jehovah, the God of the Old Testament, was an evil God who brought destruction on God's people. According to this view, Jesus is a teacher of the God of good. He is spiritual, whereas Jehovah is physical and earthly. As an example of this connection between dualism and Gnosticism, consider the theology of one of the most influential Gnostic teachers, Marcion. We know from his writings that he rejected the entire Old Testament, as well as most of the gospels, because they were too Jewish and because they were influenced by the teaching about Jehovah. Marcion taught that Jehovah is the enemy of true spirituality—that he is a worldly and evil god. Marcion based his canon principally on the writings of Paul. Influence of dualism on the *Gospel of Judas* is found in the section already mentioned in which Jesus tells the apostles, "the cattle you have seen brought for sacrifice are the many people you lead astray" (GJ, p. 39). The *Gospel of Judas* paints the picture of temple sacrifice as blasphemously sinful. If "Judas" is right, then Jehovah is evil.

Lastly, but perhaps most profoundly, Gnostic writings such as the *Gospel of Judas* are influenced by Greek philosophy—especially neo-Platonism. Greek philosophy from the time of Pythagorus through Plato and, most significantly for Gnosticism, Plotinus, had created a picture of the earth as a physical and therefore a very evil place. The goal of every human was to escape the physical world through Mystery religion practices or through philosophical speculation, in order to move to the higher, spiritual plane of existence. In diametric opposition to this picture, the Old Testament, confirmed by the New Testament, creates the picture of the created world as being essentially good (Genesis 1:31: *"God saw all that he had made, and it was very good."*). Not so with Gnostic neo-Platonism. The physical world, as represented by Jehovah or by Adam, is essentially evil. The goal is to escape the physical to experience the spiritual quintessence. This explains the central teaching of Gnostics about Jesus. According to them, Jesus was not a physical being at all. He could not be. The person we recognize as Jesus was an illusion, or perhaps he was a shell which was temporarily occupied by the entirely spiritual Jesus Christ. Thus we find the statement of Jesus to Judas as mentioned above: "For you shall sacrifice the man that clothes me." In the *Gospel of Judas*, Jesus is a spiritual being who has been trapped in a physical body. The body is not Jesus. In that case, Jesus was not killed on the cross. Therefore, Judas did a favor to Jesus by freeing him from the sinful, gross physical reality of a human body.

Of course, this is in diametric opposition to what is the commonly accepted theology of virtually all of those who call themselves Christians today. From the beginning, the church has taught that Jesus was both God and a human being. This well-established doctrine was put in writing at the Council of Nicaea in AD 325. It is just this heretical teaching (that Jesus was not flesh) which is being opposed in 1 John 1:1: "*That which was from the beginning, which we have seen with our eyes, which we have looked at and our hands have touched—this we proclaim concerning the Word of life.*" In Gnosticism (and in neo-Platonism), the true, spiritual God is a lofty being, far separated from the world. This "God" is certainly not interested in a personal relationship with human beings. This is the God of the Gospel of Judas. The real God is so distant from human beings that out of his thoughts he created lesser beings, known as "aeons." These neo-Platonic "aeons" are the same beings identified by Jesus as he speaks to Judas in the recently published letter. One of the aeons is Sophia (Greek for wisdom), also known as Barbelo. Both names are found in the Gospel of Judas. To Gnostics, Sophia's thoughts led to the creation of an evil god, Ialdabaoth (also known as Nebro), who later created the god of Genesis, YHWH, Jehovah. All of these neo-Platonic characters are found in the Gospel of Judas. This bumbling, evil god created a disastrous world in which little sparks of the divine are trapped inside an evil body. From neo-Platonism, we get Gnostic philosophy/religion, from which we get the *Gospel of Judas*. The line of connection is absolutely clear.

In the final analysis, Gnostic "Christianity" is not Christian at all, and neither is the *Gospel of Judas* Christian. This statement is true if we define a Christian teaching as one which is based on the teachings of the historical person Jesus Christ. Gnostic belief is based on an amalgam of the popular philosophy and religion of the Eastern Mediterranean, with only a thin veneer of pseudo-Christian teaching. Gnostic teachers are called antichrists in 1 John chapter two, and for good reason, because *"no one who denies the Son has the Father."*

How Is This Discovery Relevant to Our Understanding of Christianity?

What is the relevance of the *Gospel of Judas* to Christianity? The simple answer is little, if any. This discovery will be of great interest to the scholars of Near Eastern religion in the Roman Empire during the *Pax Romana*. Such scholars already have a number of such documents, especially from the *Nag Hamadi* library, but the Gospel of Judas will be an interesting addition to the extant Gnostic literature. Having said that, we will learn nothing new at all about Jesus, his life, his teaching, his ministry or the teaching of his apostles from this obvious Gnostic treatise because it has virtually no basis in the life of Jesus Christ. If we read the recent *National Geographic* article, announcing the completion of the restoration and translation of the *Gospel of Judas*, we will get a very different picture. The editors of the article imply that there were a number of competing versions of Christianity as well as a number of competing written gospels in the second and third centuries AD. The Marcionites, the Ebionites, the Gnostics, the Carpocratians and what we now consider the orthodox Christians all had more or less equally valid interpretations of the teaching of Jesus, if *National Geographic* is to be believed. By extention, the Gnostic writings, including the *Gospel of Judas*, had equal footing with the canonical Matthew, Mark, Luke and John. To quote the NG writer, "In fact, it is unclear whether the authors of any of the gospels—even the familiar four—actually witnessed the events they described."

The problem with this viewpoint is that it is completely disproved by the facts as we know them. Those who seek to stir up trouble for crusty, conservative, old, boring Christian belief (the kind through which people will be saved) want to create the false impression that these alternative gospels and other apocryphal writings have equal authority with the accepted New Testament books. Let us consider the evidence.

First, we need to bear in mind that the Gnostics were stepchildren of the Mystery religions. The practitioners of the Mystery cults used mythical stories as an allegorical means to tell a deeper story. For the Gnostic, the use of myth and symbolic story, with no basis in actual historical fact, was standard operating procedure. When one reads the *Gospel of Judas*, it is worth bearing in mind that the author did not expect the reader to take the story as history. This certainly is not the case with the writers of the four canonical Gospels. For example, in both his Gospel and the book of Acts, Luke went out of his way to mention places, the names of rulers, the direction of travel from one place to another and the specific titles of leaders of different cities. Historians and archaeologists have confirmed many of Luke's facts. To date, not a single one of his historical details has proven false. Luke interviewed eye-witnesses (Luke 1:1-3). All the Gospel writers included minute details in the events they described (30 pieces of silver, details of distances, time of day and so forth), creating an unmistakable sense that they were historical accounts. One gets the strong impression that the Gospel writers were including such small details as if to say, "If you are not sure, ask the people who were there."

The author of the *National Geographic* article on the *Gospel of Judas* tries to instill doubt about whether the Gospels are indeed reliable. One means to that end is to create the impression that the Gospels were not written until the second century. The problem with this is that the evidence does not allow for such a late composition of the canonical Gospels. Support for this comes from at least two sources. First, we have a number of actual manuscripts of New Testament writings from as early as the second century. The earliest confirmed date for a manuscript is the Rylands Papyrus, which has been dated by both Carbon-14 and by script style to about AD 125. In addition, there exist a large body of letters written by the early church "fathers" such as Clement of Rome, Polycarp, Justin Martyr, Irenaeus and others. These early Christian writers from the very late first and the second century AD quoted extensively from every part of the New Testament. The letters known as the *Epistle of Barnabus*, the *Didache* and the *Letter of Clement of Rome* have all been dated from around 100 AD. These authors quote from Matthew, Mark, Luke, Acts, Romans, I Corinthians, Ephesians, Titus, Hebrews, I Peter and others. The early church father Ignatius was martyred in 115 AD. In a set of letters he composed on his way to his execution in Rome, he quoted from nearly every New Testament book. One could continue by mentioning the much more extensive writings of Justin Martyr from around 150 AD, and those of Irenaeus, from near the end of the second century. Justin called the four Gospels the "memoirs of the apostles." Experts have claimed that using quotes from early Christian writers in the second century, one could reconstruct nearly the entire text of the New Testament. Many scholars agree that Matthew, Mark and Luke were written before AD 70. John was almost certainly written before AD 90, and probably at least ten years before that.

Let us compare the evidence for the early authorship and accurate history of the canonical Gospels to Gnostic works such as Thomas and Judas. There is no evidence that these or any of the dozens of Gnostic letters were given any authority at all by the early church. The only time the early church writers referred to such books was to show why they were heretical. It is interesting to note that the earliest actual list of inspired books is that of the Gnostic leader Marcion. Because he rejected the God of the Old Testament, the only Gospel he included in his accepted list of books was Luke, but we can tell from his writings that he was aware of the other three. What is notable is that even Marcion did not include any of the pseudepigraphical Gnostic writings in his canon. Presumably, even the followers of the Gnostic

Reliability of the Biblical Text

philosophy were aware that the Gnostic letters did not have apostolic authority. Please do not be confused by those whose goal is not to discover the truth, but to confuse the minds of those who put their faith in the Bible as the inspired Word of God. There is no justification for putting the *Gospel of Judas* in the same category as the four Gospels.

Summary

The *Gospel of Judas* is an interesting discovery, especially to scholars who study Gnosticism and the influence of Greek philosophy and Near Eastern religion on heretical Christian groups. Those who have implied that this book represents a story of the life of Jesus which is to be taken as seriously as the traditional gospels are flat wrong. The bizarre story of Judas being the favorite of Jesus apostles—the one to whom he entrusted the secret, deep knowledge (gnosis) is simply not credible. This story was made up out the imagination of a Gnostic writer, with the intent of putting the precepts of non-Christian Gnosticism into the mouth of Jesus. The four canonical Gospels are eyewitness accounts of the actual events in the life of Jesus Christ, with apostolic authorship or the stamp of apostolic approval. To compare the *Gospel of Judas* to the Gospel of Matthew is to commit a gross error of logic and of scholarship.

—John Oakes, PhD

QUESTION:

I was talking to a Muslim and he told me that the word that was used in the original Hebrew New Testament for the cross actually meant stick, and that the word has changed over time to mean cross. Is this true?

ANSWER:

I am afraid to say that your Muslim friend does not know what he is talking about. That is a bit strong, but I say this because the original New Testament was in Greek, not Hebrew. I assume your friend is quoting from an imam who has filled his head with nonsense. He has heard anti-Christian rhetoric which does not bother with good scholarship. The Muslims have a very strong stake in trying to prove that Jesus was not crucified. The Koran says that Jesus was not crucified. If in fact he was, then that is further evidence that the Koran is not inspired by Allah. This is a very important point because the Koran calls the Old and New Testament *Injil* and implies these writings are inspired by God. If we can show beyond reasonable doubt that the Koran unambiguously makes statements which contradict the Old or the New Testaments, then there is a fundamental contradiction in the Koran. In this instance, the Koran is blantantly wrong in denying the crucifixion of Jesus. Who should we trust—a Muslim who is doctrinally required to believe Jesus was not crucified, or the eyewitnesses in the early church, who should have known what happened to Jesus? And even if you do not trust the Christians, you can listen to the historians Josephus, Tacitus and others. Josephus and Tacitus were non-Christian historians from the first century. Both agree that Jesus was crucified. If you want some more specifics, including primary sources, you should read **RFB** ch. 3. There is not the slightest doubt that Jesus was crucified. Muslim apologists cannot be trusted on this one.

By the way, the Greek word used in John 19:17 (he carried his cross) is the word *stauros*, which means cross. The common word for stick in Greek was *kalamos*. I have seen no evidence at all that *stauros* ever meant anything other than cross.

QUESTION:

I have heard that Mark 16:9-20 was not in the original letter of Mark. Why and by whom were these verses added later? Why was Jesus described as riding on a donkey? Could it be because the writer knew it would be seen as a fulfillment of Old Testament prophecy and would therefore bolster his Messianic status? Much as you obviously yearn to believe that every word in the Bible is divinely inspired, I am sure that you have read too much not to have the slightest misgivings. I have no quarrel with anyone who takes up the self-denying path of the charismatic teacher, Yeshua. He calls us still to be the highest and the best that we can be and presents us with a standard of conduct that we can only struggle to achieve.

We have, however, one small torch to guide us through the surrounding gloom, and that is REASON, and we cannot afford to lose it. Religion wanted Galileo to assent to a geocentric earth and deny that the earth rotated round the sun. I stand with Galileo *"Eppure, si muove!"* [Author's note: this is translated as, "But still it moves."]

ANSWER:

About Mark 16:9-20, yes, I agree with you that the manuscript evidence leans toward excluding that section from the original Mark. This is one of the very few significant manuscript issues in the New Testament. The other fairly significant questionable passages are John 8:1-11, 1 John 5:7 and Acts 9:37. All are discussed in some detail in **RFB** ch. 6. In the case of the Mark 16 passage, the three most important early manuscripts, Codex Vaticanus, Codex Alexandrinus and Codex Sinaiticus all do not include this passage. Codex Bezae, from about the same time period (AD 350), does include this passage, but this manuscript is not considered as authoritative as the other three. None of the very early church fathers quoted from this section. It may be a genuine piece of apostolic writing, perhaps even from Mark, which was "pasted" on to the end of Mark. It is also possible that a copyist simply added an ending of his own to Mark. Scholars speculate that Mark 16:9-20 was added to the end of the book because it ends rather abruptly if one stops at Mark 16:8. As to the correct final conclusion, I am not sure. The germane point on this is that only a miniscule proportion of the New Testament text is in doubt. The twelve verses at the end of Mark 16, as well as the three single verses mentioned above, represent the entire list of significant disputed New Testament passages. Virtually the entire New Testament text is considered to be a reliable part of the original writings. I believe that whether one includes Mark 16:9-20 does not have a significant impact on one's understanding of the gospel message. No important teaching of Jesus is added or changed if we include it, and none is lost if we do not use this passage.

In my opinion, the reason Jesus was described as riding into Jerusalem on a donkey is that he rode into Jerusalem on a donkey! What possible reason would the Gospel writers have in making up this story if it were not true? The fact is that, in the 60s AD, there were still thousands of eyewitnesses to the events recorded in the Gospels still alive who could easily have refuted the Gospel accounts if they included falsehoods. If the Gospel writers were trying to bamboozle people, they would have been better advised to not include such easily refuted details, unless, of course, they were actually true. Luke quoted Jesus as saying, *"Everything must be fulfilled that is written about me in the Law of Moses, the Prophets and the Psalms"* (Luke 24:44). Jesus was well aware that he was fulfilling all the messianic prophecies. One could argue that he cynically went about fulfilling the prophecies so that he could claim to be the Messiah. One problem with this is that the Messiah had to be born in Bethlehem (Micah 5:2), which was hard for Jesus to arrange. The Messiah had to be "sold" for 30 pieces of silver (Zechariah 11:12). He also had to be crucified (Psalms 22:16). It would have been hard for Jesus to have arranged these events (unless he is the Son of God)! The skeptic can argue that these facts were made up, but there is no evidence to support this contention. Besides, the fact that Jesus was born in Bethlehem and that he was crucified are attested to by non-believers in the first and second century. No, I do not believe it is reasonable to assume that the Gospel writers were liars. I cannot absolutely prove it, but I believe the most reasonable explanation of the Gospel account, including the description of Jesus riding into Jerusalem on a donkey, is that this is what actually happened.

Do I have misgivings? Do doubts ever enter into my mind? Yes they do. I am a careful thinker. I am a scientist. I keep a mental list of difficulties. What I have found is that, over time, as I do research into historical background, as I study the original texts more carefully, as I consider scientific implications of Bible statements, I find that most of my questions are solved in that the Bible is shown to be accurate—to be inspired by God. Are all my questions answered? No. However, with time and study, the overwhelming evidence for inspiration has given me more and more reason to give the Bible the benefit of the doubt concerning things which I cannot prove. Can I prove that Esther chapter three verse eight is inspired (to choose at random)? No. Is the case for inspiration overwhelming? Absolutely yes! Should I remain cautious? Certainly I should.

As Jonathan Swift said, "It is impossible to reason a man out of a belief he was not reasoned into in the first place." I teach a class on deductive and inductive methods of reason. I regularly honor philosophers such as Kant, Hume, Descartes and others who used reason to analyze human knowledge—to study epistemology. I agree with Thomas Aquinas that if something is true, it must be reasonable. I believe that the only reasonable conclusion of the matter, based on the evidence, is that the Bible is the inspired word of God. Having said that, I am glad that reason is not the only torch we have to live by. Reason is a very powerful tool given to us by our Creator, but he has given us an even more powerful light—the gospel of Jesus Christ.

I am a huge fan of Galileo. I just taught about him in my

Reliability of the Biblical Text

philosophy of science class today. Galileo said, "The Bible was written to tell us how to go to heaven, not how the heavens go." I agree with him. I agree with Galileo that we should not read the Bible as a science book, but that we should allow nature, the creation of God, to speak for herself. Like Galileo said (to paraphrase from *The Letter to the Duchess Christina*), God is revealed alike in the inspired Word of God and in his creation. Galileo acknowledged that God revealed himself in scripture and in the beauty of his creation. I agree with Galileo on this. By the way, the Bible never said that the earth does not move. Unfortunately, Catholic theologians, beginning with Thomas Aquinas, took the word of Aristotle on this. We should not make that mistake. For your information, many believe that the story of Galileo saying, "but it moves" is apocryphal. I am not sure on that one. Galileo was a stubborn man (for good reason), and this is the kind of thing he may well have done.

QUESTION:

How can only Matthew through Revelation be considered divine scripture? What about the Apocrypha? What about the thousands of other writings? Besides, it was man who canonized scripture and man is not perfect, so that would obviously mean that scripture runs the risk of not being perfect, right? What I am really struggling with is the reliability of scripture.

ANSWER:

First of all, we have in our possession a number of apocryphal books by Jewish writers, some of which are included in the Old Testament of the Roman Catholic and other Bibles. Examples include books such as Ecclesiasticus, First Maccabees, Tobit and so forth. In addition, there are many books such as Third Maccabees, Second Esdras and so forth which are of more of less the same genre, but which were never included in the Old Testament Apocrypha. I will not discuss these, as they are relevant to the question of the Old Testament canon, not the New Testament, and you appear to be asking about the New Testament. You will find a detailed discussion of the Old Testament Apocrypha in my book **Daniel**, Appendix 1.

In addition, there exist a great number of books and letters which were written primarily in Greek in the second and third centuries AD. Some of these are considered to be "apocryphal." We should make some careful distinctions. There are literally hundreds of letters written by early church leaders such as Polycarp, Ignatius, Clement of Rome, Justin and Origen. These letters are not usually called apocryphal because they were generally never thought of or passed off as possibly inspired texts. There is a fairly small second category of texts. These include the *Didache*, and the *Epistle of Barnabus*. These are very early Christian writings from about AD 100 which some church leaders proposed to have apostolic authority. These were rejected, not generally because of any false doctrines, but because the consensus of the church was that they were not of sufficient authority to enter the New Testament canon. They were considered beneficial but not to have apostolic authority.

Lastly, there is a third category of non-canonical writings which made the rounds of early Christian groups. These writings are sometimes called apocryphal. Included in this group are letters such as the *Gospel of Thomas*, the *Gospel of Peter*, the *Gospel of the Hebrews* and the *Gospel of Judas*. The evidence for many of these books is that they were produced in the second and third centuries by heretical groups, most commonly by Gnostics. The Gnostics were a loosely defined movement which rejected the humanity of Jesus and promoted mystical "deep" knowledge (and thus the word gnostic, which means knowledge). These groups tended to have secret rites at which initiates were given this deeper knowledge. Anyone who tries to create the impression that books such as the Gospel of Thomas are somehow on par with the canonical New Testament books is either deceiving their hearer or is guilty of extremely poor scholarship. They are to be rejected for several reasons. First, in virtually every case, they were written long after the apostles were dead, and therefore clearly do not have apostolic authority. Second, there is no evidence that the early church leaders of the mainstream church (excluding heretical groups) ever accepted any of these books as canonical. Third, if you read these books for yourself, which I would recommend you do, you will see that they generally are of very inferior quality.

Let me return to the New Testament books themselves. It is true that humans both wrote these books and accepted them for inclusion in the New Testament canon. The Bible itself never pretends to be written by angels, although in places, it has direct revelation and dreams imparted by angels (Revelation, Zechariah, etc.). Instead, the Bible clearly presents itself as having been written by human beings. The Bible claims for itself that it is inspired by God (2 Timothy 3:16, 1 Thessalonians 2:13). Peter claims that it was the inspiration of the Holy Spirit which led the human writers of the Bible to speak for God (2 Peter 1:20-21). He also stated that the writings of Paul were *"Scriptures"* (2 Peter 3:16). As for the books chosen for inclusion in the New Testament, these books were chosen because, by consensus, they were the ones considered by the churches to be inspired and to have apostolic authority. It is apparent, both from the New Testament quotes by early church fathers and from lists of accepted books we have (such as the Muratorian fragment from about AD 175), that the list of New Testament books was becoming fixed by about AD 150. It is also apparent from the evidence that the four gospels were circulating as a group by AD 100 and that most of the letters of Paul circulated as a group by AD 90. The point is that, other than a couple of books (for example 2 and 3 John, 2 Peter and Revelation), there was little controversy over which were the inspired books in the second century.

In the end, for myself, I believe the books we have are inspired for a few reasons. First, I have confidence because of the facts we have about how they were chosen. Second, I believe these books are inspired because of the quality of the content of the books themselves. If you struggle with this, I suggest you take some time to find copies of some of the apocryphal "gospels" or even some of the letters from the early church fathers. You will see immediately that there is no comparison in the quality! Third, I believe the books which have come down to us are inspired simply because I have faith that God, who is all-powerful, had every interest in directing the process of assembling our New Testament. I admit that this is a matter of faith, not evidence. But common sense tells me that God had sufficient interest to make sure that the books which came down to us were the ones he wanted to be included. There is more than enough evidence of inspiration in general, and faith fills in the gaps for me.

QUESTION:

I was recently reading material from a conspiracy theorist named David Icke, and tried to look into what he believes and preaches. I ran into a number of articles that try to debunk Christianity and the Bible. I am highly offended by his work, and although he seems to have put a lot of research into it, I felt that he is just another false prophet trying to twist what has been taught in the Bible and about God. His website is http://www.davidicke.net/religiousfrauds/menu.html. He claims that the stories of Christianity are a "pious fraud." He says that the intent of the Christians was to convert anyone and everyone by any means possible, including lies. I am highly skeptical of this guy and was wondering if you could please shed some light on some of this speculation about God, the Bible and Christianity?

ANSWER:

I have spent a bit of time checking out the material at Mr. Icke's web site. I, too, find myself getting a bit angry as I see such lies and disrespectful attacks on Jesus Christ written by this person. It is tempting to vent my feelings, which would be to lower myself to the intellectual level of this writer. Let me avoid doing this, in the spirit of 1 Peter 3:15-16, which says, *"Always be prepared to give an answer to everyone who asks you to give the reason for the hope that you have. But do this with gentleness and respect, keeping a clear conscience, so that those who speak maliciously against your good behavior in Christ may be ashamed of their slander."*

In keeping with this advice from the apostle Peter, what I will do is take just four little quotes from the first article at this web site, titled "The Origins of Christianity and the Quest for the Historical Jesus Christ." This article is actually by the infamous Acharya S. (go to **EFC** and search for Acharya S.). It seems that her article is representative of the philosophy of our Mr. David Icke.

The first quote I would like to analyze is as follows:

"The most enduring and profound controversy in this subject is whether or not a person named Jesus Christ ever really existed."

First of all, there is no controversy whatsoever among legitimate scholars on whether the man Jesus of Nazareth ever lived. We have it on good authority from a number of non-Christian historians of the first and early second centuries, including Tacitus, Pliny, Josephus, Seutonius and many others, that Jesus was a very much a real person. Tacitus includes the information that "Christus" (as he calls him) was put to death by Pontius Pilate. Even the Jewish writers of the Talmud do not deny the reality of Jesus. And no one in the early centuries had more reason to deny the existence of this man than the Jews. In the Babylonian Talmud (second-century AD), the writer confirms that "Yeshu" (his Hebrew name) was hanged on the eve of the Passover. For more first and second century historians, as well as primary source information, go to **RFB** ch. 2, 3. We know for a fact from non-Christian authorities that there were many thousands of believers in Jesus Christ in the first century AD who accepted the literal fact of his life, his miracles and his resurrection. It is beyond reason to believe that these people were completely tricked into believing in a mythical man who did not even exist, when there were literally thousands of eyewitnesses living in the area at that time. Bottom line, anyone with the audacity to call into question whether or not Jesus even lived is not to be taken seriously as a scholar or teacher. Such a person is either a purposeful deceiver or refuses to accept what is absolutely obvious. It would not be wise to listen to such a person.

Below is a second quote taken from this article:

> This controversy has existed from the very beginning, and the writings of the "Church Fathers" themselves reveal that they were constantly forced by the pagan intelligentsia to defend what the non-Christians and other Christians ("heretics") alike saw as a preposterous and fabricated yarn with absolutely no evidence of it ever having taken place in history. As Rev. Robert Taylor says, "And from the apostolic age downwards, in a never interrupted succession, but never so strongly and emphatically as in the most primitive times, was the existence of Christ as a man most strenuously denied." Emperor Julian, who, coming after the reign of the fanatical and murderous "good Christian" Constantine, returned rights to pagan worshippers, stated, "If anyone should wish to know the truth with respect to you Christians, he will find your impiety to be made up partly of the Jewish audacity, and partly of the indifference and confusion of the Gentiles, and that you have put together not the best, but the worst characteristics of them both." According to these learned dissenters, the New Testament could rightly be called, "Gospel Fictions."

This is a blatant example of use of logical fallacies to make arguments. In a philosophy of science class I teach, we discuss the nature of logical fallacies. As I peruse this article, I find liberal use of a variety of the standard repertoire of illogical arguments. For example, Acharya S. makes a straw man argument by quoting Mr. Taylor out of context. What he (Mr. Taylor) is saying is that the early church argued over the nature of Jesus. Some said that he was entirely human and entirely divine. Some said he was entirely divine (the Gnostics, for example). Still others said that he was entirely human. What no one EVER argued was whether or not he really existed. The author is trying to make someone say something which he never said. Taylor is not saying that people have argued over whether Jesus was real. Such manipulative abuse of a person's statement to prove a point is inexcusable. Second, she takes a quote from Julian "The Apostate" to prove that he said Jesus never existed. The problem with this is that Julian does not say in this quote that Jesus did not exist. I am confident that Julian believed that Jesus Christ was a real person. If you look carefully at her argument that it was commonly believed back then that Jesus did not live, you will see that she cannot give a single example.

Let us analyze a third quote from this article:

A century ago, mythicist Albert Churchward said, "The canonical gospels can be shown to be a collection of sayings from the Egyptian Mythos and Eschatology." *In Forgery in Christianity*, Joseph Wheless states, "The gospels are all priestly forgeries over a century after their pretended dates."

First of all, simply telling us that "mythist" Albert Churchward said that the Gospels are a collection of myths is not evidence that this is so. Acharya S. and many of the articles by David Icke try to prove something is fact by quoting a number of people who say it is so. This is not evidence. A quote from an eminent scholar in the field may carry some weight, but who is Albert Churchward? Now, the claim here is that the Gospels were all written more than a century after their "pretended dates." In other words, this person has the audacity to claim that the Gospels were all written after AD 150. What she refuses to notice is that there is not a single serious scholar who supports this opinion. The reason is that the evidence is absolutely overwhelming that it is not true. For example, one papyrus fragment of the book of John is known as the Rylands Papyrus. This fragment of John has been dated to around AD 125. Other fragments of all four Gospels have been found from a period before Acharya claims these books were written. Actually, this is not even the strongest evidence that these books were written in the first century. The fact is that a number of church fathers, including Polycarp, Ignatius, Clement of Rome, the writer of the Didache and others, quote extensively from all four Gospels, as well as almost all of the New Testament books, all before AD 120. Some even wrote before AD 100. Acharya tries to create the impression that the apocryphal gospels (such as the pious fraud Gospel of Thomas) are of about equal worth to the canonical Gospels. This is not just an unsupported opinion. It is an outright lie. None of the apocryphal gospels is ever quoted by the very early church fathers. This is mainly because they were not even written yet. It is settled fact that all four Gospels were written before AD 90. Almost certainly they were written at least twenty years before that, with the possible exception of John. This argument does not hold water. Yet, the author speaks as if she had authority.

The fourth quote is a reference to what you address in your question.

Forgery during the first centuries of the Church's existence was admittedly rampant, so common in fact that a new phrase was coined to describe it: "pious fraud."

Of the four claims, this is the only one which is at least in part true. It is true that by the middle of the second century AD a number of "pious fraud" apocryphal letters came to be written and to circulate. Most, or more likely all of them, were produced by members of heretical sects. Most commonly, they were produced by Gnostic groups. Such heretical teachers promoted ideas that Jesus was a spiritual but not a human person. They believed in special, hidden knowledge which was only available to the initiates of their individual groups. Gnosticism was even becoming a problem in the first century, as can be seen by the book of first John which is clearly written, at least in part, to oppose Gnostic influence: "(him) *which we have seen with our eyes, which we have looked at and our hands have touched*" (1 John 1:1). The claim of Acharya S. and of David Icke is that the canonical Gospels of Mark, Luke, John and Matthew are also pious frauds. What they lack is evidence to support this contention. We know for a fact that the church accepted these letters as being inspired writings in the first century. We know that the very early church believed these were factual accounts of real events at a time when those who were eyewitnesses to the events were still alive. This is absolutely not the case with the *Gospel of Thomas* or any of the dozens of other apocryphal gospels. None of the church fathers in the first two centuries ever quoted from any of these pious frauds. If you struggle with this claim, the solution is simple. Read these "gospels" for yourself. Study what honest scholars say about these books. Compare the evidence to the four Gospels. You will find that the claim that the book of Matthew is a pious fraud does not stand up to the facts. In fact, the only way to support this claim is to either avoid looking at the evidence or to purposefully cover up the truth in order to deceive the reader.

The statements I have made in this little response are pretty strong, but I believe they will stand up to any reasonable scrutiny. The deceitful writings of Mr. Icke do not deserve to be treated as legitimate scholarship.

QUESTION:

The instructor in my religious class at college (VCU) teaches that 1 and 2 Timothy, Titus and 2 Peter were written in the early second century. Why do they think that? How do we know the letters really were written by the apostles? What would it mean to us if they were written in the second century? Would they still be scripture? (My feeling is that they couldn't be inspired if it says they were written by an apostle but not, because that would be lying, and God's word can't lie.) Anything that will help my faith in these letters would be great!

ANSWER:

It is quite common for theologians and Bible scholars to make the charge that certain New Testament letters were written well into the second century AD. Those doing so generally make this claim, not because of the evidence, but because of their own notions of what was taught at what time, as the early church evolved over time. In other words, they speculate that a certain idea did not enter Christianity until the second century. They then find this teaching in a book such as 2 Timothy. Then, using circular reasoning, they conclude that 2 Timothy was written in the second century. The fact is that there is no physical evidence whatsoever to support a claim that any of the New Testament books were written in the second century, while there is a lot of evidence to support a claim of first-century authorship.

The evidence for the more conservative date of writing (for example, a date of about AD 63 for I Timothy) is of varying quality, depending on which New Testament book one is discussing. For example, for the Gospels and some of the major letters, we have extremely good evidence for an early date of writing. One piece of evidence which supports a first-century date is the wealth of quotes of the early church fathers from most of the letters. Early church fathers such as Polycarp, Ignatius and Clement of Rome wrote letters in which they quote from almost every New Testament book. For example, Polycarp is a bishop who was martyred in AD 156. He met the apostle John when he was a young child. In his letter to the Philippians (about AD 120), he quotes or refers to the books of Matthew, Mark, Luke, Acts, 1 and 2 Corinthians, Galatians, Ephesians, Philippians, 1 and 2 Thessalonians, 1 and 2 Timothy, Hebrews, 1 Peter, and 1, 2 and 3 John. Clement of Rome wrote his first letter in AD 95 or 96. Similarly, he quotes from 10 of the 27 New Testament books. Ignatius (about AD 110) quotes from Matthew, John and Luke. Other examples can be given.

For books such as the Gospels and almost all of Paul's letters (including 1 and 2 Timothy), we can say from those who referenced them that all these books were written by the end of the first century. 1 Peter falls in this category as well. Some books are very likely to have been written in the first century, but it would be a bit too strong to call this proved. Examples would include 2 Peter, Jude, Hebrews and Revelation. Titus may fall into this second category.

This begs the question, "Why would the instructor in your religious studies class claim that these books were written in the early second century? I have read a number of authors who make this claim. Their argument is indirect. What they say is that the things taught in the Pastoral Epistles represent a later point in the history of Christianity. For example, they will point out that 1 Timothy has a list of rules for appointing elders. Both letters seem to be a bit more formulaic in giving advice than Paul's other letters. I believe that the reason for this trend in 1 and 2 Timothy and Titus is that Paul is addressing an evangelist, giving practical advice for how to direct the churches, whereas in the general epistles, he is addressing the church as a whole. I would say that in the absence of other information, the argument your professor used would be a reasonable one. In fact, it is a reasonable one even in light of what we know. However, I believe that in light of the totality of evidence, the final conclusion that the letters to Timothy were not written until over 40 years after Paul died is on thin ice. It is my strong belief that those who reach this final conclusion do so more because of a theological agenda than because the evidence points in this direction.

Now that I just made a pretty strong statement, let me say that this is not a fundamental issue. It is possible to be saved and to still be in some doubt as to the date at which these books were written. Still, the evidence weighs very strongly toward the conservative view, which is that they were written in the 60s or, at the latest, the 70s AD.

You say that if these books were not written by Paul and Peter, it would imply they were not inspired. I am not sure that it is as simple as that. Let me describe a scenario. It is not that I believe this scenario, but I use it to explain my answer. Let us imagine that an inspired writer wrote 1 Peter, but that the author was not Peter. Let us imagine that, by the second century, this inspired letter had been passed around for two or three generations without a signature, but many claimed it was from Peter. Let us extend this scenario a bit more. Let us imagine that a scribe added the phrase at the beginning, "Peter, an apostle of Jesus Christ"—not because it was inspired, but to explain to those reading who was commonly believed to be the author. In this scenario, the letter could be inspired but not written by Peter. I am not saying this is what happened, but I am saying that it is not absolutely required that Peter be the author for the book to be inspired. I agree that God does not lie, but scribes do make mistakes. We know this because some of our manuscripts do have mistakes in them.

In conclusion, I believe that all these books were written in the first century. The case for all but Titus is solid, and even with Titus, I believe it is strong. Whether or not it is provable that Paul and Peter wrote these letters is on slightly less stable ground, but on balance, I believe these are the most likely conclusions.

QUESTION:

I have a theory regarding the passages in John 8 and Mark 16 not being in the Codex Vaticanus and Sinaiticus that I would like you to comment on. Isn't it possible that the previous version, from which these were copied, had John 8 and Mark 16 torn out, resulting in incomplete manuscript copies? Maybe younger Codex like Bezae and Alexandrinus were copied from more complete versions (i.e. these sections weren't torn out/missing). Bezae and Alexandrinus didn't have to be based on Sinaitcus and Vaticanus. Does this scenario make sense?

ANSWER:

My answer to your question will differ depending on which passage you are talking about. In the case of Mark 16:9-20, there is some evidence that this was in the original Mark. One piece of evidence which supports this is the fact that the Vaticanus manuscript you refer to has a blank column left, apparently on purpose, after Mark 16:8 and before Luke 1:1. There are different possible interpretations of this. Perhaps the scribe in this case was aware of these verses but did not think they were part of the original, but left a blank space anyway. This would indicate that, even if these verses were not in the original Mark, they predate Vaticanus (about AD 350). Further evidence in support of Mark 16:9-20 being original (or at least very old) is a direct quote from this passage being found in the writings of Irenaeus. The quote is from his work titled "Against Heresies" from AD 180 (Book 3, 10:5-6). The quote from Irenaeus is: "Also, toward the conclusion of his gospel, Mark says, *'So then, after the Lord Jesus had spoken to them, he was received up into heaven and sits on the right hand of God.'*" Eusebius, the first church historian, confirmed the genuineness of Mark 16:9-20 in the second half of the 300s AD. On balance, I believe it is fair to say that whether this passage was in the original Mark is debatable. For this reason, I would not base an argument for a particular important biblical teaching solely on Mark 16:9-20. Fortunately, there is no need to, as there is no important New Testament teaching which relies solely on this passage.

The case with John 7:53-John 8:11 is different. As with the Mark passage, only the Codex Bezae of the very early manuscripts includes this passage. However, it does not have the corroborating evidence in its support as do the Mark verses. None of the early Christian authors quoted from this passage. This implies it was not in the version of John read by the church in the second century. The other manuscripts which have this beautiful story of Jesus and the woman caught in adultery place it in different locations in the Gospel. For example, other manuscripts put it at the end of John, after John 7:36, or even after Luke 21:38. Based on the evidence, I believe it is reasonable to assume that the story of the woman caught in adultery is a genuine tradition from the life of Jesus, but that it was not in the original letter by John. Perhaps early disciples were so enamored with this wonderful (probably genuine) story that they included it into different manuscripts in a place which seemed appropriate to the scribe.

In conclusion, your thought that these passages were accidently removed from the original cannot be dismissed. Our conclusion should be based on the other available evidence. In one case (Mark 16:9-20), the evidence leaves me believing this just might be the case. In the other (John 7:53-8:11), I believe this is almost certainly not what happened.

QUESTION:
Who was the author of Ecclesiastes?

ANSWER:
The general consensus of conservative scholars is that King Solomon wrote Ecclesiastes. The introduction certainly implies this. It describes the author of the book as "the Teacher, son of David, king in Jerusalem." There is only one person we know of who was described in his own time as the Teacher, who was a son of David and who succeeded him as king. That was Solomon. Another clear reference to Solomon is found in Ecclesiastes 12:9, which seems to be an epilogue to the book. It describes the author of the book by saying, *"Not only was the Teacher wise, but also he imparted knowledge to the people. He pondered and searched out and set in order many proverbs."* Again, we can see Solomon in this description. Another section in Ecclesiastes also seems to clearly reflect Solomon's life. This is Ecclesiastes 2:4-9, in which the author of Ecclesiastes describes the works he undertook in his lifetime. The details, including the statement that "I became greater by far than anyone in Jerusalem before me," are an obvious reference to Solomon. Besides, the style of Ecclesiastes is similar in many ways to parts of the Proverbs.

Some scholars discount the genuine authorship of Solomon. Such things, ultimately, cannot be proved beyond a reasonable doubt. We should be honest that it will forever remain impossible to prove Solomon wrote Ecclesiastes. Although the authorship cannot be proven beyond a doubt, the author definitely implies that he is Solomon. Therefore, either the book was written by Solomon or it is pseudepigraphic; which means that it was written by someone who was pretending to be Solomon. Given the inspired nature of the Bible in general, this seems to be a very unlikely explanation. The most likely explanation of the book is that, as it clearly claims, it was written by King Solomon, son of King David of Israel. However, we should be careful and admit that this is not proven by the evidence and must be accepted on faith. Even if King Solomon wrote the book, we can tell from 12:9-14 that a later editor put the book in its final form.

Reliability of the Biblical Text

QUESTION:

Isn't it proven that parts of the Gospels were not written from eyewitness accounts, but only from things heard from other Gospel accounts? Doesn't that mean we should question whether they are inspired?

ANSWER:

The extent to which the four gospels are the accounts of eyewitnesses varies with the four books. It is true that Luke's account is entirely second-hand as Luke did not even meet Jesus of Nazareth. Perhaps, in some cases, Luke is even third hand as he may have interviewed those who knew the eyewitnesses. Mark almost certainly was an eyewitness to the Gospel events, as he places himself in the Garden of Gethsemane (Mark 14:51), but he was not privy to them all. Even Matthew was obviously not an eyewitness to the birth of Jesus. The question you will have to ask yourself on this one is do you trust the accuracy and good faith of the writers? I believe that these books have every mark of inspiration. So did the apostles and the early church leaders. The question is not whether every single event mentioned is from an eyewitness. That would have been literally impossible, even if Jesus himself had written the Gospels! Even he did not witness every scene in the Gospels. The question is whether God has offered enough evidence to you, through the books themselves, to conclude that these are inspired. For myself, I have studied these questions very carefully and, hopefully, with a skeptic's eye. As a scientist, I am trained to be skeptical. And I answer with a resounding "yes"! I will leave your response up to you.

QUESTION:

Who wrote the book of Hebrews?

ANSWER:

The answer is that no one knows who wrote this book. It is one of my three or four personal favorite books in the Bible, but bottom line, the book is not signed. We can assume that the very early church considered it to have "apostolic" authority, as it was included in the very early list of inspired books, also known as the "canon" of the New Testament.

Many have speculated about the author of Hebrews. Probably the most common person to be attributed as author is the apostle Paul. It is impossible to disprove this claim, but at least at first glance, the style of writing seems to be dramatically different from anything we have from Paul. Others have mentioned Timothy. Some have even speculated that a female disciple wrote the book. We can probably assume that it was written before AD 70 because of what is written in Hebrews 8:13. This passage seems to imply that the destruction of Jerusalem (by the Roman general Titus in AD 70) was immanent but had not happened yet when the book was written.

I suggest you find a good commentary on the book of Hebrews. In the introductory portion (assuming it is a good commentary), you will find a section discussing most of the major theories on the authorship of the book. In the end you will have your favorite theory, but you will probably conclude with the scholars that you do not know who wrote this great book.

QUESTION:

Someone told me that most scholars say that Revelation was written after AD 70. Where can I find what scholars say regarding the date of writing for Revelation? If it's after AD 70, is it possible that most of the prophecies in Revelation have not yet been fulfilled, which is what some people I have heard say? From what I understand personally, I believe it was written more so for the first-century Christians, though there are some prophecies that have not happened yet.

ANSWER:

The book of Revelation does not come with a date, so scholars have to make a reasonable assumption about the date of the book from the context of the material in it. If you want to find out some scholar's ideas about the date when the book was written, you can buy or borrow from a library a good commentary on the book. I like the commentary by Jim McGuiggan. Another very good one by Gordon Ferguson is *Mine Eyes Have Seen the Glory* (available from www.ipibooks.com). Any good commentary will mention the range of scholar's opinions as well as the reason for their opinions. Most conservative scholars (defined as ones who accept that the Bible is inspired by God) date the book sometime after AD 75 and before AD 100. It is my opinion that the book was written during the reign of Roman Emperor Domitian (81-96 AD), probably in the second half of his reign. I reach this conclusion because John tells us that he has been exiled on the Island of Patmos. We know from Eusebius that this exile occurred as part of the persecution of Domitian, which happened toward the end of his reign. In Revelation chapter 17, Domitian is the king who yet will come (17:8). This eighth emperor is the eleventh emperor of Daniel chapter seven. This is described in my book **Daniel** Ch. 9.

In addition, we can see from chapters two and three what the issues in the churches in Asia were at the time, which can help. If you are serious about trying to determine the date the book was written, you really need to do your own research using at least a couple of commentaries.

As far as the issue of the prophecies in the book, there certainly are a wide variety of opinions about that. Let me share my belief, but encourage you to do your own research. I believe that virtually all the apocalyptic/prophetic writing in the book concerns things which happened during the time the book was written, or fairly shortly after. The book is about the persecution of the Christian Church by the Roman Empire and about God's judgment on those who attacked the Church. Specifically, the angel told John that the vision was about things which were soon to take place (Revelation 1:1) and that the time was near (Revelation 1:3). It seems easy to interpret the meaning of these passages to me! Besides, all the prophecies are easily understood as involving the Roman Empire. It is a big stretch to apply most of the book to future times. The exception is at the very end of the book, from Revelation 20:7 to the end of chapter 22, which seem to me to involve a shift to end times. A key question concerns the thousand years of Revelation 20:1-6. It is my belief that this is a description of the time between the persecutions under Rome and the end of days, the thousand years being an apocalyptic and symbolic representation of a long but indeterminate period of time.

Besides reading Revelation carefully, along with two or three solid commentaries, I suggest you spend some time doing some research into the history of the Roman Empire and the early church. Between these three sources, I believe you will reach a conclusion at least somewhat similar to my own, but I leave it up to you. Sorry to give you such a tough assignment, but digging deeper will be a fulfilling endeavor.

QUESTION:

Since human beings wrote the Bible, how can we trust it? How do we know the right books ended up in the Bible? The Bible is generally used as the primary reference for Christians. Even if I accept that the Bible is actually God's word, you have to admit that it was put on paper by humans. And since humans are imperfect, how do you put such faith in the Bible?

ANSWER:

Yes, indeed, the Bible was written by human beings—imperfect ones at that! In the end, what we have is this—the Bible claims for itself to be inspired by God. To prove this (not that it is inspired, but that it is claimed to be inspired), one can refer to 2 Timothy 3:16-17: *"All Scripture is inspired by God..."* as well as to 2 Peter 1:20-21: *"No prophecy of Scripture came about by the prophet's own interpretation. For prophecy never had its origin in the will of man, but men spoke from God as they were carried along by the Holy Spirit."*

The Bible claims for itself that its authors were *"carried along by the Holy Spirit"* as they wrote. Now, this is a claim, and you must personally decide what to do with this claim. I can see immediately that you are not the type to blindly accept this claim. That is a good thing. Either the claim is true or it isn't. What you must do is investigate the question of inspiration with a healthy level of skepticism, combined with sufficient open-mindedness that you are able to accept either conclusion. Personally, I began that search when I was in college, beginning as an atheist. I certainly was not predisposed to assume that the Bible is in fact inspired by God. However, my studies and thoughts over the years have inexorably led me to conclude that the claim is true. There is, for me, an overwhelming weight of evidence that the Bible is inspired by God.

My simply making that statement, of course, does not do much for you! Let me suggest a couple of areas you can investigate for yourself. First, I would encourage you to consider the messianic prophecies in the Old Testament. You will find a lot on this in **FSTR** Ch. 8 and **RFB** Ch. 4. There is no reasonable explanation of Psalm 22 (crucifixion, gambling at his feet, bones unbroken), Zechariah 11:10-13 (30 pieces of silver, the potter's field) and many other clear prophecies of the Messiah in the Old Testament fulfilled in the life of Jesus, unless one considers that the one who put the prophecies in the Old Testament caused them to be fulfilled in the life of Jesus. I would point out to you the uncanny scientific information in the Bible (**ITAG**), as well as the supernatural historical accuracy of both the Old and the New Testament (**RFB** ch. 7). The prophecies in Daniel (**Daniel**), the type/antitype fulfillments in the Old and New Testaments (**FSTR**), the consistency of message and lack of clear contradictions... the list can go on almost indefinitely. The case for the inspiration of the Bible is a slam dunk in my opinion, but you must do your own research.

Let me summarize by asking you to be willing to keep the question simple. There are many things which could be said for or against the Bible, but bottom line, either the evidence leads toward the conclusion that it is from God or it does not. Of course, it is true, as you say, that human beings wrote the Bible. The question is not whether it was written by human beings, but whether or not God inspired the writers—determining what got into the accepted scriptures. As Peter claims, the writers were *"carried along by the Holy Spirit"* (2 Peter 1:21). Whether or not this claim is to be believed is to be determined by the evidence. I believe the evidence gives a resounding yes.

QUESTION:

My question revolves around the true role of the Council of Nicaea. Some have argued that the council canonized certain texts to fit their purposes. I have heard the counter argument that the council merely canonized what was already widely accepted as inspired, but even this wide acceptance does little to guarantee that the New Testament is indeed God's inspired Word. I do not have much trouble with the Gospels and Acts, but why should I believe the Pauline Epistles and the other epistles are infallible? Saying that God wouldn't allow anything erroneous to enter the Bible only further confuses the argument because any religion can make the same argument about their "scripture." I understand that, but can you clarify the question of the inspiration of the epistles.

ANSWER:

The argument that the council of Nicaea changed the canon of scriptures is specious. There is absolutely not a shred of evidence that they did anything to change the content of the accepted canon of New Testament scripture. For someone to argue that such and such book is not inspired may or may not be valid, but the claim that the council of Nicaea changed the canon to fit their own idea of orthodoxy simply does not agree with the facts we have available. The "canon" of the New Testament was basically fixed by around 200 or, at the absolute latest, AD 250.

In regard to the letters of Paul, Peter and John, I'm afraid the seemingly circular argument you refer to is in fact the strongest argument for these books being inspired. The fact that the entire Bible as a whole shows marks of inspiration is evidence that God had a hand in determining what ended up in the Bible. The skeptic may find this argument unconvincing, but in the end, I believe it is compelling. It is logical (although the skeptic will not accept this logic) that if God is able to create and put together a group of, say, 80% of the Bible books which are inspired, that he would also be able to influence the whole thing. Proved inspiration of one part makes belief in the other parts (those about which we have no direct evidence for inspiration) more believable. I understand that this is not the kind of proof acceptable in a court of law, but I believe it is a logical line of reasoning.

When I discuss this matter, I will always concede that I cannot prove that every verse in the Bible is inspired. However, let me suggest one more approach. I suggest you spend some time reading the apocryphal books—those which did not make the cut. I would suggest reading the OT apocrypha (available in any Roman Catholic Bible) as well as some of the very early church father's letters which did not make the cut, such as the *Didache*, the letter of Clement of Rome, the letters of Ignatius and Polycarp. I believe that if you read these books, the difference between an inspired book and a useful, but uninspired book will make itself plain to you. Didache is good reading, but the Bible reader will be able to tell the difference immediately. These writings are available in any good library, so you can do the research for free. I am convinced that your faith in the inspiration of 1Timothy or 2 Peter will be increased by this sort of study.

QUESTION:

In the Gospel of John, the story of Jesus and the woman caught in adultery is not found in the most reliable sources such as Codex Sinaiticus and Codex Vaticanus. Why is the story in our Bibles today if it was not in what is considered the most authoritative documents on biblical manuscripts? The story has the feel of being true, but Matthew 5:18 says that not the smallest part of the Law will disappear. The Word of God should be flawless, so I am curious; if someone later inserted John 8:1-11, then how can that Gospel be inspired?

ANSWER:

This is a good question! What you are referring to is the fact that good Bible translations will note that the story of the woman caught in adultery in John chapter eight is not found in the earliest and most reliable manuscripts. It seems to me that this issue comes down to two questions. First, is the account in John 8:1-11 a genuine and accurate account of what happened? Second, was this passage in the original Gospel of John? If we answer these questions, we are ready to deal with the question of overall biblical inspiration as it relates to this passage. The fact is that nearly all the later manuscripts include the passage in John 8. Of the thousands of Greek New

Testament manuscripts, there are only three important ones which do not include John 8:1-11. The problem with this, however, is that the three which do not include the story of the woman caught in adultery are the earliest and most reliable.

One question is how did the passage get into the Book of John and why? After thinking about this question quite a bit, the conclusion I have reached is that the story of the woman caught in adultery is a true story—probably one which was often told by the apostle John himself. I am guessing that this story became so strongly associated with John that, because of this consensus, at some point an editor put it into the Gospel of John. It is also possible that, with the original Gospel of John, there were two versions, one with and one without this story, but this explanation seems less likely to me. In any case, as you imply, everything in this story has the feel of a genuine incident in the life of Jesus. I can think of no significant doctrine or teaching in the Bible which would be changed either by including or by excluding this passage.

Let us assume that the above speculation is true—in other words, that the story of the woman caught in adultery is true but was not in the original book of John. Does this somehow make the Bible less inspired by God? Did every inspired passage ever written find its way into the Bible? Obviously not! By the way, the passage you reference in Matthew chapter five is not speaking about whether some single word or phrase would or would not be lost in the New Testament. Jesus is saying that none of the requirements in the Law of Moses will be removed by his ministry. Jesus did not remove the Law of Moses, but rather he fulfilled the requirements of the Law of Moses. The Word of God is flawless, and I see nothing about the passage in John 8 which would negatively impact my belief about the inspiration of the Bible.

Let us consider for a moment the worst-case scenario. If the story of the woman caught in adultery was not even a true story, yet was included in the later manuscripts of the New Testament, even that would not make the original uninspired (not that I believe this is the case, personally). The fundamental question is whether the original writings of the Bible authors were inspired by God. To illustrate this point, consider 1 John 5:7-8. There is a little section here which found its way into later Greek manuscripts (and therefore into the King James translation) but which was not found in any of the earlier manuscripts. This section was almost without question added by a later editor, not because John wrote this passage, but in order to support their own doctrine of the Trinity. That is why most translations only include this little passage in the margins. The point is that even if some sincere but misguided editor added his own little comment into a New Testament book, that fact would not bring into question the inspiration of the original writing, which is the principle question at issue. All the evidence I have seen is that God has managed, despite the imperfect efforts of humanity, to pass on to us both an Old and a New Testament text which is essentially the same as the original. I discuss this question in detail in **RFB** ch. 6. To summarize, whether or not John 8:1-11 was in the original book of John has no effect on our conclusion about whether the original writings of the Bible were inspired by God.

QUESTION:
How do scholars date the ancient manuscripts and written records from the past, and are their methods accurate?

ANSWER:
Scholars use a number of methods to determine the age of a manuscript. You might think that Carbon-14 dating, which gives an objective date for when the papyrus or vellum or other material was produced, would be the principal method, but actually it is not. Carbon-14 isotopic dating requires the destruction of at least a small portion of the manuscript material. For obvious reasons, scholars do not like to do this. Besides, it is only accurate to plus or minus about fifty to one hundred years. For this reason, more indirect methods of dating are generally used. Scholars compare types of paper or parchment material, styles of script and other types of evidence from the manuscripts themselves. The composition of the ink used provides more useful evidence for the date of composition. Greek texts changed over time from using all capitals (uncial manuscripts) to having both capitals and small letters. The shapes of hand-printed letters tend to change with time. The types of materials used for inks tended to change with time as well. In general, scholars believe they can determine the date of copying for a manuscript about as precisely from ink, paper and writing style as they can using Carbon-14 dating, without needing to destroy part of the manuscript.

As to the precision of dates scholars give for the age of manuscripts, that is a good question. One thing to look for is whether a number of scholars from different perspectives have studied a document and all are tending to agree fairly closely on a date of writing. If that is so, you can be fairly confident. For example, the Rylands Papyrus, a small fragment of John which has been dated to about AD 125, has been studied closely by a great number of scholars. Those who look at the paper, the script style and the C-14 data are in fairly good agreement. For this reason, you can probably assume that this date is correct within perhaps 25 years or so. A more recent manuscript of Mark, known as the Magdalene Manuscript, has been dated to around AD 68. This is a very exciting find, but it has not been studied as carefully or by as many scholars, so I would advise caution about the date of this very interesting manuscript. Very likely, it is from before AD 150, but a date of pre-AD 100 is a bit tentative for now, pending more study.

QUESTION:

What evidence do we have which points to the conclusion that the Gospels were written by the apostles themselves? The first one who believed that they were written by them was Irenaeus in 180 AD.

ANSWER:

It is impossible to prove absolutely that the apostles wrote the letters of the New Testament. Actually, you should be aware that Luke, Acts (written by Luke), James (brother of Jesus, not the apostle), Jude (brother of Jesus), Mark (right-hand man to Peter) and perhaps Hebrews were not written by apostles. Apparently, for the church fathers, the question was not whether a book was written by one of the thirteen apostles (including Paul), but whether the books had apostolic authority. In fact, it is (in general) impossible to prove conclusively that the writings of such famous ancient authors as Herodotus, Cicero, Tacitus and so forth were actually written by these men. The strongest evidence we have in general is that the contemporaries accepted their writings as genuine. This is the case with the New Testament. The strongest evidence we have that these writings were apostolic is that they were accepted as such by the very earliest church as a whole.

You are not correct to say that Irenaeus was the first to claim that the letters of Paul, Peter, John and the Gospels were written by the apostles. For example, one could mention the letter known as The Shepherd of Hermas, as well as the letter of Clement of Rome to the Corinthians, both of which were written in the last decade of the first century AD. Both letters quote extensively from the letters of Paul, the Gospels and the letters of Peter, giving credit to the apostles for the books. The same could be said for the letters of Ignatius of Antioch who wrote in the last decade of the first century and the first decade of the second century AD. Another important witness is the letters of Polycarp. This early church father was a personal acquaintance of the apostle John. One can assume he would know if John had written the Gospel of John. Polycarp quotes from the Gospel of John. A small manuscript known as the Muratorian Fragment has been dated to about 170 AD. It mentions all the New Testament except Matthew, Mark, Hebrews, James, 1 and 2 Peter and 1 John as being inspired, and therefore having apostolic authority. Matthew and Mark are implied because this fragment calls Luke the third Gospel. In AD 180, Irenaeus was only quoting fairly long-standing tradition when he mentioned the apostolic authority of the letters and the Gospels.

In the end, we must rely on the authority of the letters themselves and the witness of those in the early church who were clearly in a position to judge whether these letters were apostolic or were considered inspired by the apostles. Although there was some debate about the apostolic authority for 2 and 3 John, Hebrews and 2 Peter in the second century, one can conclude with confidence that, in nearly every case, the traditional authors of the letters in the New Testament are those for whom they are generally attributed. A couple of helpful references on this subject are *The New Testament Documents: Are They Reliable?* by F. F. Bruce and *How We Got the Bible,* by Neil Lightfoot and a short book by Mike Taliaferro entitled, *How We Got the Bible and Why You Can Trust it?*

QUESTION:

I have a question about your website article on the NT canon. You said that the Muratorian Fragment is the earliest list of NT letters, but that it did not contain Hebrews, James or 1 John. Since Origen was also skeptical about these, should we be? Is there any proof to believe that these are inspired also?

ANSWER:

A certain level of measured skepticism is called for in everything, of course. However, with sufficient evidence, one is advised to let down one's guard somewhat when it becomes clear that something is true beyond a reasonable doubt. I believe this applies to the New Testament canon. You mention that Origen was skeptical about some of the books. It would be more accurate to say that Origen conceded that certain books were debated by some. In other words, Origin did not necessarily doubt the inspired nature of these books, but rather he admitted that some still debated their place in the officially accepted list of canonical writings. The fact that Origen mentions the debate, even though he believed they were apostolic, proves that he was a careful thinker, not a demagogue, which makes his statements more reliable.

If one understands the process by which the New Testament canon was created, the fact that certain books were accepted into the final list later than others is only natural. Although we do not have detailed accounts of the thoughts of Christians from this time, it might be useful to speculate about what the list of universally accepted inspired writings were in 65, in 85, in 105 and in 125 AD. In AD 65, not all the books were even written, never mind all accepted as part of what we now call the New Testament. By AD 85, most likely the last books were either recently written or perhaps would very soon be written (possible "last" books include Revelation, 1, 2 or 3 John or even the Gospel of John). By AD 105, all the books had certainly been written, but insufficient time had passed for every book to have been passed around the churches and carefully read in order to allow all of them to be clearly understood as inspired and belonging to the official list. By AD 125, sufficient time had passed that one can imagine official lists already being generated, although we do not have an extant copy from that time frame. By 150 AD, this process was almost completed. Only a very few books were still debated, and books such as the *Didache* and the *Gospel of Barnabus* had already been recognized for what they were—useful for additional reading and study, but not inspired books with apostolic authority. Even if, for some reason, the early church had erred in this natural process of collecting those letters with apostolic authority, it seems reasonable to believe, in the end, God would have stepped in and made sure that the books he wanted included made it in there one way or another!

QUESTION:

Regarding the Q-Source, Do you believe that there was a Q? If so, then was God's inspired word lost?

ANSWER:

The Q-Source is a hypothetical document containing primitive sayings and accounts from the life of Jesus. This document has been hypothesized in order to explain both the similarities and the differences between Matthew, Mark and Luke. Was there a written source of sayings and acts of Jesus available before Mark or Matthew wrote their Gospels? I would assume almost certainly there was. Did Mark draw upon this written source? I cannot prove so, but logic and common sense would lead one to assume that such documents existed and that the Gospel writers may very well have used such sources to recall and organize their information. More specifically, did the Q-source exist? I would take some of the arguments and conclusions of the theologians, and especially the liberal theologians, with a big grain of salt, but I do believe that some written sources were most likely available. Was there one identifiable source which we now call the Q-source? I have no idea, and I believe scholars do not either. There is a huge amount of speculation and argument among scholars about the Q-source.

Let us suppose for just a moment that Q was a real document, and that it was inspired. How should we feel about that? I speculate that there were a number of inspired writings which did not make it into our Bible. We know that Paul wrote other letters. Presumably other apostles wrote letters in addition to the ones we have in the New Testament. The question is not so much whether every inspired word ever uttered ended up in the Bible. The question is whether the ones we have in our canon of scripture are from God. The evidence says yes.

QUESTION:

I've heard different information about the earliest New Testament manuscript. Is the manuscript from John (125 AD) the earliest? And what about the Magdalene Manuscripts and those from Mark (46 AD) found in Egypt? Are these the earliest MS?

ANSWER:

The manuscripts you refer to are the Rylands Papyrus and the Magdalene Manuscript. The Rylands Papyrus has been thoroughly studied and dated to about 125 AD. It is a fragment of John. The Magdalene Manuscript is so-called because it resides in Magdalene College at Oxford. It is a very small fragment of Matthew 26. Dr Carsten Thiede has tentatively dated it to AD 65/66 by comparison to writing styles of several well-known manuscripts of the same period. His analysis involves looking at the papyrus fibers, the angle of the stylus used to lay down the ink and so forth. I am not sure where you found the date AD 46. It is fair to say that Thiede's conclusion is still quite tentative. It may be wise to wait for some more studies to confirm the date of writing of this manuscript. However, if the date holds up, this would clearly be an astounding find, as it would be a manuscript from within less than a generation of the original writing of the letter—perhaps within less than ten years. Other very early manuscripts have been analyzed as well, including a manuscript fragment from Luke which has been tentatively dated to AD 100. This, too, is only a preliminary finding about which we should be very cautious.

If I were asked to give a direct answer to the question, I would prefer to be cautious and say the earliest confirmed manuscript is the Rylands Fragment of John from AD 125. In addition, a fragment of Luke has been dated to AD 100, and the Magdalene fragment of Mark 16 as early as AD 65, but both are very tentative. These are fun and exciting times for those who study the New Testament document record.

Chapter Two

Archaeology, History and the Bible

QUESTION:
What is your view on the claim that the conquering of the Canaanites at Jericho is not supported by the archeological excavations and finds at Jericho? The Israelites were supposed to have entered Jericho in 1407 BC, but many archeologists believe they didn't enter until 1230-1220 BC. Kathleen Kenyon's research in 1952-1958 concluded that Jericho was destroyed in 1550 BC (probably from an earthquake, as Jericho sits on a fault line), and there was no city to conquer by the time the Israelites arrived. What about DNA evidence that the Canaanites and Israelites were the same people?

ANSWER:
There are two common views of the timing of the conquest of the Promised Land by Joshua. Actually, there are three, given that some deny that this event happened at all. I will not go into the reasons I reject the third theory at this time. The two common dates given for the conquest are some time near the end of the 15th century BC—about 1410 BC—and some time in the 13th century BC—about 1240 BC. It is true that Kathleen Kenyon concluded in the 1950s that Jericho was destroyed in 1550 BC. However, her conclusion was based on what she did NOT find, which was imported pottery from Cyprus. More recent work by Bryant G. Wood ("Did the Israelites Conquer Jericho?" *Biblical Archaeology Review* September/

October 1990, p. 45-59.) provides two kinds of physical evidence which makes Kenyon's conclusion questionable. First, the Canaanite pottery shards found in the ruins of Jericho from the time it was burned put the date of the destruction around 1400 BC. Second, Carbon-14 radiometric dating showed that the city was burned around 1410 BC. The evidence supporting this as the date of the destruction of Jericho is looking very strong.

Those who prefer a later date for the destruction of Jericho of about 1240 BC do so perhaps partly because, until the past 15 years or so, many believed that the date of the second half of the fifteenth century BC was ruled out. Once archaeologists commit themselves to a particular theory, it can be hard for them to change their views. In addition, many archaeologists are skeptical that the Hebrews could have been in Canaan as early as 1400 BC, causing them to prefer a later date. I cannot absolutely rule out the later date, but given the physical evidence in Jericho and the most likely chronology of biblical events, I believe the earlier date is most likely correct.

There is other physical evidence for an earlier date of around 1410 BC for the conquest of Jericho. This is found in the ruins of Hazor. According to the account in Joshua, there were three cities destroyed completely by fire at the time of the conquest. The three were Jericho, Ai and Hazor. Ai has not yet been definitively located, but Hazor has been found. This city has been excavated carefully by the archaeologist Yigael Yadin. At Hazor, he found evidence of a massive destruction by fire. To quote Yadin, "There is evidence of a massive destruction. I once called it the mother of all destruction" (see Randall Price, *The Stones Cry Out* (Harvest House, 1997) for references, as well as my book **RFB**). This destruction at Hazor occurred in the latter half of the 15th century BC, consistent with the data from Jericho.

About the genetic similarity between the Canaanites and the Israelites, I would have to see the evidence there. I am not sure what study you are referring to. It would be extremely difficult to genetically define a Canaanite in a modern context. Perhaps the study you heard about is of present-day Palestinians or of Arabs from Jordan or Palestine. The Jewish people have mixed their bloodlines with many peoples of the Middle East. I would not be surprised at all to find that there is a lot of genetic similarity between Ashkenazi Jews and other people in the Levant. Abraham lived in Canaan and many of his family members, which included servants from Canaan, would have had genetic similarity to the tribes in that area. I am not sure what one could conclude from genetic similarity between some modern Jews and Palestinians. That is exactly what one would expect.

There is quite a bit of other evidence which supports the general description of the events of the Exodus and the conquest of Canaan by the Hebrews. More information can be found in my book **RFB** and *The Stones Cry Out* (reference above). It would be an overstatement to say that the conquest is proven in detail by archaeology. It is more accurate to say that archaeology supports, but does not prove, that the events described in the Old Testament happened near the end of the 15th century BC.

QUESTION:

I am currently a college student and have taken several religion courses. Some things about these classes bother me. One is that the teacher is often very biased. What has been bothering me recently is some information that has been presented to us, and claimed as factual. It is said that, in their early history, the Jews actually worshipped many gods, and only later on picked out one to completely worship (*Yahweh*). I find this a bit challenging to my faith, and I was looking for some other information concerning it. Also, these teachers claim that there is much inconsistency in the Old Testament, where God declares himself as "one," and at other times, there is plural use (let us make man in our image). My professor says this is due to the fact that there were multiple gods worshipped in the beginning. I can't help but find some of this information bothering me, and I would like to find somewhat of a detailed response to this. Thanks for any help!

ANSWER:

Your experience is not an unusual one. The majority of those who teach religion courses in colleges and universities in the United States are non-believers. In light of this obvious bias, you should take what the teacher says with a grain of salt, although you will be able to learn a lot of interesting and useful information even from a non-believing religion instructor.

In analyzing the viewpoint of your religion professor, you should bear in mind that he/she makes an assumption in analyzing the data. He or she is assuming that there is no God and that it is therefore impossible the Bible is inspired by God. Given that this assumption is false (and I believe that it is patently false!), it is understandable that such teachers and the theologians or historians they use as sources are bound to misinterpret the available information. If you assume that Jesus was just a human being, then this will surely influence how you interpret the biblical account of the feeding of the five thousand. If you assume that the Jews were just another loose confederation of tribes who invented monotheism—that the story of Moses is a pious fable—this will surely affect your interpretation of the story in Exodus of the parting of the Red Sea. As you listen to your religion professor, remember that he or she has a bias which makes it impossible for him or her to interpret much biblical information correctly.

Let me get to the specific question. Based on his/her pre-assumption that there is no God, your religion instructor is assuming that the Jews evolved in a way analogous to all other ancient peoples. No wonder he or she reaches the conclusion that the Jews evolved from polytheism to monotheism! The real question is what is the evidence? Let me be honest about this. We do not have a lot of information from history or archaeology about the Jews before about 1000 BC. There is an inscription from about 1250 BC in Egypt known as the Shishak Inscription. It mentions the Hebrews, but gives us no information about their religious practices. We know from copious archaeological evidence that, by the early part of the first millennium BC, the Jews were worshipping *Yaweh*—that they were formally monotheistic, but that they definitely were still involved in idolatry. Of course, we know this from biblical references as well.

So, the question is how to extrapolate archaeological evidence of monotheism (with remnant polytheism) further into the past. It is not at all surprising that your religion professor speculates that Jewish monotheism evolved from polytheism. The evidence does not prove this, but "common sense" comparison to other cultures naturally leads to the logical conclusion that the very early Hebrews were polytheistic.

Bottom line, your professor is speculating based on a reasonable analysis of the evidence. Now, let us bring the Bible into the equation, and let us consider the possibility that it is in fact inspired by God. Let us at least allow for the possibility that it is accurate history. You must understand that your professor assumes that it cannot possibly be either of these. He or she is reasoning logically from an incorrect assumption, which makes the final conclusion inevitable. I believe, because of the evidence, that the Bible is by far the most accurate ancient historical document we have. I believe that there is overwhelming evidence that the Bible is inspired by God, including evidence from prophecy, from historical accuracy, from internal consistency and so forth. For a person who is open to the possibility that God is real and that he can work in human history, I believe that the story of God's people and of his working with them since the time of Abraham is compelling truth and wonderful evidence of God working miraculously with the Jews. You do not need to be intimidated by your religion instructor. You can probably learn a lot from this class, but you must bear in mind the entire time that you are hearing information from a person who is biased and, for whatever reason, rejects the obvious truth that the Bible is God's word. If you can listen with a wise eye to detect that bias, your experience in the class can be worthwhile.

I almost forgot your last question. It is true and a bit disconcerting at first that the very early part of Genesis has God using the word "we" when speaking. If we allow for the fact that the Father, the Son and the Spirit are all present at the creation (Genesis 1:1: *"and the Spirit of God was hovering over the waters"*) this makes sense. In the rest of the Bible, it is true that God speaks of himself in the singular, so this use of first person plural in the first chapters of Genesis is a bit surprising. But if one applies the idea of the "trinity," it is readily explained. What we can say for sure is that there is no strong evidence for polytheism anywhere in the Bible, even with the passages in Genesis one. Most conservative scholars recognize this fact, but those who assume that the Bible is entirely a human creation are bound to reach a different conclusion. This is not because of the evidence, but because of a bias.

QUESTION:
Were people literate in the time of Jesus?

ANSWER:
This is a good question. The answer will depend on whom you are talking about— whether the Jews themselves, or the Romans, Greeks or other neighboring peoples. Ancient peoples did not measure or record rates of literacy. We have no data to go by. For this reason, we must use indirect evidence to reach conclusions about literacy rates. By the time of Christ, the chief social/religious institution among the Jews was the Synagogue. The Synagogues encouraged the acquisition of at least a rudimentary level of Hebrew literacy, at least for the more well-off male Jews. I have found what seems to be a fairly careful scholarly study. It is at http://faculty.biu.ac.il/~barilm/illitera.html.

The scholar Meir Bar-Ilan makes calculations of literacy rates for the Jews using a couple of pieces of data. First, he notes that the Soferim, the Jewish Scribes of the early centuries AD, required that for a Synagogue to form, a reader of the Torah was required. He uses data on the population and the number of Synagogues in some of the smaller cities in Palestine at the time, which was presumably limited by the number of qualified readers, along with some assumptions about the male/female literacy rates to conclude that the literacy rate among the Jews in the cities was between 2-15%, but probably in the 2-3% range, and much lower in the country. This is probably higher than literacy rates of some of their neighbors. Literacy rates in ancient Egypt have been estimated at about half of one percent.

In the reference above, Meir points out that we have no reliable data from the first century on literacy. This is one statistic that, as far as we know, none of the ancients thought of as worth gathering. To show how poor our data is, the author referenced above is reduced to using data from Egypt around AD 1900 to make guesses about Egypt two millennia ago. The bottom line is that we do not know the literacy rate you ask about, but we can say with fair certainty that it was low.

One way to judge literacy is to look at records of how many copies of books were made. For example, in the time of the Renaissance, when the great universities had been open at Paris, Florence and other locations for two or three hundred years, important new books such as Galileo's *"Dialogues of the Two Chief World Systems"* had an initial run of only a couple of thousand books. Trying to extend this data to times before the printing press (introduced to Western Europe by Gutenberg in 1455) is problematic, as one can assume that, before the printing press, copies were passed around more due to the astronomical cost of copying books by hand.

My personal speculation is that, with the emphasis of the rabbis on Hebrew study, the literacy rate among the Jews may have been slightly higher than the 1.5% estimate by the author above. For well-to-do Jewish males, it may have been quite high, but certainly the overall rate was very low by modern standards.

QUESTION:

Is there hard, physical evidence for Christ, or is it all reasoning?

ANSWER:

The answer to this question will depend on what you mean by hard, physical evidence. What sort of evidence would this be? How would we judge the authenticity of such "physical" evidence? Perhaps you are thinking of a piece of clothing or a bone or a manuscript signed by Jesus. Of course, we do not have such items. In fact, even if we did, it would almost certainly be impossible to confirm a claim that an individual piece of hard evidence is genuine. As a general rule, except in extremely rare cases, we do not have hard, physical evidence of ancient peoples. One exception is the mummies of Egyptian Pharaohs, which can be identified by inscriptions in their tombs. Clearly, we do not have such a thing from Jesus, as he resurrected from the dead! We do have sculptures of some important ancients. Unfortunately for archaeologists, the Jews did not make statues or pictures of themselves because the second of the Ten Commandments prohibited making carved images of human beings. The answer, then, is that we do not have actual, physical objects which prove that Jesus was a real person.

Perhaps this is not really the question you are asking. Perhaps what you are really asking is whether there is strong evidence of a historical nature that the person known as Jesus Christ lived. In this case, the answer is absolutely "yes." The vast majority of historians, including those who do not accept the biblical picture of Jesus, accept that Jesus was a real person. There is considerable debate about exactly what he did and what he claimed, but the fact that Jesus lived is not in doubt. There are several reasons we can say this with confidence. First of all, non-believing historians from the first and second generation after Jesus lived reported the life of Jesus and supplied some details in agreement with the New Testament documents. For example the Jewish historian Flavius Josephus (AD 38-100) wrote his *Antiquities* about AD 94 under Domitian. Josephus was a Pharisee and a fairly reliable historian. His *Testamonium Flavium* comes from *Antiquities 18:3.3*. Josephus says concerning Jesus:

> About this time there lived Jesus, a wise man, *if indeed one ought to call him a man*. For he was one who wrought surprising feats and was a teacher of such people as accept the truth gladly. He won over many Jews and many of the Greeks. *He was the Messiah*. When Pilate, upon hearing him accused by men of the highest standing amongst us, had condemned him to be crucified, those who had in the first place come to love him did not give up their affection for him. *On the third day he appeared to them restored to life*, for the prophets of God had prophesied these and countless other marvelous things about him. And the tribe of Christians, so called after him, has still to this day not disappeared.

There is good reason to believe the italicized section are an interpolation from Christians, but the consensus of scholars is that probably the unitalicized material is original to Josephus. Agapius, an Arab Christian in 9th century probably quotes the original, leaving out the parts in parenthesis. Note the passage reads grammatically well without the parts in parenthesis. There is little doubt that Josephus wrote the passage as it presents Jesus in a light Christians would never accept. Note: Josephus also reports the martyrdom of "James, the brother of Jesus who was called the Christ" (*Antiquities 20:20*). From Josephus, we get the feeling that it was common knowledge that Jesus was a Jew who lived in Palestine, that he worked apparent miracles and that his followers made messianic claims about him. Tacitus, Seutonius, Pliny the Younger, Thallus and other Roman historians of the late first and early second century confirm the existence of Jesus, mentioning that he was executed and the fact that it was claimed he was a miracle-worker. In addition, the Jewish Talmud, a document of the first few centuries AD, also mentions Jesus, although these writers definitely do not accept that he was the Messiah. See **RFB** ch. 2 for references.

All these confirm the reality of Jesus. However, the most convincing evidence is the New Testament and the hundreds of eyewitnesses who became Christians in the first few years after the death and resurrection of Jesus. We know that several of the New Testament books were written by AD 60. Probably most of them were written by AD 70. There is little chance that a myth of Jesus could have arisen out of nothing in the same region where he lived in so short a time. We know from historical evidence that many, including the apostle James, were martyred in the first century. Within a generation of his death, followers of Jesus were killed for their faith in the persecutions under Nero and Domitian. In the face of this evidence, one cannot credibly claim that Jesus was not real.

There is not any reasonable doubt that Jesus was an actual person. You ask if we can only believe in him by "reasoning." The answer is that the only logical conclusion is that Jesus did in fact live. He did in fact die in Jerusalem under Pontius Pilate. There is no doubt at all that a group of believers existed in the first century who were devoted to him and believed in the literal resurrection of Jesus from the dead. Other aspects of the life of Jesus and his claims in the Bible are debatable because they are only recorded in the New Testament, but the basic outline of his life is not in doubt.

QUESTION:

I have just read an article in which you have stated that a box containing the remains of "James, the brother of Christ, the son of Joseph" had been discovered. Could you please let me know where to find more evidence on this, and other such finds?

ANSWER:

The best place to look for material on the "James Ossuary" is probably from the *Biblical Archaeology Review*. This journal presents both sides of the issue on whether the ossuary is a fake or whether it is the actual box used to contain the bones of James, the brother of Jesus. You can probably find back issues of the journal at any large university library. The issue has been argued back and forth in this journal for the past three years.

Let me summarize my take on this issue. First of all, the ossuary in question is almost certainly genuine. In other words, it is in fact a bone box from Palestine at a time more or less contemporary with the first century. The question is whether the inscription on the box is original or whether it was made in more recent times. It is my opinion that the inscription is a clever fake. I am cautious about making this statement, as I am not an expert at any of the technical aspects of examining the inscription. The scientific aspects of the question include the patina or coating built up on the article over time, as well as the style of the writing/script and the technical aspects of the actual instrument used to make the inscription. For me, the bottom line of this question is that the person who produced this box is a dubious character who is now suspected of producing many sophisticated fakes, throwing much doubt on a number of recent discoveries. I am open-minded, but lean toward the conclusion that this item is not the ossuary used to keep the bones of James, the brother of Jesus.

QUESTION:

First Kings records a massive outpouring of light and cloud when Solomon's temple was dedicated. Is there any record of such an event occurring when the second temple was dedicated? Can you think of any spiritual implications of whether such a miraculous outpouring happened?

ANSWER:

As far as I know, there is no direct evidence of the sort of miraculous outpouring of the Holy Spirit/light/clouds/etc. which happened when Solomon dedicated the first temple occuring at the dedication of the second temple. Of course, lack of evidence does not prove anything, but it is worth noting that there is no such mention of a miraculous outpouring at the dedication of the second temple. Having said that, let me mention the scene in Ezekiel 43. This is a vision of Ezekiel in which he sees God enter the second temple in Jerusalem in all his glory: *"The glory of the Lord entered the temple by way of the gate that faced east."* Bear in mind that this is a vision Ezekiel received of the second temple, which occurred about 50 years before it was actually built. This is not evidence for a visible miracle at the dedication fifty years later, but it certainly implies that, at least on a spiritual level, God did indeed enter the second temple in all his glory. I would cautiously and tentatively conclude that a dramatic, visible event probably did not occur, but that God definitely was present in the second temple in some fashion.

I believe that there is not a lot we can conclude from the assumption that there was no highly visible event signaling the time of God entering the second temple. Clearly, God was in Solomon's temple all along (unless the Bible is wrong), and the miraculous outpouring of light and smoke only happened at the dedication as far as we know. Therefore, we know that it was normal that God did not produce such a display on an ongoing basis. Why God chose not to put on such a miraculous display when the second temple was built (assuming that it did not happen, which is not proven) is a matter for speculation. Perhaps God was moving more toward spiritual rather than physical manifestation in general. Perhaps the lack of the ark in the second temple was a factor. I hesitate to conclude that God never "occupied" the second temple. In fact, I believe he did occupy the second temple, as well as the rebuilt temple of Herod. The tearing in two of the temple at the time of the death of Jesus (Matthew 27:51) was symbolic of God leaving the temple for good at that time.

In conclusion, the idea that no miraculous outpouring occurred at the dedication of the second temple is not proven, although it seems likely to me. The implications of this are a matter of speculation.

QUESTION:

Could you summarize the evidence to support the Luke 2 account of the census decreed by Caesar while Quirinius was ruling Syria? This is the census that would have forced Joseph and Mary to go to Bethlehem from Nazareth. I have read quite a bit about the topic. I do see support that the census could have happened. However, there is a lot of controversy about it since some people doubt Caesar's decree would have been enforced at that time in Palestine. Quirinius was shown to be governor at a later time in Syria, and Joseph would not have been forced to return to Nazareth. *Time* and *Newsweek* have both done cover stories on the subject of Christ's birth with a very skeptical view of the historicity.

ANSWER:

First of all, the overall accuracy of Luke as a historian, even in the smallest details, has been reinforced time and time again by an almost unlimited number of historical and archaeological discoveries. There is hardly a single point of fact recorded in Luke or Acts which has not been challenged for its accuracy by one skeptic or another. Luke's writings hold up just fine to the criticism. Sir William Ramsay began his career as a skeptic of the historical reliability of the Bible. The world-renowned archaeologist was converted by the evidence. About Luke he said (Sir William Ramsay, *St. Paul, the Traveler and the Roman Citizen*, Hodder and Stoughton, 1920), "I found myself brought into contact with the Book of Acts as an authority for the topography, antiquities and society of Asia Minor. It was gradually borne upon me that in various details, the narrative showed marvelous truth. In fact, beginning with a fixed idea that the work was essentially a second-century composition, and never relying on its evidence as trustworthy for first-century conditions, I gradually came to find it a useful ally in some obscure and difficult investigations." Ramsay concluded concerning Luke's writing, "Luke is a historian of the first rank; not merely are his statements of fact trustworthy; he is possessed of the true historic sense. In the smallest details, such as whether a particular ruler is a tetrarch, proconsul, governor, imperial legate, politarch or any of a great number of local names for rulers, Luke has been proven correct time and again." The same applies to the passage from Luke which is relevant to your question.

Consider Luke 2:1-3: *"In those days, Caesar Augustus issued a decree that a census should be taken of the entire Roman world. (This was the first census that took place while Quirinius was governor of Syria.) And everyone went to his own town to register."* This is followed by the account of Mary and Joseph traveling to Bethlehem. Critics have claimed that Caesar Augustus never issued such a decree. They have also claimed there was no way people would have been required to travel long distances to their home district for such a census in any case. To top it off, critics say that Quirinius was not governor of Syria at the time in question. Conclusion of the critics: This never happened and Luke's story of the birth of Jesus is a fable.

There are two problems with this conclusion. First, our knowledge of the uncanny accuracy of Luke, as mentioned above, makes it perfectly reasonable to assume that if Luke said it happened, almost certainly it did. Some might call this circular reasoning, but the fact that Luke was a brilliant and careful historian lends great credence to his claims about the census and the travel of Joseph and Mary. In fact, I would go so far as to say the evidence I am about to mention supporting belief that this event happened is not as reliable as the account of Luke itself!

This brings me to the second reason for accepting Luke's account, which is the external evidence that the census and the requirement to travel agrees with recent discoveries. On all three points, archaeological evidence has proven Luke to be accurate. More recent archaeological discoveries have proven that Augustus did in fact decree censuses every fourteen years. The first census was in 23-22 BC. The second was in 9-8 BC. Being in the far reaches of the Empire, the census may not have reached Palestine until 7 or 6 BC, the latter being a probable date for the birth of Jesus.

As to the need for Mary and Joseph to travel to Bethlehem from Galilee, a papyrus has been found in Egypt. On it is written: "Because of the approaching census it is necessary that all those residing for any cause away from their homes should at once prepare to return to their own governments in order that they may complete the family registration of the enrollment and that the tilled lands may retain those belonging to them." This papyrus provides wonderful confirmation of Luke's account of the birth of Jesus. Or perhaps it would be more accurate to say that the more reliable source (the New Testament) confirms the accuracy of the less reliable source (the papyrus found in Egypt).

As far as Quirinius is concerned, again historians doubted Luke because it was known from the writings of Josephus that Quirinius was governor in Syria after 6 AD, which is definitely too late for the birth of Jesus Christ. This argument was eliminated when an inscription was found in Antioch ascribing to Quirinius the governorship of Syria in 7 BC. [*Elder, Prophets, Idols, and Diggers*, (Bobbs Merrill Co., New Youk, 1960), p. 159,160 and Joseph P. Free, *Archaeology and Bible History*, (Scripture Press, Wheaton, Illinois), p. 285]. Apparently, Quirinius had two tours of duty in Syria. He was a Roman consul from 12 BC, ruling in Galatia and Cilicia, in the region just west of Syria, from about 6 to 3 BC. In his other tour of duty in the East, he served in Syria after 6 AD as an imperial legate. By the way, Luke got Quirinius' title correct, as usual.

It is my opinion that those who claim today that the account of Luke is dubious historically have to purposefully ignore the evidence. As far as I know, every single time skeptics have attempted to disprove the accuracy of Luke, they have been proven wrong, or at the very least, the jury is still out. Luke was a very careful chronicler of events, down to the smallest detail. Yes, there was a census in around 7-6 B.C. Yes, Quirinius was governor in the area at the right time. Yes, it makes sense that Joseph and Mary had to go to Bethlehem—yes, yes, yes! Some people doubt that the decree found in Egypt applied to Palestine. These skeptics should bear in mind that before the decree was found, some doubted that Augustus ever ordered a census! These skeptics keep shifting their criticisms. If I have to choose between the skeptics (who have an extreme bias, and whose goal is to prove the Bible to not be inspired) and Luke, the careful historian who interviewed the people who were involved in the events, I will trust Luke. If there was evidence that Luke was a shoddy historian, I would say that the skeptics have a good reason to question the accuracy of his statements. But the fact is that Luke was a very good historian who, in addition, was a disciple of Jesus. He would not lie.

QUESTION:

I do not see the Ark of the Covenant mentioned in the Bible after the time of Solomon. What happened?

ANSWER:

You are correct, as far as I know. During the times of the Kings is the last time the the Ark is mentioned and existed. Of course, there has been a great amount of speculation about the location of the Ark. Some in the Coptic church have claimed that the Ark is located today in a monastery in Axum in Ethiopia. In order to keep speculation alive, the Coptic Christian monks in charge of this monastery do not allow any outsiders into the place they claim holds the Ark. In my opinion, it is a very dubious claim. As mentioned below, it is very unlikely that the Ark survived the wars in Judah. Besides, if the Ark really was in Axum, those who have possession would stand to gain hugely from showing proof of its existence.

What happened to the Ark of the Covenant? It is my belief that it did not survive the various times that Jerusalem was conquered throughout its history. Pharaoh Neco defeated Judah and took tribute in 609 BC (2 Kings 23). The tribute may have included the Ark or other items in the temple. More likely, the Ark was taken when Jerusalem submitted to Nebuchadnezzar in 605 BC or when it was destroyed by his army in 586 BC. It seems very likely that the Ark was destroyed and its gold melted down at this time, as even the existence of the Ark would have encouraged hope for revival of Jewish worship. The fact that there has been no legitimate evidence for the existence of the Ark for well over 2,500 years seems to support the idea that it was destroyed at this time.

Would it be significant if the Ark of the Covenant were found?

For archaeologists, it would be very significant. It would represent a coup as significant as the discovery of King Tut's tomb, assuming the identity of the Ark could be confirmed. For believers in the Bible, it would be a great encouragement, of course. What would be really interesting (although extremely unlikely) would be if the remains of the manna in the Ark were found. What is the organic content of manna? However, given the great deal of archaeological evidence in support of the Bible, it is not obvious that it would represent a great increase in reasons for belief in the historical veracity of the Bible. We have more than enough physical evidence to prove that the Bible, on the whole, is an accurate historical account.

QUESTION:

I was having a discussion with a friend recently who says he prefers to read the New Testament over the Old Testament because the latter is less historically accurate. He cited as an example the Hebrew exodus from Egypt. His claim is that the Egyptians recorded all important historical events carefully and that there is no Egyptian or other extra-biblical historical record of the Hebrews being enslaved by the Egyptians. I had no answer since I am a bit rusty on my Egyptian history. Can you help? How would you answer this argument?

ANSWER:

What your friend says is true, at least to some extent. What I mean is that there is no clear record in extant Egyptian sources which confirms details of the Exodus account. We do have the Tel el Amarna letters which were found in the city of Amarna in Egypt. These were letters from local rulers in Canaan to Pharaoh Ahkenaten, who ruled in the fifteenth century BC. Some of the letters report the attacks of the "Hapiru" in Canaan which occurred at about the same time that biblical chronology implies that Joshua brought the Hebrews into the Promised Land. One letter pleads for military assistance: "The Hapiru plunder all lands of the king. If archers are here this year, then the lands of the king, the lord, will remain; but if the archers are not here, then the lands of the king, my lord, are lost." The identification of the Hapiru and the Hebrews is controversial. Personally, I believe they are one and the same, but I would admit that I am biased, to some extent. There are other tantalizing finds which support the Exodus account, such as the nature of the destructions of Jericho and Hazor as revealed by archaeological findings, which are in dramatic agreement with the account in Joshua. See my book, **RFB** ch. 7 for more details.

The one statement that your friend made which is patently false is that the Egyptians recorded everything which happened. Or, to put it a bit more carefully, we do not now have an extant record of everything the Egyptians did. In fact, it would be fair to say that we have an extremely spotty record of goings-on in Egypt in the second millennium BC. The Egyptians did not keep detailed historical records, and we clearly have only a small part of what they did write down.

For one to say that the lack of clear confirmatory evidence of the Exodus is evidence that it did not happen is simply not a good line of reasoning. We do have many records of Canaanites living in northern Egypt at the time. We also know of the raids of the "Peoples of the Sea" (the Hyskos) which may very well have led, in part, to the ouster of the Canaanites, including the Hebrews from Lower Egypt. Clearly, the Jews were not a powerful or influential group in Egypt at this time, and there is no compelling reason to expect them to show up in the histories of Egypt, which tend to focus on dynastic intrigue, external warfare and so forth, not on the details of life of the lowly slaves such as the Hebrews.

Your friend is making the claim that the Old Testament is not reliable history. I would counter with the argument that the Old Testament is the most accurate and reliable general historical account we have from the ancient world—by far. Again, I would refer you to **RFB** chapter seven for a detailed argument for the accuracy of the Old Testament as history. Time and again, the skeptics have attempted to "prove" that the OT is full of myths and legends, only to be disproved on the specifics. Opponents of Bible belief, when proven wrong on details, such as with the discovery of the el Amarna letters, simply move on to the next supposed "mistake" in the Bible.

QUESTION:

I have heard that the Old Testament was written by Jewish priests just a couple of hundred years before Christ, and that it is very unreliable historically, with lots of religious fables and myths. How can I be sure about this?

ANSWER:

Two hundred years ago, it would have been somewhat challenging to produce hard evidence to prove the skeptics wrong when they make such claims. Before the discoveries of modern archaeology, belief in the truly ancient character of the writings in the Old Testament was based primarily on faith. This is certainly not the case today. Since the mid-nineteenth century, there has been an ever-increasing amount of material discovered in the Near East which provides abundant and dramatic proof of the historical accuracy of the Old Testament. At the same time, the historical reliability of the Old Testament text has strongly supported belief that most of it was written in a time frame relatively close to the actual events described. In other words, the historical reliability of books such as Exodus strongly support belief, not only that it is accurate history, but that it was written using materials from a time close to the original events. The cultural knowledge found in Exodus reflects Egypt in 1400 BC, not Palestine in 400 BC.

Many examples could be cited to support this claim. See **RFB** ch. 7 and Randall Price, *The Stones Cry Out* (Harvest House Publishers, 1997) for further examples. I will list a small number here.

1. The Hittites.

As recently as the late nineteenth century, many scholars doubted the very existence of these people known as the Hittites, despite the fact that they figure so prominently in the Bible. Many considered the Hittites, Horites, Jebusites, Amorites and so forth as simply historical fiction. That was until 1906, when the German archaeologist Hugo Winkler began excavating the site of the ancient city of Hattusha in present-day Turkey. He excavated five large temples, as well as a citadel. Ten-thousand clay tablets containing what is now known to be the Hittite language were also discovered. A great number of other cities which were once part of the great Hittite Empire have since been excavated. The Hittites were the dominant power in the Near East, along with Egypt and Assyria for well over a thousand years. So much for the Bible being a historical fantasy!

2. The Tel Dan Inscription.

As recently as the 1990s, skeptical Bible critics claimed that the person known in the Bible as King David was a pious fiction, created in the fifth-century BC by Jewish teachers. This claim was shown for what it is by the discovery in 1993 in the ruins of the city of Dan in northern Israel of what is now known as the Tel Dan Inscription. This inscription was found in a wall of the city. It is in Aramaic, and has been dated to about 800 BC. It was recorded by the king of Aram, Hazael, not by Israelites. This statement by King Hazael mentions the Aramaic King Ben Hadad, as well as King Jehoshaphat of Judah and King Ahab of Israel. In the inscription, Ben Hadad claims to have killed Ahab in battle. Actually, Ahab was wounded, but died later of his wounds (1 Kings 22:34-36). Presumably, Bible skeptics no longer claim that Ahab and Jehoshaphat are pious frauds. Most significantly for us, the inscription mentions King David; referring to "King Jehoshaphat of the house of King David." Thus we have an enemy of Judah confirming, not only that David was a real king, but that the rulers of Judah were descended directly from David.

3. The Sennacherib Cylinder.

This "cylinder" is actually in the shape of a five-sided prism. It is also known as the Taylor Prism. It was found in Nineveh. Events recorded on the prism imply that it was carved in 686 BC. It reports the attack and siege of Jerusalem by Sennacherib. These events are related in detail in 2 Kings 18:17-19:37. The writer of 2 Kings states that, after conquering all other cites of Judah, Sennacherib's army put Jerusalem under siege. After preparing the defenses of the city, King Hezekiah prayed to God for deliverance. As described in 2 Kings, that night the army of Sennacherib was slain by an angel of God, and Sennacherib retreated back to Assyria. The account of the siege as recorded on the Sennacherib Cylinder is as follows:

> As to Hezekiah, the Jew, he did not submit to my yoke. I laid siege to 46 of his strong cities, walled forts, and to the countless small villages in their vicinity. I drove out of them 200,150 people, young and old, male and female, horses, mules, donkeys, camels, big and small cattle beyond counting and considered [them] booty. Himself I made a prisoner in Jerusalem, his royal residence, like a bird in a cage.

Surely, if Sennacherib had actually defeated and captured Hezekiah, it would have been mentioned on the cylinder. Apparently, both 2 Kings 18 and 19, and those who recorded Sennacherib's accomplishments, agree that he put siege to Jerusalem, but that he left Canaan without overcoming Jerusalem.

Dozens of other examples of archaeological finds which support the accuracy of the Old Testament as history could be listed. Another important factor supporting the reliability of the Old Testament text is that the cultural and legal details found, especially in Genesis, are in agreement with cultural and legal environment appropriate to the time of the events. For example, Genesis records Laban chasing Jacob down when he left, not so much to get his possessions back, but to recover his household gods. Archaeologists have found a law in ancient Babylonia, at the appropriate time, stating that those who were in possession of the household gods retained possession of the family wealth. Such a tradition was not in force over a thousand years later, when the critics claim that Genesis was written. The great volume of archaeological evidence has made it clear that the Bible is the most accurate ancient historical document in existence today. Those who claim it was written hundreds of years after the supposed events, and those who claim it is full of fables and unreliable history, are either misinformed or are not willing to consider the obvious evidence revealed by archaeology. The fact is that, the more we learn, the more we become confident that the Bible is an extremely reliable historical account of the events which affected God's people throughout their history.

QUESTION:

I was looking for some credible evidence for the historicity of Jesus. Two main historians who wrote about Jesus, Thallus and Josephus, are controversial. It is not clear if or when they wrote about Jesus. Are there records which date to the first century in which scholars are sure that they refer to Jesus Christ?

ANSWER:

The historicity of Jesus is about as well established as is the case for any single person in the ancient world. The number of authors from the first and second century who mention Jesus is approximately the same as those who mention the emperor Tiberius. This, of course, does not include the many Christian writers who mention details about Jesus. No serious scholar would even entertain the claim that the existence of Jesus is a myth (exceptions such as Robert Price are so radical that we are justified in questioning whether they should be counted as serious scholars). In fact, we are entitled to assume that anyone who claims that Jesus did not live is either misinformed about the facts or extremely biased. You refer to Josephus and Thallus being controversial. Josephus was a Jewish historian who lived from about AD 35 to AD 100. He wrote for the emperors in Rome at the time. It is not at all controversial that Josephus mentions Jesus in his work, *Antiquities of the Jews*. He refers to Jesus and the Christians in a few places. He also mentions specifics about the execution of the apostle James. Having said that, there is one passage in Josephus which is controversial. This passage mentions both the crucifixion of Jesus and his resurrection. Scholars have proposed that Christian writers interpolated part, but probably not all, of this famous portion of Josephus' writings. This claim may be true. For more on the passage from Josephus, see **RFB** ch. 3.

To summarize on Josephus, it is not controversial whether

he mentioned Jesus. What is controversial is the specific wording of one of the passages in his writings whose authenticity some scholars question.

As far as Thallus goes, we know of him only from a third century Christian historian named Julius Africanus. From Julius Africanus we know that Thallus wrote a three-volume treatise of world history in the 50s AD. In discussing the darkness at the time of the resurrection of Jesus, Julius Africanus mentions that in the 3rd book of Thallus' history, he mentions the darkness and calls it an eclipse of the sun. Africanus believes that Thallus is wrong. Whether or not this source proves the darkness at the time of Jesus' crucifixion is dubious, but it does seem to support the idea that even non-Christians were aware of the resurrection as early as the 50s AD—at about the time the first book of the NT was written. It also supports the claim, not necessarily of the darkness having occurred, but of the darkness having been claimed and believed by the Christians. Because we do not have Thallus' history and because we have a Christian interpreting rather than quoting it, this is somewhat weak support to Christian claims. However, the consensus of scholars is that he did in fact refer to Jesus in his original writings.

You ask whether others in the first century mention Jesus. The answer is definitely "yes." For example, both Tacitus and Pliny the Elder, well-known Roman historians of the first and second century AD, mention Jesus. Tacitus mentions his execution under Pontius Pilate. He called Jesus "Chrestus." Besides, a number of Jewish rabbis mention the life of Jesus during the first three centuries. For example, Jesus is mentioned in the Babylonian Talmud *Sanhedrin 43a*. These Jewish writers mention the miracles of Jesus, but of course do not acknowledge that he was the Messiah. They claim that the miracles of Jesus were the work of sorcery, which is reminiscent of the sayings of Jesus' accusers during his lifetime. Details of these claims may be found in **RFB** ch. 2 and 3.

You may be well assured that Jesus was a real person who lived in Palestine, who performed many public signs, who was crucified under Pontius Pilate and about whom it was claimed that he was resurrected from the dead. These things are verified by such a wide variety of witnesses that they can be taken as proved. You cannot prove all the sayings and acts of Jesus from sources outside the New Testament, but the facts mentioned above are certainly true.

QUESTION:

I recently watched a television show about Moses. It was discussing the Red Sea crossing. They claimed that Moses never led the children of Israel through the "Red Sea," but through an unknown sea. They also said the original Hebrew for Red Sea was *Yam Suph*, which meant Sea of Reeds, and the "Red Sea" name was mistranslated in the Greek. Is this argument true? Also, did Moses really cross the Red Sea, or was it another sea? How reliable are the facts to support the crossing of that sea?

ANSWER:

You bring up a question which is the subject of much debate and current research. Most of what was reported in the show you refer to is true. *Yam Suph*, or Sea of Reeds, is indeed the correct wording in Exodus for the body of water which Moses and Israel crossed when escaping the Egyptian army. The fact is that no one knows absolutely for sure where this crossing occurred. Many will confidently support their personal theory about what the term "Sea of Reeds" is referring to, but there is no conclusive proof that I have ever seen which can nail down the location of the miraculous crossing of God's people. If you look at a map carefully, you will see a smaller body of water just to the northwest of the Red Sea which some have proposed as the crossing site. This is a shallow, very muddy area which is essentially a large salt marsh rather than the single large body of water which seems to be described in Exodus. The fact is that this salt marsh is full of reeds, and is a possible site for the crossing referred to in Exodus. You should be aware that the maps in the back of your Bible are only showing speculation as to the route taken by Israel when they escaped from Egypt. Many Bibles will show the traditionally accepted site, which is the Red Sea.

Another more recent theory is that the famed crossing occurred across the Gulf of Aqaba near the tip of the Sinai Peninsula. This theory puts the biblical Mount Sinai in northwestern Saudi Arabia (rather than the traditional Mount Sinai in the Sinai Peninsula) at the mountain known as Jebel el Lawz. Other mountains in northwest Arabia have been proposed as the biblical Sinai as well. Claims have been made that chariot wheels were discovered at the supposed crossing place at the entrance to the Gulf of Aqaba, but these are unsubstantiated. Some interesting finds have been made at Jebel el Lawz. If you are interested, a book on the subject has been published by Bob Cornuke, *Mountain of God* (Broadman and Holman, 2000). Cornuke's claims are certainly not conclusive, but they are interesting. A similar theory has been put forward by Colin Humphreys in his book *The Miracles of Exodus* (Harper Collins, 2004). Humphreys identifies Mount Sinai with Mount Bedr.

In the end, it is not possible for anyone to say with absolute certainty where Moses and the people of God crossed the *Yam Suph*. We have on the extremely good authority of the Bible itself that this crossing did take place. We also have archaeological evidence, such as with the *Tel el Amarna* letters, substantiating the entrance of Israel into the Promised Land. However, hard evidence for the exact location of the miraculous events of Exodus 14 is lacking as of today. I am sorry to give you what may be a somewhat unsatisfactory answer, but if we are not sure where the crossing occurred, we may as well be honest about it. If you are interested in the subject, I encourage you to get a copy of one or both of the books I referred to above. You can also do an Internet search concerning Jebel el Lawz. You would be wise to be open-minded but also to maintain a healthy skepticism concerning new and exciting theories.

QUESTION:

What evidence do we have that the stories of Christianity are real?

ANSWER:

I am not sure what you mean by "stories" of Christianity? Perhaps you mean to ask how we can know for sure that the events recorded in the New Testament actually happened. Or you may be asking how sure can we be about the historical events recorded in the Old Testament. Let me supply a general answer. I would say that, without question, the Bible is the most accurate book of history we have from the ancient world. The writers of both the Old and the New Testaments paid meticulous attention to details. The histories in the Bible are more honest about both the victories and the defeats of their heroes than their contemporaries; especially in Old Testament times. The greatest historians of the ancient world, such as Herodotus and Thucydides, were careful writers, but even Herodotus' writing contains much which is obviously myth, legend and exaggeration. He was also very biased in favor of his mother city, Athens. The Bible has been subjected to more scrutiny, by far, than any other ancient book, yet its accuracy as history has held up time and time again.

Having said that, in the end, one must take some of the details in both the Old and New Testament on faith. For example, in the Old Testament, when it reports a particular war or a particular king, you would be quite safe in assuming that the war actually happened and that that king actually lived. However, some particular dialogue between David and one of his sons will obviously not be confirmable by any other ancient source. One is left, at least to some extent, to trust the accuracy of the Old Testament writers because we will obviously never be able to confirm every single detail. In the end, despite the amazing proof of the historical reliability of the Bible, one will always be left filling the rather large gaps in the external proof by accepting the implications of the fact that the Bible is, as it claims, the Word of God (2 Timothy 3:16). Did Isaiah really say the prayer recorded in such and such chapter? He said he did and it is in the Bible, so I assume he did by faith. Rationalists may scoff at those who fill in the gaps of fact with faith, but at some point, the overwhelming evidence justifies giving the Bible writers the benefit of the doubt.

So, I wish I could say that I can prove beyond a reasonable doubt that every single detail of every single story reported in the Bible is an accurate account. I cannot make that claim. What I can say is that, to the extent the Biblical stories have been compared to reliable external sources, it has proven itself to be the most reliable book of ancient history we have. However, in the end, one is still left filling in the gaps by assuming that, as claimed, the Bible is inspired by God. The massive evidence in support of the claim for biblical inspiration makes this leap of faith to not be a blind one. History and archaeology support the Bible, but they do not prove the Bible.

QUESTION:

What happened between the Old Testament and New Testament?

ANSWER:

You should get a copy of my book **Daniel**, which has lot of material on the history of the Jews between the Testaments. Another source is the books of *First and Second Maccabees*. These books are part of the Old Testament Apocrypha. They are part of the Roman Catholic canon and are included in the *New American Bible* and the *New Jerusalem Bible*. Although these books are not part of the accepted Jewish canon of the Old Testament, both supply useful history of the Jews during the fourth through second centuries BC. A third source I recommend is Charles Pfeiffer, *Between the Testaments* (Baker Books, 1959).

To give the briefest possible summary:

- Persians dominate Palestine: 538-335 BC
- Alexander the Great conquers Palestine, ending the Achaemenian Dynasty: 335 BC

- Palestine ruled by Greek Ptolemaic dynasty: 321-205 BC
- Greek Seleucid Kings control Israel: 205-164 BC
- Desecration of the Temple and severe persecution of the Jews by Antioches Epiphanes: 167-164 BC
- Maccabean rebellion, re-consecration of the temple in Jerusalem: 164 BC
- Jewish Maccabean/Hasmaonian dynasty rules Judea: 164-63 BC
- Palestine conquered for Rome by Pompey: 63 BC
- Brief rule by the Parthian (Persian) Empire: 41-37 BC
- Jerusalem retaken by Rome, Herod the Great made puppet king by Octavian: 37 BC
- Jesus of Nazareth born: 6 or 5 BC

QUESTION:

I'm reading *"Genesis and the Big Bang"* by Gerald L Schroeder, PhD. He has a biblical cumulative age for the Earth after Adam of 5,763 years. I've noticed that the Jewish people also use this age, but when you add up the dates in the Bible, it comes out closer to 6,000. I've asked Jewish people about this, and the incongruity comes from the fact that they consider the Egyptian bondage to have lasted only 200 years rather than the 400 years which the Bible states. I was just wondering if you have heard this and how you would respond.

ANSWER:

When you say that the Bible states the time in Egypt was 400 years, I assume you are thinking of the statement of Paul in Galatians 3:17: *"The Law, introduced 430 years later..."* This passage does not actually say that the Jews were in Egypt for 400 years, but it puts the time between the promise to Abraham and the giving of the Law at Sinai to Moses at about 430 years. Given the time between the reception of the promise by Abraham and the entrance of Jacob and his descendants into Egypt, a sojourn in Egypt of less than 400 years is possible.

To answer your question, no, I have not seen the time in Egypt estimated to be as low as 200 years. I believe 200 years would be pretty low for the Israelites to have expanded from the couple of hundred or so who entered Egypt to the 1-2 million who left. In fact, that would border on impossible, unless one questions the census data in Numbers. Let us think about the numbers involved. First, I will estimate the descendants of Abraham who entered Egypt. Including children, grandchildren, great-grandchildren, servants and so forth, about 500 people is a reasonable number. If we allow the number of Israelites to double every thirty years, which is fairly rapid growth, the population would reach one million in about 330 years. Clearly, these numbers are gross estimates, but they do seem to make 200 years too short a time for Israel to stay in Egypt.

A similar question is the length of time for the period of the Judges. I have heard estimates for the period of the Judges as low as 200 years and as high as 400. Given that Saul took the throne in about 1050 BC, this puts the time of the conquest of Canaan between 1450 and 1250 BC. Because Judges does not give a clear chronology, a fairly wide range is possible. In the end, one is wise to not be dogmatic about the dates. However, thinking about them and trying to discover a reasonable chronology can be helpful, both for your faith and in order to answer the questions of others.

QUESTION:

Many scholars have used the writings of Josephus the Jew as historical evidence for Jesus. But there are a lot of critics who say that the writings of Josephus didn't even exist until the sixth century. In other words, Josephus couldn't have written them. What do you know about this?

ANSWER:

I have not personally heard the sixth-century date, but I am aware of some of the issues which have been brought up concerning Josephus' writings. An important section in one of the works of Josephus known as the *Testamonium Flavium* refers to Jesus and his resurrection. Some have claimed, not without reason, that part of this important statement was an interpolation of later Christians. I am going to guess that the critic you read was confusing the evidence that a very small portion of Josephus' writings were interpolated several centuries later and incorrectly turning it into a statement that all of his writings are from several centuries later. That Josephus is a true person who wrote histories for Roman emperors is not in doubt at all. Careful scholars are unanimous as far as I know that *The Jewish Wars* and *Antiquities of the Jews* (his most famous works) were written by Josephus.

Josephus, whose complete name was Joseph ben Matthias, was born in AD 37 and died about AD 100. He was a Pharisee and a Jewish zealot. He fought on the Jewish side in the wars with the Romans under Vespasian. He was captured by the Romans at the fortress of Jotapata in AD 67. After his capture, Josephus switched sides, becoming an adviser to Vespasian and Titus when they attacked and eventually destroyed Jerusalem in AD 70. Josephus wrote his histories under imperial sponsorship. *His Wars of the Jews* was published in about AD 78. Antiquities of the Jews was published in AD 93. Josephus published other works as well.

There is little doubt about the authenticity of the works attributed to Josephus. The sixth century you heard is not possible as a date of its writing. In fact, many Christian writers referred to Josephus and his writings long before the sixth-century date you mention. As to the accuracy of his histories, Josephus had a tendency to exaggerate numbers and his accounts of the distant past are not reliable, but the general outline of events he described after about 200 BC has held up well to scrutiny using other sources.

The difficulty with Josephus as a source of information about Jesus is that there is some legitimate doubt about whether the most important reference to Jesus may have been tampered with by early Christian writers. There is one particularly interesting section in *Antiquities 18:3:3* in which Josephus describes Jesus as "a doer of wonderful works" and says concerning him, "and when Pilate, at the suggestion of the principal men among us, had condemned him to the cross, those who loved him at first did not forsake him." He continues by mentioning belief of the early church in the resurrection. This passage clearly provides support to the claims of Christianity, and perhaps for this reason alone has caused some to wonder if it is a later interpolation of Christians into Josephus' original writings. I have read a number of authors on this subject. Based on the balance of the evidence, I believe the most likely conclusion is that the reference in Antiquities in question was in the original work of Josephus, but that it was amplified by a later editor—probably a believer in Jesus. In other words, Josephus mentioned Jesus and the Christians, but not necessarily all of the statements in our current text of the book.

In summary, I am not sure exactly what you have heard, but it is fair to say that the existence of Josephus and his writings in the first century AD are not in doubt, but there is some debate about whether certain of his writings may have been changed somewhat by others after his death.

Chapter Three

Supposed Inconsistencies in the Bible

QUESTION:
How do you account for the inconsistencies and mistakes in the Bible?

ANSWER:
Which inconsistencies and mistakes? It is easier to claim that the Bible is full of inconsistencies and mistakes than it is to find one which will stand up to careful study. Claiming that the Bible is full of errors and inconsistencies is the standard approach of many Bible critics.

Of course, there are many good questions one can ask about the Bible. What about the different versions of creation in Genesis 1 and 2? What about the fact that Matthew 27:5 says that Judas hanged himself, while Acts 1:18 says that he fell headlong into a field and his body burst open? The fact is that each of these seeming inconsistencies is fairly easily explained in a way which is perfectly satisfactory to any open-minded person.

I deal with the general question of supposed contradictions in **RFB** ch. 9. Let me give you a very brief summary of that material. The types of supposed errors and inconsistencies include:

1) Claims that what is taught in two different passages is contradictory.

2) Identical events described by two different authors have details of facts which appear to contradict.

3) Numbers of objects, people or years in two different passages do not agree.

Let me suggest a couple of questions one can ask to sort through and answer apparent biblical contradictions.

Is this a legitimate contradiction? In other words, is there a perfectly reasonable explanation of the supposed contradiction which can be found simply by reading the relevant passages in context?

Is there any chance that a scribal error can explain the apparent discrepancy? This will be a particularly relevant question if the supposed contradiction involves numbers from the Old Testament text.

Is it possible that the two passages, rather than contradicting one another, actually complement one another? In other words, is it possible that the two apparently discrepant scriptures actually create a fuller picture of what God is trying to communicate when taken together?

I will supply just a few examples of supposed contradictions I have come across to demonstrate the different categories and the questions which can be used to resolve them.

1. "Genesis 7:17 says that the flood lasted 40 days, but Genesis 8:3 tells us that it lasted 150 days."

This is an example of a supposed contradiction which is very easily eliminated by simply reading the relevant passages in their context. Genesis 7:17 describes 40 days of rain, while Genesis 8:3 states that the duration of the flood was 150 days. Apparently after the rain stopped, there was a significant amount of time before the waters receded.

2. "As to the death of the apostle Judas, Matthew 27:5 states that Judas took the money that he had obtained by betraying Jesus, threw it down in the temple and then 'went and hanged himself.' However, Acts 1:18 reports that Judas used the money to purchase a field and 'falling headlong, he burst asunder in the midst, and all his bowels gushed out.'"

This is an example of a supposed contradiction which is removed by reading the two relevant passages and simply thinking carefully how they might be resolved. What actually happened is that, out of remorse, Judas brought the money given to him to betray Jesus and threw it down at the feet of the elders and chief priests who had put him up to the betrayal. In Matthew 27:3-10, we see that the chief priests "decided to use the money to buy the potter's field as a burial place for foreigners." After returning the money, Judas hanged himself. After only a few hours in a hot climate, and hanging from a rope, his body became extremely bloated. That would explain why, when he was cut down, "his body burst open and all his intestines spilled out." In summary, Judas returned the money, it was used to buy a field, he hanged himself, and when cut down, his body burst open. There is no contradiction.

3. "David took 700 (2 Samuel 8:4) or 7,000 (1 Chronicles 18:4) horsemen from Hadadezer. Which is correct?"

This is an example of a contradiction which was produced by a scribal error. In other words, almost certainly in the original 2 Samuel and 1 Chronicles, the numbers agreed. When numbers are recorded in Hebrew, it is extremely easy for an error to occur. Similar to Roman numerals, letters are used to represent numbers in Hebrew. Some of the letters which represent numbers are very similar, making copy errors over long periods very likely. A mistake by a factor of ten (seven hundred versus seven thousand, for example) are even more likely to occur. The reader of the Old Testament should be cautious in assuming the numbers found in our text are identical to the original writing. Bottom line, a copying error is not a Bible contradiction.

4. "In Genesis 37:36, it says that Joseph was sold into Egypt by Midianites, while in Genesis 39:1, it says that he was sold by Ishmaelites."

Would it be a contradiction to say that George Bush is a Texan and at the same time that he is an American? The Midianites were an Arabic tribe. A common general name for Arab tribes in ancient times was Ishmaelites, showing that they were descended from Abraham's first son, Ishmael.

5. "Exodus 20:8, 'Remember the Sabbath day by keeping it holy,' contradicts Isaiah 1:13 'Your... Sabbaths and convocations—I cannot bear...'"

This is an example of two passages which, when understood together, deepen our understanding of a biblical teaching. It only appears to be a contradiction to a person who does not understand the intent of the writer in each case. God commanded his people to observe the Sabbath. The writer of Isaiah definitely does not deny that. In fact, the book of Isaiah includes many admonitions to keep the Sabbath. The point in Isaiah 1:13 is that God was very displeased with their worship. They were committing blatant sins, worshiping idols, committing sexual immorality and so forth. They were then hoping that by ritualistically performing a religious ceremony they could somehow be right with God. Religious hypocrisy makes God angry. The solution was not to stop observing the Sabbath, but to repent of their evil ways.

In summary, there are different kinds of apparent contradictions and inconsistencies in the Bible. It is my experience that virtually all of them are easily explained. In many cases, the answer actually provides deeper insight into biblical truth. We need to be honest and open-minded about criticisms of the Bible. We should not ignore them. In doing so, our faith will be deepened.

QUESTION:

I had a question regarding Numbers 3. Why does there seem to be an inconsistency between the sum of the males counted in the Levite clans (7,500 + 8,600 + 6,200 = 22,300) in Numbers 3:21-34, and the number listed in Numbers 3:39 (22,000)? It would seem to pose a problem when (in vs. 40-51) the people of Israel are to "redeem the 273 firstborn sons of Israel who are in excess of the number of Levites" with five silver pieces for each. Wouldn't the sum from the first count put the number of Levite males above the firstborn Israelites (22,273) by 27? A footnote in my Bible mentions that "in Numbers 3:28, some Greek manuscripts read 8,300; see total in Numbers 3:39." However, this doesn't explain why the translators chose to include the 8,600 rather than the number that would have helped v. 39 add up correctly. Do you know of the manuscript evidence for choosing one number over the other, even though it seems to not add up?

ANSWER:

I cover the topic of Hebrew numbers and the problems for scribes in copying these numbers in **RFB** p. 165. To summarize, the Jews represented numbers using Hebrew letters. Their system was somewhat like Roman numerals. The problem is that some of the Hebrew letters used to represent different numbers are very similar to one another. For example, the Hebrew letters *kaleth* and *resh* look almost identical, yet they represent different numbers. For this reason, when copies of the Hebrew were made, it was very easy for accidental errors to slip into the manuscripts. Therefore, one would expect that our Hebrew Bibles will have a significant quantity of copying errors with respect to numbers, which would reduce our general confidence in the numbers in the Old Testament. For example, if one saw in a particular passage that there were 500 soldiers, it would be hard to rule out that the original might have been 530 or even 5,000. One would be well advised to not base any strong claims based on the numbers found in the Old Testament. Exceptions to this rule would include the command to circumcise on the eighth day, or the 40 years in the wilderness, both of which are found in numerous places in the Old Testament, making it extremely unlikely that those numbers were not in the original.

By contrast to numbers, mistakes in spelling of words in the Hebrew are fairly easy to detect and to correct. Using an example in English, if one was making a copy of a manuscript and saw the letters *thougt*, it would be easy to discover the mistake and correct it, especially if the context implied that the word *thought* fit in the passage. Number copying errors are not so easily detected or corrected, and once they occur, it is difficult to establish from either context or spelling rule which of two different manuscripts is correct. Given the difficulty in copying Hebrew numbers, it is fortunate for us that it is not important to know the exact number of Levite men in order to teach the Christian gospel.

About the specific example you raise, it is possible that a scribe made a mistake in copying Numbers 3. It is my guess that the most likely place that a scribe might have made a mistake would be in 3:23-28 or 34. The footnote you find in your Bible says that some manuscripts of the Septuagint have 8,300 in Numbers 3:28. Given that the Septuagint is a Greek translation from the Hebrew made in about 200 BC, my first guess (and probably the guess of those who created the NIV translation) is that the Septuagint manuscripts with 8,300 represent an attempt by a scribe to "improve" or "correct" the apparent error in the Hebrew manuscript he was copying. It is possible, but unlikely, that the Septuagint is the correct original, as this implies that the accepted Hebrew Masoretic text represents a later copying error. In the end, without more data, it will be difficult to reconstruct what the cause of the different totals in the two halves of Numbers is. This will have to remain one of the fairly low numbers of copying mistakes we have in our Hebrew Old Testaments which will be difficult to correct. You can probably assume that, if we had the original documents, the discrepancy would disappear. Clearly, however, no important teaching or doctrine is affected by this copying error.

QUESTION:

What about when words of Jesus in one Gospel do not match exactly the words of a parallel account in another Gospel? The temptation of Christ is an example. The accounts of Satan's efforts to tempt Jesus in the desert do not match exactly. Wouldn't the Holy

Spirit record the words of Christ verbatim, which would make the words match in each Gospel? The different words in Matthew and Mark when Jesus was tempted seem like an error. Is there a reasonable answer to this?

ANSWER:

You ask a good question. What we have in the Gospels is four independent accounts which corroborate one another. Each of the Gospel accounts of events in the ministry of Jesus brings out different aspects of what happened. In the case of Matthew and John, and perhaps Mark as well, we have separate eyewitness accounts. Although Luke was obviously not an eyewitness, he was the most careful and systematic researcher of the four. If the Gospel accounts were not independent, then we would expect them to agree exactly in details. However, because they are truly independent accounts of the events, we get a somewhat different perspective from all of them. The vast majority of supposed "contradictions" are not contradictions at all. In many cases, the appearance of contradiction is the result of having different eyewitnesses who have different perspective on the same events. This gives stronger support to the Gospel's accuracy rather than producing reason for doubt. When several witnesses report what they observe concerning the same event, there will always be differences of detail, but there is a common thread. If the four Gospel accounts were the same verbatim, then their testimony would not provide additional support for the accuracy of the Gospels. If they were identical, most people would simply assume that each writer quoted from the first to write, and that they were not complementary, independent accounts of the events.

I was on a jury two summers ago. Each witness to the terrible events in question reported significantly different details. In some cases, the testimony even seemed to contradict. For us in the jury, we did not feel that anyone was lying, but that they reported those aspects of what happened which caught their attention. In the end, we felt that the seemingly contradictory testimony, when taken all together, produced a fairly clear picture of what happened at the scene of the crime.

One account says that John and James asked Jesus for something, another says that it was actually their mother who did the asking for them. These do not contradict; they complement one another. John and James asked Jesus, but they were too proud to do it themselves, so they got their mother to do it for them. You can assume that the sayings of Jesus in the New Testament are not necessarily absolutely precise word-for-word quotations of the exact words said by Jesus, but are a faithful account of the essence of what he said. Very slight differences in wording are not a sign of a lie or a lack of inspiration, but they reflect the nature of how the eyewitnesses were able to reproduce what they observed to the best of their ability, aided by the inspiration of the Holy Spirit.

Let me discuss the example you used. The accounts of the temptation of Jesus in the desert do differ somewhat. For example, Matthew 4:2 has Satan saying, *"Tell these stones to become bread,"* whereas in Luke 4:3 he says, *"Tell this stone to become bread."* One uses the singular, while the other uses the plural. Clearly, these accounts are not verbatim transcripts. We can assume that Matthew was not present for the scene, but Jesus told him about it later. In the case of Luke, he must have gotten his information from someone else concerning what Jesus had said. Do not expect the quotations of people in the New or the Old Testament to be verbatim. Besides, the conversation in question probably happened in Aramaic, while the books of Matthew and Luke are in Greek. If nothing else, they will differ because conversations we read in the New Testament are a translation by the writer from Aramaic to Greek. We can assume that the quotations from Jesus and others in the New Testament are a fair representation of what they said, but not an exact word-for-word transcription. We need to allow room for God to work here. We can assume that if the exact words and their order were important, God would preserve these words.

Another factor to bear in mind is that the Near-Eastern writer 2,000 years ago did not think the same way we do. We tend to think in a linear way. We think more literally in general. We expect facts to be delivered chronologically, where the Near-Eastern writer did not feel as tied to a strict chronology. It is harder for us to think of a quotation being a summary or a paraphrase of the original. The Near-Eastern writer was concerned with catching the meaning of what was said, whereas those of us of the Western mindset are more likely to expect an exact representation of the original. It is important when interpreting the Bible to bear in mind the standard way of thinking and of verbal expression at the time the material was written. I hope this is helpful.

QUESTION:
An atheist friend of mine claimed that there are many contradictions or prophetic misinterpretations in Matthew. What is your response? The list is Matthew: 1:22-23, 2:15, 2:23, 8:16-17, 12:18-21, 12:23, 12:40, 16:4, 24:44, 27:9.

ANSWER:

These are fairly common criticisms of the reliability of the Bible. I am guessing that someone was visiting an anti-Christian web site. Here are my responses.

Matthew 1:22-23 is one of the most commonly used examples of an "error" in the Bible. The claim is that Matthew is making an error because he says Isaiah called the woman in Isaiah 7:14 a virgin, when the actual Hebrew word is young woman, not virgin. This example works well as long as one does not engage the passage in context and apply a bit of common sense. When the Jews created the first Greek translation of the Hebrew Bible, known as the Septuagint, Isaiah 7:14 was translated by the Jews themselves as "virgin" for the obvious reason of the context, which is that this birth is described in Isaiah as a "sign." If a woman who is not a virgin has a child, this would not be much of a miracle. It is a prophecy of the Messiah fulfilled by Jesus, who was born of a virgin. Of course, it is one of the weaker examples we can use to support the claim that Jesus fulfilled all the messianic prophecies because, unlike many of the messianic prophecies fulfilled by Jesus, it is really hard to "prove" that the birth of Jesus was from a virgin. I suppose all we really have is the word of Mary and Joseph on this.

Matthew 2:15. I do not see what the contradiction is here. Some have said that Matthew is pulling Hosea 11:1 ("Out of Egypt I called my son") out of context. I believe that this is because they do not understand how the Jews used the Old Testament. Some messianic prophecies were of a definite historical nature. Others are historical foreshadows. Matthew 2:15 is an example of the latter. For example, when God freed his people from Egypt, using Moses as his instrument in that case, it was a physical foreshadow. The physical liberation of Israel from slavery in Egypt by Moses is a foreshadow of the spiritual liberation of spiritual Israel (the church) from slavery to sin by Jesus. Like God said to Moses in Deuteronomy 18:18, *"I will raise up for them a prophet like you from among their brothers."* Jesus is like Moses in dozens of ways. It just so happens (not a coincidence) that Jesus literally came out of Egypt as a child, but this is not the main point of Matthew or of the original Hebrew writer. It is a misunderstanding of the intent of the passage which causes skeptics to mistakenly charge Matthew of taking this prophecy out of context.

Matthew 2:23 (in which Matthew says that Jesus fulfilled the prophecy that the Messiah will be called a Nazarene). Again, this is a rather shallow example which is often used by atheists, but a simple knowledge of Hebrew prophecy makes the meaning clear. Jesus was called a Nazarene in three senses. First of all, he was literally a

Nazarene. In other words he was from Nazareth. Second of all, he was by type/antitype a *Nazirite* (Numbers 6:1-21). However, it is in the third sense that Matthew is telling us Jesus fulfilled this prophecy that the Messiah will be called a Nazarene. The Hebrew word *nazar* means branch. There is more than one prophecy in the Old Testament that predicts the Messiah will be the "branch." Specifically, he will be the branch of Jesse—the father of David. In other words, the prophecy that Jesus would be the branch is a prophecy that he will be descended from David. One example of a prophecy fulfilled by Jesus in this sense, as mentioned by Matthew is Isaiah, 11:1. Other prophecies calling the Messiah "the Branch" include Jeremiah 23:5, Zechariah 3:8 and Zechariah 6:12. Again, this charge that Matthew is mistaken is a result, not of an error by Matthew, but of a shallow reading of the gospel.

Matthew 8:16-17. I do not see the problem here.

Matthew 12:18-21. Jesus rather obviously did fulfill this prophecy. What is the criticism here?

Matthew 12:40. Jesus did fulfill the physical prophecy of the death and resurrection of Jonah from the big fish. Of course, if one takes a purely naturalistic viewpoint, the story of Jonah is impossible, but if we are deciding whether the Bible is true, to take as an assumption that there is no supernatural, that would be to decide the result before doing the investigation, which is circular reasoning. Even if the story of Jonah was a fable, which I believe it is not, then Jesus still did fulfill the prophecy of Jonah, both in offering salvation to the Gentiles, as did Jonah and in being resurrected from the dead on the third day.

Matthew 16:4. Jesus certainly did give the sign of Jonah when he was resurrected from the dead. I believe the evidence for this resurrection is quite strong--but that is another argument to be made.

Matthew 24:44: I do not see a contradiction or problem here.

Matthew 27:9. Jesus fulfilled the prophecy in Zechariah 11:9-13. Because this is really rather nice proof that Jesus is the promised Messiah, I am a bit surprised that a skeptic would be so bold as to bring up this one.

QUESTION:

(This is a response and subsequent question from the previous question) I believe that in the last 6 cited scriptures, you missed, or addressed the wrong aspect of the issue in question. If you could clarify your response to these I would be grateful, because I think there are legitimate concerns raised. Matthew 8:16-17, what is translated as *"diseases"* in Matthew is rendered *"sorrows"* in Isaiah.

Quite different at a glance. Matthew 12:18-21: Matthew shortens and changes four lines of text in Isaiah into 2 lines of this quote. Why should he have changed it? Matthew 12:40: Jesus claims that Jonah was three nights and three days in the fish (correctly) and so he will also be three nights and three days in the earth. My understanding was that he was only in the grave 2 nights and 3 days. Matthew 24:44: Perhaps this is a misquote attempting to question Mt. 24:29. This reference is quoted as if it was one source, but is footnoted as two distinct sources, which in context appear to be referring to separate events. Are we to understand this as a paraphrase more than a direct quotation? Is it even referring to prophecy? Matthew 27:9: The question here is why the author cites Jeremiah for a prophecy which is (as you pointed out) much more aptly attributed to Zechariah.

ANSWER:

I just finished teaching a class on Biblical inspiration and inerrancy. I am quite confident that the doctrine of Biblical inspiration is well established by the evidence and can be defended both from scriptural and from evidential basis. The question of inerrancy is more nuanced. For example, I do not believe that when Jesus or anyone else for that matter is quoted in the Bible, that it is necessarily an exact transcript, but that it is at times the hearer's best recollection and reconstruction of what Jesus said. Often the sermons presented in the gospels will be a reconstructed version of sermons and lessons he gave innumerable times. The question is not whether the quotes are an exact transcript, but whether the author is speaking under the influence of the Holy Spirit. The same can be said for New Testament quotations from the Old Testament. For example, quite often New Testament authors quote from the Septuagint translation rather than from the Hebrew original. Does this mean their letters are not inspired? I think not.

Also, I believe that occasionally New Testament writers paraphrase and do not give exact quotes. This does not imply that what they wrote is a "mistake" or evidence that the Bible is not inspired. I would apply this principle to Matthew 8:16-17, Matthew 12:18-21 and Matthew 24:44. Now, if we look into the subtleties of the Greek word for diseases and the Hebrew word for sorrows, we might find that the apparent distinction when rendered in English is not as large as we think. Nevertheless, we should allow Matthew, or perhaps Jesus, some latitude in translating and interpreting the original and not apply a Western-style analytical approach, which is out of character to a Near Eastern mentality.

About Matthew 12:40, Jews used *"three days and three nights"* as an idiom to stand for any part of three days and three nights. This is a well-founded discovery of scholars. As to whether Jonah was literally in the fish for 72 hours, I personally doubt this, as the Jewish author was most likely working within the same idiomatic framework. I think there is no contradiction here. Jesus certainly did not see one, and he was the one who was in a position to know.

Matthew 24 deserves a bit more comment. The entire section of Matthew 24 and 25 is an extended prophecy which is rather difficult to break down analytically. This is, in part, because it is both a prophecy about the "coming" of the kingdom when Jerusalem was destroyed by the Romans (esp 24:9-21, and Daniel 9) and the coming of the kingdom when Jesus comes back at the end of time. Biblical prophecy can be a bit more complex than we would prefer as the coming of the kingdom has occurred and will still occur in various ways. The biblical prophets tend to comingle such comings in their prophecies. There are many examples of this.

About Matthew 27:9, I will admit that I do not have a ready and convenient answer to this question. Matthew tells us that the prophecy of the purchase of the potter's field comes from Jeremiah, whereas we know that this prophecy is found in Zechariah 11:13. Did Matthew get it wrong? Is he simply mistaken? This seems to draw into question biblical inerrancy and perhaps even biblical inspiration. It represents one of only about two or three apparent "contradictions" in the entire Bible for which I simply do not have a ready and rather obvious answer. Did Jeremiah also prophecy this, but we do not have it recorded in our book of Jeremiah? This is possible but it is also speculation. In fact, to the skeptic it will appear to be a rather convenient and perhaps even suspicious speculation. I would like to say that there are literally zero unresolved examples of apparent contradictions in the Bible, but the fact is that there is a very small number of cases for which I must resort to some sort of speculation. In fact, the only two claimed contradiction/mistakes which I know of which I find hard to explain are this one and Matthew 10:10 and Luke 9:8 vs. Mk 6:8. These raise the question of whether Jesus said to bring a staff or not. That's it! End of story, at least as far as I can tell. Such examples, which can be resolved, but which require relatively unfounded speculation to resolve, are so rare that the paucity of examples is good evidence of the inspiration of the Bible.

QUESTION:
Did the Gospel writers borrow material from one another? Did they plagiarize?

ANSWER:

Dozens of books and hundreds of ThD dissertations have been written on the subject of the sources of the Gospels. Much of this is almost pure speculation—sometimes even an unfounded and biased attack on the veracity of the New Testament. Some of the research on possible biblical sources is good scholarship which can be helpful to understanding the New Testament. One example of somewhat speculative but not unreasonable attempt at reconstructing the sources of the gospels is the supposed document Q. Many, if not most scholars believe that the Q document, possibly in Aramaic, was the principle source document from which the synoptic Gospel writers (Matthew, Mark and Luke) drew their material.

Despite the fact that many biased critics have used claims about the sources of the New Testament to discredit the authenticity of the Gospels, the question of sources is still a legitimate area of inquiry for the serious student of the Bible. Which Gospel was written first? Did Matthew have a copy of Mark in front of him as he wrote, and did he use it as a source for his material? Even if the existence of document Q is unsubstantiated, what, if any written records of the sayings and acts of Jesus were in existence before the Gospel accounts were written down? All of these are legitimate questions. The answers may provide us with some insight as to why Luke included or excluded certain specific events in the life of Jesus and so forth.

When one reads the Gospels, one can discover hints as to who wrote first and who borrowed from whom. Logically, one might thing that Mark, being the shortest and most succinct of the writers, may have recorded his Gospel first. However, some commentators believe Matthew wrote first. If that question is important to you, you should consider getting a couple of good commentaries to the Gospels and consider the arguments of the scholars. I believe it is fair to say that no one will ever resolve beyond a reasonable doubt the question of sources or who wrote first. Therefore, although it may be helpful and interesting to think about why Luke does or does not include a certain detail and whether he had Matthew as a source, in the end, you will be left with some guesswork and nothing really solid you can hang your hat on.

As to plagiarism, it would not be "unethical" if Mark included certain passages straight out of Matthew—or if he borrowed from Matthew. It is not as if they had copyright laws back then, in the modern sense. Mark certainly did not make a profit from his little book. Having said that, the evidence is that all four Gospel authors wrote essentially independent accounts of the life and sayings of Jesus. This is proven by the great number of examples in which Matthew, Mark and Luke describe the same event in significantly different ways. That is not to say that their accounts contradict. Their accounts appear to be truly independent eyewitness or second-hand reports of the same events. We also forget that the gospel writers recorded messages that Jesus presented multiple times. This is common in a dynamic and growing ministry. It goes without saying that he would also adapt his messages for different audiences depending on their needs. In the same fashion the gospel writers will never be able to duplicate the exact message but only the highlights.

Let me use one example. When James and John came to ask Jesus for the right and left hand place with him in heaven, Mark describes them going directly to Jesus to make the request (Mark 10:35-45). When Matthew records the same event, he has their mother making the request (Matthew 20:20-28). In Matthew's account, James and John are waiting in the wings and are confronted by Jesus for making this request through their mother. Most likely, Mark is simplifying the account, not bothering to mention the role of their mother. Is this a significant difference? No. Whether or not they asked their mother to voice their desire, it was James and John doing the requesting, even if they hid behind their mother. The point is this: these accounts do not contradict one other; rather, they show signs of two different witnesses reporting the same event from their own independent perspective.

Did Luke do some borrowing from Matthew? Possibly. Would it really matter a lot if he did? The fact is that, on the whole, all four Gospels show clear evidence that they are more or less independent accounts of the same general events in the life of the most amazing man who ever lived, Jesus Christ of Nazareth.

QUESTION:

In Leviticus 11:20, it says the Israelites must not eat "four-legged" insects. I was wondering what the Hebrew for "four" meant in that passage and if all insects were considered four-legged literally?

ANSWER:

My English translation says *"all flying insects that walk on all fours are to be detestable to you."* I would take "all fours" to be an expression generally meaning an animal which does not walk upright. No one should take this verse to mean that the Bible is teaching that insects have four rather than six legs. I would assume that the writer of Leviticus was well aware that insects have six rather than four legs, but that he is using an idiom meaning insects which crawl around.

QUESTION:

If you place so much faith on the reliability of the synoptic Gospels and refuse to accept that they are not plain eyewitness statements, how do you account for the blatant contradiction between John 19:17 and Matthew 27:32?

ANSWER:

The two passages you mention are both about the carrying of the cross to Calvary. All the Gospel accounts either say directly or imply that Jesus carried the cross-beam to the scene of his execution. Notice it says in Matthew 27:32, *"As they were going out."* Most likely, Jesus was so exhausted from being nearly beaten to death that it became apparent that he would not be able to carry it to the crucifixion. It would have been very embarrassing to the Roman soldiers if Jesus died before reaching the place of execution. The public wanted to see a spectacle. He had to be crucified. For this reason, when Jesus collapsed, they chose an innocent bystander, Simon the Cyrene, to carry it for him. I will admit that, to some extent, I am relying on the standard Roman Catholic version of events. I do not know for sure that Simon of Cyrene was forced to carry it the rest of the way specifically because Jesus had collapsed, but it is a reasonable conjecture. What is for sure is that the eyewitnesses reported that Jesus carried his cross (John 19:17), and that Simon was forced to carry it part of the way (Matthew 27:32 and Luke 23:26).

As I have said before, the differences in the eyewitness accounts is evidence, not of mistakes, but of independent witness. I believe I shared with you earlier that I was a juror in a trial two years ago. Each eyewitness to the brutal beating provided dramatically different details, yet we, as jurors, felt the correct overall picture was created by listening to all the witnesses. In fact, Mark provides additional details. He tells us that Simon the Cyrene was the father of Alexander and Rufus. Most scholars believe Mark provided these details because Simon and his two sons were very well known Christians in the first century. It is quite possible that the Rufus in Romans 16:13 is the same man. Scholars consider it probable that Mark was in Rome, as Paul specifically mentions him in 2 Timothy 4:11. If that is true, Mark, the Gospel writer, mentions Rufus and Alexander because they were friends of his. It is as if he is saying, "If you are not sure about this, ask Rufus."

QUESTION:
How do you reconcile Genesis 14:14 with Judges 18:29?

ANSWER:
I can see how one might see a possible contradiction here. The reason is that Genesis 14 identifies the location to which Abraham pursued his family as the city of Dan. Judges 18:29 has the same location, Dan, receiving its name much later, at the time the Israelite tribe Dan occupied the city. This event happened hundreds of years after Abraham lived. If you assume that Genesis was written by Moses or even earlier, then there is a problem. There is a long tradition that Moses wrote Genesis, but I do not accept this tradition. It is possible that he had some sort of influence on this book, but as far as I know, there is no evidence for Moses being the author of Genesis. Personally, I believe Genesis was put into its final form, probably in the early kingdom period, from much earlier written and/or oral materials. It makes perfect sense that the Genesis compiler/editor used the common name for this city so that his readers would get the connection, while the writer of Judges is giving us an accurate account of how it got that name. Again, if you assume that Genesis was written in its final form some time around 1400 BC, then there would be an apparent contradiction. However, I do not believe this is the case, as it is more likely Genesis took its final form some time after 1000 BC.

QUESTION:
Please explain the apparent contradiction between Acts 9:7 and Acts 22:9.

ANSWER:
The relevant passages are as follows: Acts 9:7 (NIV)—*"The men traveling with Saul stood there speechless; they heard the sound but did not see anyone."* Acts 22:9 (NIV)—*"My companions saw the light, but they did not understand the voice of him who was speaking to me."* I do not understand what the perceived contradiction could be in this case. The companions heard a great noise and saw a great light. However, they did not see the "person" speaking to Paul. Neither could they understand the words spoken. They knew something extraordinary had happened, but did not see or understand. Apparently, God somehow allowed Paul to see and understand what they could not.

QUESTION:
I'm trying to reconcile an apparent discrepancy/contradiction between Matthew's and Mark's accounts of the Gerasene demoniac. Matthew says there were two while Mark says there was just one. Matthew was an eyewitness, and Mark wrote the memories of Peter, another eyewitness. How can I resolve this?

ANSWER:
This apparent "contradiction" is one which is brought up fairly often. It therefore deserves a careful answer. The evidence from the Gospels is that they represent separate, independent, largely eyewitness accounts of what happened in the life and ministry of Jesus of Nazareth. This is the case even with the Gospel of Luke, which was largely gathered second hand from eyewitnesses to the events. The significant difference in details between the parallel accounts of events in John, Luke, Matthew and Mark show that the authors did not rely on one another, at least not principally, as they wrote their accounts of what happened. This is the case with the demoniacs in the region of Gerasene. If one wants a more rounded account of what happened, one must find a way to reconcile what might at first appear to be contradictory details. When the accounts are reconciled (assuming that all the witnesses are telling the truth), the story is more fully understood. I assume that Matthew and Mark chose to mention different aspects of what happened.

Let me share how I personally reconcile the two versions of the story. I assume that when Jesus arrived on the scene in the boat, he found two men who were possessed by demons wandering in the tombs. I believe that one of these men was extremely violent, that he was the one who broke his chains, shouted out and fell at Jesus' feet (Mark 5:1-8). Matthew's account (Matthew 8:28-34) includes the detail that there were actually two demon-possessed men among the tombs. Most likely, one of these two was much more violent and loud than the other, although both were possessed and needed healing. Mark mentioned the one who got everyone's attention, while Matthew mentioned both men. The fact that the accounts differ, yet all can be readily reconciled, gives evidence of separate, reliable eyewitness sources for the Gospel stories.

QUESTION:
Have you noticed there are two accounts in the Bible of Jesus cursing the fig tree and when Jesus drove the money changers out? In one account, Jesus drove the money changers out and then cursed

the fig tree the next day (Matthew 21:10-22). And in the other account, he cursed the fig tree first and then drove the money changers out the same day (Mark 11:11-26). If the Bible has verbal, plenary inspiration, I do not see how these two stories can be inspired. [Author's note: By *verbal plenary inspiration*, the questioner means that the actual, individual words of the entire scripture in its original language are as God determined them to be.]

ANSWER:

Scholars generally agree that Matthew created a dramatic description of the ministry and words of Jesus without giving great care to reproducing the exact order and timing of the events. Luke, being an accomplished historian, created a consciously more chronological account of the events of Jesus' life. Most likely (although I cannot prove it), when Matthew presents Jesus' monologues, he is bringing together some of the actual statements from different lessons of Jesus into a single monologue for dramatic effect in order to explain Jesus to his hearers. In other words, when one reads a monologue by Jesus in Matthew, one is not necessarily reading a word-for-word transcript of a single speech. This is not evidence of a lack of inspiration, but is simply one way to present the Gospel material. The fact that different witnesses report slightly different aspects of the same events supports the belief that the four Gospels are independent accounts of the same events. This is not evidence of a mistake or of a lack of inspiration, but of truly independent accounts of the life of Jesus, which is just what one would want of multiple Gospels. The point, when one reads Matthew or Mark, is that one is seeing a God-breathed glimpse of the words and ministry of Jesus. Every event is recorded with great care by Matthew and Mark to give an accurate account of what transpired. I believe that both the general description and the details of Matthew's and Mark's accounts are true to what happened, and that is all that I require to view it as accurate history and as inspired by God.

Nevertheless, this does not make your question go away. It remains a possibility that one might find irresolvable contradictions in the Gospel accounts. If Matthew said Jesus was killed by beheading and Mark said that he was crucified, this would clearly bring the accuracy of the accounts into question! Therefore, the question is whether the specific example you raise is this type of irresolvable discrepancy.

As I look at Matthew 21 and Mark 11, I simply do not see a contradiction. Matthew reports Jesus at the temple, driving out the money changers in vs. 12-15. After that, Matthew has Jesus *"early* in the morning" causing the fig tree to wither. Knowing the fact that Matthew is not always careful to present every situation in strictly chronological order, I would not be shocked if it turned out that the events in Matthew 21, although accurate, are not in the actual order they occurred. However, when I go to Mark, I see Jesus, after driving out the money changers, coming across the fig tree, cursing it and the tree withering. The only significant difference in the two accounts is that Matthew reports only the second visit to the fig tree, while Mark reports both the first and the second visit to the tree. I also think it is highly likely that over a three year span of ministry Jesus cleared the temple more than one time and this would account for some variation in the accounts as they are describing more than one event.

My own harmonization of the accounts is that Jesus, on the day of the temple-clearing, pronounced a curse on the tree for not bearing fruit, as described in Matthew. Then, on the following day, Jesus actually spoke to the tree, causing it to wither before the very eyes of the disciples. It is possible that Mark was not aware that Matthew and others actually saw the tree wither before their eyes on that particular day, and that all he was aware of was the original statement to the tree and the subsequent withering of the tree the apostles saw the next day. Simply put, the accounts do not contradict if we simply ask how the two might make sense when taken together.

QUESTION:

How do you reconcile the accounts in Matthew and Luke regarding the events immediately following the birth of Jesus? In Matthew, Jesus is brought to Egypt from Bethlehem and then later to Nazareth after the death of Herod. In Luke, he is brought from Bethlehem to Jerusalem and then immediately to Nazareth. The way Matthew and Luke are written (or should I say translated in English), it creates the impression that the events narrated happened immediately after Bethlehem.

ANSWER:

Matthew provides more information than Luke, but the two accounts do not contradict one another. We can assume that Mary and Joseph did many things which are not recorded in either account. For example, Matthew says that the wise men came to see Jesus at the house where they were living (Matthew 2:10), yet Matthew does not report the move from the cave/stable where Jesus was born. Obviously, all the authors of the Gospels leave out huge amounts of information about Jesus. When one reads any of the Gospels, one gets the impression that it was a normal narrative technique at that time to report incidents which were separated by a significant amount of time as if they were successive events. For example, for dramatic effect, Mark often begins a new scene in Jesus' life with "Then the..." (such as in Mark 10:35, Mark 12:18 and many others), implying that the events followed immediately upon one another when we know that this is not literally true. This dramatic means of telling a story was common at that time, although it may catch us off guard because we are not used to it.

Luke 2:39 is no exception to this rule—that Near-Eastern writers made sudden transitions to the next scene in their story (by the way, the Greek text of this passage is very similar to the NIV translation). It seems, at first, that Luke implies the return to Galilee followed immediately after finishing all the formal ceremonies at the temple. However, given the common mode of narrative we find in the Gospels, we should be hesitant to assume that nothing significant happened before the move to Galilee. When one reads Matthew, one finds the additional information that Joseph and Mary fled for safety into Egypt for a time before returning to Nazareth. Luke obviously could not relate everything that happened to Jesus and, apparently, he chose not to include the escape into Egypt. There is no contradiction between the two Gospel accounts.

QUESTION:

Why does the miracle of turning the water into wine and the temptation of Christ in the wilderness take place at the same time if you read the story in two different books of the NT? Why is the list of ten rules found in Exodus 20 and Exodus 34 not the same?

ANSWER:

It took me a while to understand your first question. I could not tell how you thought the two events happened at the same time. However, upon careful reading of Matthew's account of the temptation of Jesus, I saw how you were caused to ask this question. If one reads Matthew 4:1-11, which describes the temptation of Jesus, it follows immediately after the account of the baptism of Jesus. The passage starts with the phrase, *"Then Jesus was led by the Spirit into the desert..."* which leads into the temptation of Jesus by Satan. When one reads John chapter one and two, it gives a more thorough account of the days which followed upon the baptism of Jesus, saying that *"on the third day"* Jesus attended a wedding, where the miracle of turning the water into wine took place. I am assuming that this is where the question comes from.

The answer to your question is that both Matthew and Mark make a consistent habit of describing events which were separated by a significant amount of time—sometimes even weeks and months—by beginning the next account with the word "then." If you thumb your way through the first two Gospels, especially Mark, you will notice this to be the style of writing. If you look carefully, you will see both of the Gospel writers using "then..." to describe events which definitely had a significant amount of time between what is described as happening. This was a literary style which, for the audience at the time, gave a sense of drama. Mark and Matthew wrote accounts of the life of Jesus which did not necessarily stress chronological order. Their dramatic and fast-moving style was appropriate considering that many or most who heard the Gospels were listening to the letters being read out loud, as the majority were not literate. I believe you can assume that the description in John represents the actual timing of the events. About all you can assume by the statement in Matthew that *"then Jesus was led by the Spirit..."* is that the events of the temptation followed after the events of the baptism of Jesus.

About Exodus 20 and 34, here is my response. In Exodus 20:1-17, one finds the "Ten Commandments" which were written on the stone tablets by God. In Exodus 34, God told Moses to *"chisel out two stone tablets like the first ones."* These are two different incidents, separated by some time, and the details are different. In Exodus 34, God wrote the same laws on the two stones as before (Exodus 34:1). We can assume these were the same ten laws that are found in Exodus 20:1-17. In addition, God dictated a number of other laws which he asked Moses to write down (Numbers 34:27). The laws God dictated to Moses in Numbers 34:10-26 are in addition to the ten God miraculously wrote onto the tablets Moses had chiseled out. If you look in Leviticus, you will find that God gave Moses many laws in addition to the famous "Ten Commandments." Perhaps the reason this made you wonder about a contradiction is that many of the laws God had Moses write down are similar in some ways to the ones he wrote onto the two stone tablets.

QUESTION:

Why do the Gospels differ in showing how Jesus called his first disciples? The book of John describes the encounter differently from the other Gospels.

ANSWER:

I am assuming that you are referring to John 1:35-42, which is obviously significantly different from, for example, Mark 1:14-20. I have always assumed that when Jesus formally called the first disciples to join him permanently in his ministry in Mark 1:14-20, this was not the first time he had met Peter, Andrew, James and John. The very first time I read Mark chapter 1, I thought that this was the first time they had ever met Jesus, because it seems a natural implication. However, the more I thought about it, the way they responded to the call seemed to me to represent men who knew Jesus fairly well and were already prepared to consider following him. This was not the first time they had met him.

Having reached this conclusion, it then becomes easy to see where John 1:35-42 fits in. This is the account of the first time these fishermen actually met Jesus. They spent some time with him at his house, witnessing his miraculous understanding of the heart of Nathaniel, hearing him speak of his ministry and so forth. Several weeks, or perhaps even several months later, when Jesus came to their home town to call them into the full-time work of following him, they were prepared by their previous knowledge of him, as described in John chapter one. When Jesus called them, he was asking men who knew him well enough to have at least some idea of what they were getting into when they left their nets and followed him.

QUESTION:

How can I understand both 2 Kings 15:30 and 2 Kings 17:1 involving Ahaz and Uzziah and their reigns? In the NIV translation of 2 King 15:30, it states: "Then Hoshea son of Elah conspired against Pekah son of Remaliah. He attacked and assassinated him, and then succeeded him as king in the twentieth year of Jotham son of Uzziah." Then in 2 King 17:1 we find: "In the twelfth year of Ahaz king of Judah, Hoshea son of Elah became king of Israel in Samaria, and he reigned nine years. He did evil in the eyes of the LORD, but not like the kings of Israel who preceded him." It appears to me that there is a difference between the numbers of years in the two scriptures. Do you know of an explanation of this apparent contradiction?

ANSWER:

It is pretty easy to get confused about the years the kings of Judah reigned. First, Uzziah ruled for something like 41 years. However, because of his illness, his son ruled as regent from about

750-742 BC. When Uzziah died, Jotham ruled in his own right. Therefore, the year of Jotham's reign is sometimes based on 750 and sometimes on 742 BC.

Both 2 Chronicles and 2 Kings agree that Jotham ruled for only 16 years. Here is what I would speculate. For some reason, the reign of Hoshea is dated from the time that Jotham ruled, beginning somewhere around 750 BC, even though Jotham had already died. Perhaps this is to take honor away from Ahaz, who was an ungodly king, as 2 Chronicles clearly states. This would put the beginning of Hoshea's reign somewhere around 731 BC. As for 2 Kings 17:1, I can conceive of two possibilities. Perhaps it reports the twelfth year of Ahaz because Ahaz was ruling as regent for a time before he came to full power, or perhaps there is some sort of scribal error in the years of reign in this passage.

We should be cautious when looking at numbers in the Old Testament. The Jews used a letter system for their numbers, somewhat like Roman numerals. To make matters even more difficult, some of the letters used for numbers are very similar in appearance, which was very likely to produce scribal errors in copying. I advise OT readers to take numbers in the text with great caution because number-copying errors are so easily made and hard to fix after the fact. In general, such number-copying errors do not introduce any issues about the spiritual meaning of the scriptures, implying that they are not significant for modern readers of the Bible.

Because of the likelihood of the number-transcribing errors, I cannot state for certain what the solution is to the problem in the 2 Kings text. By the way, a fairly trustworthy Bible archaeology book I have on hand lists the years of reign for the relevant kings as:

Judah:
>Uzziah 783-742
>Jotham 750-735 (note; as regent for about nine years)
>Ahaz 735-715

Israel:
>Pekiah 737-736
>Pekah 736-732
>Hoshea 732-724

If there is a number-transcribing error, then Hoshea began to rule in about the fourth year of Ahaz. If there is a hidden regency, then Ahaz became regent around 743.

QUESTION:

How can I understand Luke 23:34 (*"forgive them father"*), Acts 2:23 (*"wicked men put him to death"*) and Acts 2:38 (*"repent"*)? It is a bit confusing to me. In Luke, Jesus asks the Father to forgive those who killed him, but in Acts 2:23, Peter accuses these same people of putting him to death; then in Acts 2:38, Peter tells them to repent and be baptized for the forgiveness of their sins. How are these consistent with one another?

ANSWER:

Out of compassion, Jesus asked his Father to forgive those in the execution detail for the horrible way they had treated him. This is certainly consistent with what we know about the heart of Jesus. He saw these men as *"sheep without a shepherd"* (Matthew 9:36). In fact, at least one of the soldiers was convinced that Jesus was the Son of God by the events he witnessed that day (Mark 15:39). It was on Jesus' heart to forgive the men for their actions, at least in part because he was voluntarily letting himself be treated in this way. God had allowed the events to lead up to this culmination, and Jesus did not want even the slightest hint of bitterness to enter his heart at this point.

The events of Acts chapter two are a very different thing. First of all, you can assume that those in the crowd at Pentecost in Acts chapter two were not the same as those who were in the execution detail on the hill of Golgotha. It is unlikely that any of the Roman soldiers were at the temple on the day of Pentecost. When Peter said *"this Jesus whom you crucified,"* he was not placing blame on the actual individuals who carried out the execution, or even those who plotted to have him arrested. In effect, Peter was saying to the crowd, "All of you who are sinners are at least indirectly responsible for Jesus being killed on the cross. As sinners, Jesus died for you and you are therefore responsible for his death." Based on acceptance of this truth, many were cut to the heart that day and willingly repented of their sins, were baptized and "added to their number that day."

There is a very unfortunate history among some Christian groups to try to lay the blame for the crucifixion of Jesus on the Jews. It is true that all, or at least nearly all, the audience of Peter's first gospel sermon were Jews. However, this fact does not give legitimate support for anyone to claim that Peter was saying Jews alone are responsible for the death of Jesus. Jesus died for everyone's sins. All have sinned and fallen short of the glory of God, and are freely justified by the blood of Christ (to paraphrase Romans 3). Perhaps the individuals in the crowd who demanded the execution of Jesus have a special responsibility before God. Personally, I doubt that, but be that as it may, the crowd in the temple on the day of Pentecost—fifty days after the crucifixion of Jesus—was no more responsible than all of us are for the death of Jesus.

Yes, it is true that Jesus asked his Father to forgive his executioners on that day. Nevertheless, even these men would have to come to grips with their sin in the end, repent and be baptized into Christ to obtain salvation. One can only hope that some of them did. If so, I will assume that they will be in heaven some day.

QUESTION:

How do you explain that Jesus called people "fools"? Wouldn't he be subject to hell fire according to his own words (Matthew 5:22, Matthew 23:17, Matthew 23:19)? Is it acceptable for us to call people fools in certain situations?

ANSWER:

The relevant passages are:

Matthew 5:22: *"But I tell you that anyone who is angry with his brother will be subject to judgment. Again, anyone who says to his brother, 'Raca,' is answerable to the Sanhedrin. But anyone who says, 'You fool!' will be in danger of the fire of hell."*

Matthew 23:17: *"You blind fools! Which is greater: the gold, or the temple that makes the gold sacred?"*

Matthew 23:19: *"You blind men! Which is greater: the gift, or the altar that makes the gift sacred?"*

This is an interesting question. To be honest, I had never thought about it in that way. In order to resolve such a question, one must look at the relevant scriptures in their context. Applying this principle to the passages in question, the word "fool" is being used in a very different context in Matthew 5 and Matthew 23. In Matthew 5:22, Jesus condemns as sinful saying to someone *"you fool."* In the context, he just finished talking about murdering someone. He is talking about angrily lashing out at someone and cursing them. Jesus would not use a curse word to make his point, so he used what was, for him, a fairly strong term of derision, if used in anger toward someone. Let me make it practical. It is not sinful to show to someone (in a calm and rational way), just between the two of you, that their actions are foolish. In such a situation, it may well be the loving thing to do. However, if we lash out at someone in the throes of anger and call them a fool—that would be sinful. Calling someone a fool in anger is like pouring gasoline on a fire in the midst of an emotional conflict.

In Matthew 23, Jesus is definitely using some strong words. He is labeling some of the hypocritical behavior of the Pharisees as very foolish. I believe we are seeing righteous anger in his pronouncements to the Pharisees, not uncontrolled rage. Even in this situation, notice the wisdom of Jesus. He is not calling out any one single individual and calling him a fool—insulting him in front of his friends. If he had done so, I believe he would have crossed the line. It is almost always unwise, or even sinful, to call someone out in a public setting and ridicule that individual publicly with strong condemnatory language, even if such a statement, if made in a calmer, private setting is more or less accurate.

Let me add one comment on Jesus' behavior. I believe Jesus was in a much better position to make strong public statements about sin than we are. He was tempted in every way, yet was without sin. Through his amazingly loving and calm response to every conceivable form of derision and criticism, he earned the right to speak to people more directly than most of us. Isaiah 42:3 describes the Messiah's behavior with the phrase, *"A bruised reed he did not break."* What was wise behavior on the part of Jesus in Matthew 23 might be foolish behavior if one of us did the same thing. We should admire and appreciate Jesus' boldness, but I do not suggest copying all aspects of his style of condemning the Pharisees, as most of us have not earned the right to speak so strongly. When Jesus said in John 8, *"let he who is without sin throw the first stone,"* he was the only person present with the right to throw a stone, based on that criterion. We would do well to admire and even imitate Jesus' boldness, but given our own sin, we should be careful how we speak about the sins of others, especially in a public setting.

The word "fool" (admittedly, a Hebrew rather than a Greek word for fool) is found 46 times in the book of Proverbs. There are many kinds of actions an individual might take which are foolish behavior according to God. It is not wrong for a follower of Jesus to pull aside a brother or sister, or even a non-believer whom they love and are trying to help, and point out that their behavior is unwise (a gentle way of saying foolish). However, even Solomon does not call out his enemy "Mr. X" as a fool in front of his friends. Public statements about what is foolish behavior is fine, but calling out an individual in a crowd and calling that person a fool is not advised or demonstrated by either Jesus or the writer of Proverbs.

One last thing: for your information, the Greek word for "fool" is the same in all three passages from Matthew. It is a simple word, meaning fool or foolish. Proverbs obviously uses a different word, as it is in Hebrew, but the connotation is the same.

QUESTION:

I was hoping you could give me a good answer why in Leviticus 11:6 the Lord told Moses that *"The rabbit, though it chews the cud, does not have a split hoof; it is unclean for you."* Technically, a rabbit does not chew the cud like a cow because it only has one stomach. On www.bible.org, it says because a rabbit chews its food so much it looks as though it chews cud. Do you think that is a good explanation of that Scripture? This question has bothered me since I read the definition of chewing the cud in the dictionary after I read an Amazon.com review by an unbeliever of a Christian evidence book that pointed out this apparent biblical error.

ANSWER:

Yes, I have heard of this one before. I would say that if this is the best example of a significant contradiction or "mistake" in the Bible, then that alone would be evidence that the Bible is an amazing book! The answer to the question is that the Hebrew words translated as "chew the cud" is not a technical term. The translation "chew the cud" is probably about the closest translation of the Hebrew word as we have in English. The fact is that rabbits do re-chew their food, but not from an extra stomach. The Hebrew does not have a sufficiently technical term to separate what rabbits do from what cows do. This is not a Bible error. Rather than create the false impression that I am an expert about this question, I will supply a link to a website where an expert on the Hebrew language will answer your question. http://www.tektonics.org/af/cudchewers.html. A brief quote from the author, James Patrick Holding, follows:

Two issues are at hand: the definition of "cud" and that of "chewing." Let's take a close look at the Hebrew version of both. Here is the word for "cud" according to Strong's: *gerah*, the cud (as scraping the throat):—cud.

There are a few factors we need to keep in mind here. First, this word is used nowhere in the Old Testament besides these verses in Leviticus and Deuteronomy. We have only this context to help us decide what it means in terms of the Mosaic Law.

Second, refection is a process whereby rabbits pass pellets of partially digested food, which they chew on (along with the waste material) in order to give their stomachs another go at getting the nutrients out. It is not just "dung" that the rabbits are eating, which is probably why the Hebrew word for "dung" was not used here.

Contrast this with what cows and some other animals do, rumination, which is what we moderns call "chewing the cud." They regurgitate partially digested food in little clumps called cuds, and chew it a little more while mixing it with saliva.

So then, partially digested food is a common element here. We suggest that the Hebrew word *gerah* simply refers to any partially digested food—the process is not the issue, just the object.

QUESTION:

Genesis 11:1 says that the world at that time *"had one language and a common speech."* However, Genesis 10:5 seems to imply that there was more than one language at that same time. Please explain this.

ANSWER:

Although Genesis 10:5 comes before Genesis 11:1 in the Bible, it is referring to a time frame which stretches past the Tower of Babel incident. The time frame which is represented by the genealogy of Japheth-Javan-Elishah-etc. may be hundreds of years. It was very common for Jewish genealogies to skip one or even several generations. Because this particular genealogy mentions peoples (the Kittim and the Rodanim) rather than individual people, it is even more likely than usual to imply a gap of time. Therefore, by the time Japheth's descendents had multiplied into many nations, such as the Rodanim, the incidents at the Tower of Babel may have been distant history. The context of Genesis 11:1-9 seems to be a few generations after Noah and his sons, but Genesis 10:5 appears to reach to many generations—well past the Babel events. Because neither account gives a definite number of years, it is hard to prove either way, but this appears to be the natural reading to me.

QUESTION:

In Luke 2:49, Jesus refers to the Temple in Jerusalem as his Father's house. Also, King Solomon built this temple for God according to his instruction. However, in Acts 17:24, it is taught that God does not live in any temple built by humans. I am having some difficulty explaining this apparent discrepancy.

ANSWER:

I can certainly see how one might see a potential contradiction in these two Bible teachings. However, if one looks at both Luke 2:49 and Acts 17:24, it will be seen that both are correct, but are talking about different aspects of God. 1 Kings 8 records Solomon's prayer upon the dedication of the temple in Jerusalem. In both the tabernacle, and later the temple, the Bible clearly states that God dwelt on the mercy seat, between the cherubim in the Holy of Holies. Yet, at the dedication of the temple, Solomon said (1 Kings 8:27), *"But will God really dwell on earth? The heavens, even the highest heaven, cannot contain you. How much less this temple I have built."* Even as he built and dedicated the temple, Solomon was aware that God was way too big to dwell in his fullness in a temple made by human hands.

What we have, then, is that an aspect, or a part of God, dwelt in the temple. When Moses entered the Most Holy Place, his face was glowing afterward so that they had to put a veil over his face (2 Corinthians 3:12-18). Moses was seeing God, but if he had seen God in all his glory, he surely would have died (Exodus 10:28). This is a deep concept. The fact is that Moses saw God but he did not see all of God. By analogy, God dwelt in the temple, but not all of God dwelt in the temple. That is why Jesus was right in Luke 2:49, but Paul was also right in Acts 17:24. God did dwell in the temple, but God cannot be limited to living in a temple.

It is also worth noting that by the time Acts 17:24 was written, God no longer dwelt in the temple in Jerusalem. Matthew 27:51 describes how, at the time Jesus gave up his last breath, the curtain in the temple was torn in two. At that time, God ceased to dwell in the Holy of Holies in the temple. Forty years later, the temple in Jerusalem was destroyed for the last time. By the time Paul wrote Acts 17:24, his statement that God does not dwell in temples built by human hands was correct in both the limited sense (as in the Temple of Solomon) and in the greater sense (i.e. God is too great to be limited to dwelling in his fullness in a human-built temple). The only remaining "temple" in which God dwells at the present time is in the bodies of saved disciples of Jesus: *"You are the temple of the living God"* (2 Corinthians 6:16). God no longer dwells in temples built by human hands, but he lives in temples built by the Holy Spirit.

QUESTION:

I have really been struggling a lot over this one, even though I believe the Bible is inspired by God. When I read the Gospel accounts of Peter's denial of Jesus, there seems to be a glaring contradiction here. In both Mark and Matthew, we see that a servant girl (or "maid" depending on your translation) confronts Peter during the first denial. In Mark, it seems that the same girl confronts him again (most translations have her saying again), whereas the Matthew account has "another" servant girl approaching him the second time. How can these two accounts possibly be harmonized?

ANSWER:

I believe the appearance of a contradiction which you perceive is created by the way that Mark is translated into the English. I am looking at my Greek interlinear which has the Greek words in the original with the English translation of the word directly below the Greek. In the Greek text of Mark 14:68b-69, the original words are, *"And he went forth outside into the forecourt and the maidservant seeing him began again to say to the [ones] standing by, 'This man of them is...'"* The sense I get from Mark is that, when Jesus went into the forecourt, there was another maidservant on duty in there who began saying to him that Peter, like Jesus, was one of "them" as had the servant girl working outside. I will admit that if I had never read Matthew, but only Mark, I might have at least considered the possibility that the maidservant inside was the same one as the one outside. The English translation would have pushed me more strongly in that direction than the Greek original. However, when I hear the parallel witness, I learn that the two women were actually different servants. The consistency and accuracy of the Bible are such that the biblical accounts deserve the benefit of the doubt. If we are presented with what looks as though it might contradict, we should look for the common thread in the witnesses and ask ourselves how their seemingly contradictory testimony may actually be a different but complimentary account of the same events. That is exactly what I see going on in this case.

QUESTION:

Please harmonize Ezekiel 18 and the punishment on Achan and his entire family. How can it be true that "the soul who sins is the one who will die," yet Achan's entire family was punished for his personal sin (Joshua 7)?

ANSWER:

This question brings out an important point of biblical theology. It was true from the very beginning that the soul that sins is the one who will die. One need only look at Adam and Eve to be sure of that. So what about Abraham? Abraham became lost when he sinned, just like the rest of us. Nevertheless, he had his sins forgiven by God's sovereign choice because of his faith. Romans 4 (the whole chapter) makes it clear that Abraham was considered righteous (i.e. forgiven of his sin) because of his faith which was shown by his righteous deeds. So yes, all who sin are destined to perish—that is, unless they are saved from their sins through the forgiveness from God which is found in Jesus Christ. Achan sinned and was judged both physically, and presumably, spiritually for his sin. Clearly, he did not have the faith of Abraham. One difficult point for us doctrinally is that some of the people who lived before Jesus, such as Abraham and Elijah, will clearly be with God in heaven, yet they were not saved in the New Testament sense. Apparently, the blood of Jesus *"slain from the creation of the world"* (Revelation 13:8) is able to save even those who put their faith in God before Jesus died on the cross. They were not saved in the same sense as we are, as they did not have the gift of the Holy Spirit living in them, but they will be forgiven by God nevertheless.

Let us go back to Achan. He and his family were judged physically for his sins. The entire family received punishment from the civil authorities. However, if we accept Ezekiel 18:14-20, which says that the son is not accountable (before God) for his father's sins, we can assume that only Achan will be punished spiritually and eternally for his sin. At first, this distinction can be confusing. Our sins in this life can cause suffering and physical judgment on our neighbors—particularly on members of our own family—but before God on Judgment Day, we will be saved or lost based on our actions alone. The difficulty here is to distinguish between some sort of physical punishment in this life (which can affect the "innocent") versus an eternal judgment which is completely a matter of one's own life. Is it sad that the entire family was punished for the sins of Achan? Definitely! Hopefully, the Israelites got the point. I assume that the children will be in heaven. The adult family members will not be judged eternally for what Achan did. Praise God for the grace of Jesus Christ. Based on our personal righteousness, no one would be saved.

To summarize, the apparent discrepancy between what happened to Achan and the clear statement in Ezekiel 18 is explained when we consider physical judgment and suffering in this life, which can fall on both the sinner and the innocent, versus eternal judgment, for which we are accountable before God for our own actions alone.

QUESTION:
How can I explain Matthew 16:28 when Jesus did not come back in the first century? In this passage, Jesus says that some of them would not die before they see him coming in his kingdom. Was he saying that he would come back during their lifetime?

Supposed Inconsistencies in the Bible

ANSWER:

Jesus did indeed come in his Kingdom during the lifetime of most of those who heard him on that day, but not in the manner you apparently anticipate. The subject of the Kingdom of God is a broad and deep one. In order to understand what Jesus meant, we must have a good definition of the Kingdom of God. I cover this in **FSTR** ch. 9. In this book, I define the Kingdom of God as anyone or anywhere over which God rules. Israel was in a sense the Kingdom of God. The church of Christ is in a sense the Kingdom of God because Jesus reigns over the Church. Heaven is the fullest realization of the Kingdom of God. When Jesus comes back in the sky at the end of time (Matthew 24:30-31), that certainly will be a coming of the Kingdom. However, I believe this "coming of the Kingdom" is not the one Jesus has in mind in Matthew 16:28.

In the context of Matthew 16:28, Jesus is talking about the Kingdom of God in the sense he most commonly uses it in the Gospels, which is the Kingdom of God on Earth in its present form, which is his rule over the Church. It is not correct to say that the Church is equal to the Kingdom of God. However, when the Church began on the day of Pentecost (as described in Acts 2), that certainly was a coming of the Kingdom. In fact, Jesus had just recently made that point in Matthew 16:17-19 where he points out the relationship between the church and the Kingdom of Heaven. Jesus appears to use the phrase Kingdom of God and Kingdom of Heaven almost interchangeably in the Gospels.

So when was the prophecy in Matthew 16:28 fulfilled? The answer is that the Kingdom of God and of the Son Jesus Christ came in a limited but very important way on the day of Pentecost, 50 days after the resurrection of Jesus. This fulfillment is found in Acts chapter two. Many prophecies, both in the Old Testament and in the New Testament, point to the coming of the Kingdom in a new and unique way on the day of Pentecost. For example, one could look at Isaiah 2:2-4, Daniel 2:44,45, Matthew 3:2, Luke 24:45-47, Matthew 16:18-20 and Matthew 16:28 which point to the pouring out of the Spirit, the first public gospel sermon and the first conversions to Christ, all of which occurred on the day of Pentecost, as recorded in Acts chapter two.

Jesus did not come visibly or physically on the day of Pentecost, but God certainly did come in the person of the Holy Spirit on that day. There are many passages which express the thought that Jesus comes to us when we receive the gift of the indwelling Holy Spirit; 1 Corinthians 15:24, John 14:15-21 and John 16:7-15 come to mind.

QUESTION:

God tells us to be merciful and loving toward our enemies (Exodus 23:4-5, Matthew 5:43-48, Luke 6:27-35). At the same time, God will send his enemies to hell for eternity (Luke 9:43-48, Luke 16:19-26, Jude 7, Revelation 20:14-15). As an analogous paradox, in the Old Testament, we are taught justice in an eye for an eye and a tooth for a tooth (Exodus 21:24), but in the New Testament, we are taught a higher more merciful standard (Matthew 5:38-42). Why in the next age will we see the same God who taught the above things inflicting infinite punishment on those who have committed finite sins? I have no problem with the idea of punishment in this age or the next, but infinite torment in the age to come in light of both the Old and New Testament ethic seems impossible to accept. How do you resolve this apparent contradiction?

ANSWER:

You ask what, in my opinion, is perhaps the hardest question one can possibly ask about Christianity. The only rival to this difficult issue, in my opinion, is the problem of pain and suffering.

First, let me deal with one small aspect of your question—the fairly easy part. I believe God always wanted and even commanded people to treat one another according to the Golden Rule. When he said *"an eye for an eye..."* he was only conceding to a lower standard for the Jews in the Old Testament because of the barbarity of the age and the stubbornness of the hearts of the Jews. He was giving a civil law to apply to all of Israel. This is similar to his allowing divorce, under certain situations, in the Old Testament, because of the hardness of their hearts (as Jesus says in Matthew 18), whereas it is clear from the New Testament that God always had in mind one man, one woman, for life. So, God always wanted us to love our neighbor, to turn the other cheek and so forth, as in Matthew 5. In Leviticus 19:18, God commands his people, *"but love your neighbor as yourself. I am the Lord."*

Let me make another point which is relevant to your question. God commands his people to love their enemies, but not to judge them. In general, God calls his people to become holy and to be like him. Here is one exception to the rule that we are to be like God. We are to be loving like God, but we are not to be a judge like him. God reserves the role of judge wholly to himself as long as we are in our physical bodies.

That brings me to your much more difficult question. How could a supposedly loving God punish anyone he created in eternal torment forever? Discipline is about love, but his is not discipline.

Supposed Inconsistencies in the Bible

This is punishment. And how is it that we will be able to enjoy ourselves in heaven, knowing that these people, some of whom presumably were our closest loved ones during this lifetime, are in that awful place?

I will be completely forthright with you: I do not have an answer which will be completely satisfying to us human beings. The Bible clearly presents God, both in the OT and the NT, as a God of love and compassion (Jonah 4:2: *"I knew that you are a gracious and compassionate God, slow to anger and abounding in love, a God who relents from sending calamity."*) and as a God of justice and vengeance for sin (Romans 12:19: *"Do not take revenge, my friends, but leave room for God's wrath, for it is written: 'It is mine to avenge; I will repay,' says the Lord."*). These two aspects of the nature of God clearly come to a head in the face of a created being such as us who are loved by God and yet who willfully sin.

For some of God's created people, the problem is solved. Jesus did the suffering and dying for our sins already, so that the Father's justice/anger/judgment do not need to fall on us. He paid the price and accepted the penalty. God's wrath fell on Jesus. Those who are saved by the blood of Jesus only have to deal with God's love. For the other folks, because of their sin, they only get to deal with God's justice and anger in the end. After Judgment Day, only God's wrath will apply to them. It is not that God does not love them, but it is that his justice requires punishment. This is a hard teaching. It is hard to accept. Personally, I do not particularly like this biblical teaching. However, it is also the truth. I cannot completely explain God to you. In the final analysis, I believe that God is God, and as it says in Romans 9:20, *"But who are you, O man, to talk back to God? Shall what is formed say to him who formed it, 'Why did you make me like this?'"*

Like you, it is hard for me to see how I will be able to sit there in heaven and be happy all the time in view of those who do not make it there. I accept on faith, based on what my God and Lord has said in the Bible, that heaven will be a place with *"no tears"* (Revelation 21). How can I blithely believe this? I believe it because God has proven his love in Jesus and because God has proven his Word to be inspired through so many types of evidence. I am left with no choice but to accept the Bible as the inspired Word of God.

I wish I could give you a simple "aha!" answer, but I do not know one and cannot in good conscience pretend that I do. In love, fear and respect, I accept God for who he says he is. I do believe that the message of both the Old Testament and the New Testament is consistent. God is a God of love to those who fear and honor him, but to those who reject him and refuse to do his will, he will appear as a God of judgment. God does not choose to send people to hell, but, unfortunately, many of us, when given the choice between a relationship with God and separation for eternity, choose hell. God accepts this choice.

Chapter Four

The Resurrection of Jesus

QUESTION:
I am doing a brief study on the foundation of Christianity for our Bible study group. Am I correct that, in accordance with Jewish burial customs, Jesus' body would have been wrapped in a manner similar to that of an Egyptian mummy? If so, would that be further evidence against the swoon theory? It seems that it would have been rather difficult to unwrap oneself given that your arms were folded across your chest and then your upper body wrapped. Matthew 27:59, Mark 15:46 and Luke 23:53 describe Jesus' body being wrapped "in linen cloth," not "in a linen cloth." John 19:40 is more specific, describing strips of linen cloth (not a single sheet, as is the Shroud of Turin), "in accordance with Jewish burial customs."

ANSWER:
It is not accurate to say that Jesus' body would have been wrapped as Egyptian mummies, especially if you mean by this the familiar burial customs in Egypt of the second millennium BC. I am sure you know that the aristocracy in ancient Egypt were elaborately embalmed and wrapped in several layers of material. This would have been a considerable impediment to a resurrected person! However, Jesus' body certainly was not treated in this way. To judge by the biblical accounts, his body was wrapped in strips of cloth along with aromatic herbs. This was normal in the Near East at that time.

If in fact Jesus had been embalmed and tightly wrapped up as were the mummies of ancient Egypt, it certainly would provide a significant additional argument against the swoon theory. However, what we know of burial customs at the time of Christ argues against this being what was done to the body of Jesus. It is worth noting that, by the Roman period, even wealthy Egyptians were no longer using such elaborate methods for preparing their dead bodies, never mind a relatively poor Jew.

Getting to your question, there is evidence beyond a reasonable doubt against the swoon theory [for the reader, this is the theory that Jesus did not die on the cross, or even when he was pierced by a lance in the heart, but that he later revived and escaped from the tomb], but mentioning the difficulty of a supposedly revived Jesus escaping from the cloth strips which were wrapped around his body does not add a lot to the argument. The idea that Jesus somehow survived crucifixion, followed by being stabbed in the heart by the Roman soldier, is ludicrous. However, if we could grant this possibility, it is not unreasonable to think that this miraculously revived Jesus might have been able to escape from the strips of linen which had been wrapped around his body. Of course, if he did, he would have had to roll a massive stone out of the way and personally defeat a cohort of heavily armed Roman soldiers. I am not saying your argument is without merit. I believe that, even if Jesus had miraculously revived, it would have been tough to escape the linen wrapping. I just would not make a big deal about this aspect. The difficulty of surviving scourging to near the point of death, crucifixion, stabbing in the heart, lack of food and water for two days and having to move the stone and fight his way through the guard—all of these arguments are stronger than the difficulty of getting out of the strips of cloth, in my opinion.

You ask a thoughtful question. I respect those who, when thinking of a potentially useful argument, take the time and mental energy to ask whether that argument will truly hold up to scrutiny. It seems that is exactly what you are doing. By the way, I notice your meticulous study in finding the description of the strips (plural) of cloth versus strip (singular) in John. In the interest of being careful, I would add that, just because John describes strips of cloth, it does not preclude the use of a burial shroud in addition, underneath the strips of cloth. For your information, the Shroud of Turin was tested by the Carbon-14 dating technique and found to be linen from the thirteenth century, so it seems to be ruled out as the burial shroud of Jesus, at least according to scientific evidence.

QUESTION:

I am writing to ask if you have any explanation for one apparent discrepancy that I have often wondered about: "three days and three nights." I have read that the "days" part of that statement was due to the Jewish tradition of counting any part of a day as a whole day in the description of passing time. However, I can't see how the "three nights" can be explained. Was it a later editorial insertion, or is there some other explanation?

ANSWER:

About the three days and nights, you are accurate in describing it as an "apparent" discrepancy. It is only apparent because resolving the discrepancy is a matter of recognizing the use of a common idiom of the Jews at that time. According to scholars, the Jews used the expression *"a night and a day"* to refer to any part of a 24-hour period. This may seem odd to us, but we should remind ourselves that there are many idioms in any language or culture which seem very strange to an outsider. For example, we say that the sun rises and sets when everyone knows (hopefully) that the sun is not moving: the Earth is spinning!

The Jews counted their days from sunset to sunset. Jesus died on Friday well before sunset (Luke 23:44-46). It is tough for those of us who are used to a new day starting at midnight, but believe it or not, by Jewish reckoning, the third day had already started any time after sunset on Saturday evening. Sometime very early the following morning (Sunday), Jesus rose from the dead. Even though, by our accounting, he was only in the tomb for parts of three days and all of two nights, it was customary usage for Jews to call any part of a 24-hour day "a day and a night." Thus, the biblical writers say correctly that Jesus was in the tomb "three days and three nights."

An analogous example of this interesting Jewish way of describing time is found in how they counted the number of years their kings reigned. If a king of Judah ruled for 400 days, and if those days happened to fall in three different years (their years started with the first of Nisan, near the time of Passover), then the Jewish historians would say the king ruled for three years. We might say he ruled for one year and one month, but that is not how the Jews counted the reigns of their kings. Historians must take this method of reckoning time into account when they try to use biblical writings to calculate the number of years between the reigns of David and Hezekiah. If they simply add up the number of years each king is recorded as having reigned in the books of Kings, they will significantly overestimate the total time.

In summary, the apparent discrepancy between the biblical accounts of the length of time between the death and resurrection of Jesus, and the statement in the Bible that Jesus was in the grave for three days and three nights, is in fact not a discrepancy at all. Any confusion is created by our lack of knowledge of Jewish idiom at that time.

QUESTION:

I am currently studying the resurrection of Jesus in an apologetic manner and have started looking into the Greek texts. Matthew 27:65 mentions the guard requested by the Jews, but I noticed that the word translated as "you have" appears to be "I have" (echo as opposed to the ete ending denoting you plural). Unfortunately, I have no biblical Greek teacher I can check this with and am learning only from books and CDs. Surely, this word would indicate definitively a Roman guard as opposed to a Jewish temple guard. Any help would be greatly appreciated. [Author's note: the NIV has *"Take a guard,"* Pilate answered. *"Go, make the tomb as secure as you know how."*]

ANSWER:

I am looking at a Greek interlinear word-for-word translation of the Greek. It does not confirm your contention. A word-for-word translation of the Greek text, in the original word order, says, *"Said to them Pilate you have a guard go make fast as you know and they going made fast the grave sealing the stone with the guard"* (using the *Zondervan Parallel New Testament in Greek and English*). I am not an expert in Greek. I am not even an amateur in Greek, so you should consider confirming this with an expert. The Greek word in question is *exete*, which is *"you have."* The NIV translates it as *"take."* The verb can mean to have, to need, to take, to hold, etc. I believe (and please do not trust my Greek grammar!) that the sentence is in the imperative, which is why the NIV uses the word *"take."* It is hard to use the imperative in English using the word *"have."*

If I am correct, Matthew 27:65 is inconclusive on whether the guard was Roman or Jewish. The traditional interpretation of this passage is that the guard was a Roman one. It may be possible that the Jews would have had the equivalent of local police, but the guard is specifically described as *"soldiers"* (Matthew 28:12). The only soldiers in the city of Jerusalem were Romans. The Jews were not allowed to have an army or a traditional armed force at all. Therefore, the most reasonable interpretation, which is the traditional one, is that the guard referred to is a Roman one. My advice is to continue to believe and teach that this was a Roman guard, but to not use the Greek in Matthew 27:65 to prove this.

QUESTION:

I have heard of a conspiracy theory which uses the argument that Jesus' body was taken by the Romans, and then some sort of stunt was pulled using someone who looked like Jesus to make the 500 eyewitnesses mentioned by Paul in 1 Corinthians 15 believe he had risen from the dead. The argument then says that church membership was increased by bribery (from the Romans). This plot was encouraged by the Romans bribing or frightening some of the apostles into supporting the plot. Probably some of the apostles would not have gotten involved for moral reasons. According to this conspiracy theory, the book of Acts is a cover-up by those who wanted to create the false impression that all the apostles supported the lie about the resurrection. How would you argue against this?

ANSWER:

This "conspiracy theory" is so outrageous and illogical that I think its mere existence reveals how difficult it is and how desperate some people must be to present any reasonable argument against the resurrection.

First, the idea that any of the twelve apostles could actually be fooled by an imposter that he was indeed the dearest friend with whom they had spent the past three years is beyond the possibility of being believed. One thing we know for sure is that Thomas was very skeptical. He demanded that he be shown the actual wounds in Jesus' body (John 20:25: *"Unless I see the nail marks in his hands and put my finger where the nails were, and put my hand into his side, I will not believe it."*). The Jesus look-alike in this conspiracy theory needed to mutilate himself in all the right places. Not only that, but he had to be able to fool Jesus' mother, brother and sisters, dozens of other very close friends and over 500 other eyewitnesses, nearly all of whom knew him well. In addition, he had to be a very good imposter, because this fake Jesus had to work a miracle with the fish in the nets, as recorded in John 21:1-14. Has there ever been such a case in human history?

Second, this conspiracy theory argues against itself by claiming that some of the apostles were bribed into accepting the theory, when the theory itself implies that the 500 witnesses were fooled into believing this imposter was actually Jesus.

The next claim of the theory you describe takes incredulity to an even higher level. This is the idea that that the Romans bribed and threatened the apostles into falsely claiming that Jesus raised from the dead. Why would the Romans bribe anyone to support Christianity? There is not a single conceivable reason for this to happen. The idea that some of the apostles actually supported this conspiracy and fought battles with those who refused to support the lie is disproved by the fact that most of the apostles were martyred for a faith that this "theory" claims all of them were well aware was a complete lie.

This "theory" is so far-fetched that I am tempted to wonder if it might have been proposed, not as a serious theory, but as a satire on some of the other somewhat less outrageous theories about the resurrection (such as the stolen body or the swoon theory). A vastly more reasonable explanation of the over 500 eyewitnesses to the resurrection is that Jesus was, in fact, resurrected from the dead. For more on the resurrection, see **RFB** ch. 3.

QUESTION:

No one other than Christians believe that Jesus rose from the dead. A few mention he was crucified, and some even admit the first Christians believe he rose from the dead. However, no one other than the Christians in the early centuries AD said that he was crucified and that he rose from the dead. There are no writings, other than by Christians, which say he rose from the dead. This is why I have doubts. I don't doubt that Jesus existed, but I cannot believe that he truly rose from the dead. In addition, with the prophecies of the Messiah which he fulfilled, how do I know that the early followers didn't make up these things so that we would believe Jesus fulfilled these prophecies?

ANSWER:

I definitely agree that it is hard to find people who believe in the resurrection who are not Christians. In fact, I have not yet met a single person who believed that Jesus was raised from the dead who does not also accept that he is the Son of God. Naturally, you will not find people in the historical record who believed in the resurrection and who were not Christians. That would be like finding people who believe in gravity who nevertheless jump off of cliffs. Such people will always be hard to find. Apparently, it troubles you that non-Christians do not believe in the resurrection of Jesus. It is not logical to let the fact that non-believers do not accept the resurrection lead one to doubt the truth of the resurrection. Of course, non-Christians do not believe in the resurrection. Acceptance of the resurrection of

Jesus as fact is tantamount to accepting the claims of Jesus and to belief in him.

By the way, more than one non-Christian author in the first and second century does mention the crucifixion of Jesus. Josephus, Tacitus and the writers of the Jewish Talmud all report the crucifixion of Jesus in their histories, and none of these were believers.

Your next point is that, perhaps, the writers of the New Testament made up things to make it appear as if Jesus Christ fulfilled the prophecies of the Old Testament. That is an insupportable claim for a number of reasons. I suggest you read **RFB** ch. 4 for more material on the messianic prophecies. In short:

1. Many of the prophecies were fulfilled by Jesus and are a matter of historical record. Psalms 22:16 predicts that the Messiah will be crucified. This is verified by the historical record. Daniel 9:20-25 predicts that the Messiah will come to Jerusalem to *"atone for wickedness"* in around AD 33, which is also matter of historical record. Isaiah 9 predicts that the Messiah will be from Galilee, a matter of historical record. Also, Micah 5:2 predicts that the Messiah will be born in Bethlehem. This one is a bit harder to prove from documents external to the Bible, but it is not likely that Mary would have lied about where her son was born.

2. If one claims that the Gospel writers were fakers and liars, this is inconsistent with the fact that not a single one of them ever denied the faith or admitted that they had falsified any of their claims. In fact, many, if not most, of the apostles were killed for their faith. In view of this fact, the idea that they would have made up facts to support a belief which they knew was a lie and which resulted in their own death is logically insupportable.

3. If the apostles were trying to put over a lie on people, then they would have provided as little detail as possible in their writings about the circumstances surrounding the fulfillment of prophecy, in order to create plausible deniability. Instead, the Gospel writers included dozens of facts which were readily verifiable of falsifiable in their accounts (sold for 30 pieces of silver, hundreds of eyewitnesses, betrayal money used to buy the potter's field, the seal on the tomb, the sword thrust in the side and so forth). The fact is that history provides us no record of contemporary people—even the Jews who were enemies of Jesus—who denied the essential facts of Jesus' life, death or resurrection as recorded in the four Gospels. None provided any evidence to deny that he worked miracles, that he lived a sinless

life, that he was crucified and that hundreds saw him alive after he was killed.

In view of these points, those who say that the writers of the New Testament made up facts to support the claim he fulfilled the prophecies need to present some facts to support their claim. By the way, we at ARS sponsored a debate in Houston, Texas, in June, 2009 between Dr. Douglas Jacoby and Dr. Robert Price titled *Jesus: Man, Myth or Messiah?* You may want to get a copy of the debate. It is available at www.ipibooks.com.

QUESTION:
I was just wondering: I believe Jesus died by crucifixion. I also believe in the resurrection. However, what is the point of the resurrection? Was it just an example of God's power? Other people have been raised from the dead. What really makes Christ's resurrection so special?

ANSWER:
There are many things which make the resurrection of Jesus from the dead very special indeed. In fact, I believe that the resurrection of Jesus is the central miracle of the Bible. After the death of Jesus for our sins, it is the second most important fact in human history. Let me give a few reasons that the resurrection is absolutely key to the entire plan of God from the beginning.

First, consider Colossians 1:18, which includes the statement concerning Jesus that he is *"the firstborn from among the dead."* It is true that the widow's son was raised by Elijah (1 Kings 17), that Peter raised Tabitha from the dead (Acts 9) and that Jesus raised Lazarus (John 11) and others from the dead. However, all of these people died in the usual way at a later time. They were raised with a perishable body. Jesus was raised in an imperishable body. He is the firstborn among many of us who will rise at the time of the end in imperishable bodies (1 Corinthians 15:50-57: *"the perishable must clothe itself with the imperishable"*). Jesus' resurrection points us toward a future everlasting life with God. His resurrection provides proof that there will be a Judgment Day. This is stated explicitly in Acts 17:31, where Paul said concerning Judgment Day that *"he has given proof of this to all men by raising him from the dead."*

The resurrection of Jesus from the dead gives all followers of Jesus hope. It gives us hope of an eternal life in heaven with God. We are reminded of this in 1 Peter 1:3: *"In his great mercy he has given us new birth into a living hope through the resurrection of Jesus Christ from the dead."* This passage of scripture points us toward another importance of the resurrection of Jesus Christ. If Jesus had simply died on the cross, that would not have been enough. The resurrection of Jesus is part of the process by which we are saved. Consider 1 Peter 3:21,22, which says, concerning baptism in water, *"It saves you by the resurrection of Jesus Christ, who has gone into heaven and is at God's right hand—with angels, authorities and powers in submission to him."* Here we see that the resurrection of Jesus is part of that which "saves" us. Romans 6:1-14 brings out this doctrine more fully. For example, in Romans 6:5 it says, *"If we have been united with him in his death, we will certainly also be united with him in his resurrection."* Also, one finds this statement in Romans 6:8: *"Now if we died with Christ, we believe that we will also live with him. For we know that since Christ was raised from the dead, he cannot die again; death no longer has mastery over him. The death he died, he died to sin once for all; but the life he lives, he lives to God."* Again, we see that the resurrection of Jesus provides for us an opportunity to be raised with Christ to live a new life. Jesus is truly the firstborn from among the dead—*"Death no longer has mastery over him."*

There are a number of other reasons the resurrection of Jesus is central to the gospel message and to the entire Bible. Let me mention just one more. The resurrection of Jesus fulfills prophecies spoken by Jesus himself as well as prophecies in the Old Testament. Jesus prophesied his resurrection a number of times. When the Pharisees demanded a miraculous sign, Jesus replied that the only sign he would give them was the sign of Jonah (Matthew 12:39-42): *"For as Jonah was three days and three nights in the belly of a huge fish, so the Son of Man will be three days and three nights in the heart of the earth."* With hindsight, this is clearly a prophecy of his death and his resurrection on the third day. Matthew 16:21 and John 2:19 (*"Destroy this temple and I will raise it again in three days"*) are two more among many prophecies of Jesus that he would be raised from the dead. When Jesus came through on this promise and was raised on the third day, this validated all of his claims about himself. For anyone else to claim to be God would be lunacy. Jesus made this claim. He also claimed to be the resurrection and the life (John 11:25). Jesus backed up these astounding claims when he was raised to life. In addition, the resurrection of the Messiah from the dead was prophesied in the Old Testament. The incident with Jonah and the great fish serves as a type, to which the resurrection of Jesus is the antitype. Psalms 16:8-11 is another Old Testament prophecy of the resurrection of the Messiah, as is Genesis 22:1-14 (see also Hebrews 11:17-19).

To summarize, the resurrection of Jesus from the dead on the third day is the central miracle in the Bible and in God's entire dispensation for mankind. It serves as proof that we, too, will rise to face judgment. The resurrection of Jesus is essential to our being raised to a new life after participating in the death of Jesus in baptism. The resurrection provides proof that the Bible is inspired by God, and it provides us with proof that Jesus had every right to say the amazing things he said about both us and himself.

Chapter Five

Biblical Prophecy

QUESTION:

I have done some studying of Psalm 22 with its supposed prophecy of the Messiah having his hands and feet pierced. My studies tell me that the word "pierced" in Psalm 22:16 can instead be translated as "lion." Doesn't this prove this is not a messianic prophecy? Why do believers place such reliance on this one word in the text to prove Christianity? [Questioner mentions a website: www.christian-thinktank.com/ps22cheat.html]

ANSWER:

No one I know places a huge amount of weight on this one passage. I certainly do not. I would say that it represents about 0.1% of my evidence that Jesus is the Messiah (just kidding on the number, of course). In fact, this passage is far more important to the skeptic than to the believer, as a single passage like this disproves the skeptic's conclusion that the Bible cannot be inspired by God, while dozens support the believer's position. Psalm 22 prophecies the crucifixion of the Messiah, and it also prophecies that his bones would not be broken. In addition, it predicts that those who crucified him would both divide and gamble over his garments. No wonder the skeptic is intimidated by this passage! It appears to be irrefutable evidence for biblical inspiration. He or she absolutely must disprove this one, which partially explains the long and convoluted argument by your ally on Psalm 22!

There is a great weight of evidence for biblical inspiration provided by messianic prophecy. First, there were a number of clear messianic prophecies in the Old Testament. The testimony of Jewish interpreters of the Old Testament who identified messianic prophecies before the time of Jesus confirms this. Second, there is the fact that Jesus fulfilled such a wide variety of prophecies. Some of the prophecy fulfillment involved acts over which he had some control (entering Jerusalem on a donkey, being silent when accused and so forth). Other prophecies involved things over which he did not have control (assuming he is not God, of course). These include being born in Bethlehem, being sold for 30 pieces of silver, being pierced after his death and so forth. The evidence for divine oversight of both the writing of these prophecies and their fulfillment is absolutely overwhelming. To be honest, I believe the only way to miss the obvious implications of the messianic prophecies is to either choose not to read the Bible or to willfully ignore the obvious.

By the way, this argument that the skeptic has more at stake than the believer in biblical prophecy also explains the non-believer's vehement attacks on the authorship of Daniel. If the historical Daniel was the author of the book we know of as Daniel, then the Bible is inspired by God (or to be more careful, certainly the book of Daniel is inspired). End of story! The believer does not particularly need the prophecies in Daniel, but the non-believer absolutely must prove bogus authorship or unbelief becomes untenable. This is why relatively few believers pour a lot of energy into defending Daniel (it is a small piece of evidence in an ocean at their disposal), while so many skeptics make a big deal about it.

Getting to the author's argument at the website you refer to, it is true that there is a Hebrew word which can, in some contexts, be translated as "lion," and in other contexts as "pierced." A rule of interpretation (hermeneutics) is that when there are two possible interpretations of a single word, the context will usually determine the correct interpretation. Let me give the two readings: *"They have pierced my hands and my feet"* or *"they have lion my hands and my feet."* Even if we completely discount what I consider to be an obvious messianic prophecy in Psalm 22, it is not at all surprising that all Bible translators use pierced, not lion, in Psalm 22:16. The sentence requires a verb, not another noun. It is helpful in this connection to note that, when the Jews themselves translated Psalm 22:16 into the Greek in about 200 BC, in what is known as the Septuagint translation, they used the Greek for pierced, not lion, even though the Jews did not necessarily see this as a messianic prophecy.

To summarize, the author you quote from is obviously a non-believer. He is not attempting to discover the best translation of Psalm 22:16. It is quite clear that he is trying to find a way to escape the obvious implications of this passage. No scholar would agree with him, unless he, too, was strongly biased against the inspiration of the Bible.

QUESTION:

I see you used Psalm 16:10-11 as a messianic prophecy in your book, *From Shadow to Reality*. How do you know this passage is about the Messiah, since David is obviously talking about himself? What hermeneutical principle authorizes you to inject additional significance?

ANSWER:

First, here is the passage in question:

> *"... because you will not abandon me to the grave,*
> *nor will you let your Holy One see decay.*
> *You have made known to me the path of life;*
> *You will fill me with joy in your presence,*
> *with eternal pleasures at your right hand."*

I see messianic implications in this passage for at least four reasons. First, there are several examples in David's writing which are obvious prophecies of Jesus (Psalm 22:15-18, Psalm 110:4 and Psalm 118:22 are examples). The existence of several clear examples that the writings of David are often messianic justifies one to consider his words in general as possibly being messianic. Second, David's body certainly did decay and he was *"abandoned to the grave."* Jesus' body did not decay, nor was it abandoned to the grave. David could not be talking about himself in this case, unless he is simply mistaken. Third (although the translation is debatable), the passage calls the person referred to "your Holy One," which makes it unlikely (but not impossible) that David is talking about himself. Besides, the author of this poem refers to a person at God's right hand. It is difficult to see David taking such liberty as to assign himself this position. The wording implies David is talking about someone far greater than he. Fourth, the inspired writer of Acts quotes the inspired preacher Peter as telling his audience that this passage is about Jesus. I understand that my fourth reason will seem like circular reasoning to a skeptic like yourself, but for a person who is already convinced that the Bible is inspired by God, it is a perfectly good reason to accept that it is about the Messiah.

QUESTION:

My question is on your interpretation of the two olive trees [Author's note: questioner is referring to Zechariah chapter 4] on page 102 of your book, *From Shadow to Reality*. You said, "The two who are anointed are a reference to the high priest Joshua and the governor Zerubbabel, both of whom were foreshadows of the anointed one: the Messiah." I was wondering why you believe them to be the two anointed men. I have read from other scholars that the olive trees symbolize the two witnesses of Revelation 11:3-11. I have also read that the two witnesses were Enoch and Elijah (Malachi 4:5-6). Also, some claim that Malachi is predicting the Christ, but I get confused at Malachi 4:5: "Behold, I will send you Elijah the prophet before the coming of the great and dreadful day of the Lord" (KJV). This bothers me because John the Baptist claimed he wasn't Elijah (John 1:21). Besides, Elijah and Enoch didn't die, so wouldn't they have to come back to die physically? If they didn't die physically, then they would be the "first-fruits" of the resurrection instead of Christ (1 Corinthians 15:20-23). How do you see these points?

ANSWER:

First of all, it does not make sense for the olive tree to symbolize the two witnesses of Revelation 11:3-11. In this case, you would have a symbol being a symbol of a symbol, which is not logical. The two witnesses in Revelation 11:3-11 are clearly part of apocalyptic writing and are certainly symbols. Now, it is conceivable that the two witnesses of Revelation 11:3-11 could be a symbol of the same thing which is symbolized by the olive tree, or by the two witnesses in Zechariah chapter four. To decide this one, we will have to look carefully at the text. Let me consider Revelation 11:3-11 first. I will confess that I am not an expert on the book of Revelation. For a more thorough and scholarly treatment of this book, I suggest my two favorites, which are Jim McGuiggan, *Revelation* (Lubbock: International Bible Resources, 1976), and Gordon Ferguson, *Mine Eyes Have Seen the Glory* (Billerica Mass: DPIBooks, 1996).

I believe the scene in Revelation chapter 11 is highly symbolic. It does not represent any actual physical war on the Earth. If the olive trees and the lampstands in Revelation are symbols, then it does not make sense that the trees and the lamp-stand in Zechariah are symbols of the ones in Revelation eleven. The symbolism in Revelation eleven is about the attacks of Rome on the young Christian church. The two witnesses, like the two olive trees in this vision, represent the fact that God is guarding his *"temple"*—that he will protect his people. I understand many commentators take Revelation chapter 11 literally, but I believe that this is not justified by the context or by the tenor of the entire book of Revelation.

Let me move, then, to Zechariah chapter four. I will admit that there is certainly some parallel in the details of the two passages. Both have two olive trees. Both have a lampstand, (although there is just one in the Zechariah passage, not two). Both have the olive trees and the lamp-stand representing the power of God. In the case of Zechariah 4, the vision gives a clear interpretation. To quote: *"He answered me, 'Do you not know what these are?' 'No, my Lord,' I replied. So he said to me, 'This is the word of the Lord to Zerubbabel: Not by might nor by power, but by my Holy Spirit, says the Lord Almighty.'"* The olive tree and the oil from the olive tree which is burned in the lampstand are defined by the Bible writer as symbolic of the Holy Spirit in Zechariah chapter four. I think it is questionable to say that the two olive trees and the two lampstands in Revelation chapter eleven represent the Holy Spirit. Maybe they do. One thing I can say for sure is that the olive trees in Zechariah chapter four do not symbolize the two witnesses in Revelation chapter eleven. That definitely does not make sense.

Your next question is whether the two witnesses (in Revelation chapter eleven?) could be Enoch and Elijah, based on Malachi 4:5-6. First of all, Malachi 4:5-6 does not mention Enoch at all. Second of all, Malachi does not identify Elijah as a witness in Malachi 4:5-6. It is a common thing for certain Bible teachers to try to spin together prophetic scenarios about the last days by cruising the Bible for little snippets from passages which they can rip out of their context to try to support their modern-day interpretation of last-day events. It is my experience that such efforts are, almost without exception, very bad hermeneutics (the science of correct interpretation). It is very common for people to fixate on prophecies of the last days. We will do well to fixate on Jesus and on becoming like him, and leave speculations about the last days to those with plenty of idle time on their hands. Bottom line, Revelation is principally about the attack of the Roman persecutors on the early Christian church. Little, if any, of the first 19 chapters of Revelation have anything to do with events at the very end of the world. I refer you to the books mentioned above for a thorough treatment of this claim.

By the way, Malachi is prophesying the coming of John the Baptist. Malachi 4:5 is a prediction of the coming of John the Baptist *"in the spirit and power of Elijah"* as a sign or witness of the coming of the Messiah (see Luke 1:17). That much is certainly true. I will admit that the reference of *"the coming of the great and dreadful day of the Lord"* is confusing here. In what sense did John the Baptist's coming precede a dreadful day of the Lord? I believe *"the great and dreadful day of the Lord"* here is a reference to the destruction of Jerusalem in AD 70. The coming of Jesus, and the rejection of him by the Jews in about AD 30, led fairly soon thereafter to a great judgment and destruction of Jerusalem in AD 70 by the Romans.

I will have to say that the fact that John appears to reject being labeled as Elijah makes this whole thing more confusing, at least at first glance. I am not sure of the correct understanding of John 1:21. One possibility is that John the Baptist was simply mistaken. Perhaps he did not completely understand his role in fulfilling Malachi 4:5. Another possibility is that John the Baptist is correct in saying *"I am not Elijah."* Clearly he was not Elijah, but he was one born in the spirit and power of Elijah, as predicted in Malachi 4:5 and as confirmed by Luke 1:17. Was John the Baptist confused, or was he being cautious and somewhat evasive in his response? I am not sure and will leave that one to you.

Elijah and Enoch are not the first-fruits of the resurrection, since they did not die. The first-fruit of the resurrection is Jesus. He is the first one to die physically, after which to be resurrected for eternity. Others were resurrected, but died later (John 11 and Lazarus for example). Others never died (Enoch and Elijah, for example), but Jesus is the first to die and later to be resurrected for eternal life. Therefore, he is the first-fruit from the dead (Colossians 1:18, 1 Corinthians 15:20-23). I will admit that this can be a bit confusing, but I believe that it is the correct resolution of the matter.

To conclude, there are obvious parallels in the details in Zechariah chapter four and in Revelation chapter eleven, but this does not mean that they are about the same thing. Either way, there is no reasonable connection between Elijah, Enoch and the two witnesses in Revelation chapter eleven. This would be to take things wildly out of context. Almost certainly, you have heard a pre-millennialist, sincere as he or she may be, misuse the scripture. Yes, John the Baptist is the Elijah who was to come of Malachi 4:5, and no, his is not the first-fruits from the dead since, as you point out, he did not die.

Biblical Prophecy

QUESTION:
Was Revelation written before or after AD 70? I have heard most scholars say it was after AD 70. How does this relate to whether most of this book has already been fulfilled?

ANSWER:
The book of Revelation does not come with a date, so scholars have to make a reasonable assumption about the time of writing of the book from the context of the material in it. If you want to find out some scholar's ideas about the date the book was written, you can buy or borrow from a library a good commentary on the book. [See the previous question for book recommendations.] Any good commentary will mention the range of scholar's opinions as well as the reason for their opinions. Most conservative scholars (defined as ones who accept that the Bible is inspired by God) date the book sometime after AD 75 and before AD 100. It is my opinion that the book was written during the latter part of the reign of Domitian (AD 81-96). I believe this because the book includes prophecies about Domitian in Revelation chapter 17. In this chapter, Domitian is the king who yet will come (17:8) to persecute the church. This eighth emperor in Revelation 17 is the eleventh emperor of Rome in Daniel chapter seven.

The prophecy about Domitian in chapter seventeen is not the only evidence for the date of the book of Revelation. In chapter one, we find that the apostle John is a prisoner on the island of Patmos. It is hard to say exactly when John was imprisoned, but this does give us one hint. The Christian historian Eusebius puts the persecution of the church by Domitian and the exile of John to Patmos in about AD 95-96. Also, we can see from chapters two and three what the issues in the churches in Asia were at the time, which can help.

As far as the issue of the prophecies in the book, there certainly are a wide variety of opinions about that. Let me share my belief, but encourage you to do your own research. I believe that virtually all the apocalyptic/prophetic writing in the book concerns things which happened during the time the book was written or shortly thereafter. The book is about the persecution of the Christian Church by the Roman Empire and about God's judgment on those who attacked the church. Specifically, the angel told John that the vision was about things which were soon to take place (Revelation 1:1) and that the time was near (Revelation 1:3). It seems easy to interpret the meaning of these passages to me! Besides, all the prophecies are easily understood as involving the Roman Empire. It is a huge stretch to apply most of the book to future end- times as so many modern Bible teachers do.

I believe that there is an exception to the rule that almost all the book of Revelation concerns things which happened during the Roman Empire. From Revelation 20:7 to the end of the book, the text seems to me to shift to the end-times. A key question concerns the thousand years of Revelation 20:1-6. It is my belief that this is a description of the time stretching from the persecutions under Rome to the end of days; the thousand years being an apocalyptic and symbolic representation of a long but indeterminate period of time.

You should not take my word for it, but should read the book for yourself. Besides reading Revelation carefully, I suggest you get a good commentary and spend time doing some research into the history of the Roman Empire and the early church. Between these three sources, I believe you will reach a conclusion at least somewhat similar to my own, but I leave it up to you. Sorry to give you such a big assignment, but I am assuming you do not just want my opinion.

QUESTION:

I understand that Psalm 2:7 is talking about Jesus, but what do the words "Today I have begotten you" mean? Is he referring to physical birth? If not, what is it talking about?

ANSWER:

I believe the most obvious place to look for an answer is in John 1:14: *"We have seen his glory, the glory of the one and only (also translated the only begotten) son."* The son of God was not "begotten" by God in the sense of being created, as God cannot create himself. Jesus Christ, being deity, was not created. As it says in John 1:1, *"he was with God in the beginning."* John 1:14 answers your question in very plain terms: *"The Word became flesh and lived for a while among us."* When the Bible describes Jesus Christ as "begotten" (a word not appearing in more modern translations), it is referring to the incarnation. The word "incarnation" is a fancy theological word which refers to God the Son coming and living in a physical human body. I am convinced that Psalms 2:7 is a reference to, and prophecy of, the physical birth of Jesus, the Son of God.

QUESTIONS:

Are Micah 5:2 and Micah 5:4-7 both messianic passages? Micah 5:2 says that the Messiah will be born in Bethlehem. After that, it goes on to speak of the Assyrians invading Israel and that he (the Messiah) and seven others will save Israel (v.4-6). How does that work, since the Assyrian Empire was gone before Jesus was born?

Biblical Prophecy

Also:

Isaiah 11:1-10 speaks of the messianic era and the peace among people of different races and places. But then it goes on in verse 10 to speak of God freeing people from slavery (physical) to the Assyrian people (v.11-16) at that time. It doesn't seem to me that it applies to Jesus.

And:

Isaiah 9:1-6 is similar. Isaiah speaks of the present time and says that the son is born and will reign (it doesn't say that he will be born and will reign, or he is born and he reigns). Can you explain this apparent discrepancy?

ANSWER:

I have always assumed that the messianic portion of Micah 5 ends with verse 5a. The section beginning with *"When the Assyrian invades our land"* seems to me to clearly be a change of subject. The context seems to demand this, including such statements as "The remnant of Jacob will be in the midst of many peoples." This seems certainly to be talking about the captivity under Assyria, which began around 722 BC. Up until Micah 5:5a, the text seems to be messianic. For example, in 5:4, it says that *"He will stand and shepherd the flock"* and *"for then his greatness will reach to the ends of the earth."* Finally, the messianic section concludes with Micah 5:5a, *"And he will be their peace."*

I believe that Isaiah 11:12-16 is an apocalyptic description of the rapid rise and expansion of Christianity which occurred in the first and second century AD. It is a mistake to take apocalyptic language literally. What I learn from Isaiah 11:12-16 is that the Kingdom of God will unite people of very different social and religious and national/cultural backgrounds, and that it will spread rapidly with God's help.

I cannot blame you for thinking that this section is not literally fulfilled as a messianic prophecy, because a simple, non-symbolic reading seems to preclude this interpretation. However, let us look carefully. We know this is non-literal, apocalyptic material from the description in Isaiah 11:6-9: "The wolf will live with the lamb; the infant will play near the hole of the cobra." This passage is about the bringing together in God's kingdom of people who would not normally speak to each other, never mind being a loving family of believers. Isaiah 11 describes *"the Root of Jesse"* as *"a banner for the peoples: the nations will rally to him"* (Isaiah 11:10). It describes God reaching out *"a second time to reclaim the remnant that is left of his people."* The first time God recalled a remnant which had been scattered was when, through Cyrus and his successors, God gathered the Jews to reoccupy the Promised Land, beginning in 538 BC. The first re-gathering of a remnant of God's people involved a physical people, Israel, occupying a physical land, Canaan. The second gathering of God's people is a spiritual remnant gathered into a spiritual kingdom (Luke 17:20-21, Acts 1:3-8). The only way to understand Isaiah 11:12-16 is to see it as an apocalyptic, and therefore highly symbolic, description of how God will gather people from a life of sin (Assyria being symbolic of sinful nations, v. 16) into the Kingdom of God.

I am not sure what problem you have with the messianic passage in Isaiah 9:1-7. In this scripture, God, through Isaiah, is using what is sometimes called the prophetic present. This is a common literary device. In English we do something like this when we speak of past events in the present tense. For example, when we describe the works of Jesus, we often say, in this situation, Jesus is doing such and such—using the present tense for a situation which the reader is obviously to understand as referring to the past. The context of Isaiah 9:1-7 clearly tells the reader that the present tense being used is a reference to the future. We can be sure of this because, in Isaiah 9:1, it says that *"in the future, he will honor Galilee of the Gentiles, by the way of the sea, along the Jordan."* The passage then proceeds immediately to use the historical present to describe the things which will happen "in the future."

QUESTION:

Matthew 2:15 quotes Hosea 11:1, implying that it was about Jesus. But is that truly a messianic prophecy? It seems that Matthew is taking this out of context. If you go a little further down Hosea, it has the same person worshipping Baal. How would you respond to this?

ANSWER:

I will have to say that this one has bothered me a bit as well. To be honest, I will admit that if I simply read Hosea 11:1 for myself, without the suggestion of Matthew, I would not see it as a prophecy of the Messiah. Let us consider the verse and its context. First, it is a good idea to go back to Exodus 4:22-23. Here one reads, *"Then say to Pharaoh, 'This is what the Lord says: Israel is my firstborn son, and I told you "Let my son go, so he may worship me." But you refused to let him go; so I will kill your firstborn son.'"* In fact, Jacob (later called Israel) was the second son of Isaac, but God arranged it so that Jacob would receive the blessing of the first-born son when Esau sold

Biblical Prophecy

his birthright for a bowl of lentil stew (Genesis 25:27-34, Hebrews 12:16-17). God worked all this out as a historical foreshadow of the spiritual equivalent, which is his first-born son, Jesus Christ (Colossians 1:15: *"he is the firstborn over all creation"*).

In God's eyes, when he called his first-born son Israel out of Egypt, it was a symbolic foreshadow of his later calling his first-born son Jesus Christ out of Egypt. It is not just coincidence that God had Joseph take his wife and son Jesus into Egypt. This was part of God's plan all along, as evidenced by the foreshadowing in Exodus 4 and the prophecy of Hosea 11:1. All this helps me to understand how, when God tells us in Hosea 11:1 that he called Israel out of Egypt, he is referring to the fact that he called his first-born Israel out of Egypt as a type, that he would later also call his first-born son Jesus Christ out of Egypt as an antitype, and that he calls us today out of a life of slavery to sin in "Egypt" through the death of Jesus, the Passover lamb.

Unfortunately, Israel was unfaithful to God, as Hosea 11:2f relates. Clearly, this does not refer to Jesus, but to the nation of Israel. Despite God calling Israel out of Egypt, they became unfaithful in the desert, as is described in great detail in the book of Exodus.

In summary, I can certainly understand your confusion when the footnote to Matthew 2:15 refers to a passage which goes back to the historical Israel and not to Jesus. However, when one considers the biblical meaning of a first-born son, one can see that the Hosea passage is referring both back to Israel when it escaped Egypt and forward to Jesus and his escape into and later out of Egypt with his parents. Matthew is very perceptive to see the type/antitype symbolism in Exodus and in Jesus, and God amazes me once again with his inspired Word in Hosea 11:1 and Matthew 2:15.

QUESTION:

I was wondering what your take on Matthew 24:14 is. Until recently, I had thought it was telling us that when the Great Commission is completed—when the gospel reaches the entire world—that is when Jesus will come back. After reading Steve Kinnard's commentary on Matthew 23-25 and Mark 13, as well as two other commentaries, I began to question my own conclusions. However, I find it difficult to accept that Jesus' "coming on the clouds" was meant to be symbolic in Matthew 24:30. The language regarding the coming of the Son of Man seems to me to be too consistent to allow for a double meaning to the prophecy. Steve Kinnard argues that Jesus was answering two questions:

1) When will the temple be destroyed (24:4-35)? and
2) When will Jesus come again and what are the signs of the end (vs. 36-51)?

My confusion is with the language. Jesus talks of "the Son of Man coming on the clouds of the sky, with power and great glory" (v. 30). Kinnard identifies this verse as answering the first question regarding the destruction of the temple, making the fulfillment symbolic. However, Jesus uses similar language in the second section ("the coming of the Son of Man," v. 37; "the Son of Man will come," v. 44; and "when the Son of Man comes in his glory," Mt. 25:31), which Kinnard says answers the second question, but he says this fulfillment is literal. How am I to understand this?
[The question refers to the book by G. Steve Kinnard, *The Crowning of the King: The Gospel of Matthew* (www.ipibooks.com)]

ANSWER:

I will happily defer to Steve Kinnard on this one, as I assume he has studied this out thoroughly. However, I have spent a fair amount of time thinking about Matthew 24 and Luke 21, and will give you my "for what it is worth" answer. From my study, I conclude that both Matt 24 and Luke 21 are principally about AD 70 and the destruction of Jerusalem. However, I feel the prophecies of Jesus in these passages have implications for the second coming of Jesus and the end-times as well. If one considers Luke 21:20, it is almost without doubt that this verse is talking about the surrounding and eventual destruction of Jerusalem under Vespasian (AD 68) and his son Titus (AD 70): *"When you see Jerusalem surrounded by armies, you will know that its desolation is near."* Looking at Luke 21:20, one can see that the language is apocryphal (its desolation is near). There is a clear reference to the abomination of desolation, prophesied in Daniel 9:27: *"...one who causes desolation will place abominations on a wing of the temple until the end decreed for him is poured out."* Daniel 9:25-27 is a reference to the events in the first-century AD as you can see from its context and its fulfillment. You should not be surprised at the highly symbolical description used in both Matthew 24 and Luke 21. This is a pattern established throughout both the OT and the NT with apocalyptic writing. Consider the description found in Joel 2:28-32, with the sun turning to blood, wonders in the heavens above and so forth. All this is applied to the coming of the Kingdom of God on the day of Pentecost in Acts 2:16-21. The coming of God in a visitation or for judgment is described in multiple places using vivid symbolism. Phrases such as stars falling from the sky and so forth are used to symbolize the falling of the enemies of God. This is the pattern followed in Matthew 24:29 (sun darkened, moon not give its light, etc.) to describe God's judgment on an unrepentant Israel, which occurred in AD 70 when Jerusalem was destroyed.

But that brings us to Matthew 24:30-31. Here the scene appears to have changed: *"They will see the Son of Man coming on the clouds of the sky, with power and great glory. And he will send his angels with a loud trumpet call, and they will gather his elect from the four winds, from one end of the heavens to the other."* Here it appears that we have a change of subject to end-times. The imagery no longer seems to be of judgment on a nation, but rather it appears to be an image of Jesus returning and of the final Judgment Day. On behalf of those who believe the entire passage refers to AD 70, I will concede that the change in Matthew 24:30 is so abrupt that I can understand see why some commentators struggle with seeing a change of subject. Jesus does not give us anything to indicate he is changing the subject. Perhaps, from God's perspective, he is not really changing subject. In either case, whether AD 70 or end-times, the passage is about judgment and about being ready.

I believe that, from this point on, including the day and hour unknown section (Matthew 24:36-51) and the parable of the ten virgins (Matthew 25:1-13), the subject has switched to end-times; to the second coming of Jesus and to Judgment Day.

It bears pointing out that there is one reasonable argument for the entire passage being about the events of AD 70. This is found in Matthew 24:34 where it says *"this generation will certainly not pass away until all these things have happened."* It just so happens that the destruction of Jerusalem by Titus did indeed happen before most of that generation had passed away. Obviously, the final Judgment Day has not yet happened. People who search for simple, logical answers will be tempted to interpret this verse narrowly, concluding that Jesus coming on the clouds happened figuratively in AD 70. I disagree. I believe that Matthew 24 and Luke 21 is a double prophecy (double in that they refer to AD 70 and to ultimate end-times). It is one of those passages which are inherently difficult to interpret with absolute certainty. The prophecy switches subject mid-stream for reasons the author did not reveal to us.

To summarize, I believe Matthew 24:1-25 is clearly about AD 70. I believe that Matthew 24:36-25:13 is clearly about Jesus coming again and Judgment Day. What Matthew 24:26-35 is referring to is controversial. The simple answer is what Steve Kinnard proposes, which is that 24:1-35 all refers to the destruction of Jerusalem. The more complicated and, in some ways, harder to defend position, which happens to be mine, is that there is some mixed reference in 26-35, at least some of which refers to the ultimate end-times, not all to the destruction of Jerusalem.

That brings me to Matthew 24:14—the passage which got you started on this subject. I believe (in the context) that he is referring to the end of Jerusalem. Therefore, it is not good exegesis to use it to teach that, if we finish evangelizing the world, Jesus will come again at that time to bring in the Judgment Day. This may be a nice preacher's point. It may even be true that, once the gospel has finally spread throughout the world, Jesus will come back. But it is probably an incorrect reading of Matthew 24:14 in its context.

So, I guess I agree with you. I agree that Matt 24:26-35 is not simple, and that it may be a mixed reference to two "comings" of God, in AD 70 and at the ultimate end of things on Judgment Day. However, I advise that we be humble about such things rather than dogmatic, especially as this passage contains no content of particular doctrinal importance. Whether about preparing for the coming of the Roman king to judge the Jews or about the second coming of Jesus, the message for us is to always be prepared for the coming of Jesus.

QUESTION:
Where in the Bible did God promise David that he would place one of his descendants on his throne?

ANSWER:
There are several prophecies which imply that the Messiah will be a descendant of David and that he will reign on David's throne. Of course, we know from Jesus that this throne will not be a physical one in Jerusalem, but that *"the Kingdom of God is within you"* (Luke 17:21). The Kingdom over which the Messiah rules is a spiritual one. As Jesus said, *"My kingdom is not of this world"* (John 18:36). Passages which give the promise concerning David's descendent include 2 Chronicles 17:12-14 and Psalms 89:4, as well as 2 Samuel 7:14-16. Other passages could be used, such as Psalms 2:7, where he is speaking through David to his "son" Jesus. Also relevant are Psalm 18:50 and 1 Chronicles 28:4-7.

QUESTION:
In light of all the messianic prophecies, why did most first century Jews reject Jesus?

ANSWER:
First of all, it is worth noting that many thousands of Jews

did accept Jesus as the Messiah. All of the early converts to Jesus were Jews. Even as the gospel spread throughout the Roman Empire, Jewish Christians continued to make up a large percentage of the converts for decades, as evidenced by the letters of Paul, as well as James and Hebrews. I would venture to guess that a larger proportion of Jews came to Jesus in the first century than any other group. Of course, this does not answer your question.

Although we do not have statistics available, surely well under half of the Jews became Christians, and it is reasonable to ask why they did not accept the Messiah for whom they had been waiting for so many years. One thing we can say for sure is that those who did not accept Jesus as Messiah did not fail to believe because of lack of evidence. Jesus said, *"Even though you do not believe me, believe the miracles, that you may learn and understand that the Father is in me, and I in the Father"* (John 10:38) Jesus worked more than enough miracles and fulfilled more than enough messianic prophecies to prove his claim to be the promised Anointed One. One amazing example of Jews refusing to believe despite undeniable evidence is recorded in John chapter eleven, when Jesus raised Lazarus from the dead. Most of the crowd that day put their faith in Jesus, but some said, *"If we let him go on like this, everyone will believe in him..."* (John 11:48). They decided to plot to kill Jesus to stop the miracles! Even raising a man dead in the tomb after four days was not enough for some.

Jesus said to the Jews that if they could not accept his message, they should believe the miracles. He performed miracles of the most astounding sort, in full view of the public. The overwhelming nature of these healings and other signs and wonders was sufficient that Peter could say in the temple in Jerusalem on the day of Pentecost, *"Men of Israel, listen to this: Jesus of Nazareth was a man accredited by God to you by miracles, wonders and signs, which God did among you through him, as you yourselves know."*

So, the problem with unbelief of the Jews was not lack of evidence. I believe the problem many of the Jews had during the ministry of Jesus and immediately thereafter was pretty much the same that people have with believing today. The problem was not lack of evidence, but hardness of heart. Jesus called people to leave their life of sin, to humble themselves before God and to follow him. This call to humility and repentance was more than many of the Jews were willing to accept, despite the overwhelming evidence. Many who saw the miracles of Jesus had the natural response: *"Forgive me, for I am a sinner."* Others refused to face up to their sin, and so rejected Jesus. Is this not the case today? Many today are willing to take the name of Jesus, but repentance is not part of their lives. Do they lack evidence that Jesus has authority to demand they give their lives to him? No. Others reject God altogether. Again, it is not a matter of evidence, but of a sinful heart. The human heart rules the mind and not vice-versa, in general. It does not come down to evidence, but to hardness of heart.

QUESTION:

Are there prophecies which still remain to be fulfilled from the Old Testament and the New Testament?

ANSWER:

Absolutely! If you think about it, you will realize this for yourself. For example, consider 1Thessalonian 4:16f: *"For the Lord himself will come down from heaven, with a loud command, with the voice of the archangel and with the trumpet call of God, and the dead in Christ will rise first. After that, we who are still alive and are left will be caught up with them in the clouds to meet the Lord in the air. And so we will be with the Lord forever."* Or consider an Old Testament passage such as Daniel 12:1-3: *"But at that time your people—everyone whose name is found written in the book—will be delivered. Multitudes who sleep in the dust of the earth will awake: some to everlasting life, others to shame and everlasting contempt. Those who are wise will shine like the brightness of the heavens, and those who lead many to righteousness, like the stars for ever and ever."* Another prophecy of the future is found in Revelation 20 and 21 in which Judgment Day is described, and in which the coming of the New Jerusalem down to Earth is described in joyous detail.

Any passage which describes the coming again of Jesus or the final Judgment Day will clearly be fulfilled in the future. The problem which arises is that many Bible teachers claim certain prophecies are of the future when in fact they are not. It is extremely common to hear prophecies from Daniel, Ezekiel, Revelation and other books taken out of context to apply to end-times or to current events with little if any justification. Much of the problem arises from an unbalanced emphasis on end-times, which is fun for the hearers but takes attention away from the basic teachings of Christ (2 Timothy 4:2-5). Another problem is that many Christians, and even Bible scholars, fail to understand the nature of biblical prophecy. In the Bible, and especially the Old Testament, there are a number of judgment days (small j, small d) in which God came to judge the nations during Old Testament and even during New Testament times. A number of premillennialist teachers, especially those who incorrectly interpret the book of Revelation, mistake prophecies of God's judgment on

Biblical Prophecy

nations who oppose his people, or judgment on God's own people, as referring to the future. Not knowing the exact cause of your question, it is hard to anticipate what passages you might be thinking of, but let me mention just a couple of prophetic passages which have already been fulfilled but which some teachers incorrectly claim are about the future.

First, one could mention Matthew 24 and Luke 21, which are primarily (although not exclusively) prophecies about the destruction of Jerusalem which occurred in AD 70. *"When you see Jerusalem surrounded by armies, you will know that its desolation is near"* (Luke 21:20) is clearly a reference to the events of AD 70, not to some future event. Another example would be in Daniel 2:41f in which feet and toes, partly of iron and partly of clay, are described. Premillenialists have traditionally claimed that the ten toes of Daniel chapter two refer to some sort of future alliance of ten countries which will be involved in the final battle of Armageddon. The problem with this is that the prophecy refers to the Roman Empire and its division, which occurred almost 2,000 years ago. This fact is made clear by the context of the prophecy, which describes the establishment of the Church during the time of Rome.

The greatest source of already-fulfilled prophecies that is erroneously applied to future times comes from Revelation. John was told that the prophecies in the book were events which *"must soon take place"* (Revelation 1:1), yet many choose to ignore the obvious implication. Over-literalizing of the apocalyptic language in the visions is a mistake. Chapter 17 is about the Roman persecution of the church in the first centuries, not about a battle at end-times.

In summary, yes, there definitely are prophecies, both in the Old and the New Testament, which remain to be fulfilled, but we would do well to be very skeptical of those who specialize in finding prophecies of the future where they do not exist.

QUESTION:

How do we know that our Christian perspective of what the Jews thought isn't gross revisionism? I have read articles by scholars who claim that the Jewish/Old Testament concept of the Messiah was of a military leader, not a worker of miracles. Many scholars claim that there is no evidence that the Jewish idea of the Messiah had him being God or dying for anyone's sins. One commentator said that Jesus did not do any of the things the Old Testament said the Messiah should do. He did not save the nation of Israel from slavery, so he cannot be the Messiah. How do you respond to this challenge? [Question included a fairly long quote from a Jewish scholar which I am not including here.]

ANSWER:

This is a very good question. The person who you quote is giving what is the most common view of the Messiah for the Jews in the first century AD. There was a fairly wide spectrum of ideas of the Messiah amongst the Jews in the first century. Some saw him as a righteous teacher. Less saw him as a suffering servant. However, the greatest number believed that the promised Messiah would be a military leader who would lead the Jews to a time of unprecedented glory and physical blessings. Many, if not most, saw the Messiah as being a godly man, but not deity. If one can assume that the common Jewish concept of the Messiah at the time Jesus was born was correct, then the passage from which you quote is accurate. If the majority of Jews at the time of Jesus were right about the Messiah—that he would lead Israel to military victory—then Jesus could not have been the Messiah.

The question, of course, is whether the common view of Jews about their Messiah is a correct understanding of the Old Testament scripture. The fact that the person you quote from doubts the actual existence of Jesus as a real person shows that he or she has not done a thorough study of the historical record. Both the Jewish historian Josephus and the Roman historian Tacitus report that Jesus was a real person. Even the rabbinical writers of the Talmud in the second and third centuries do not deny that Jesus was a real person, although they clearly deny that he was the Messiah. Scholars may legitimately argue over the details of what Jesus said and did, but any self-described scholar who does not believe that Jesus was a real person can reasonably be dismissed.

It is God himself who revealed the coming of the Messiah in the Bible. In order to discover the true mission of the Messiah, one must consult the Old Testament, not Jewish opinion in the first century AD. Jesus certainly saw himself as the fulfillment and culmination of all the prophecies of the Messiah. Luke 24:44 has Jesus saying, *"Everything must be fulfilled that was written about me in the Law of Moses, the Prophets and the Psalms."* Isaiah 53 describes a Messiah who will suffer at the hands of sinners—one who will be silent before his accusers. Zechariah 11:12-14 describes a Messiah who will be sold for 30 pieces of silver (the exact price given to Judas). Psalms 22:16-18 describes a Messiah who will be crucified and whose garments would be divided and gambled over. These messianic prophecies make the claim of the author whom you quote very questionable indeed. The Messiah is presented in the Old Testament as more than a military conqueror.

Biblical Prophecy

It is possible to defend the view of the author from whom you got this quote if one chooses to look only at a limited number of messianic prophecies. If fact, if we limit ourselves to considering only the two most familiar messianic predictions—familiar to the Jews at the time of Jesus, that is—we can make a pretty good case that the Messiah was to be an earthly savior. One of these is Micah 5:2, which says that the Messiah will be born in Bethlehem. It also describes him as *"ruler of Israel."* The other is Isaiah 9:1-7, which describes the Messiah as being from Galilee, and as ruling on the throne of David. Both of these passages can be read to fit the Jewish concept of a Messiah who will rule as a physical king of a physical Israel. On the other hand, they can also be taken as beautiful descriptions of a spiritual king of a spiritual Israel. Besides, Isaiah 9:6 describes a child who will be called *"Wonderful Counselor, Mighty God, Everlasting Father, Prince of Peace."* This clearly does not fit the description of the Messiah from the person you quote, who neither sees him as deity nor as a man of peace. If we take all the clear messianic prophecies together—including Micah 5:2, Isaiah 9, Zechariah 11:12-14, Psalms 22 and dozens of others—we discover a figure who is born as a child but who is God-in-the-flesh. We find a savior of Israel who nevertheless suffers and dies for his people. The common Jewish view of the Messiah is quite simply not consistent with the full range of messianic prophecies in the Old Testament. The Christian view of the Old Testament Messiah is not gross revisionism. Paul describes the prophetic writings of the Old Testament as a mystery, hidden for ages but now revealed to us through Jesus Christ. For hundreds of years, the true, complete nature of the Messiah was not understood by the Jews, but for those who were willing to accept him, Jesus revealed the true Messiah, hidden in the Old Testament all along.

In addition, I recommend that you study the subject of prefigures and foreshadows of the Messiah in the Old Testament. My book, **FSTR** covers this subject. Prefigures of the Messiah, such as Moses, Joseph and David, show us a Messiah who leaves the right hand of a king to suffer and to save God's people. From historical foreshadows such as the Passover and the Day of Atonement, we learn that the savior of Israel will sacrifice himself to bring about forgiveness of sins.

Chapter Six

The Book of Daniel

QUESTION:
   What is the earliest proven evidence for the date Daniel was written? Are the Dead Sea Scrolls relevant? Was any part of Daniel found in the Dead Sea Scrolls, and if so, what is the accepted date of those manuscripts? This seems important to arguments about prophecy, as it depends on them being written before they were fulfilled.

ANSWER:
   That is a good question. In my book **Daniel**, I discuss this subject of manuscript evidence in some detail. The book covers both the evidence from the Dead Sea Scrolls and the Septuagint translation. More detailed information on the Dead Sea Scroll evidence for the date of the book can be found in an excellent article at http://www.christian-thinktank.com/qwhendan3a.html. Let me give you a synopsis.
   The answer is that, among the Dead Sea Scrolls, we have both Daniel manuscripts and quotes by non-biblical authors at Qumran from Daniel. It is very significant to note that the quotes in the (Essene?) writings at Qumran clearly imply that Daniel was already accepted as scripture when they wrote. It is obvious that a number of years were required from the time a book was written before it was

accepted into the Jewish canon of scripture. The fact that the residents of Qumran accepted Daniel as scripture in the second century BC almost unquestionably pushes the date of writing of the book into the third century BC, which defeats attempts of skeptical theologians who want to place it after 160 BC.

The actual Daniel manuscripts from the Dead Sea Scrolls have been analyzed. The date of composition for the various fragments has been estimated to be from the second half of the second century BC to the first half of the first century AD. In other words, the fragments of Daniel are from about 130 BC and later. There are a total of eight known manuscript fragments from Daniel found thus far in the Dead Sea Scrolls, including fragments from every chapter except Daniel 12. In addition, a passage from Daniel 12 is quoted by a non-canonical author in one of the Dead Sea Scrolls. This confirms the existence of the entire letter at this early date.

From this information, we can say that the book of Daniel was written and already definitively accepted as inspired and canonical by about 150 BC. This makes the claim that it was written by a fake Daniel around 160 BC impossible to support by credible argument. The likelihood that a pseudepigraphal (i.e. a fake autobiographical) Daniel would have been circulated and accepted by the Jews as a whole as scripture within ten or so years of its composition is essentially zero. In fact, the Dead Sea MSS evidence argues for a date of writing at least before 250 BC, and most likely 100 years before that date. A summary of the Daniel DSS manuscripts is found in the table below, taken from an article by Flint at the web address mentioned above.

Item	Manuscript	Number	Content Range	Date Copied
1	1QDan(a)	1Q71	1:10 to 2:6	Herodian
2	1QDan(b)	1Q72	3:22-30	Herodian
3	4QDan(a)	4Q112	1:16 to 11:16	Mid-1st c. BCE
4	4QDan(b)	4Q113	5:10 to 8:16	Ca. 20-50 CE
5	4QDan(c)	4Q114	10:5 to 11:29	Late 2nd c. BCE (note: Ulrich, DJD 16)
6	4QDan(d)	4Q115	3:23 to 7:23?	Ca. mid-1st c. BCE
7	4QDan(e)	4Q116	9:12-17?	1st half of 2nd c. BCE (but this is presumably a typo; dated elsewhere to Late 2nd c.)
8	Pap6QDan	6Q7	8:16? To 11:38	Ca. 50 CE

To give you an idea of how biased liberal scholars are when they assume a date of post 164 BC for the writing of Daniel, consider the quote below:

> We need to assume that the vision [of Daniel 8] as a whole is a prophecy after the fact. Why? Because human beings are unable accurately to predict future events centuries in advance and to say that Daniel could do so, even on the basis of a symbolic revelation vouchsafed to him by God and interpreted by an angel, is to fly in the face of the certainties of human nature. So what we have here is in fact not a road map of the future laid down in the sixth century B.C. but an interpretation of the events of the author's own time, 167-164 B.C...
> (Daniel Towner, *Interpeter's Bible*, John Knox: 1984, p. 115)

Given the manuscript evidence (and much more besides, to be found in **Daniel** Ch. 2), we can conclude that those who claim that Daniel was written around 160 BC do so because they assume a late date, not because the evidence supports the conclusion. The only reason to believe Daniel was written about 160 BC is because one assumes, *a priori*, that the Bible cannot be inspired by God. Such circular reasoning is not worth the paper it is printed on.

Besides, if we study Daniel, we will find absolutely clear prophecies of events well into the first-century AD! Daniel seven is a prophecy of the beginnings of Roman persecution of the church under the eleventh "king" of Rome, Domitian, who ruled from AD 81-96. This prophecy provides stunningly accurate details of the rule of this boastful king. For more on this, see **Daniel** Ch. 9. If Daniel prophesies with such accuracy events of the late first-century AD, then the argument of Daniel Towner and others like him falls apart.

QUESTION:

In your book on Daniel, in the section on the 10 horns, with the 11th horn being Domitian (Daniel 7), what historical sources can you site that show that Vespesian and/or Domitian subdued Otho and Galba? I have only been able to find sources for Vitellius' overthrow by armed forces that supported Vespasian. Could the three who were subdued actually be ordinal? For example, perhaps the little horn subdued the third king, instead of all three?

ANSWER:

One source I have used recently is Michael Grant, The Roman Emperors: *A Biographical Guide to the Rulers of Imperial Rome 31*

B.C.-A.D. 476. It is true that we only have direct evidence of Domitian helping to defeat Vitellius. The source above specifically mentions Domitian's part in defeating the third of the trio of short-lived emperors who ruled before Vespasian. I would agree with you that it may be more accurate to say that we know Domitian defeated the third of *"the three."* Daniel 7:8 has "three of the first horns uprooted before it." I am confident that this is a reference to "the three" (i.e. Galba Otho and Vitellius). The exact meaning of "uprooted before it" is unclear. We cannot rule out the possibility that Domitian was involved in defeating Galba and Otho as well, but that we do not have the information recorded, but this would be speculation. In any case, I still see the replacement of these three by Vespasian as an amazing fulfillment of Daniel's prophecy. Thanks to your question, I will be a bit more careful how I describe the fulfillment of this prophecy.

QUESTION:

In Daniel 2:44 it says that "...it will crush and put an end to all those kingdoms, but it will itself endure forever." In what way will the kingdom of God "crush" the other kingdoms? Is he talking about when Christ returns and destroys the physical realm or about the kingdoms in Jesus' time?

ANSWER:

That is an intriguing question. I have thought about it some and cannot give you an absolute and definitive answer. The most likely interpretation is one you allude to. At the end of days, all the earthly kingdoms will come to an end and the eternal Kingdom of God will exist on *"a new heaven and a new earth"* (Rev 21:1). At that point, all earthly "kingdoms" will come to an end and be "crushed," but the Kingdom of God will endure forever.

Having said that, I am inclined to see a double-fulfillment of this prophecy. Some feel that any historical, predictive prophecy has only one unique fulfillment in the future. These people do not allow for both a primary and a secondary fulfillment of predictive prophecy. I am not of that opinion. The secondary fulfillment of this prophecy came when each of the four kingdoms in Nebuchadnezzar's dream was in fact judged and destroyed by God. Babylon was destroyed by Cyrus in 538 BC and Persia was destroyed by Alexander the Great in 331 BC. The last of the Greek dynasties established by Alexander's successors, the Ptolemies, was destroyed at the Battle of Actium in 31 BCE. The Western Roman Empire was destroyed (more or less) in AD 476 by the Visigoths, while the Eastern Roman

Empire was overcome by the Ottomans in AD 1453. During the time of the Roman kings, a kingdom was established, beginning in Jerusalem. This was the Church of Jesus Christ. The church—the Body of Christ—is a manifestation of the Kingdom of God. The Church which was set up by Jesus has indeed endured to this very day and has outlasted all those other kingdoms. If the Church has "crushed" any of those kingdoms, it is only spiritually or metaphorically. One could argue that, when Rome became "Christian" after the time of Constantine, it was crushed by the Church, but this seems like a stretch to me, as the political transition was relatively smooth and the empire endured many generations after the conversion.

So, as I see it, the passage in Daniel chapter two finds its principle fulfillment at Judgment Day, but it is fulfilled secondarily in the arrival of the Church and its ultimate endurance forever in the face of the worldly kingdoms, all of which will be destroyed, while the Kingdom will endure forever. Sorry to give you a somewhat complicated answer, but that is how I see it.

QUESTION:

About Daniel 9:24-27, is it possible to look at the last of the 70 weeks as taking 70 years instead of seven? That way, the last week would cover from the birth of Jesus until the destruction of the temple. In that case, Jesus would be crucified about the middle of the last week. I have another question about Daniel. I read that the end of chapter 11 is referring to Augustus' death, which means that "at that time" in Daniel 12:1 is within the lifetime of Jesus, while he "grew in stature and wisdom." Then the time of suffering referred to in Daniel 12 is the crucifixion (not the destruction of the temple), and the deliverance in Daniel 12 is the atonement of Jesus, and the multitudes are those who were raised in Matthew 27:52. Do you have a comment?

ANSWER:

Let me answer your first question. I believe that your idea cannot be completely ruled out. Let me state a couple of reasons that I personally would not take it as the most likely explanation of Daniel 9:24-27. I assume you have read my book on Daniel. First, if one takes the beginning of the 70 weeks to be the decree of Artaxerxes in 458 BC, then the seventieth week began in AD 26 (plus or minus a year). In that case, assuming Jesus was born about 5 BC, he was born in the 66th week, not the seventieth. Applying your idea, the last week would end in the year AD 95, which would be 25 years after Jerusalem was destroyed and animal sacrifice was brought to an end, once and for all. Last, it is a bit tough to accept the first 69 weeks being seven years and the last week being 70 without any evidence or suggestion in the text. I know of no case when one "day" is ten years. I will admit that the explanation I give (Daniel Ch. 11), with a 40-year hiatus during the last week, is somewhat speculative as well, but it just so happens to fit the time-line quite well. It also fits God's very common use of 40-year or 40-day periods of waiting, found in many places throughout both the Old and the New Testament. So I appreciate your thought, and I would not rule it out, but I believe the evidence does not support this interpretation of the vision.

As to your second question, I agree that Daniel 11:36-45 deals with the conflict between Augustus Caesar (known as Octavian at that time) and Marc Antony, which resulted in the death of Antony and the accession of Octavian to the undisputed throne of all Rome. What I am not sure about is your apparent interpretation of Daniel 11:45, *"yet he will come to his end, and no one will help him."* I cannot see how this can be a reference to Augustus. His reign ended in peace and his son succeeded him to the throne. God did not judge Augustus as far as I can tell. He certainly did not persecute the Church. More likely, Daniel 11:45 is a prophecy of the end of the Roman power to persecute the Church of God. Also, when we move on to Daniel 12:1, we are fast-forwarding to the end of days. I believe that that the phrase *"Now at that time..."* marks a jump to end-times, when the resurrection and judgment of mankind will take place. The visions in the book of Daniel take large jumps in time without warning a number of times. There are over 100 years between Daniel 11:35 and 11:36. Other examples can be given. Adding to this, in God's eyes, time is not really a factor, so when he says "Now, at that time," he may be referring to the next great event after the end of Rome, which will be the end-times.

In either case, the events referred to in Daniel 11:36-45 happened in the 30s BC, before Jesus was born. In order to know how to interpret Daniel 12, we need to let the context of the chapter determine what it is talking about. Like I say in my book, I believe that reading Daniel 12 will almost certainly lead one to assume he is talking about end- times, not the time of the death and resurrection of Jesus. For example, consider Daniel 12:2: *"And many of those who sleep in the dust of the ground will awake, some to everlasting live, but others to disgrace and everlasting contempt."* The parallel to Revelation 20:11-15 seems hard to ignore. I can see how you saw Matthew 27:52 here, with the people coming out of their graves at the time of the death of Jesus, but I just do not see the context of Daniel 12 working to support this view. One will find reference to the end-times more than once in Daniel 12.

Please do not take my opinion as the end-all of the discussion. I think you have some good insight here. I suggest you continue asking good questions and seeking solid answers.

QUESTION:

1. Why did Daniel become a prophet? 2. What did he do that was so important? 3. When and where was he born and where did he live? 4. How did he go about doing God's work? 5. Why do you think Daniel was able to talk with God?

ANSWER:

I answer all these questions in my book Daniel, especially in the first chapter. I will give a brief answer to your questions here. Daniel was not a prophet, at least not in the classic sense that Elijah, Isaiah, Micah and others were prophets. He did not declare "Thus says the Lord" to Israel, as the others did. In fact, his ministry was primarily to pagan kings and their courts. Several of the prophets were specifically called by God to their ministry—for example Isaiah (Isaiah 6) and Jeremiah (Jeremiah chapter 1)—as you can see in their own writings, but Daniel was not called to be a prophet, at least as far as we know. He received dreams and visions and the interpretation of dreams directly from God. That is how he became a "prophet," if indeed one could call him a prophet. The closest one can come to a commission for Daniel is found in Daniel 1:17: *"God gave knowledge and understanding...And Daniel could understand visions and dreams of all kinds."*

Daniel set the example for all Israel of how to behave righteously while held as a captive under both Babylon and Persia. He was the ultimate example of a man of God living in a world dominated by pagan religion and ungodly politics. In addition, he brought to Israel and to us a great number of incredibly accurate predictions of future events such as predicting when Jesus would come to Jerusalem (Daniel 9) and when Jerusalem would be destroyed (70 AD, also in Daniel 9), as well as the great persecutions under Antiochus Epiphanes (167-164 BC, Daniel 8, 11), thus proving that the Old Testament is inspired by God. Many other significant contributions of Daniel can be mentioned.

Daniel was taken captive as a youth from Jerusalem to Babylon after Jerusalem was attacked under Nebuchadnezzar (Daniel

1:1-2) in 605 BC. Presumably, he was somewhere between 12 and 20 years old at that time, so he was probably born between 622 and 617 BC (approximately). Daniel continued to minister to Babylon and Persia until his death, some time after 536 BC.

Daniel did God's work simply by being a righteous man in every situation he found himself. His specific job description was adviser to the kings of Babylon and prime minister to the Median king, Darius. Often, God put Daniel directly into situations (such as Nebuchadnezzar having an amazing dream) in which he was able to use his talents to interpret dreams, but one can assume he was simply a very powerful man who trusted in God on a daily basis, which is why God was able to use him.

The Bible does not say that Daniel talked to God. God communicated with Daniel through angels (Daniel 8:13, 10:10, etc) and possibly directly through Jesus Christ (Daniel 10:5-8), but there is no evidence God the Father ever spoke directly to Daniel.

QUESTION:

In the book of Daniel, it says that the beast with eleven horns will be destroyed. However, the Roman Empire was not destroyed after only eleven kings. Domitian was the eleventh king, and there were many after him, including ones that persecuted the Christians. Why does Daniel only mention eleven kings and then destruction?

ANSWER:

At the time the New Testament book of Revelation was written, Domitian was either the current emperor or was soon to take that position. Domitian was either the eighth emperor (Revelation 17:11) or the eleventh emperor (Daniel 7:7-8), depending on if you include the mini-kings Galba, Otho and Vitellius. Because Domitian was the first of the emperors to bring about a systematic persecution of the saints (Nero instigated a very brief persecution against the Christians, only in Rome), God chose him as representative of all the persecutors who came after him. Of course, it is true that there were many more than eleven emperors of Rome. Some, such as Diocletian, brought about much greater persecution than Domitian, but God chose to let the first persecutor represent them all. I cannot think of a better way God could have prophetically represented to the readers of Daniel what would happen to the disciples of Jesus in the distant future other than how he did it in Daniel seven. In God's eyes, from the time Domitian began to attack the saints, Rome and its persecuting emperors were already judged. God did not bring to completion the destruction of Domitian and of the persecuting power of Rome for over 200 years. This is not unique in biblical history. God pronounces judgment on a person or nation. In his eyes, it is a done deal; although in human terms, he may not carry out that judgment for many years. It is good to remember the main point of Daniel chapter seven and Revelation chapter 17. God will allow his people to be persecuted, but only for a limited amount of time (for a time, times and half a time). However, God will judge the persecutors, and their judgment will be eternal. For this reason, God's people should stay faithful. God is in control.

QUESTION:

After talking of the destruction of the fourth beast, Daniel says that the other beasts were given some time to live after that (Daniel 7:12). What does that mean?

ANSWER:

The power of the first beast, Babylon, was taken from it in 538 BC when Cyrus the Persian conquered the city of Babylon. The power of Media/Persia was taken away in 332-331 BC when Alexander conquered the entire Persian Empire under Darius III. The power of the successor Greek empires was finally ended in 27 BC when Rome overcame the remnant of the Ptolemaic Dynasty. Although the power of these kingdoms was destroyed at that time as prophesied by Daniel, these nations did not completely disappear. Instead, their power and influence were greatly reduced. Babylon remained as an important satrapy within Persia. Persia's power was partially revived in the Parthian and Sassanian kingdoms. In fact, Babylon (Iraq), Persia (Iran) and Greece are all independent nations, even today. However, as prophesied by Daniel, none of these peoples ever returned to the glory which God had taken from them. The fourth beast, Rome, also had its power destroyed by God. Unlike the others, once Rome lost its power, it was never revived, unless we consider the Papal States or modern Italy as remnant Roman powers.

QUESTION:

In the book of Revelation ch.17, it has the other 10 horns being together in the fight, against the people of God, with the 11th horn. So the other kings helped Domitian?

ANSWER:

That could be confusing, I have to say. The answer is that the ten horns/kings in Revelation 17:12 are not the seven (or eight) kings in Revelation 17:7-8. The vision in Revelation 17 describes the seven kings in verse seven as past kings, while the ten persecuting kings in verse twelve are ones *"who have not yet received a kingdom, but who for one hour will receive authority as kings along with the beast."* It is important to note that Revelation was probably written either immediately before Domitian took the throne or during his reign (AD 81-96). This helps us to separate the seven former kings (who did not persecute the Church) in Revelation 17:7-8 from the ten persecuting kings (*"They will make war against the Lamb"*) who followed Domitian, as described in Revelation 17:12. By the way, many premillennialists used to identify the ten kings of Revelation 17:12 as the ten nations of what used to be known as the EEC (European Economic Community). Now that the EEC is the EU, with at least twenty-seven countries, none of which attack the saints, they have presumably stopped making this identification.

QUESTION:

What was the birthplace of the prophet Daniel?

ANSWER:

The best I can tell, the Bible gives no direct information as to the lineage of Daniel, or where he was born. For this reason, one is left to speculate based on the limited information available. Speculation should always be taken with a grain of salt. However, let me speculate.

We know that Daniel was taken to Babylon from Jerusalem with a relatively small group of hostages when Nebuchadnezzar conquered Jerusalem for the first time in 605 BC (as proven by Daniel 1:1-2). Larger deportations of hostages did not occur until the second and third attacks on Jerusalem in 595 and 587 BC. Additional information is that Nebuchadnezzar took Daniel and his three friends Shadrach, Meshach and Abednego into service in his palace. We know all this from Daniel chapter one. This tells me that these four were definitely not commoners.

For this reason, I believe that Daniel and his friends were children of the nobility of Jerusalem. In other words, it seems to me that they were taken by Nebuchadnezzar to Babylon as hostages. Their being taken as hostages was meant to insure the good behavior of Jehoiachin and the other leaders left behind in Jerusalem. If they did not pay the annual tribute to Nebuchadnezzar, the threat would have been that the lives of the valued child hostages would be forfeit. To some extent, I base this speculation on the fact that this was a common practice in the ancient world.

So if I am right (and remember that this is somewhat speculative), then Daniel was taken as a young hostage to Babylon from Jerusalem. He was most likely from a very influential family of the nobility which either lived in Jerusalem or which was closely associated with Jerusalem.

QUESTION:

As far as the Bible being 100% in agreement with history, Daniel is at odds with the historical record, and the details are not minor. According to Daniel, Nebuchadnezzar was king of Babylon, then Belshazzar his son, then Cyrus, then Darius the Mede. However, according to the historical record (the Behistun Inscription, the Letter of Nabonidus and other accounts), Nebuchadnezzar was king of Babylon, then Abel-Marduk his son, followed by Nabonidus his general (after a coup), then Belshazzar, the son of Nabonidus (not of Nebuchadnezzar). The other records say that Cyrus was next, then Cambyses I, then Darius I and so forth. The account of Nebuchadnezzar given in Daniel is in line with what is known about Nabonidus' reign, not Nebuchadnezzar. Not much is known about his reign during the 40 years or so. How do I reconcile what's known in the historical record with what's written in Daniel? (By the way, Darius was not a Mede, but a Persian).

ANSWER:

You bring up so many issues with the book of Daniel that it would take many pages to answer them. Fortunately, I have answered every single one of the questions you raise concerning the book of Daniel in my book, **Daniel**. Every claim of historical error you mention is completely unfounded. For full answers, you might want to get a hold of my book, but I will supply a brief answer below. First of all, you are correct about the external sources with respect to Nebuchadnezzar, Abel-Marduk, Nabonidus and Belshazzar. Nabonidus was a powerful general under Abel-Marduk, who apparently instigated a coup to take power. However, what you may have missed is that Nabonidus married the daughter of Nebuchadnezzar in an attempt to impart legitimacy to his blood line. For this reason, Belshazzar is the grandson of Nebuchadnezzar through his mother, not his father, and by Near Eastern ways of describing family relationships, he was in fact the "son" of Nebuchadnezzar. It was standard practice in ancient genealogies to call grandsons and even great grandsons the "son" of their father. There is no contradiction between the description in the book of Daniel and the histories of Herodotus and others. It is true that Daniel does not mention Abel-Marduk or Nabonidus. This is because nothing of sufficient importance happened to Daniel during the reign of Abel-Marduk. The events of Daniel chapters 1-4 happened during the reign of Nebuchadnezzar. There is a space of quite a few years between the events of Daniel chapter four and chapter five. The events and visions of Daniel chapters 5-12 all happened rather late in the life of Daniel—after 555 BC. A lack of mentioning a person is not evidence of a mistake.

It is worth noting that historians used to attack the book of Daniel for mentioning Belshazzar as the king of Babylon because no ancient records listed him as a king. Then an inscription was found at the Ziggurat in Ur which proved that Belshazzar ruled as regent for his father Nabonidus who spent most of his time in the desert on a religious quest. This explains the offer of Belshazzar to Daniel in chapter five to give him the third (rather than the second) highest position in the kingdom. King Belshazzar occupied the second place in Babylon. This fact undermined the criticisms of the non-believers and provided dramatic evidence for the accuracy of Daniel.

Second, you claim that we know very little about Nebuchadnezzar's reign from history. This is definitely not true. There is more material from Herodotus and others on Nebuchadnezzar than any of the others. Besides, the Bible, the most accurate and reliable history book of the ancient Near East we have, mentions him more than the other Babylonian rulers as well. (I realize this is circular reasoning, but it just so happens that the Bible agrees with the external sources).

About Darius the Mede, it appears that when Cyrus conquered Babylon, he left a Median noble named Darius in charge of the province (satrapy) of Babylon, which was the largest one in his empire. This is not at all surprising, as the empire was technically a dual government of the Medes and the Persians. Giving Darius the Mede charge over the satrapy of Babylon, the largest in the empire, made perfect sense. The Darius who succeeded Cambysses I was a Persian, but clearly he was a different person. Daniel never describes Darius the Mede as ruler of the entire Persian/Mede Empire. In fact, it says of him that he "was made ruler over the Babylonian

The Book of Daniel

kingdom." Clearly, Daniel does not have him as a Persian emperor. I am well aware that critics of the Bible have attempted to prove error in Daniel at this point, but there is no error. The details in Daniel match up perfectly with what we know from external sources. Daniel mentions details other historians do not mention (such as the name of the first satrap of Babylon), while Herodotus and others mention details not in Daniel (such as the fact that Abel-Marduk succeeded Nebuchadnezzar.

You should be aware that there are a significant number of scholars who scan the Bible with the purpose of trying to prove that there are many historical errors there. Time and time again, such biased attempts have been proven for what they are through subsequent discoveries by historians. The discovery that Daniel was correct about Belshazzar is a good example of this. The critics of the Bible, naturally, did not publish apologies or acknowledge that the Bible was right again. They just moved on to other unfounded claims of biblical historical error.

Chapter Seven

Science and the Bible

QUESTION:
You state in your book, *Is There a God?*, that "comparison of Genesis one with scientific knowledge implies a transcendent source for the creation story." Why only limit it to Genesis one? What about Genesis two? Not so brave there—you have to fall back on faith. How can you explain the contradiction between the two creation accounts?

ANSWER:
I do not limit the claim of evidence for a transcendent source to Genesis one at all. I believe that the medical evidence from Leviticus implies a transcendent source of that book. I believe that the foreshadow content in Leviticus also argues for transcendent reality. I believe that the prefigure/foreshadow content in the story of Abraham in Genesis is compelling evidence for transcendent reality. I can go on with dozens of examples, including specific ones from the book of Genesis.

I also believe that Genesis two is consistent with transcendent reality, but the evidence in this particular case is not as compelling as with Genesis one, simply because there is less scientifically relevant information in the second chapter. I can say the same about the book of Esther, but there, too, the supportive evidence is not absent, it is just considerably less compelling. I agree that it requires more faith to believe that Ruth is inspired than is required to believe that Isaiah is inspired. So what? I will freely admit the uneven distribution of evidence in the Bible. Some of the books of the Bible are "obviously" inspired because of the evidence, but by the nature of their topic and material, others do not contain a lot of internal evidence for inspiration. It is the overall case which proves the conclusion. The lack of compelling evidence for inspiration in the fourth chapter of 1 Samuel is not a logical argument against the transcendent nature of biblical inspiration as a whole.

By the way, although the creation content in Genesis chapter two (I would include Genesis chapter three, as the second and third chapter form a single narrative) may not have the same compelling scientific evidence for inspiration as the first chapter, the story of Adam and Eve is not without evidence for transcendent authorship. There is much prefigure and foreshadowing in this story which anticipates both specific events and teaching in the New Testament. Adam is a pre-figure of Christ. See **FSTR** p. 62-63 for more on this.

QUESTION:

How can you explain the contradiction in the Genesis story, which has the sun and the moon being created on the fourth day, if there was already day and night on the first day of creation? Isn't this an example of the Bible being contradicted by science and by common sense?

ANSWER:

I have studied current theories of the early Earth and its atmosphere. Scientists use the chemical makeup of very old rocks (oxygen content, for example) to make reasonable guesses as to the content of Earth's atmosphere at the time the rock formed. Such models predict that the early atmosphere of the Earth had much higher quantities of sulfur dioxide, carbon dioxide, methane, ammonia and so forth than today. It is likely that the sun and the moon remained invisible from the surface of the Earth until life on the planet had significantly changed the chemistry of the atmosphere. Photosynthetic life had to evolve (or be created by God) before the atmosphere contained a significant amount of elemental oxygen. The planet Venus today is an analogous example to the early Earth atmosphere. The heavenly bodies are not visible from the surface of Venus. In other words, the sun, moon and stars were not visible until the third or fourth "day"

Science and the Bible

of creation. Obviously, I do not believe that these "days" are literal 24-hour periods, but that they represent periods—eras—over which God did his creative work.

So, day and night existed on the first "day," but the heavenly bodies were not visible. The oceans and the atmosphere formed on the second "day," and life appeared on the third "day," but the sun and the moon were still not visible. The life God created changed the chemistry of the Earth, so that the heavenly objects appeared in the sky on the fourth "day." As I have said before, the outline of information in the Genesis creation account is in remarkable agreement with the current models used by scientists today. Your example is a good question, but it does not change my conclusion.

Let me add:

As a side note, I strongly agree with Galileo who said, "The Bible was written to tell us how to go to heaven, not how the heavens go." In other words, if you read the Bible in order to discover statements about the laws of nature, you will be disappointed, as that was not the purpose of the writers. It was also not the purpose of the ultimate writer—God. However, what is required is that the content of the Bible not directly and incontrovertibly contradict what we know to be true from science. For Galileo, the issue which raised conflict with the religious authorities was whether the Earth moves. The Bible described the sun rising and setting. Does that mean that the sun moves around the Earth? I say no. It is common usage even today to describe the sun as rising and setting. We obviously know that the sun does not literally set and rise. It is the earth that spins, not the sun that moves. Galileo believed in the Bible and in the inspiration of the scriptures, as is made clear from his writings. To try to apply rigorous methods of scientific analysis of the Bible is to miss the point. Galileo was right. The religious "experts" of his day were wrong. The Bible does not state that the Earth does not move or that the sun moves around the Earth. A skeptic/critic trying to prove the Bible is in error can use the fact that the Bible describes the sun moving across the sky to prove that the Bible is not inspired by God. Such an example does not prove this at all.

Now, if the Bible were to say that the Earth is hollow, or if it were to say unequivocally that there are only three planets, or if it were to say that there is life on Venus, that would be the kind of statement which could be used to test the scientific accuracy of the Bible. The fact that the Bible metaphorically describes "days" of creation does not disprove the inspiration of the Bible. Again, the Bible is not a science book. Neither does the fact that the Bible describes the actual visual appearance of the lights in the sky at the beginning of the fourth "day" prove error in the Bible. Now if it said the moon was created on the sixth day, then that would constitute a scientific error in the Bible.

Even if you cannot agree with my conclusions, I hope you can at least understand the logic of my thinking on this. Like I already said, science does not prove the Bible. It could conceivably be used to prove the Bible is of human origin (hollow earth, Atlas holding it up, etc.), but it just so happens that it does not. The best I can tell, and I have received many questions on this, the Bible is not proven incorrect by any scientific discovery.

QUESTION:

I would like you to explain two statements I found in your book "Is There a God." First, "Belief in Adam and Eve can only be by faith," and second, "If it were not for what is recorded in the Bible, I would probably accept the evolutionist's conclusions about the origins of man."

ANSWER:

For the first statement, although one can imagine compiling evidence, indirectly, for special creation of humans, it will almost certainly remain impossible to find historical evidence to confirm the existence of the persons Adam and Eve. Historical records simply do not exist earlier than about 2500 BC. We may be able to argue indirectly that human beings were created, but even that will probably be impossible to "prove" scientifically. What direct, hard-evidence proof could we find for special creation of humans? I believe it is possible to provide indirect evidence, but not a piece of physical evidence for special creation of humans. Think about it. What physical evidence can we imagine digging up which would prove special creation? As for Adam and Eve, I believe that there is no conceivable physical evidence which we could find which would prove that they actually lived in a specific place. Again, what could we find? An inscription: "Adam and Eve slept here?" I believe that the first man and woman were real people who actually lived. It is just that there almost certainly will never be physical proof of this. Therefore, belief in Adam and Eve is reliant on trust in the accuracy of the biblical account.

As for the second statement, when I look at the physical evidence, I see no absolutely compelling proof beyond a doubt that humans did not evolve. I am not saying that humans evolved from apes. I am simply being honest about the evidence. I am not trying to argue for evolution of human from apes; absolutely not. I simply am saying that belief in special creation of humans is not proved by scientific evidence. To say that special creation of human beings is proven by the evidence is to be dishonest about the data. Just because one can poke some holes in the evolutionist's assumptions does not mean that you can prove absolutely (scientifically) that evolution of humans is untrue. As a scientist, I struggle to think of an experiment I could do or evidence I could find to prove God created humans by supernatural power. Perhaps my statement made you uncomfortable. My intention is to encourage believers to realize that faith in the reliability of the Bible is part of the reason for what they believe. I believe some creationists create a false impression about this question. Science supports the Bible, but science does not prove the Bible.

QUESTION:

What is your opinion on the Earth's approximate age? Creationists believe it to be not more then a few thousand years, whereas scientists claim that the earth is about 4.5 billion years old. The evidence I have seen used by creationists includes the current rate of space dust accumulation on the Earth's surface. They say that if 4.5 billion years is correct, the buildup by now would reach the moon. Another evidence I have seen used for the young Earth is the claim that there were human fossils found in the same layer as dinosaurs, proving dinosaurs did not go extinct 65 million years ago. I do not see how scientists could get it so wrong. Could the six days of creation in Genesis be six eras of time?

ANSWER:

I can see from the way you ask the question that you have thought about these ideas for yourself a lot. Let me say that, in general, I agree with your line of thinking here.

First of all, I answer your question in great detail in my book **ITAG**. I am a chemist and a physicist, but not a biologist, so I will address these areas primarily. I have looked at the evidence carefully and have read numerous books by young-Earth creationists. I have reached the conclusion that every piece of physical evidence which we have points toward the conclusion that the earth is very old. The fact is that a number of methods (radiometric dating of moon rocks, radiometric dating of meteorites, earth/moon distance and several others) all give about 4.5-4.6 billion years old. This consistency makes it reasonable to conclude that this is the probable age of the Earth, although it is a good idea to hold to some skepticism on the exact age.

I agree with you that it is reasonable, especially given our knowledge of Jewish literary forms, to conclude that the "days" of creation may be metaphorical days, referring to periods of time. I believe that we should not be dogmatic about this. I cannot rule out the possibility that God created the Earth "with an appearance of age." However if God created the Earth out of nothing just a few thousand years ago, then he seems to have gone through a lot of trouble to make it appear to have a scientifically verifiable age of 4.5 billion years. Many facts support the belief that the universe and the solar system are very old. There is the apparent distance of galaxies; some as much as ten billion light years from us, implying the light left these galaxies ten billion years ago. This means that the light left these extremely distant objects before the Earth was formed. Other evidence, including uranium/thorium/lead-dating, the Earth/moon distance and more, points to an old Earth.

Young-Earth creationists are forced to distort or ignore a massive amount of evidence which supports great age, and to misuse or misrepresent a smaller amount of evidence they claim supports a young Earth in order to make it appear to less knowledgeable readers that the scientific evidence supports a young Earth. Bottom line, there is literally zero evidence that the Earth is 6-10 thousand years old. I suggest you do your own study of this claim. I also recommend that you read at least one book by an author in the young-Earth camp so that you can understand their arguments for yourself. You should not take my word for it!

As for the specific examples you give, there is no reliable example of human and dinosaur fossils being placed together in situ in rock strata. Claims to the contrary are unfounded or even deceitful. The argument on space dust hitting the Earth is specious, and the careful creationists do not even use this argument any longer. The numbers do not support their conclusions. Anyway, it is not my desire to attack those believers who support a scientific young-Earth view. I agree with you wholeheartedly—this is not a salvation issue. Old Earth or young, Jesus is Lord of the heavens and the Earth. It is more helpful for us to move on to weightier matters such as the salvation of human souls for eternity. By God's grace, we will.

QUESTION:

How long has mankind lived on the Earth according to the Bible? If one does the math, using biblical genealogies, one gets a little over 6,000 years. This subject fascinates me, and I would like to hear your opinion on it.

ANSWER:

You ask a good question. I would agree with you that one could "do the math" and calculate how long ago Adam and Eve were created from the numbers provided in Genesis. However, there are some problems with this sort of calculation. The fact is that, for the Jews, genealogies often skip generations. When the Old Testament calls someone the father of someone else, it may refer to a grandparent or even a more distant relationship. This was common practice for the Jews. In Luke and Matthew, the genealogies skip many generations. There are other specific examples one can point to in the Old Testament. For material on this, I would refer you to a book by Doug Jacoby, *Genesis, Science and History* (available at www.ipibooks.com). Because of uncertainties about the generations, one will do well to not push the Genesis account to imply a definite amount of time. It is wiser to say that the numbers provided in Genesis can be used to calculate a minimum possible age for humanity. The conclusion from reading Genesis with an understanding of Hebrew literature is that Adam and Eve lived more than 6,000 years ago, and probably considerably more than that.

This brings one to the question of scientific evidence. What about Neanderthal or even Homo erectus? Scientific evidence seems to constantly push back the age of supposed human ancestors. Anthropologists put modern humans back to about 100,000 years ago. If we count Neanderthal as human, the age goes back to about 250,000 years. Neanderthals had average brain sizes about the same as modern humans, they made tools and they cared for their sick and elderly. Were these beings people? Were they descendants of Adam and Eve? If so, how far does that push the creation of mankind back? Homo Erectus, Homo Habilis and other pre-humans had much smaller brains. Their status as humans is debatable at best.

Another intriguing possibility is that God took an already created/evolved proto-human creature and put a soul and spirit into two of these people, creating Adam and Eve in his own image. On the face of it, this seems to contradict the literal interpretation of the statement that God "formed man from the dust of the ground." However, it is not completely clear how literally to take this statement, as all of us are, ultimately, made from the dust of the ground. To be completely honest, I am a bit of an agnostic on these questions. I am not sure. I would refer you to the book by Douglas Jacoby mentioned above as a great resource. I accept the story of Adam and Eve in Genesis principally on the weight of the evidence of the Bible being the Word of God as a whole. I do not believe we will ever find direct forensic evidence of the first two humans. For this reason, I prefer to not be dogmatic about the age of human beings and the timing of the Adam and Eve event. I do believe on the solid evidence for the reliability of the Bible that the events described in Genesis 2 and 3 did indeed happen.

I am sorry to leave you with a somewhat vague answer, but since I am not certain, I prefer to be honest about that. By faith, I believe in the account of Adam and Eve, but I do not know exactly where the story fits in the history of hominid existence on the Earth.

QUESTION:
What is "the breath of life" breathed into Adam in Genesis 2:7b? Is it air or spirit/soul?

ANSWER:
Those who specialize in biblical interpretation advise that, when in doubt, we should let the obvious meaning of a passage stand. The writer of Genesis chapter two seems to be saying that God made the inanimate Adam alive, and he began to breathe. Whether or not God put a spirit/soul into Adam at this point in time is a matter of speculation. One might even go so far as to say it seems likely that Adam received a soul at this time, but the Bible does not say this, so one would do well to stick with the obvious.

Many have suggested the possibility that Adam was a previously evolved intelligent *Homo sapien* into whom God breathed a soul, making him into the image of God at this point. I cannot rule out this possibility, but again, I feel it is always best, when in doubt, to let the Bible speak for itself. So I believe that the most obvious interpretation of Genesis 2:7 is that it is saying God made Adam alive physically at this point, and that he began to breathe.

QUESTION:
A teacher I heard recently made an interesting claim which relates to the question of when dinosaurs and other ancient creatures lived, which also preserves the idea that the dinosaurs lived many millions of years ago. This teacher said that, in between Genesis 1:1 ("In the beginning...") and Genesis 1:2 ("Now the earth was formless and empty..."), there was a time-gap of many millions of years, between "In the beginning" and "Now." Can you shed some light on this theory?

ANSWER:

What you are describing is known as the "Gap Theory" explanation of Genesis chapter one. There are several proposed approaches to resolving the creation account in Genesis with what is known from science. Let me give a brief synopsis of some of the most common approaches to understanding the Genesis creation account.

One approach is to assume that the creation of the universe, the Earth and all life on Earth occurred within six, literal 24-hour periods just a few thousand years ago. This is the simplest and most straightforward reading of Genesis chapter one, but it does not agree at all with the scientific evidence. All the evidence we have at our disposal implies that the Earth and the universe are very old—almost certainly billions of years old. This in and of itself does not disprove the literal 24-hour approach, as God certainly could have created the Earth a few thousand years ago, already appearing old. The problem comes when creationists claim that scientific evidence agrees with the earth being young. This is simply not the case.

Another approach is known as the day/age theory. In this approach, the "days" of Genesis chapter one are not literal 24-hour periods, but are symbolic of great periods of time over which God did the things described in Genesis. For example, in the first period of creation, presumably over great periods of time, God created the heavens and the Earth. In the second period of time, represented by the second day, God created separate land and seas as the Earth cooled and so forth. This approach can be seen to agree well with observable data. Scientific evidence agrees in outline with the description in Genesis chapter one, if one can accept that the "days" are symbolic of great periods of time. However, some are uncomfortable with allowing what appears to them to be literal 24-hour periods to be taken as symbolic of a greater period of time. Both of these theories are discussed thoroughly in my book **ITAG**, ch. 6.

A third approach has been proposed, which is known as the Gap Theory. This is the one you heard about. This explanation of Genesis chapter one proposes a great period of time—a gap—to exist between the creation of the Earth and the first "day" in Genesis 1:1. In other words, this theory allows for the great age of the Earth, but still assumes that the 24-hour periods of Genesis are literal. Gap theorists imply that trilobites, dinosaurs and so forth lived a very long time ago. However, God chose to wipe the Earth clean and re-create almost from scratch several thousand years ago. The apparent advantage of the Gap Theory is that it allows for the obvious great age of the Earth while preserving the literal meaning of Genesis chapter one.

The Gap Theory appears, at first, to be the best of both worlds; agreeing with scientific evidence of an old Earth and preserving literal days. However, I believe that, in reality, it does neither very well. First of all, there is not a shred of evidence that the Earth was wiped clean and life was recreated a few thousand years ago. There is nothing at all scientific about the Gap Theory. Second, there is no theological or biblical justification for the claim that God wiped the slate clean just before Genesis 1:2. The Hebrew word translated "Now" certainly cannot justify this. Gap theorists have tried to support their theory by proposing very speculative ideas about a rebellion of the angels in heaven. They have used a dubious interpretation of Isaiah 14:12. Gap theorists take the passage "How you have fallen from heaven, O morning star, son of the dawn!" to imply the fall of Lucifer, or Satan. There are at least two problems with this. First, the passage is about the fall of Babylon, not of Lucifer. Second, it is speculative in the extreme to imply that this passage can support the Gap Theory. Those who propose the Gap Theory are attempting to find a middle ground where there probably is none. Either one accepts the scientific evidence to say what it says, or one believes that God created the Earth and universe with an appearance of age. In saying this, I do not mean to ridicule the Gap Theory or those who believe in it. I simply am saying that I do not believe this is a theory which is theologically or logically consistent, so personally I reject it.

QUESTION:

What is the meaning of the word "made" in Genesis 1 and 2? I have heard that the Hebrew word actually means appointed rather than made. This could be used to imply that God appointed Adam from a species which was already walking upright, and that God formed him with dust into what we now know as humans. What do you think of this?

ANSWER:

My Hebrew dictionary defines the Hebrew word *asa* as "to do, to make, to be done, a generic action." Some of the translations of the Hebrew word, including the number of times they are translated that way in the NIV, are do (405), did (286), made (270), make (161), doing (61), does (55), follow (39), prepare (30), celebrate (25), deal (24), built (22), obey (22), maker (21), show (21), carry out (20), be done (18) and so forth. Way down the list, asa is translated as appointed four times.

Anyone claiming this word means appointed rather than

made is clearly stepping out on a limb. Asa is translated as "made" far more often than as "carry out" (which seems to me similar to appoint). One example in which asa is translated "appoint" is in 1 Samuel 12:6. If you look at this passage, you will see why the context caused the translators of the NIV to use "appointed." As with any attempt to translate from one language to another, the context determines the word to be used. In the context of Genesis 1:26, *"let us make man"* seems to fit better than *"let us appoint man."* Genesis chapter one describes God making the Earth, the heavenly bodies and life. In the same way, and using the same word, it describes God making man. If God merely appointed mankind, did he merely appoint the universe? Did he merely appoint life itself? If so, who made the universe and who made life? It is best to let the Bible and its context speak for itself. Although I do not know the person who made the point you read, I suspect this is a case of a person starting with a conclusion and trying to fit the evidence to the conclusion, rather than vice-versa.

This brings us to a second aspect of your question. Is it possible to interpret Genesis 1:26 to mean that God took an already-evolved, very intelligent descendant of the apes and put his Spirit into that being, making the first true human being? Whether one translates asa as "made" or "appointed," this interpretation of Genesis 1:26 may still be possible. I suppose we cannot rule out this understanding. One can argue that, for a scientifically unsophisticated Jewish audience, Genesis 1:26 is a reasonable description of God putting a soul into an evolutionally-advanced being. This may be true, but to be honest, it seems a bit of a stretch to interpret Genesis chapter one in this way. Personally, I do not agree. However, I feel it is not appropriate to be dogmatic on this particular question. You may be right. In the end, I am not sure that any truly essential doctrine is irreversibly affected by the exact means God chose to create the first human beings. I would caution you to not force your own pre-conceived notion onto your interpretation of the Bible, but leave you to decide what you believe on this question.

QUESTION:

Did Adam and Eve's children commit incest? Where did Cain's wife come from in Genesis 4?

ANSWER:

First of all, the Bible states that Adam lived 930 years. We do not know how long Eve lived or how long her child-bearing years were, but we can probably assume both were far greater than what is normal today. Presumably, Adam and Eve had many children, including daughters.

It is true that, in the Law of Moses, blood siblings were prohibited from having sexual relations and therefore from being married (Leviticus 18:9). The question is why God gave this prohibition to Israel, and whether such a prohibition would have applied to Adam and Eve's children, given that they were not under the Law of Moses. The answer to these questions is not obvious, because the Bible does not tell us. First, one must ask why God outlawed "incest" for the Hebrews. Was it because it is inherently an evil thing to do, or was it to protect these people from the danger of genetic disease?

To answer this question would require some speculation. It may be helpful to divide the commandments in the Mosaic Law into those which were clearly a sin issue and those which may have been imposed to protect the health of the Israelites. For example, God outlawed the killing of others, idolatry, stealing, profane use of God's name and so forth because he hates these things. They are inherently sinful. Seemingly different from these examples are the prohibition against eating certain types of meat. God outlawed the eating of pork, shellfish, rodents, carnivores and so forth. I believe there is nothing inherently sinful about eating these types of meat, but it just so happens that eating these particular types of meat exposes people to a number of very dangerous diseases. With our modern scientific knowledge, we are aware of the relatively greater danger of eating carnivores, shellfish, rodents and pork, as we can trace each of these to specific diseases. Besides, using our knowledge of these diseases, we can cook these meats in such a way to make them not nearly as dangerous. Christians are free to eat these meats (Mark 7:19). In Exodus 15:26, God tells his people that if they follow his Law, *"I will not bring on you any of the diseases I brought on the Egyptians, for I am the Lord who heals you."*

The next question is where does the proscription against sex and marriage to one's sibling fit into this picture? Is "incest" inherently sinful, or is it a matter of God protecting his people from disease? Given our knowledge of the causes of genetic disease—especially those gene-linked diseases which are recessive—it is very easy to see how the prohibition against incest was one of the ways God protected his people against "the diseases I brought on the Egyptians." Bear in mind, that there is at least an element of speculation here, as I certainly am not a direct spokesperson for God, but I am assuming that marriage with one's sibling was outlawed by God under the Law of Moses, not because God hates this practice, but in order to protect his people from any of a host of genetic diseases.

This brings us back to Adam and Eve, and more specifically to their children. When God created human beings, he saw that his creation was good (Genesis 1:31). I assume that Adam and Eve were created without genetic defect. The natural process of DNA replication inevitably leads to mistakes in copying which produces mutations, the vast majority of which are definitely not beneficial—some of which cause genetic disease. The way I understand the question you ask is to assume that Adam and Eve's children were allowed by God to marry and to produce children because there was no possibility of genetic disease. The reason for God giving the law in Leviticus was an attempt to protect his people from harm. This cause simply did not exist for Adam and Eve's children. Because there was no risk to be prevented, God did not see "incest" as "sinful" for the earliest descendants of Adam and Eve.

This discussion involves two assumptions of which you should be aware:

1. The prohibition in the Law of Moses against incest was enacted by God to protect his people, not because incest is inherently sinful. This is a likely conclusion, but it is impossible to prove.

2. Adam and Eve, and therefore their children, did not have defective genes in their DNA, making the threat of genetic disease be small or non-existent. This, too, is impossible to prove, although it is a logical inference.

Because there is an element of speculation in my argument above, I suggest you consider these thoughts, do a little research of your own and come to your own conclusion. But this is how I have viewed the interesting question you bring up.

QUESTION:

If the God of the Bible is all-knowing, why didn't he initially know that Adam would need a helpmate? Why didn't he just make Adam and Eve at the same time, if he is omniscient, knowing no animal would satisfy Adam?

ANSWER:

God did know that Adam would need a companion. In order to understand this passage, you need to bear in mind the literary style of the early part of Genesis. The first few chapters of Genesis have God speaking specific words. One should not take this literally. It is doubtful that, as described in Genesis 1:3, God literally said the Hebrew words for *"Let there be light."* God does not have lips, and besides, there was no one for him to speak to, at least in the human sense. You should take the descriptions of God speaking in Genesis chapters one and two in a metaphoric sense. Does God talk to himself as described in Genesis. This is a description of God, given in a form understandable to people. Did God literally talk into the air and say to himself, "It is not good for man to be alone." Or is the writer of Genesis describing in human terms how God decided to give Adam a suitable mate to take care of his emotional/relational needs and with whom to procreate and populate the Earth?

It seems reasonable to assume that the description in Genesis 2 is put in human terms so that the original hearers, as well as present-day readers, can understand in broad terms God's plan to create people whom he could love and with whom he could have a relationship. A similar example is found in Genesis 6:6, which says about God that, when he "saw" the condition of man in the time of Noah, *"his heart was filled with pain. So the Lord said, 'I will wipe mankind whom I have created, from the face of the earth...'"* Does God have a "heart" in the sense people do? Maybe! Did he literally tell himself, in Hebrew, that he was going to wipe mankind out? Again, the Bible writer is using human terms to express what God did. The application of human characteristics to a non-human thing is called anthropomorphism.

Perhaps describing Genesis 1-3 as being somewhat metaphorical will make you feel you are on slippery ground. Is there any point of fact at all to take from Genesis? Is the story of Cain killing Abel literal, or is it just a metaphorical description? I may not be able to give a definitive answer to every possible question, but let me make at least a preliminary attempt. When the Bible describes an action of a human being, one should, in general, take it literally. When it says that Cain killed Abel, or that Noah did something, one should assume that the author intends us to take this at face value. However, when the Bible describes something that God said or did, one should generally assume that the Bible is using human terms to describe in a non-literal way something God did, "said" or felt. When the Bible says that Eve reached out her hand and ate the fruit, it probably means literally that she reached out her hand and ate what she touched. Could this story be metaphorical as well? I am not sure we can rule this out, but it seems unlikely. When the Bible says that God reaches his hand down to help the weak, we should assume that it is meant metaphorically. In Genesis 2, God did not suddenly realize his mistake and decide to make a woman as well. That would be to over-literalize the text.

As for why Adam was made first, then Eve, we can look to 1Timothy 2:13-14 for a hint about that. From this passage, it appears that God made Adam first as a symbol of the fact that, in marriage, a husband would have authority over his wife. Should we take the creation of Adam before Eve literally or metaphorically? You can decide for yourself, but because it is describing a human event, I take it literally.

QUESTIONS:

Is the order of creation in the Genesis 1 and 2 accounts contradictory? It seems that the order of the creation of man and of the animals is reversed in the two creation stories. Also, I have heard that Genesis chapter one and Genesis chapter two are contradictory stories of the creation, written by two different authors. Is this true?

ANSWER:

No and maybe.

"No" to the first question! Genesis chapter one is the story of the creation of the universe and more specifically of the Earth and the life on the Earth. Genesis 2 (actually starting in about verse 4) is the story of the creation of man. So Genesis 2:4-25 describes a part of what happened on the sixth "day" in Genesis 1. Viewed in this way, there is no irresolvable contradiction between the two creation accounts. Many have claimed that there is, but the supposed contradictions disappear if one simply starts the account of the creation of Adam and Eve with Genesis 2:7 (remember that the chapters in our Bibles are arbitrary divisions, not included in the original writings). By the time we get to Genesis 2:7, the animals, plants and so forth are already created. If you read Genesis 2 after verse seven, it never says that the shrubs, plants, animals, etc. were created after Adam and Eve. Probably the phrase in Genesis 2:5, *"no plant of the field had yet sprung up,"* is a reference to the fact that at that point no agriculture had taken place. One problem people have with this passage is that, in most Bible translations, Genesis 2:7 is in the middle of a paragraph.

About the authorship of the two creation stories, no one knows who wrote the book of Genesis. Although tradition holds that Moses wrote Genesis, the evidence is that, at most, he may have been involved in putting it in its final form, but almost certainly he was not the actual original writer of the entire book. The historical content of Genesis bears signs of authorship well before the time of Moses.

Many Bible scholars claim that the writing styles of the first and second chapters of Genesis are sufficiently different to imply that there were two different authors. Based on the content of the two accounts, the Hebrew used and the stylistic differences, I believe it is very likely that the two accounts were written by two different authors, but the case is not conclusive. If that is true, then a later editor combined the two accounts, as well as other material, to put together what we call the book of Genesis. I am not sure why it would be important to the question of inspiration whether there were two separate authors, given that there is no contradiction between the two creation accounts.

QUESTIONS:

Did dinosaurs really live? Did they live at the same time as people? Could this be the "leviathan" in the Old Testament?

ANSWER:

What one can say with certainty is that there are fossils of dinosaurs found scattered across every continent on the globe, including Antarctica. Did dinosaurs ever live? The obvious answer is "yes"—they lived at a time in the very distant past. The only conceivable alternative argument is that God created the Earth with an appearance of age with dinosaur fossils already in the ground. Although this claim would be impossible to disprove, very few would be willing to defend it.

Did dinosaurs and people ever live at the same time? The simple answer is "no"! Some creationists have claimed to have found human and dinosaur imprints in the same location, but these claims have not held up to independent scrutiny. The fact is that the sediment layers in which dinosaur fossils are found—without exception—do not contain fossils of such modern animals as bison, antelope, rabbits, elephants, humans and the like. Besides, in places where dinosaur and more modern fossils, especially mammals, are both found, the supposedly more modern fossils are universally found on top of the apparently older layers which include dinosaur fossils in the fossil sediments. Please, let us put aside the bogus claim that humans and dinosaurs lived at the same time.

How long ago did the dinosaurs live? Scientists use several methods for dating rocks in which fossils are found. Most common is the use of radiometric dating such as potassium/argon and uranium/lead isotope pair measurements. According to the scientific evidence, dinosaurs lived in the Triassic, Jurassic and Cretaceous eras, or about 250-65 million years ago. It is a good idea to be somewhat skeptical of the exact ages quoted by scientists, but unless evidence to the contrary can be presented, one can assume that the dinosaurs lived a very, very long time ago!

Is the leviathan of the Bible (Job 3:8, Job 41:1, Psalms 74:14, Psalms 104:26, Isaiah 27:1) a dinosaur? Perhaps it is, but not likely. One should keep in mind that the writing style of the Bible passages which mention leviathan are all poetical. The description of leviathan is a bit hard to pin down. It would be a good idea to leave it at that.

QUESTIONS:

Does the third law of thermodynamics imply the big bang theory is wrong because things tend to decay, rather than grow in complexity?

ANSWER:

The law you are referring to is the second law of thermodynamics. This law certainly is relevant to understanding the creation of life, but it is not particularly important in telling us whether or not the Big Bang Theory is correct. The second law of thermodynamics states that for any spontaneous process, the net entropy of the universe increases. In order to make this law understandable, we need a practical definition of entropy. Basically, entropy is a measure of randomness or freedom of motion. To put the second law more simply, nature tends toward disorder and "decay." By this law, it is not natural for highly ordered systems, with a lot of information, to build up out of less ordered matter. For example, a building will never be constructed out of raw materials spontaneously. Only with the intelligent input of energy can such an ordered thing (with such low entropy) as a building ever be created.

By this same law, it is impossible for a living thing to be created spontaneously out of the simple atoms and molecules which would compose any natural system in the universe. Even the simplest conceivable living thing which could live on its own must be incredibly complex—requiring the creation of thousands of different large and delicate molecules such as proteins, nucleic acids and so forth. This requires that the original living things in the universe must have been created by some sort of intelligent Creator. We call this Creator God. This is not a simple argument, and it may not convince the hard-line atheists, but as a chemist and physicist, I see no possible "natural" answer to the origin of living things. All this is discussed in great detail in my book **ITAG**, ch. 4.

Getting back to your original question, I have never seen any contradiction between the second law of thermodynamics and the Big Bang. In fact, cosmologists who create models for the Big Bang use the second law to describe how the universe expanded and cooled with time; evolving into the much cooler universe we live in today. There is no contradiction between the second law and the Big Bang Theory.

QUESTION:

Please comment on N. F. Gier's claim that the Bible writers believed in a solid "firmament" surrounding the Earth. You can find his material at the University of Idaho website, under his name in an article titled, "God, Reason and the Evangelicals" (ch. 13).

ANSWER:

I read the chapter. It was interesting. There is a lot of good scholarship here. Gier makes some good points about the blatant errors, for example, in the Koran, the Hindu scriptures, etc. What he fails to do is prove that the author of Genesis chapter one believed in a solid firmament. [Note to reader: many of the ancients believed the stars were imbedded in a solid crystal "sphere" which rotates around the Earth. Gier claims that the Bible reflects this incorrect assumption.] Such things certainly can be proved with the scriptures of other religions, but not with Genesis one. I agree with many "evangelicals" (to quote Gier) that a large proportion of the references to nature in Psalms and Job, for example, are poetic and are not to be taken literally. This is the normal hermeneutics of poetry. One could perhaps take the poetic descriptions in Job and Psalms and create a questionable case that these poets believed in the crystal sphere, but even with the poetical passages, the conclusion is questionable. On the other hand, the Genesis creation account is not poetry. In general, statements in Genesis should be taken literally. The problem with Gier's theory is that the Genesis writer does not make statements which imply belief in a solid crystal sphere.

Bottom line, the author reaches his unjustified conclusions because of some assumptions he makes. I will quote him:

> "We must use the doctrine of 'sharable implications,' which means that we cannot impute to authors knowledge or experience which they could not possibly have had."

In other words, the author assumes that the writer of Genesis could not have had supernatural influence. Like I say in **ITAG**, we must look at people's assumptions. If the author assumes that the writer of Genesis could not possibly be inspired, no wonder that he concludes that the author is not inspired.

Another quote from Gier's article:

> "We can assume that they borrowed much from their neighbors."

Here we go again. The author makes unfounded assumptions. His conclusions are not reliable, because he proves that Genesis is not inspired by assuming it is not inspired by God.

Another quote:

> "Why should the Hebrews, who had no special expertise in ancient science and who borrowed heavily in other areas, have had a view different from other ancient peoples?"

This is the logical fallacy known as "begging the question." If one argues that the writer of Genesis does not have special knowledge by stating that he could not have had special knowledge, that is called "begging the question."

In conclusion, I believe this author raises some very good issues. However, the example he uses to debunk the Bible actually supports the conclusion that the Bible is inspired. It is absolutely incredible that a Jewish writer could write an account of creation which does not contain the things Gier says that it logically should, if it was written according to human knowledge. The author assumes the answer before doing the investigation. Your champion of skepticism provides a great deal of information which supports belief in the Bible. Virtually all ancient peoples believed in this solid firmament, but the writer of Genesis does not (or perhaps he did, but God prevented his false belief from entering the biblical text). Genesis is not a scientific description. I agree with the theologians quoted by Gier that the purpose of Genesis 1 was not to describe the science of creation. The purpose is to give credit to God for his creation. Nevertheless, the fact remains that the biblical account is not at all like the creation story of any other ancient people.

QUESTION:

I was re-reading your article on the ID debate [note: this article is included below] after reading through an interesting article at http://philsci-archive.pitt.edu/archive/00002583/. It made me reconsider your statement: "There is no experiment one can even conceive of which can test the design hypothesis." I began to wonder if there aren't other scientific "theories" that are taught in schools that are also not falsifiable or testable. The author mentions String Theory and Newtonian Physics. He mentions that one is not testable and the other has been proven false. Yet, they are both taught as theories. He also speaks to the matter of science vs. truth. His conclusions seems to say that if, in fact, science is bound to methodological naturalism, no amount of evidence in the world in favor of the supernatural would ever be considered valid since it is presupposed that it cannot be counted. If, as you say, "the goal of science is to find an explanation which is consistent with the experimental evidence," and "[an] acceptable theory is one which is at least as consistent with the evidence as rival theories," on what basis is ID disqualified? Has a strict Darwinian evolutionary theory ever been tested and proved? Are there other common theories in science which are not really scientific by this criterion?

ANSWER:

I went to the website and read the article you mentioned. I appreciated the perspective of this person and find myself in the same camp. However, I have problems with several of the points he makes. Perhaps my difference with what he says has more to do with my being a scientist and his being a philosopher than with a fundamental disagreement over what is true. We both believe that there is an intelligent designer and that it is convincing from observation of nature that there is a God. We differ significantly, however, over what is the nature of science and of the scientific method of discovery. To some extent, this is an argument over definition. I believe scientists are probably in a better position to define science than philosophers! Basically, what this person says is that there are many ways of knowing something, and that experimentally determined truth is not the only way to discover knowledge. Of course, I agree with this. However, he seems to want to broaden the definition of science to include any conceivable way to infer information about nature, including use of logic or speculation or other lines of reasoning. As a scientist, I know that the scientific "method" is limited. The scientific approach to acquiring knowledge, by definition, does not allow one to consider supernatural causes. This does not mean that supernatural events cannot happen. It just means that science must remain silent on this subject when speaking "scientifically". The author uses what I believe to be a poor example in an attempt to prove that it is possible for science to be able to do an experiment to prove that supernatural events are possible. Bottom line, science is limited to creating models which are testable by experiment and which can be refuted by some conceivable experiment.

Do scientists ever break their own rules? Have scientists, historically, passed off as science theories which, perhaps not unlike intelligent design, do not meet the criteria described above? The answer is yes. However, we need to be careful to analyze examples to discern what is going on. Let me consider an example—String Theory. I will be honest with you and admit that I do not have a thorough grasp of this theory. However, from what I can see about the string model, it is quite speculative. It is somewhat on the edge of even being a scientific theory. There is no scientific experiment which can directly observe these "strings." Arguably, this theory will remain impossible to prove by direct experiment indefinitely. This might appear to put it in a league with Intelligent Design. However, I would argue that there are major distinctions between ID and String Theory. First of all, String Theory is a model which can be used to make specific, testable predictions. Even if the existence of strings cannot be demonstrated directly, the implications of the model can be shown to be either consistent or not consistent, at least indirectly, with experiment.

The same could have been said about the Atomic Theory of John Dalton. This theory was proposed in 1804 to explain a number of empirical laws in chemistry. Yet, the existence of atoms was not considered proved until the explanation by Einstein of Brownian Motion in 1905. For about 100 years, Atomic Theory could not be demonstrated directly by any experiment. Yet, its power to explain well-known experimental phenomenon was so great that it was a very successful theory.

I believe it is fair to say that String Theory is significantly more speculative than Atomic Theory ever was, and that it is a bit "out there" as science. Despite this, it is not in the same category as ID. Intelligent Design is a very powerful model which can explain the reason for many observable phenomena, such as the size of the electrical force, the gravity force and so forth. However, it cannot be used to predict yet-unknown physical laws. It cannot be used to explain any experiments. It cannot be disproved by experiment. In the end, String Theory will stand or fall according to how well it can explain experimental evidence. Intelligent Design will not be able to explain experimental evidence. What it will be able to explain is the question of ultimate causes. It is very important to ask the big questions of why the universe is the way it is. Arguably, this is a far more important question than any answered by science. However,

ID cannot be confirmed by experiment or disproved by experiment. It is not scientific.

Let us consider another example—evolution. When Darwin proposed evolution by natural selection in 1859, there were a few aspects of the theory which put it somewhat on the fringe. In 1859, it was debatable whether the theory was refutable by any experiment. It dealt with things which happened in the distant past. It is not clear that this theory could be tested directly by any experiment in the laboratory back in the nineteenth century. I do not believe that it was an unscientific theory, even in 1859, but it was somewhat unique in that it did have broad predictive powers about the past, but not about experiments which could be performed in the lab at the time. Having said that, the evidence behind the Theory of Evolution has grown dramatically in the past 150 years. Since the time of Charles Darwin, as I am sure you know, the discovery of DNA has greatly changed the situation. Evolution as a theory of origins of species is now easily refutable. Genetic similarities between related species can be looked at. These experiments do not prove evolution of all life from a single initial life form, of course, but they do broadly support the theory of evolution. In addition, in recent decades, a number of experiments have been done showing evolution occurring in the laboratory. Of course, these experiments only show relatively minor changes in the genomes of rather simple species. Nevertheless, although evolution is far from "proved" (as some claim), it has certainly moved into the category of a solid scientific theory in that its claims can be tested by experiment and it can be refuted by scientific discovery.

Getting back to two examples you raise. First, the author you mention is absolutely right that String Theory is not proved. I believe no theory can be "proved," as science does not lend itself to final proof. Having said that, String Theory is highly speculative, barely warranting being described as a scientific theory. Even with that, though, it is still in a different category from ID. As for the author's comment about Newtonian Physics, I do not agree with his assessment of this theory. Newtonian Theory has not been disproved. It was also never "proved" in the past. Like any scientific theory, it is only as good as its ability to explain phenomenon and to predict experiments. The reason scientists still teach Newton's classical mechanics is that it is still able to explain a wide variety of phenomenon extremely well. Newtonian mechanics breaks down for extremely small objects, such as atoms and electrons. It also breaks down for objects moving very fast. For very small objects, quantum mechanics is far better at explaining the data. For very fast objects, relativity works much better than Newtonian mechanics. Newtonian mechanics is neither right nor wrong; neither proved nor disproved. The same can be said for quantum mechanics. There are phenomena which are not fully described by quantum mechanics. The fact that a particular theory cannot explain all phenomena does not make it unscientific.

None of this is true with Intelligent Design. Please remember that I am absolutely convinced that there is an intelligent designer, and that his fingerprint is all over creation. It is just that supernatural design does not lend itself to confirmation or denial by experiment. It never will. The author you mention wants to redefine science. He wants to broaden the definition of science so that it can include a theory like Intelligent Design. As they say, it is a free world, and he is certainly allowed to use any definition he likes. I predict, however, that he will not be able to change how scientists define what they do. It is my opinion that it is not helpful to redefine science in a convenient way to shoe-horn questions about deity and supernatural events into the realm of science.

The following is my essay on intelligent design as mentioned in the question above:

The Intelligent Design Debate

From Kansas to Dover, Pennsylvania to Baylor University, a debate has been raging across the United States over whether or not the theory of Intelligent Design should be taught in schools. Recently, televangelist Pat Robertson said of the voters in Dover, Pennsylvania who turned down a pro-ID school board, "If there is a disaster in your area, don't turn to God. You rejected him from your city." Is a decision not to include Intelligent Design in school curricula equivalent to rejecting God? What should the "Christian" position be on this divisive debate? Much of the angry rhetoric is the result of a failure to understand the nature of the evidence, pro and con, as well as a lack of insight into scientific methodology. Another major cause of misunderstanding is that many do not understand that there are two distinct and fundamental questions which must asked about the Intelligent Design hypothesis. This essay is an attempt to delineate and separately answer these two questions. They are:

1. Does the evidence support belief in an intelligent designer of the universe and of life on the Earth?

2. Should Intelligent Design be part of the required curriculum in public school science curricula?

Of course, if the answer to question number one is "no," then the answer to the second question is also "no." It is this author's belief that many, if not most, of those who are involved in the emotional debate over ID fail to address the two questions above separately on their own merits. Most supporters of Intelligent Design assume that if there is valid reason to believe in an intelligent designer, then automatically this implies that it should be taught as the principle, or at least an alternate, paradigm of science. Of course, it should not surprise us that those who say "no" to the first question react strongly and negatively to those who push a positive agenda to put Intelligent Design into required school curricula.

IS THERE SUFFICIENT EVIDENCE OF AN INTELLIGENT DESIGNER?

Let us begin by addressing the first question. Does the information we have at hand regarding the nature of the physical world require, or at least support belief in a designer? The emphatic answer is "yes"! The evidence from nature for a designer of the universe and of life is overwhelming, and it is increasing. In fact, the evidence is so strong, that there is a developing movement among scientists toward accepting the Anthropic Principle. The Anthropic Principle is a basic paradigm[3] regarding the laws of nature. The anthropic paradigm is a way to answer the basic "why" regarding the laws which govern the universe. It can be simply stated as follows: **The laws of the universe are what they are and the fundamental constants have the values they have because this is what is required for advanced forms of life to exist. In other words, the reason for the existence of gravity, of the electromagnetic force, of the conservation of mass/energy, the law of entropy and so forth are because a designer created them so that "we" can exist.** The same would apply to the fundamental constants which determine the size of the four fundamental forces, the mass of the elementary particles and so forth. The gravity force, the electromagnetic force constant and the size of the strong and the weak nuclear force is finely "tuned" to allow for galaxies, stars, planets, atmospheres and living systems to be self-sustained by those laws.

An example of the inexorable move toward belief in the Anthropic Principle is the recent "conversion" of one of the world's most renowned agnostics, Antony Flew (for a recent interview, go to http://www.biola.edu/antonyflew/). Flew's change of mind was a direct result of the fact that he could not refute the Anthropic Principle. However, it is not all roses for the believers in Intelligent Design, as we all know. There has been a determined backlash against deism from many scientists as well as organizations such as the Smithsonian Institute, the NSTA and others, but the quiet and unheralded fact is that, although most scientists are afraid to mention

Science and the Bible

it publicly for fear of the backlash, a majority of scientists believe in design. Why? Because of the evidence!

But let us return to that evidence. Knowledge of the fundamental laws of nature is what leads scientists to the Anthropic Principle. The size of the gravitational constant is in tune with the energy in the original big bang to an incredible degree. If it had been larger by one part in 10^{60}, the universe would have collapsed in just a few million years without forming stable galaxies, stars or planetary systems. If it had been smaller by a similar one part in 10^{60}, then galaxies and stars would have never formed, and therefore no life. If this is luck and not a matter of conscious design, then it is luck of the highest imaginable order. No one would be foolish enough to play the lottery if they understood that their chance of winning was one part in 10^{10}, never mind one part in 10^{60}! There are over 20 fundamental constants and important ratios in basic physics, including the size of the electromagnetic force, the nuclear strong and weak forces and many more, all of which must be finely tuned to a value within a very small range of the actual values we measure for life to exist in the universe. For more information on this subject, see **ITAG** (ch. 5).

There is much more evidence for design in the universe beyond the incredibly precise fine tuning of the fundamental constants of the universe. One could mention the amazing and unique properties of water, without which life would not exist. Other very lucky accidents of nature (lucky, that is, if there is no designer) include the unique but absolutely necessary properties of carbon, iron, uranium and several other elements for life to exist. Knowledge of biochemistry offers us a seemingly unlimited number of examples of design, including the amazing structure of DNA, which just happens to carry a code to instruct the synthesis of proteins, while proteins are required to construct DNA. There are literally hundreds of properties and laws in the physical world; each of which is necessary for advanced life forms to exist; each of which are either outrageous coincidences or the product of a designer. No wonder that many scientists have been forced into the position that design is the organizational principle to explain the laws of nature.

From all this, we can conclude that Intelligent Design is real. It is not the product of religious presupposition, but the only reasonable conclusion from the evidence. Those who persecute the supporters of ID would do well to consider the facts. But then again, most of them approach the question already predisposed toward materialism and the assumption that only "natural" explanations are to be accepted as valid. No wonder that people who assume the answer (only random, "natural" explanations are allowed) before looking at the data reach this conclusion. Intelligent Design is the only reasonable answer to the question "why" as it is applied to the physical world.

SHOULD INTELLIGENT DESIGN BE PRESCRIBED IN PUBLIC SCHOOL CURRICULA?

As stated in the introduction, the question of whether Intelligent Design is correct is not the only important one we should ask. Just because something is true does not automatically mean it needs to be included as curriculum in science classes. Scientific theories which are consistent with experimental evidence are what should be discussed in science classes. Many assume that the validity of Intelligent Design automatically means that it must be taught as a scientific theory. We must look at this assumption carefully.

First, let us consider what makes for a good scientific theory. When scientists create theories, their goal is not to discover "the truth." In fact, scientists are not in the business of discovering the truth. When the partisans of evolution declare that "evolution is a fact," they are either ignorant about how science is supposed to work, or they are manipulating their hearers. Rather, the goal of science is to find an explanation which is consistent with the experimental evidence. An acceptable theory is one which is at least as consistent with the evidence as rival theories. There are two requirements for a theory to work in science.

1. The theory must be testable by experiment.

2. The theory must be falsifiable.

What does it mean for a theory or hypothesis to be falsifiable? It means that it must be possible to refute the theory by some experiment. An irrefutable hypothesis is not a scientific one.

This is where the theory of Intelligent Design runs into trouble for scientists—even those like me who believe in design. There is no experiment one can even conceive of which can test the design hypothesis. What could one do in a laboratory to test whether a system was designed? Intelligent Design "researchers" do not do experiments. The question one must ask is not whether the universe shows evidence of design, but whether design can be positively proved by experiment.

The Intelligent Design idea fails the second test of a scientific theory as well. Not only is there no experiment which can be done to test the theory, there is no conceivable way to disprove design. Design is a paradigm, but it is not a scientific paradigm. Perhaps it is a theological paradigm. Perhaps it is a philosophical paradigm. Bottom line, creation is a supernatural event which does not lend itself to reproducible experiment. Science does not, nor can it preclude the supernatural. It just does not know how to deal with it.

If it is true that nature was designed—that the evidence is consistent with the Anthropic Principle—and it is also true that this has profound implications for how we view the physical world, what are scientists to do with this dilemma? Should they pretend that they do not know what they know? Evolution is a theory, but Intelligent Design is a fact.

I am a professor who has taught physics and chemistry for more than 25 years. I have taught everything from biochemistry to organic to physical chemistry to calculus-based physics. There is hardly a course I have taught in which I do not have the opportunity to point out the evidence for design. I do so freely in my classes and have for many years. However, when I consider where I would put Intelligent Design into my curriculum, the answer is "nowhere." I cannot think of any experiments we could do. Which course would I put the design theory in? Chemistry? Biology?

I do teach a class where Intelligent Design definitely does belong. I teach a class on the history and philosophy of science. In this class, we do a chapter on science and religion. We cover the Anthropic Principle, we discuss the evidence for design, we mention that science came about as a result of believers in a monotheistic God looking for order in the universe. Intelligent Design definitely belongs in a class on the philosophy of science. It probably would be appropriate in a philosophy class or a theology class, but I struggle to see where it belongs in a science class.

Bottom line, intelligent design is not a scientific theory. It is truth. It is a beautiful organizational paradigm which explains the underlying "why" of the physical world, but it is not science. It definitely deserves a place on the lips of every science teacher, but should a unit on design be a required part of public school science classes? I say "no."

What about evolution? Is the theory of evolution from Satan? Is it a conspiracy promoted by demons? No! Evolution is a model which fits the proper criteria as a scientific theory. Contrary to the polemical cries of some, evolution is not a fact. There are many unresolved "problems" with the claim that all life on the Earth evolved by random forces from a single original randomly created life form four billion years ago. Nevertheless, evolution is a powerful scientific theory. It can be successfully used to explain much of what we know from genetics. It can and has been tested by experiment. Mutation and natural selection has been shown in the laboratory to work for very simple life forms such as bacteria. Evolution is not a fact. Design is. However, evolution is a good scientific theory and design is not. I, for one, deeply respect those who have been at the forefront of the ID movement. Michael Behe, Hugh Ross and many others have braved the undeserved wrath and even hatred of a small but extremely vocal part of the scientific community. Some have been fired from university positions and been blacklisted for simply stating the obvious—that the universe is the product of a very powerful and intelligent designer. Such behavior against believers is reprehensible. I believe, however, that efforts to "prove" design scientifically are doomed to failure, although I respect those who make the effort. I believe that our energy should not be turned to forcing design into high-school curricula. Rather, we should take the opportunity, through science, to show to any who will consider that *"The heavens declare the glory of God; the skies proclaim the work of his hands. Day after day they pour forth speech; night after night they display knowledge"* (Psalms 19:1-2).

—John Oakes, PhD

QUESTION:

I just finished reading an article you wrote regarding the "evidence" for an intelligent designer. I found it so intellectually dishonest that it inspired me to write you. I hope that someday you come to see the "folly" that comes with accepting ideas such as the Anthropic Principle. Someday, I think you will see that the universe does not exist for our benefit, but rather that we exist more or less in spite of its seeming "brutality." I believe that life exists more or less within a balance of harmony and disharmony and without the need for an intelligent designer offering us support. There simply is no evidence for the existence of such a being in spite of the clear evidence we have for needing such support. Can I disprove his existence? No, but then again, the burden of proof does not lie with me, right? Tell me, what major discovery or explanation for how the universe operates was made assuming an intelligent designer? Is it not clear from the Bible and other religious texts that this same "intelligent" designer inspired man to write down erroneous statements regarding the nature of the universe? Was God simply "checking" to see if we were doing some thinking of our own and not relying on his servants Moses or Joshua for our modern view of biology and astronomy? Certainly, there are things that were written which were later supported by the evidence, but it's a mixed bag to say the least. To say that our existence within this universe clearly points to intelligent design would be a highly dishonest statement. Instead, I ask you to make a hypothesis that can be tested to prove or disprove this Anthropic Principle.

ANSWER:

Let me share with you a couple examples of discoveries which were made by assuming an intelligent designer. The first example is science itself. If you read the writings of Roger Bacon, Nikolai Copernicus, William of Ockham, Galileo and any of the very early philosophers of science, what you will find is that their starting point was the assumption that the universe is ordered, based on their belief in a single, unchanging God. In other words, the origin of belief in order and predictability in nature was belief in God—in the Anthropic Principle. It is fair to say that this prediction has proven to be true. To take it farther, based on his concept of God and of beauty, Roger Bacon predicted in the 13th century that nature would follow mathematically precise laws. Again, this prediction was proved true over time. I believe the reason his prediction has proved true is that the assumption he based his prediction on—namely, that there is a single, unchanging God who created an orderly universe—is true.

You will find in my essay, if you read it carefully, that I freely state that the Anthropic Principle is not strictly "scientific" because it is not refutable and because it cannot be used to predict the results of specific experiments. I am being quite intellectually honest here. Given that I make such an open admission, I am confused that you accuse me of being intellectually dishonest. In fact, you accuse me of making "a highly dishonest statement." Which statement is highly dishonest?

Let me make a "scientific" prediction using the Anthropic Principle. Here we go. In the next few decades, scientists will discover dozens of additional facts/constants about how the physical world works which, by "coincidence," happen to have what seem to be ideal values in order for advanced life forms to exist.

Let me make another prediction using the Anthropic Principle. This one is more specific, so it probably comes closer to being a hypothesis. In the next generation or so, neuroscientists will discover that the human brain is amazingly "designed" (to use a biased term) to allow humans to have religious/spiritual experiences. They will discover a number of facts about brain chemistry, structure and function which have relatively little evolutionary advantage, but which are of great relevance to the experience of "spiritual" reality.

I absolutely agree with you that the burden of proof for belief in God is on the believer. I have stated that many times in many places, including in my books. You are right about this.

It is my understanding that the Anthropic Principle is literally the only principle by which we can explain why the universe we live in has the properties it has. Of course, it is also possible that there is no reason for the universe to have the properties it has. It is possible that it is completely random. I will freely admit (and I do so in the article you read) that I cannot scientifically prove the Anthropic Principle. Nevertheless, the Anthropic Principle is clearly consistent with the data. For you to say that I am intellectually dishonest, you must show evidence that my thinking is not consistent with the data. The amazing good luck of having a nuclear strong force exactly tuned to allow both hydrogen and heavier elements to exist, the long list of unique properties which water and no other molecule has—without which there would be no life, the precision with which the energy of the big bang is matched to the gravitational force in order to allow for long-lived stars to form—all of these do not prove the Anthropic Principle in the sense that a scientific experiment can support the law of gravity. However, the fact is that the design worldview is in dramatic agreement with the facts. Is it possible that this is all just luck? I suppose so. However, this requires a coincidence of such magnitude that atheist physicists have been forced to speculate that there are an infinite number of universes. Now that is unjustified speculation. I say that to reach the conclusion that the laws of nature are not designed to allow advanced life to exist shows greater evidence of unclear, intellectually dishonest reasoning, given the evidence. Just four years ago Michael Flew, the world's most renowned atheist, "converted" to deism because of the power of the Anthropic Principle. Of course, his change of mind does not prove anything. However, if you read his reasoning, I challenge you to accuse him of being intellectually dishonest.

You imply that the Bible contains many erroneous scientific statements. I have studied the Bible carefully for many years. I have a PhD in chemical physics. Thus far, I have failed to find incontrovertible scientific errors in the Bible. It is easy to say that there are many erroneous scientific statements in the Bible. It is much harder to come up with examples of such errors.

It is not an intellectually dishonest statement to say that the universe shows evidence of design. In fact, I believe that for a scientifically well-informed person to claim that there is not good evidence of design in the universe requires a great degree of bias. I will not go so far as to call this dishonest thinking, but it requires one to explain away a lot of undisputable facts.

QUESTION:

Should oxygen be on your list (along with carbon) of elements whose properties are required for life?

ANSWER:

Yes, this element has unique properties, without which advanced life forms, in need of a very efficient metabolic source of energy, would not be possible. In fact, one can go through the periodic table and make arguments for the absolutely essential need for many of the elements in order for life to exist. One could mention iron, with its magnetic properties, which are essential to protecting the Earth from very harmful cosmic particles. One could mention lithium and beryllium, which play unique roles in creating carbon, nitrogen and oxygen in stars. The uniquely long lasting radioactivity of uranium is required for earth to have a viable atmosphere. One could mention nitrogen and, of course, oxygen as playing unique and absolutely essential roles allowing life to exist. The need for a pair of ions such as potassium and sodium to regulate nerve impulses, the role of helium in allowing for release of nuclear energy... one could go on. As a chemist, when I look at the periodic chart of the elements, I see the fingerprint of God all over it.

About oxygen, it has a couple of properties which are absolutely essential to the existence of complex life forms in the universe which no other element has. First of all, oxygen is the only element which has two stable molecular forms which exist as gases. One of these is ozone, with the formula O_3. Ozone is the only gaseous substance with sufficient ability to absorb the short ultraviolet radiation which reaches the Earth from the sun. Without the ozone layer, hard UV rays from the sun would reach the Earth with sufficient intensity to destroy all life on land and near the surface of the ocean (with the possible exception of some bacteria which are UV resistant). No oxygen, no ozone, no complex life.

Of course, the more common form of oxygen is diatomic O_2. This molecule is unique and has essential properties as well. It is the element which sustains combustion, which allows humans to live in cold areas. More importantly, it is the element whose reaction with molecules provides almost all the energy for animal life. It was only when photosynthesis began on the Earth that sufficient oxygen was found in the atmosphere, and only then could a metabolic pathway arise which releases sufficient energy for complex animal life to function. Yes, you can add oxygen to your list of elements which has at least one property unique to that element, without which life would not exist.

QUESTION:

Why did God create the other planets? Also, if stars are meant to give us light, what about other stellar phenomena such as nebulae and black holes? Why did God create such seemingly unnecessary things?

ANSWER:

In the final analysis, I cannot speak for God about why he created planets. However, when scientists look at nature, a pattern emerges. It appears that everywhere we look, there are signs that nothing about how nature works is accidental. Nearly every observable phenomenon is essential to life or is caused by a property of the universe which is essential to life. The forces of nature appear designed to allow advanced life forms to exist. This explanatory rule is known as the Anthropic Principle. Like I already said, I am not in a position to answer the question of why God created other planets, but it just so happens that the existence of other planets in our solar system provides another good example of the Anthropic Principle of design because their existence is essential to protecting life on the Earth.

When God designed the universe, one of the forces he created was gravity. It is this force which causes the "stuff" of interstellar media to condense in order to produce stars. As the material which forms stars collapses toward a center, some of it does not end up in the central star. This is fortunate for us; otherwise there would be no Earth to live on. Life requires a very hot source of energy, but life cannot exist in the hot place where the energy is produced. The extra material surrounding the star coalesces by the same gravity force which produced the star to form planets. What I am saying is that the universe was created in such a way that the formation of stars and planetary systems was inevitable. Evidence gathered by astronomers in the past ten years has revealed what we expected to see. It is now known that it is a common thing for planets to circle stars. Hundreds have been observed in the past few years.

There is an anthropic aspect to the other planets in our particular star/planet system. For the inner planets, most of the lighter elements such as hydrogen and helium are lost due to the higher temperature and the smaller size of the inner planets. The atmosphere of the Earth is composed of somewhat heavier molecules such as nitrogen, oxygen and carbon dioxide, all of which are necessary to sustain advanced life forms. The outer planets are much larger and colder. These larger planets provide gravitational protection for the inner planets, including the Earth. Astronomers tell us that without the much larger planets such as Saturn and Jupiter, the Earth would be subject to occasional collisions with large asteroids. By occasional, I mean every few million years, not every few years. Nevertheless, if it were not for the protective presence of the gas giants, catastrophic collisions by asteroids would have wiped out all or nearly all advanced life forms on the Earth a number of times. In fact, it was the impact of an asteroid, slipping past the gravitational protection of the outer planets sixty-five million years ago, which is believed to have wiped out the dinosaurs and about 80% of all species. The impact of the Chixlub Asteroid, which struck in the Yucatan Peninsula of Mexico, has been identified as the cause of this destruction. So you can see that, although God did not tell us why he created other planets, there is wisdom in his plan as he created laws of nature which provide for other planets to protect the one on which he created life.

You also ask about black holes. I would add supernovae to the list. According to the laws of physics, the existence of black holes and the occurrence of supernovae (stars which explode spectacularly, creating and throwing heavier elements out into interstellar space) are an inevitable consequence of the formation of certain types of very massive stars. It is now believed that the formation of spiral galaxies depends on the presence of super massive black holes at the center of these swirling galaxies. If there were no black holes we would not be here. If it were not for supernova events, stars with a sufficient concentration of heavier elements (necessary to form life) would not have been created. Supernovae are required to create all the elements heaver than carbon. Of course, life could not exist without some of the heavier elements such as iron, copper and uranium. As a physicist, I see great wisdom in God's plan to create the universe with its wonderful natural laws. Without black holes, supernovae and gas giant planets, we would not be here.

QUESTION:

If we all come from Noah, how are there so many different races?

ANSWER:

We do not know when the flood happened, but presumably it was at least several thousand years ago. I assume that human beings evolved the different "racial" characteristics over the past several thousand years. In a gene pool with a fairly broad genetic diversity, the physical characteristics which lead to the greatest survival rate will become dominant in an area in just a few generations. Clearly, darker skin is a strong survival trait in parts of the globe where the sun is nearly directly overhead at noon the entire year, as UV radiation causes skin cancer and other health problems for the light-skinned. In regions of the world where there is relatively little direct sunlight, very dark skin results in a chronically low level of vitamin

D, making lighter skin predominate over just a few generations in parts of the globe farther from the equator. Of course, skin color is not the whole story on "racial" characteristics, but you can assume that genetic diversity and natural selection has worked to produce the wide variety of physical characteristics you see in humans.

Some have claimed that the different races were created depending on which of Noah's sons they are descended from. My experience is that many of those making such claims are themselves racists. I see no scientific or biblical support for such a view of the races.

QUESTION:

Jeremiah 31:37 says, *"This is what the LORD says: 'Only if the heavens above can be measured and the foundations of the earth below be searched out will I reject all the descendants of Israel because of all they have done,' declares the LORD."* I am a physics grad student at UC Berkeley. From my studies, it seems that we have measured the heavens. We know the distances to the visible objects in the sky such as Andromeda Galaxy very accurately. We have put a mirror on the moon and measured the distance using a laser with great precision. We have penetrated the atmosphere and measured the cosmic microwave background radiation with astonishing accuracy. From my vantage point, we have essentially measured the heavens. Am I missing something here?

ANSWER:

First of all, when we interpret a particular passage in the Bible, it is important to bear in mind the kind of literature involved. Good hermeneutics demands that we do not interpret every part of the Bible by the same set of rules. It makes sense to interpret the clearly symbolic/apocalyptic language of parts of Daniel and Revelation differently from the straightforward history of the Samuels or Acts, which is to be interpreted differently from doctrinal passages such as Colossians, or emotional/poetic passages such as the Psalms or Song of Songs. The passage in Jeremiah you quote is clearly poetical. Jeremiah is not giving an authoritative statement about cosmology. This passage is not a source of doctrine, but an expression of love. Jeremiah is expressing an emotion from God toward his people.

Having said that, the idea behind what Jeremiah said in this passage just happens to be literally true. The universe remains to this day immeasurable. The universe does not end in the sense that a road has an end or the Milky Way Galaxy has an edge. If

Science and the Bible

cosmologist's models of the universe are correct, then the "size" of the universe will never be measured, despite the fact that we can measure the distance to the moon to within one meter (that was a really cool experiment). The universe is expanding at the speed of light and we are unable to see the edge, if it has one. Like you, I am impressed at the amount we have learned about how God set up this amazing universe we live in, but we will never "measure the heavens." Perhaps we will one day be able to literally drill to the center of the Earth, but I doubt it, as the center is too hot for any drill! Thus far, our knowledge of the "foundations of the earth" (a clearly poetic phrase) is based on conjecture, theory and indirect evidence from such data as earthquake waves.

I believe that God, through Jeremiah, is not trying to literally say that the universe is not capable of being measured by a yardstick, or that one cannot go to the center of the Earth. I believe Jeremiah is delivering a spiritual message through this beautiful poetry. Has God ever rejected all his people? No! Will he ever? No! That is the message of Jeremiah 31:37. Let us not take emotional poetry as literal fact unless the context demands such a thing. This is a basic rule of biblical interpretation.

QUESTION:

Can discoveries of self-replicating molecules explain how life began on the Earth? Can supercomputers calculate the probability?

ANSWER:

I try to keep up as much as possible with the new discoveries in evolutionary/molecular biology. I am not sure exactly which area of research into self-replicating molecules you refer to. For example, there are prions, which are the cause of Kreutzfeld-Jacob (mad cow) Disease. These molecules are not truly self-replicating, but when they are inside a living cell, they have the interesting (and dangerous) property of being able to direct the cell to replicate themselves. I am sure there are other examples of molecules which, in certain chemical environments, automatically make copies of themselves. I would need you to identify which system you refer to in order to give a specific response.

In the absence of a particular example from you, let me give a generic response to what I have seen to be out there. As far as I know, molecules are not truly self-replicating. They need to be in an environment with other complicated molecules in order to have the tools to reproduce themselves. DNA is not truly self-replicating because it requires the presence of protein molecules to be replicated. To use a crude analogy, one could imagine designing a robot which is able to make copies of itself, but someone would have to assemble the original robot. In the end, even if scientists discover a truly self-replicating molecule which can be built spontaneously out of much simpler molecules, it would not change my answer all that much. I believe if scientists find some sort of fairly simple self-replicating molecule, then that alone will not even begin to solve the problem of the origin of life. Life requires the existence of information. Do these self-replicating molecules have intelligent information in them? There is a detailed description of the problem of spontaneous generation of life in my book **ITAG** (ch. 4 and the appendix).

Let me give a brief summary of the problem of creation of life from self-replicating molecules. In order for life to be created by a spontaneous chemical accident, as atheists and scientists committed to materialist explanations assume, several things must happen which simply cannot happen. First of all, a genetic code capable of storing information would have had to have been created by accident. Second, molecules capable of storing that coded information would have had to have been created by chemical accident. Third, millions of pieces of information capable of creating an actual living thing would have to have been created spontaneously. Fourth, thousands of protein molecules, capable both of building these molecules and, in turn, being synthesized by these same coded DNA molecules, would have to have been created at the same time. All these tens of thousands of molecules would have to have come together inside a non-polar cell membrane bi-layer—all of this by accident. This is the extremely brief summary, but perhaps it gives you at least the beginning of the picture of what would have to happen for life to be created by random accident. Bottom line, this cannot happen. Life was created. If a biochemist were to discover some sort of presumably fairly simple self-replicating molecule, this would do nothing significant to bridge the gap required for the spontaneous generation of life.

You mention calculating the probability on a supercomputer. It is not possible to calculate the probability of an impossible event. Those who claim that a supercomputer can calculate the probability of a series of accidental but believable events producing a living thing are not telling the truth. Such a calculation would require a long series of speculative guesses which could not produce a believable number. Life was created by God. That is the end of the story, in my opinion.

Science and the Bible

QUESTION:
Does the Big Bang Theory contradict what the Bible says?

ANSWER:
As I would assume you know, this is a matter of opinion. More accurately, it is a matter of Bible interpretation, as the truth is not affected by human opinion. Since you asked, I will explain to you how I interpret the relevant biblical passages.

The Big Bang model was created by scientists, many of whom were predisposed to assume that the universe was not created. Physicists such as LeMaitre and Gamov created this theory because the evidence demanded it. The "red shift" of light approaching the Earth from very distant objects in the sky demonstrates clearly that the universe is expanding. The more distant objects from us are receding from us at a faster rate than those which are closer. This fact was discovered in the 1920s and 1930s by Hubble and Humason. Further evidence, including the discovery of a nearly homogeneous background microwave radiation which fills the universe (Penzias and Wilson, early 1960s), all points to the validity of the Big Bang model.

The Big Bang model implies that the universe was "created" as an unimaginably hot and dense flash of light which, as it expanded, cooled and condensed into the fundamental particles, and eventually into atoms, galaxies, stars and planets. What we can say for sure is that the Genesis creation account implied all along that the universe and everything in it were created at some point in the past. As the Hebrew writer put it, *"By faith we understand that the universe was formed at God's command, so that what is seen was not made out of what was visible."* (Hebrews 11:3) The universe we live in has not always existed according to the creation story in Genesis chapter one. Cosmologists caught up with this correct claim of the Bible in the 20th century. If our best scientific models are correct, the universe had a beginning. It was created as a super-dense flash of light. From this super-hot beginning, expansion led to cooling—which led to clumping of matter due to gravity—which led to the formation of galaxies and stars in those galaxies. As these stars exploded and reformed, heavier elements were created, allowing for rocky planets such as the Earth to form around second-generation stars such as our sun. As the Earth cooled, an atmosphere and a liquid ocean formed. As the "crust" further cooled, buckled and folded, allowing lighter silicate rock to rise above the oceans, life appeared in water first, followed by life on land.

The point of this description is that, in outline form, the

Genesis creation account is in good accord with science. Good accord, that is, if one allows for the "days" of creation to be eras of indefinite length, rather than literal 24-hour periods. Whether or not the literary and grammatical Hebrew context of Genesis allows for this interpretation is something for the experts in Hebrew to decide. My study has led me to believe that this is not an unreasonable interpretation of the text. I would suggest you pick up a copy of the book *Genesis, Science and History* by Douglas Jacoby (www.ipibooks.com). Dr. Jacoby goes into more detail than I am qualified to do with regard to both the theology and language of the Genesis creation account.

In summary, the Big Bang model was forced on scientists—believing or unbelieving—by the evidence. It just so happens that this model and the data we have is in general agreement with the Genesis creation account. This is in dramatic contrast to the "creation myths" of other cultures. Does this information (about the creation and expansion of the universe) contradict Genesis chapter one? I say no, but will freely acknowledge that others disagree with me on this. I will leave you to do a more in-depth study of the Hebrew scripture so that you can make your own decision.

QUESTION:
How does Carbon-14 dating work? I have heard that it is inaccurate, so it is unreliable to tell us the age of the Earth.

ANSWER:
Carbon-14 dating works on the basis of the fact that, in naturally-occurring carbon dioxide in the atmosphere, there is a very small but predictable level of the radioactive isotope of carbon, C-14. The rate at which radioactive particles are emitted from this element are very predictable, making it rather easy to measure the level of the isotope in a sample. The fact is that C-14 has a half-life of about 5,740 years. If one can assume that the level of C-14 in the air is approximately constant, then one can measure the amount of C-14 in any sample of organic matter and calculate how long ago the material was alive. The calculation and even the method are quite simple and are a standard technique used today to date archaeological finds. By the way, there are a number of cases in which archaeologists have been able to compare C-14 dates from materials created by events whose dates they are confident of for other reasons. They have discovered that the levels of C-14 are not constant. They have changed slightly, probably due to changes in the solar cycle. Scientists now make a small correction due to

this additional information. Having said this, isotope dating using carbon-14 is considered to be fairly reliable.

You should be aware that the method is only useful for relatively young samples. For objects more than about 30,000 years old, the level of C-14 is so low that the method is not useful. Therefore, Carbon-14 is not relevant to such issues as how old the Earth is, or how long ago such creatures as the dinosaurs lived or even of the most ancient early human remains. You imply in your question that this method is extremely inaccurate. That is simply not true. It is possible to take samples whose age we know from other sources (dates of pottery shards, dates of destruction of cities and so forth) and the method turns out to be accurate to within less than ten percent. Beyond about 3,000 years of age, the method has to become somewhat less certain simply because we do not have solid historical markers to compare, and because it is difficult to prove beyond a reasonable doubt that the C-14 levels have remained constant. Nevertheless, it is perfectly reasonable to assume that C-14 dating is at least acceptably accurate out to the maximum range of its effectiveness—about 30,000 years.

The persistent rumor that C-14 is an unreliable method is, unfortunately, at least partially supported by defensive "Christian" groups who are trying to defend a very recent creation date for the Earth. Whether or not the Earth is actually young or old will ultimately not be answered by C-14 dating, since it is only good to several thousand years, but it is unfortunate that Christians have made false statements about the reliability of C-14 dating because they are not willing to accept the implications of what we learn from this important scientific tool.

QUESTION:
Is there life on other planets?

ANSWER:
The answer to your question is really quite simple. I do not know. At this point, no one knows for sure about life on other planets, leaving the entire issue up to speculation.

But since it is a matter of speculation, and since I am a scientist, please bear with me as I give my opinion. First of all, there is at least some pretty good (but inconclusive) evidence for life having existed on Mars. A meteorite which was expelled from Mars was found several years ago in Antarctica. NASA scientists studied this meteor carefully. We know it is from Mars from the isotopic abundance of certain elements in the rock which serves as a fingerprint to tell us which planet it came from. The rock is much younger than other Martian meteorites (1.5 versus 4.5 billion years). It contains certain iron compounds which are only known to form in nature in the presence of water. The meteorite also contains a class of organic compounds known as polycyclic aromatics which are typically only associated with water and with life. In addition, when the Martian meteor was studied under magnification, features which are identified as microfossils were seen in this rock. They look remarkably like micro bacillus bacteria. All this evidence has been carefully documented, but the conclusion that this proves life once existed on Mars is hotly debated by scientists. It is fair to say that the result is inconclusive.

Since NASA studied this interesting meteorite, the Mars Pathfinder has proved conclusively that Mars was once far wetter than it is today. Mars had a much thicker atmosphere, including carbon dioxide and enough water for liquid to stand on the surface. From this evidence we can conclude that the conditions on Mars (temperature, water, sufficient atmosphere) were once sufficient to support at least primitive life forms such as bacteria.

Given the established fact that a meteorite can travel from Mars to the Earth, I would assume that whether life began on the Earth or on Mars, the other planet would have been seeded eventually. Therefore, I am prepared to climb out on a limb and state that I believe life probably existed on Mars at one time. If I were a betting person, I would go so far as to bet that there is even life still there, buried under ground. We have found life buried thousands of feet under ground on the Earth, in Antarctica, at the bottom of the ocean and in hot springs with temperatures of 100 degrees centigrade. I believe that extremely simple life forms will eventually be found on Mars.

What about other planets, even planets on other stars in the Milky Way or in other galaxies? Given that God created life here, might he have created life elsewhere? It may be possible that life from a planet on one star could spontaneously seed planets on another star. It has not yet been proven, but the evidence is suggestive that there are other rocky planets in the universe with sufficient water and in the appropriate temperature range to support life. Let us just say that this is an interesting question, the answer to which we are simply not able to determine at this time.

In the end, whether or not life exists on other planets, it will have little if any impact on Christian belief. It is apparent that the universe was created with laws which allow for advanced life forms to exist. Whether or not God chose to create life on another planet or in another galaxy is a very interesting question to ponder, but it is one which we will not be able to answer. Presumably, if it were important, God would have told us.

QUESTION:
What did God say to Job about water molecules and where do I find it in the Bible?

ANSWER:
I am going to guess that the passage you are referring to is found in Job 36:27. Here, Elihu says, *"He draws up the drops of water, which distill as rain to the streams; the clouds pour down their moisture and abundant showers fall on mankind."* In this passage, Elihu appears to have knowledge of the water cycle, which was not "discovered" by modern science until the 19th century. This is one of many examples in which the Bible exhibits apparent knowledge of science about which the ancients were ignorant. It supports belief in the inspiration of the Bible. However, I do not believe one can accurately claim that Job or any other writer of the Old Testament showed knowledge of the existence of individual water molecules.

QUESTION:
What evidences are there on elements having a half-life? Is matter eternal?

ANSWER:
First, there are just less than 300 stable atomic isotopes. The atoms of these isotopes do not decay radioactively at all. According to science, they are "eternal." This is the scientific perspective, but from a theological point of view, this does not mean that the same omnipotent God who made the universe and all the matter in it could not do whatever he wants to with the matter he created! Such a thing, however, would be outside the range of discussion for scientists. Stable isotopes include Carbon-12, Nitrogen-14, Hydrogen-1 and 2, Helium-4 and so forth. In addition to these stable isotopes, there are some atoms with an unstable arrangement of neutrons and protons in their nuclei. Samples of these isotopes will be changed through radioactive decay into more stable isotopes, with the emission of alpha, beta, gamma or other particles in the process. Some of the more famous radioactive isotopes are Carbon-14 and Uranium-238. These unstable isotopes have a very predictable rate of decay which can be measured easily in a laboratory. They are said to have a half-life because no matter the size of the sample and no matter the

concentration of the isotope, and even no matter the temperature, the time it takes for half of a sample to decay to other isotopes is the same. For example, the half-life of Carbon-14 is about 5,700 years, while the half-life of Uranium-238 is 4.5 billion years.

In 1907, Ernest Rutherford proposed determining the age of a sample by measuring the concentration of both the original (parent) and final (daughter) isotope in a sample. Using this information and knowledge about the half-life, it is a simple matter to calculate the age of the rock or cloth sample, or whatever. Carbon-14 dating has been used to show that the famed Shroud of Turin was not the burial shroud of Jesus Christ, as it was created out of flax about AD 1200. Uranium-238 dating has been used to show that rocks in the crust of the Earth are as much as 4.15 billion years old.

Therefore, some atoms are "eternal" if you will, while other atoms are temporary. That is the scientific answer. Having said that, God can certainly do what he wants with the matter he created. Scientists can only discover the laws of nature which are obeyed under "normal" circumstances. God can break these laws any time he so chooses, especially since he created the laws of nature which scientists discover in the first place. If God says that at the end of times, *"the elements will be destroyed by fire,"* (2 Peter 3:10) I believe it.

Chapter Eight

Evolution

QUESTION:
Doesn't denying macroevolution fly in the face of much hard evidence and research? Isn't it simplistic and naïve of creationists to say that scientists such as Richard Dawkins and others are deceived about this?

ANSWER:
This is a very good question. The simple answer is "yes" and "no." If you are speaking of some of the "simplistic and naive arguments" of some sincere but scientifically uninformed creationists, then, yes, you have a good point. It is certainly true that some people treat the Theory of Evolution as a satanic force to be treated as the enemy of Christianity. This is not a wise way of dealing with one of the most successful ideas in science. There are some creationists who attack evolution without giving fair consideration to the predictive power of the theory or to the growing experimental evidence underpinning the evolutionary model. The solution to this problem is for us to avoid using simplistic and naïve arguments based more on our religious presuppositions than on the evidence.

Having said that, the answer is "no"—it is not necessarily true that criticisms of the evolutionary theory fly in the face of the evidence and research. It is definitely not "incredibly simplistic and naïve" to say that Dawkins is a deceived individual. Please let me explain. Richard Dawkins brings an assumption with him when he considers scientific evidence to explain the origin of species. Dawkins and many others like him assume out of hand that there cannot possibly be any supernatural intervention in the universe. When a person assumes that God does not exist and that life evolved by entirely "natural" processes, then we can be sure what that person's conclusion of the matter will be. Such circular reasoning is not an effective way to ask and answer the legitimate question of special creation. If, in fact, God does exist and if God has created different species in the past, then Dawkins and friends are sure to be deceived when they interpret the evidence.

A fairly thorough description of the underlying evidence for organic evolution is found in my book **ITAG** (ch. 9). To summarize extremely briefly, the genetic evidence generally supports the evolutionary model in that species which appear to be related by descent generally have genetic information similar enough to make the belief that they evolved from a single earlier ancestor a reasonable working assumption. The fossil evidence can go both ways on this question, but we can say that the fossil evidence provides at least some broad support for the idea of evolution over great periods of time as well.

Having said this, there is evidence which will cause any open-minded person to seriously question the pre-assumption of materialist explanation for the origins of all species from the first life. Dawkins himself has pointed out that the fossil record generally does not show the gradual change predicted by Darwin. In fact, the evidence reveals long periods of fairly small change and adaptation, followed by leaps of change, which puts the idea of evolution by natural, random mutation and natural selection in doubt as a way to explain the fossil evidence. Scientist such as Stephen Jay Gould and Niles Eldridge have proposed the idea of punctuated equilibrium in an attempt to explain the surprising nature of the fossil record. The fact is that, although there is quite a bit of evidence for evolution of existing species in the fossil record, the data generally supports sudden and very rapid "change," followed by long periods of fairly stable species. This is the little secret which Stephen Gould was a key figure in pointing out. The Theory of Evolution predicts generally that, as the fossil record grows, the gaps should fill in. The reality is that some of the gaps in the fossil record have been filled but many remain unexplained.

Another problem for the completely materialistic view of evolution is the Cambrian explosion of life. Evidence from paleontology implies this "explosion" happened about 540 million years ago. In this profusion of new life forms, all five animal body patterns appeared in virtually zero time geologically. No new body pattern (phyla) has since emerged. In 3.5 billion years of time over which life has existed on the Earth, all the animal phyla were created in essentially zero time, geologically. This suggests (but certainly does not prove) special creation. There were no complex animals before the Cambrian explosion. In fact, it is extremely difficult to conceive how the species in the fossil record before this explosion can serve as predecessor to the amazing flowering of species which followed.

A lot more can be said on this. It is fair to say that if one allows for at least the possibility of supernatural intervention, then one will find the fossil evidence to make a lot more sense. I believe that the available data can support the idea that different species have been created at different times in the past, after which these species changed gradually through a natural process we call evolution. The laws of thermodynamics tell us that almost certainly the original life form was created by divine intervention, but that is another story.

Please bear in mind that such a "theory" (special creation of species) is not "scientific." By definition, any supernatural explanation is not scientific. However, I believe that the evidence is consistent with allowing for divine creation of species.

I do not believe that we will ever be able to prove by experiment that different species were created. Supernatural creation is not subject to experiment. However, to assume that creation of life did not occur, and to proceed from that assumption to argue against creation of species, is to use circular reasoning. This is what Dawkins and others do. Such circular reasoning can lead to being deceived, especially if the assumption is not true.

Those who believe in creation should not be defensive. I do not deny that evolution has occurred. I believe that evolution is an elegant theory which can explain a great deal of the evidence. I do not deny that "macroevolution" (a word which is difficult to define) may have occurred, but I do deny that random natural forces are sufficient to explain either the existence of life itself or the evidence from the fossil record. I hope that my analysis of the evidence is neither simplistic nor naive. Having said that, I do not believe that Dawkins is simplistic or naïve either. However, I do believe that he is very biased against the possibility of divine influence in the origin of species, and that this bias causes him to miss the obvious. God's fingerprints are to be found in the origin of species.

No matter what your analysis of the data, for a scientist to say that "evolution is a fact" is deceptive. For one to say that evolution is a powerful theory which is our best scientific model to explain the existing evidence is to speak accurately. However, we cannot travel back in time. It will forever remain impossible to "prove" the claim that evolution by natural forces can explain the origin of all species.

QUESTION:

What about evolution? Is there any way evolution and the Bible can both be true?

ANSWER:

This is probably the most controversial question which relates to science and the Bible. In fact, many Bible believers have divided along the lines of this controversy. In addressing this question, one would do well to remember the words of Paul in 2 Timothy 2:23-24: *"Don't have anything to do with foolish and stupid arguments, because you know they produce quarrels. And the Lord's servant must not quarrel; instead, he must be kind to everyone, able to teach, not resentful."* We should not let this controversy divide us as believers, and we should not allow disagreement over this question to keep non-believers away from God

What about evolution? Is there any way evolution and the Bible can both be true? The answer will depend on your definition of evolution. If one takes as his or her definition the full-blown, atheist/naturalist version of evolution, the answer is perhaps no. The fully naturalist/materialist view of the origin of life and of evolution can be described something like this: In some early environment on the Earth, a living thing spontaneously arose from inorganic matter by a random, natural process without any interference by a supernatural power. This original one-celled life form was transformed through a fully random, natural process of evolution into every species of plant, animal and so forth which has ever inhabited the Earth.

I believe the first half of this naturalistic assumption can be shown to be scientifically untenable. No scientist has been able to put forward a believable model by which random processes could produce a living thing, and I personally believe they will never be able to do so. Whether or not the second half of this statement, the hypothesis of common descent without the intervention of God, is scientifically possible is more debatable. Nevertheless, if it is true, then it seems that there is no obvious way that the fully naturalistic neo-Darwinist evolutionary assumption can be reconciled with the Bible. Genesis chapter one, and indeed the Bible as a whole, creates the clear impression that life was created by the supernatural

Evolution

command of God. Genesis one also seems to imply that, at different times, God created various "kinds" (to use the non-technical Hebrew term) of plants, animals and so forth. Again, this certainly seems to be irreconcilable with the fully materialist view described above.

So the completely naturalistic creation of life and evolution of that simple life form into human beings seems, at least on the face of it, to be incompatible with the Bible. A better question, perhaps, is whether a belief in macro-evolution is compatible with what the Bible teaches. The answer will depend on one's view of Genesis one. If one interprets Genesis chapter one to imply an Earth only a few thousands of years old (one which was created in six literal 24-hour periods), then the answer is a definite no. There is no way that any really significant evolutionary change could occur in such a short time frame. Perhaps a dog could have "evolved" from wolves in that time frame, but certainly humans and chimps could not have evolved from some common primate ancestor in that amount of time, never mind mammals from fish.

If, on the other hand, one allows for the "days" of Genesis chapter one to represent great periods of time, then a significant amount of evolution by random mutation and natural selection may be consistent with the Bible. The question of the actual mechanism by which evolution occurs would still remain, but that would be something for the scientists to solve. The fact is that the fossil record can be seen to be consistent with a group of trees rather than a single tree of evolution. In other words, the fossil record is consistent with the possibility that the Creator produced various species at various times in the distant past of the Earth, followed by evolution of those created species. In fact, Darwin himself, in his earlier editions of Origin of Species, allowed for the possibility that there may have been a number of different original species. The most well known example in the fossil record of species seeming to appear virtually out of nothing on geological timescales is what is known as the Cambrian explosion. In the fossil record paleontologists have discovered that 540 million years ago all five animal body forms found on the earth appeared in the fossil record, with no obvious precursors, in virtually zero time.

Do cats and lions have a common ancestor? Almost certainly they do. Genetic information certainly supports this conclusion. Could all fish have evolved from some sort of original created fish? Quite likely they did. Did the original one-celled organism evolve into human beings? The Bible seems to say no, but we cannot rule out the possibility that the means by which God created all the "kinds" in Genesis one is through an evolutionary process. At first glance common descent seems to be ruled out by Genesis one, but, given that the creation account is not intended to be a scientific treatise, perhaps common descent can be seen to be consistent with the first chapter of Genesis. God created every "kind," but how did he do it? Might evolution be a guided, theistic, but largely natural process? The fact remains that the Bible does not answer each of these questions in detail. Therefore, it is wise for individuals to investigate the question carefully and reach their own conclusions, but to not be overly dogmatic about areas which are debatable.

This is obviously only a cursory introduction to answering this question. Let me suggest a few references which may be helpful. These authors take a variety of positions on the question you raise.

Gerald L. Schroeder, *The Science of God.*
Michael J. Denton, *Nature's Destiny.*
Michael J. Denton, *Evolution, a Theory in Crisis.*
Darrel Falk, *Coming to Peace With Science.*
Francis Collins, *The Language of God.*
Denis Lamoreux, *Random Designer.*

QUESTION:
What is your take on mitochondrial Eve?

ANSWER:
My take on "mitochondrial Eve" is that there is evidence that all human beings are related by direct descent to a single female progenitor from about 200,000 years ago. The fact which forms the basis of this theory is that all humans have virtually identical mitochondrial DNA. The mitochondria are the principle energy-producing organelles in all animal cells. Mitochondria have their own DNA which is passed from parent to daughter cell, independent of sexual reproduction. Unlike in meiosis, crossing over of genetic material between parents does not occur during this process. Sperm do not carry mitochondria, so the mitochondrial DNA is passed directly from mother to child, whether the child is male or female. Since the rate of "evolution" of mitochondrial DNA can be estimated by looking at isolated human populations, scientists can provide a rough estimate for the age of this first theoretical mother of the current human race. This can be done by looking at the amount of variation in human mitochondria today, which gives us the apparent amount of evolution in mitochondrial DNA which has happened.

This result may have relevance to the Genesis creation account. However, it is my opinion that we should be careful not to push the science in the Genesis account too far. We do not know when Adam and Eve lived. How does the flood fit into this? Might the mitochondrial date be used to support the Genesis account? Perhaps, but we should be very cautious about this. Evolutionists will tell us that there may have been a bottleneck in human population in the distant past, and that the apparent mitochondrial age reflects this bottleneck, certainly not special creation of Adam and Eve. The mitochondrial Eve data is one of those "hmmmm…" sort of facts which just so happen to be in at least a broad agreement with biblical claims but certainly does not prove them.

QUESTION:
How do you know evolution isn't real?

ANSWER:
The answer is that I do not know it isn't real. Evolution happens. It is real. We know this from experiment. Scientists have studied very simple life forms such as bacteria and viruses and observed them "evolving" in the laboratory. By doing genetic studies, they can infer (but perhaps not directly observe in the laboratory) evolution in higher plants and animals. I do not know what you have been taught, but let me inform you that evolution is very real. The definition of evolution is "change." Through random interchanges of DNA and through mutation, the average genetic pool of a given species changes with time. This is evolution. It is not the message of the devil, designed to destroy your faith in the Bible. It is a conclusion one can reach by looking at the evidence.

[Note: the original answer to this question repeats much of that from the previous two given here, so much of it is being skipped, to give the conclusion to this question.]

So, evolution is real, but blind, random, non-theistic evolution is not sufficient to explain the evidence we have at hand, especially from the fossil record. As a scientist, I do my best to maintain an open mind. However, I believe, first, that the evidence for special creation of life is overwhelming; second, that evolution is real—it really happens; and third, that the evidence in support of fully non-theistic evolution is inconclusive.

QUESTION:
Was Darwin an atheist, an agnostic or a Christian? I grew up, like most American Christians, assuming he was an enemy of Christianity. The Christian "right," such as Orrin Hatch, John Ashcroft and Pat Robertson, demonize Darwin to make political advantage.

Then I learned that he was educated to be an Anglican priest. In addition, there is the story of his death-bed conversion and his sister's denial of the whole thing. Now I am questioning my assumptions. Why do people make such a big deal out of this? It seems to not be important to us personally.

ANSWER:

Of course, I agree that both sides in the evolution debate use and abuse Darwin as they like. Darwin was relatively quiet about his religious convictions. It is interesting to note that the founding fathers of the United States were deists/Universalists, not necessarily Christians. Noted deists include Benjamin Franklin, Thomas Jefferson, George Washington and Alexander Hamilton. Deists define God as the Creator, but are not usually tied down to any single concept of God. Perhaps Darwin was a believer in God in the later point of his life, but if so the evidence is that he may have been a deist, but not a Christian. He was a skeptic with regard to the Bible. I assume he also was a skeptic about Jesus being the Son of God and about his resurrection from the dead. Everything I have read about Darwin leads me to believe he was a very good person and I'm not surprised that, at his death, some religious people expressed a profound respect of Darwin. I believe his life warranted that kind of respect.

Having said this, unless I am wildly mistaken, Darwin was not a Christian by any definition of the word which could be made to align with the Bible. For me, the label Christian implies faith in the divinity of Jesus and in his bodily resurrection. By coincidence, just today in my Science 110 class, I read a quote from Darwin very similar to the one you allude to. Darwin freely acknowledged the beauty and order in nature, and often made comments which could be described as deistic. Let us not abuse Darwin, but give a reasonable and honest interpretation of him, which is to say that from what he wrote he seems to have wavered between agnosticism and deism. He was definitely not a Christian, at least in the last 30 years or so of his life. Those at his funeral could proclaim him a "good Christian," but in so doing, they did not make it true.

Of course, I agree with you that the religion of Darwin is not really all that relevant to anything, except possibly his eternal destiny, which is not any of our business anyway. That is between him and God.

I, too, find the reactionary position of many believers in Christ to be very disturbing. Creationism (by that I mean young-Earth creationism) is somewhat questionable theology and it is bad science. It makes Christianity look foolish when it is presented as being "Christian" science. Believe me—being an apologist, and having written books on the subject, I face very strong creationists on a regular basis. Such people are occasionally irrational in their defense of the literal interpretation of certain passages. Let us find a way to argue this non-essential question with respect, patience and love, not with dogmatic declarations.

Chapter Nine

The Genesis Flood

QUESTION:
Did the flood in Genesis 6-9 really happen? If so, was it a worldwide flood or just a local phenomenon in Mesopotamia? Is there any evidence for the flood happening?

ANSWER:
This question has certainly brought about a lot of debate over the years. Many have scoffed at the "myth" of the flood in the time of Noah. One reason many intellectuals scoff at the story of the flood is they have a predisposition to assume that supernatural events cannot and do not happen. It is easy to see that, if one assumes before even examining the question that miraculous, supernatural events do not happen, then one will end by assuming that the flood never happened.

However, the flood is an inescapable part of the inspired word of God—the Bible. Jesus did not hesitate to accept it as a literal event which actually happened (Matthew 24:38). Neither did Peter (2 Peter 2:5) or the writer of Hebrews (Hebrews 11:7). Should the Bible believer accept the flood as literal truth as well? We should at least be open-minded enough to check out the evidence. If the worldwide flood recorded in Genesis actually happened, there might be some evidence of the event which one could point to. If one were to search for evidence consistent with the flood, what could one expect to find?

Some claim that the flood created most of the sedimentary layers on the Earth—up to 25,000-feet thick in places. They claim, for example, that all the layers which can be observed at the Grand Canyon were laid down in a single, universal flood, and that the canyon itself was carved out as the waters of that single flood receded. This claim is not credible. In fact, if a universal flood occurred, it would, at most, redistribute a significant part of the top soil, sand and gravel at the surface of the Earth, leaving perhaps as much as a few dozen feet of mud in some places and eroded top-soil in others. Therefore, the physical signs of a great, worldwide flood in any single location would be similar to those of a major local flood. In Mesopotamia, flood layers up to 15 feet thick have been discovered. Some have attributed these to the flood in the days of Noah. This may well be, but it is difficult to prove, as major floods occur naturally in Mesopotamia from time to time.

If physical evidence will (probably) remain unconvincing, what evidence does one look for to confirm or deny the flood described in Genesis? One significant fact is that nearly every ancient culture has a record of a great flood. Traditions of a singularly massive flood are found in cultures in Australia, China, Egypt, Sub-Saharan Africa, Mesopotamia, North, Central, South America and Europe. No other ancient event is remembered in every part of the globe. This fact is very strongly suggestive that some sort of great, worldwide flood actually happened. Due to their presupposition against the possibility of a supernatural event, most intellectuals are extremely unlikely to accept this hypothesis.

Although the common record of a great flood from every region of the globe is quite suggestive, it is worth remembering that ultimately, for the Bible believer, faith in the account of the flood in Genesis is based primarily on belief that the entire Bible is inspired by God. The Old Testament has many marks of inspiration by the Creator. Peter reminded his readers (2 Peter 3:5-7) that the ground for belief in the return of Jesus is the same as the reason for belief in the flood. Both are based on the Word of God.

Another common question about the flood is whether it was truly worldwide. One answer is that the account in Genesis certainly seems to imply that it was. In Genesis seven, one can find the words "every" and "all" used throughout. Besides, as already pointed out, there is a similar record of a great flood found in every part of the globe, lending credence to its being worldwide in its effect. Some have proposed the "Local Flood Theory" to explain the Genesis flood account. The idea is that the flood of Noah was a massive flood in the Mesopotamian area only. The problem with this theory is that there is no reasonable way to explain how the water could rise so high for 150 days only in Mesopotamia, without spreading to surrounding areas. The Local Flood Theory creates more problems than it solves, which is a good reason to reject it. Others have proposed pseudo-naturalistic explanations of the flood such as the "Canopy Theory." This is the theory that, in the early Earth, there was a massive canopy of water in the upper atmosphere which was released in the flood. This theory is easily dismissed as it defies several well-known physical laws.

In the final analysis, the flood described in Genesis is clearly a miraculous event. It is plainly described as a judgment for mankind's sins. Any attempt to find some sort of "natural" explanation is bound to fail. Exactly how God caused the flood we do not know. Unfortunately, many possible questions about the flood will probably remain unanswered. Did literally every kind of animal come to the ark? What happened to the water? Could the flood have been worldwide in effect but leave at least some creatures behind in various parts of the world? Did God recreate certain species after the flood? Because the Bible does not provide specific answers to some of these questions, one can speculate, but it is unwise to be dogmatic about any one specific opinion. More on this can be found in **ITAG** ch. 10.

QUESTION:

If Noah's Ark landed on Mt. Ararat, how did animals get to North and South America?

ANSWER:

I am afraid I am going to have to plead ignorance on this one. You ask a very good question which is very difficult to know how to answer. Because you ask the question, I assume you already see the difficulty of explaining how animals could have attained their present distribution in the world if the only living species after the flood were in the ark. For example, I see absolutely no way that a koala bear could migrate from Australia to get on the ark, nor any way for the koala to make its way back to Australia after the flood, leaving behind no koalas anywhere besides Australia. It is simply impossible for koalas to swim across the ocean. Besides, the land-bridge argument definitely does not work because there is no route from Asia to Australia which does not involve crossing very deep water. I have thought of two possible explanations of the current distribution of animals on the Earth, assuming the flood story in Genesis is true, neither of which I can prove from the Bible or from any other source of evidence.

1. One possibility is that, after the flood, God miraculously recreated the animals in places such as South America and Australia, animals which were wiped out in the flood and obviously could not migrate to the ark to be saved. By this picture, the animals on the ark with Noah and his family were those which lived within some sort of reasonable distance from the ark. Again, I cannot prove this claim, and the Bible does not say that this is what happened. I just believe it is a reasonable explanation of the facts which would also agree with what the Bible says.

2. Another possibility is that when Genesis describes a worldwide flood, it is indeed true that the flood had a worldwide effect, killing off animals across the surface of the Earth, but that the destruction was not absolutely total—leaving at least some remnant populations in different parts of the world. I personally do not like this explanation as well as the first, as it calls into question (at least to some extent) some pretty clear statements in Genesis chapters seven and eight which picture a flood that wiped out literally all creatures. However, I do not think I can rule it out. It is possible that God was describing the flood in general terms, but not mentioning some details such as some survivors in different places.

In the end, it is hard to make an absolutely clear and unambiguous statement in answer to your question. You will need to reach your own conclusion. By the way, there is a third explanation of the Genesis account. This option is that it is just a myth and that one cannot expect it to agree with evidence, because it simply did not happen. I reject this view for several reasons. First, the Bible has proven itself to be inspired by God through such a mountain of evidence that, when I am confronted with a question I cannot answer definitively, I give the Bible the benefit of the doubt. I accept on faith, based on the great volume of evidence of inspiration, that the parts of the Bible I cannot prove by evidence are also inspired. Second, there is some evidence of this flood (see the previous question and answer). I do not believe the Genesis flood is a myth.

QUESTION:

Some argue that Noah's flood was only local. What's your view on this?

ANSWER:

In my experience, those who have proposed a local flood have done so in order to provide some sort of reasonable, semi-natural explanation of the flood, making it more easily acceptable to skeptics of the Bible flood story. The problem with these attempts is that, in general, they create more problems than they cause. The Bible, in Genesis 6-8, describes a flood of massive proportions which lasted for about half a year. Even if one were to not take absolutely literally that the water covered the entire Earth as high as Mt. Everest, one is clearly and unavoidably left with the impression from the flood account that this involved an unprecedented amount of water which covered the ground to a great depth: *"For forty days the flood kept coming on the earth, and as the waters increased they lifted the ark high above the earth"* (Genesis 7:17).

In order for water to cover Mesopotamia to a depth sufficient to lift the ark high above the Earth for more than 150 days, it would be physically impossible for the flood to be strictly a local event. Gravity does not allow for this. The only possible way this explanation can work is for God to have put some sort of wall around the area, allowing the water to rise locally but not spill out to other areas. This argument violates Ockham's Razor—the rule that the simpler explanation of a phenomenon is usually the correct one. It is simpler and more reasonable to simply accept that if the flood story is true, then the flood affected the Earth on a massive scale. This requires that the flood involved a miraculous creation of water and the later miraculous removal of the water. It is not surprising that atheists and Bible critics, in general, have a problem with this. However, for those who believe in the awesome, divine power of God and who accept the Bible to be the inspired Word of God, the idea of God judging the world through water is reasonable.

I prefer not to be dogmatic on such things, but that is how I understand it.

QUESTION:

When God destroyed the Earth with a great flood, all the creatures of the ground and air were destroyed (Genesis 7:22-23), but what about the creatures of water? Were they also destroyed?

ANSWER:

There is no evidence in Genesis that creatures which lived in water were destroyed wholesale by the flood—be they fresh or saltwater life. It would not be surprising at all that salt water creatures were able to survive, as their environments were affected, but not drastically. Fresh-water creatures would be able to survive a massive flood as well, even if they cannot tolerate salty water. This is true because the fresh rain- water would flow downhill. Because fresh water is considerably less dense than salt water, it can exist on top of salt water without mixing for a considerable time. There is no mention of sea creatures being on the ark because there was no need for these animals to find refuge there.

QUESTION:

How could Noah's ark have contained two of every single creature? There are many, many different species in the world.

ANSWER:

You ask a question which has no easy answer. Any answer will involve some speculation, so forgive me as I speculate!

First, your claim is certainly true. There are literally millions of species on the Earth. Estimates vary widely on the total number of species, because one can assume there are more waiting to be discovered than have been described to date. In any case, even if one were to count only land-animal species, and even if one were to exclude insects, worms and other rather simple land animals, every single species of mammal, bird, reptile and amphibian could not have fit on the ark at one time.

Given this fact, one is left with two possible views. One possibility is that the flood account is a myth; or at best, a gross exaggeration. The other view is that it is not to be taken in the fullest possible literal sense. In other words, not "literally" every creature was on the ark. Personally, I am convinced, through an overwhelming body of evidence, that the Bible is inspired by God. In addition, I note that the same man who rose from the dead on the third day, Jesus Christ, also believed that this flood happened: *"As it was in the days of Noah, so it will be at the coming of the Son of Man. For in the days before the flood, people were eating and drinking, marrying and giving in marriage, up to the day Noah entered the ark; and they knew nothing about what would happen to them until the flood came and took them all away"* (Matthew 24:37-39). For these reasons, I am compelled to believe that the flood really did happen. I just need to try to understand what happened to the animals which were not on the ark, given that God did not tell us.

A possible explanation of the seeming inconsistency between the most straightforward literal interpretation of the flood account

The Genesis Flood

and the facts of science with regard to the numbers and distribution of animals might be that the ark only contained local animals and that God somehow recreated or protected other animals from complete destruction. The Bible is trustworthy, but it does not answer every question we can ask. You may have to think about this one yourself and decide what the most reasonable conclusion is in light of what you know. It is good to remember that the exact resolution is not particularly significant to how we lead our lives in submission to the Creator. Having said this, it is a good idea to bear in mind the words of Jesus in Matthew 24. As the people in the days of Noah, we need to be prepared for Jesus to come back: *"At that time the sign of the Son of Man will appear in the sky, and all the nations of the earth will mourn. They will see the Son of Man coming on the clouds of the sky, with power and great glory. And he will send his angels with a loud trumpet call, and they will gather his elect from the four winds, from one end of the heavens to the other...As it was in the days of Noah..."* (Matthew 24:30-31, 37).

QUESTION:

How do you explain the similarities between the Babylonian Gilgamesh Epic and the flood account in the Bible?

ANSWER:

First of all, let us acknowledge that there are significant similarities between the *Gilgamesh Epic* and the flood account in Genesis, which seem to defy coincidence. For example, in Gilgamesh, a god speaks to a man named Utnapishtim in a dream, telling him to construct a boat because of a great flood which is coming. Although the stories are not identical (for example, when God spoke to Noah, it was not in a dream), there is obvious parallel to the biblical flood account. In the Gilgamesh Epic, Utnapishtum took his family and some friends, as well as many animals, on the boat. Again, one can see parallels but also differences in the accounts. To deny any possible common root to these two flood stories seems unrealistic.

There are five logical explanations I can think of for the admittedly striking similarities between the two accounts:

1. It is coincidence.
2. They are completely separate records of an actual event (even if semi-mythical as described by the Babylonians).
3. The Jews borrowed their account from the Babylonians.
4. The Babylonians borrowed from a more primitive and accurate flood story, which was also the source of the Jewish story.

5. The Babylonians borrowed from the Jewish flood story.

I reject explanation number one as defying believability. The Gilgamesh Epic has a flood coming from a god as a judgment for man's fall. It also has a family and their animals entering a boat to be saved from the flood. Perhaps most telling, the Noah character in the Gilgamesh Epic, Utnapishtim, sends out three birds to know when the flood had subsided. He sent a dove and a swallow which did return, followed by a raven which did not return because it found a home. Once reaching dry land, Utnapishtim offered a sacrifice to the gods. There is too much in common between the Gilgamesh Epic and the biblical flood account for coincidence to be a reasonable explanation.

For chronological reasons, I hesitate to accept explanation #5, but I cannot absolutely rule it out, as Abraham lived around 1850 BC. The Gilgamesh Epic was written down in ancient Akkadian, somewhere around 2000 BC, according to scholars. We do not know how far back the Hebrew account of the flood goes, perhaps as an oral tradition.

Between explanations 2-4, I prefer explanations #2 or #4, as the Hebrew account has less of the feel of a classic myth. The superior story cannot be borrowed from the inferior story. For example, the Gilgamesh Epic has a number of gods disagreeing over the fate of Utnapishtim. After the flood, Utnapishtim and his wife become like gods, and are transferred "to the mouth of the rivers." For this reason, it does not make sense to me that the Jews borrowed straight from Gilgamesh. That the Jews may have worked from a more primitive and accurate source makes more sense to me. I will admit to you that my predisposition to believe that the Bible is inspired may cause my interpretation of the information to be biased. I am sure you can reach your own conclusion! It is my belief that God influenced, by inspiration, the Genesis account of the flood. The point is that Gilgamesh has all the marks of a myth. The Genesis flood account has a very different feel to it. It has the feel of a realistic human story. The similarity between the Gilgamesh Epic and Genesis 6-8 cannot be coincidental, but the superior account is that of the Jews, without a doubt, at least in my opinion.

QUESTION:

Did Israel receive "Noah's flood story" from the Babylonians while in captivity? I recently saw a documentary which made this claim.

The Genesis Flood

ANSWER:
I am assuming that this documentary was referring to the *Gilgamesh Epic*. As to the Israelites receiving the story from the Neo-Babylonians while in captivity, I find this explanation very unlikely for a few reasons. First of all, the *Gilgamesh Epic* circulated in the time of the first Babylonian Empire, about 1800 BC, not during the Neo-Babylonian Empire under Nebuchadnezzar, around 600 BC. Second, there is sufficient evidence to conclude that the book of Genesis was written in essentially its final form well before the time of the captivity (586-538 BC). This would make the claim that it was borrowed from Neo-Babylonian sources during the captivity untenable. The Hebrew flood account was in existence long before the Jews went into captivity.

QUESTION:
Do the quick-frozen mammoths which were found with their last warm-weather food frozen in their bodies support the Hydroplate Theory? [Note to readers: the Hydroplate Theory is an attempt to explain the flood of Noah. According to this theory, at the time of the flood, huge volumes of water which had been stored under the Earth were released suddenly, flooding the Earth.]

ANSWER:
It is true that scientists have examined mammoths who were extraordinarily preserved by a rapid freezing process which seems hard to explain by any "normal" process. These carcasses have meat which is preserved more than 10,000 years after the animals died. They have been found in Siberia and in Alaska. I have read some of the background on these and am not sure I can answer how the mammoth bodies were so remarkably well preserved. Perhaps some catastrophic event caused this. Perhaps even a catastrophic event of miraculous and biblical proportions was the cause of their preservation.

Actually, if we look at the evidence, it is not quite as amazing as some creationists have implied. Almost all these quick-frozen mammoths have flesh which is quite decayed. Contrary to urban legend, the flesh is not sufficiently preserved for human consumption. Usually, only a small portion of the original flesh is preserved. Some of the quick-frozen carcasses have shown evidence of dying in the spring. Others have evidence of death in the summer, while still others appear to have been killed in the winter. If they were killed in a single event such as the flood, this evidence is hard to explain.

The use of the quick-frozen mammoths by some creationists to support the Hydroplate Theory is evidence that this is pseudoscience. It is a common strategy of pseudoscientists to use an unexplained mystery as evidence of a theory which is not supported by any actual scientific evidence. Just because we have an unexplained (or partially explained) mystery with the surprisingly well-preserved mamoths, it does not mean that this mystery is evidence for some half-baked creationist idea such as the Hydroplate Theory. All the evidence surrounding the wooly mammoth carcasses imply that these animals were frozen during an ice age. The last ice age almost certainly predated the flood of Noah. I have read the writings of hydroplate theorists. Their supposed scientific evidence for this idea does not pass muster as a scientific theory. So, yes, it is true that the quick-frozen wooly mammoths are interesting. Arguably, they are not yet fully explained. However, it is a great leap from there to claim that the wooly mammoth findings are legitimate evidence for the Hydroplate Theory. To be honest, I see no connection between the unproved existence of hydroplates and the quick freezing of mammoths (for a book which supports the hydroplate theory, see *In the Beginning*, by Walt Brown. Although I disagree with his conclusions, it is fairly well written).

Chapter Ten

Miracles

QUESTION:
How can we be sure that Jesus really worked the miracles which are recorded in the Gospels?

ANSWER:
I answer this question thoroughly in **RFB** ch. 2. I will give a synopsis here. The reason for belief in the miracles of Jesus can be separated into two principal categories, which are;

1. The reliability of the Gospel witnesses.
2. The testimony of non-Christian authors.

The first point is that the Gospels have every sign of being a reliable account by honest eyewitnesses of actual events. It is important to bear in mind that many of the original public witnesses to the miracles of Jesus and to the resurrection were martyred for their faith, yet none of them ever relented: none of them ever said, "Sorry, we were just kidding." The evidence is a bit spotty, but we can say with some confidence that most of the apostles were killed for their faith. No one has ever given a single believable piece of evidence that any of these eyewitnesses were anything other than truthful and accurate. And not a single one of them ever backed down on their claims, even upon pain of death.

Perhaps it is possible that a few men and women could have cooked up some deceitful bogus claims about the miracles of Jesus, although this is very difficult to believe, given the well-known character of these men and women. However, it is simply not credible that every single one of these conspirators would have refused to relent, even though their lives were at stake. Oral traditions about the acts and miracles of Jesus passed around for twenty or more years before the gospels were written. There was every opportunity for the actual eye-witnesses to correct any errors or exaggerations. Can anyone imagine Peter, after having made up a bunch of miracles to support belief in a fake Messiah, being willing to die for such a lie? Could every single witness hold up in such a situation? This is not credible. The opponents of Christianity may not have accepted the message delivered by the apostles, but they could not deny the character and honesty of the men. That is part of the reason the opponents were so frustrated when they persecuted the early church leaders.

In addition to the public claims of the apostles and thousands of eyewitnesses for whom Jesus worked great marvels, wonders and signs (Acts 2:22), a few historians who definitely were not followers of Jesus reported the same sort of things, although they did not combine them with faith.

One of these non-Christian authors who referred to the miracles of Jesus was Flavius Josephus. Josephus was a Pharisee, as well as a commander of the Jewish forces whose rebellion ultimately resulted in the destruction of Jerusalem in AD 70. Josephus wrote about Jewish history for a largely Roman audience. He had an ambivalent attitude toward Christianity. In Josephus, one can find the following passage (Flavius Josephus, Antiquities, book xviii. chapter iii, verse 3):

> About this time there lived Jesus, a wise man. For he was one who wrought surprising feats and was a teacher of such people as accept the truth gladly. He won over many Jews and many of the Greeks. When Pilate, upon hearing him accused by men of the highest standing amongst us, had condemned him to be crucified, those who had in the first place come to love him did not give up their affection for him, for the prophets of God had prophesied these and countless other marvelous things about him. And the tribe of Christians, so called after him, has still to this day not disappeared.

It is worth bearing in mind that there is some controversy about whether part of the Josephus passage were interpolated by Christians, but in the version quoted above, I have removed the controversial phrases. Josephus reports that Jesus was a "doer of wonderful works," an obvious reference to his miracles. Josephus was born in 37 or 38 AD. He published his Antiquities in 93 or 94 AD. As a Pharisee, he surely knew many who were eyewitnesses to some of the events which are recorded in the Gospels.

Another source of testimony from non-Christians is the writings of the Jewish leaders who were vehemently opposed, both to Jesus Christ and to the movement which he began. For example, a very interesting passage can be found in the Talmud. The Talmud is a set of rabbinical teachings and commentaries on the Old Testament produced in the first centuries AD. In one section of the Talmud, known as the Baraila, one can find the following comment about the person Jesus:

> On the eve of the Passover they hanged Yeshu and the herald went before him for forty days saying (Yeshu) is going forth to be stoned in that he hath practiced sorcery and beguiled and led astray Israel. (Babylonia Sanhedrin 43a)

The writer of the Talmud continues by informing his reader that Jesus was ultimately hanged (crucified). What is interesting is that, in this passage, it is stated that Jesus practiced sorcery. In other words, the Jewish leaders were not able to refute the well-established fact that Jesus worked many wonders. They simply accused him of doing them by the power of the devil.

Between the reliable witnesses and the testimony of non-believers, one can reasonably conclude that Jesus was indeed a worker of miracles, wonders and signs.

QUESTION:
Did miracles occur or were they the perspective of the observer? For example, did the sun stand still like it says in Joshua?

ANSWER:
The Bible describes miracles which certainly cannot just be the perspective of the observers. When the Red Sea parted, forming dry land, that was not just a "perspective" of the witnesses. Lazarus' body was already exuding the putrid odor of death when Jesus called him out (John 11:38-43): *"But, Lord' said Martha, the sister*

of the dead man, *'by this time there is a bad odor, for he has been there four days.'*" In this case, the smell of death was not just the perspective of the observers. Neither was the fact that Lazarus came out of the tomb. Some commentators have searched for semi-natural explanations of the miracles recorded in both of the Testaments. Such efforts are bound to fail. No, these miracles are not a matter of perspective. There are two possibilities. Either the Bible records bona-fide miracles, or the authors are liars.

This brings me to the example you have in mind, when *"the sun stopped in the middle of the sky and delayed going down about a full day"* (Joshua 10:13). From a scientific perspective, even a miracle would not allow the sun to come to an instantaneous stop in the sky. That would mean that the Earth suddenly stopped spinning. Objects now moving at 1,000 miles-per-hour (because the Earth spins that fast, at least at the equator) would become 1,000 mile-per-hour projectiles if the Earth screeched to a halt. I will be honest with you that I am not sure exactly how to understand what is described in Joshua 10 from a physical perspective. Perhaps God miraculously allowed time to seem to stretch way beyond the normal. Perhaps God did indeed gradually slow the spin of the Earth, and later gradually sped it back up. Either way, what one has in Joshua chapter 10 is a miraculous victory won by God's people through the miraculous intervention of God by throwing the enemies into confusion, causing a huge hailstorm, and by somehow (but I am not sure exactly how to interpret the somewhat vague, non-technical wording of Joshua) slowing down the day so that his people could win the victory.

QUESTION:

Are Satan and the Devil two different persons? I have heard that the Hebrew word for Satan in the Old Testament is completely different from the New Testament word for devil. Some claim that they are two different beings. Also, how do you explain Catholic miracles such as stigmata, statues crying, holy oil and so forth? Many believe that these are legitimate miracles from God occurring today. I have heard accounts like this from people I trust. If these really happen, how do we know if they are from God or from the Devil?

ANSWER:

It is difficult to nail down absolutely a doctrine of Satan, as the Bible is occasionally somewhat enigmatic in its description, but there are a few things we can be confident of. First of all, the statement that there are two completely different names for the Devil and Satan (and therefore two separate beings) is not true. Naturally, the word in the Hebrew Old Testament and the Greek New Testament are not exactly the same, as they are different languages. However, the words are almost identical. Let us look at the relevant words. First of all, there is the Hebrew word which is translated as Satan, for example, in Job 1:6, Zechariah 3:1 and so forth. In this case, the Hebrew word is literally *satan*, which means adversary or accuser. In the New Testament, the word Satan is found in many passages; for example, Matthew 4:10, Mark 3:23, Acts 5:3 and others. In this case, the Greek word is *satanas*, which means hostile opponent. Obviously, these are one and the same name.

There is a second common name used for Satan in the New Testament, which is not found in the Old Testament. This is the word "devil." This word is found in Matthew 4:1, Luke 8:12, Acts 10:38 and many more. The Greek word is *diabolos*, which means malicious slanderer. It seems to me that the meaning of devil and Satan are almost identical. The Hebrew Satan means adversary or accuser, while the Greek word devil means malicious slanderer. Perhaps we could describe Satan as the accuser's personal name, and devil as a description of what he is. Proof that these words refer to the same person is found in Matthew 4:1-11. In this passage, there is no doubt that Satan and Devil are used of the same person—the one who tempted Jesus in the wilderness.

There is one reference in Isaiah chapter 14:12 to a *"shining morning star"* which has fallen from the heavens. Some have said that this is a reference to Lucifer; another name for Satan. This is almost certainly not correct. The passage is an apocalyptic reference to the destruction of Babylon—the enemy of Israel. There is no evidence in the Bible that Lucifer is a name for Satan or any other spiritual evil person.

There are a lot of things we can conclude about Satan. He is a deceiver (Genesis 3:1-6). He is an accuser (Revelation 12:10). He masquerades as an angel of light (2 Corinthians 11:15). He prowls the Earth, looking for souls to devour, wanting to cause them to go to hell (1 Peter 5:8). One thing you can be assured of is that anyone who claims Satan and the Devil are two different people is not correct. We know from Matthew 4 (and other passages as well) that they are one and the same person—the deceiver, the prince of this world (John 12:31).

Your second question is about the supposed miracles commonly claimed by Roman Catholic believers. These include stigmata—wounds that are similar to those on Jesus' body after the crucifixion which supposedly appear on sincere believers. Another category of Catholic-inspired "miracles" includes phenomena such as statues, idols and paintings which supposedly cry or bleed. I believe we need to be careful in characterizing such phenomena, as it is difficult to say with absolute certainty what is going on. Let me mention a few possibilities and leave you to decide. As for the stigmata, I believe some of these are the result of mentally unstable people who have hysterical reactions. I cannot say this is true in every case, nor do I feel it is my place to say so, but I am confident that some of this is self-induced emotional trauma. Some cases of apparent wounds caused by hysteria have been documented scientifically. In each example which I have seen described, the subject was a psychologically very troubled person. However, it is always a good policy to be careful, and, to be honest, I cannot say unambiguously that every case of stigmata is explainable as a psychological phenomenon.

As for statues which supposedly cry or bleed, let me remind you that God is not pleased with the worship of idols. The idea of God working a miracle through a Roman Catholic idol defies biblical common sense. It is my opinion that some of these supposed Catholic miracles are hoaxes. Others may be perfectly natural occurrences of some sort which are magnified by gullible people into a "miracle." People see pictures of the "Virgin" on grilled-cheese sandwiches, on drive-in theatre screens and so forth. Given that these phenomena are being observed by believers in a form of Christianity which is far from biblical truth, I believe we need to be extremely skeptical. Could some of these events be real miracles? Perhaps, but more likely they are from Satan. Paul tells us in 2 Thessalonians 2:9 that the working of Satan will include false miracles, signs and wonders.

In the end, I am sure I will not be able to explain all such phenomena. I have painted a very negative picture of these supposed miracles. I should be careful here. It is really not my place to judge such things, especially ones which I have not witnessed personally. I cannot absolutely rule out the possibility that God might work some sort of miracle such as those which Roman Catholics report. What I can say is that this seems to be unlikely. I cannot see God supporting a distorted version of Christianity by working a miracle, but God does not consult me about such things.

It is my personal experience that we do not gain much by denying other's belief in the miraculous. Our place is to teach the accurate gospel. Many people are thoroughly convinced of the validity of such things. Such beliefs are usually emotional rather than rational. For this reason, logical arguments are not likely to be persuasive. I believe it is more likely we will be able to bring people around to a correct understanding of the gospel by exposing them to real Christianity, not by trying to prove that their anecdotes of the miraculous are bogus.

Chapter Eleven

The Relationship between Christianity and Other Religions

QUESTION:
What about other religions? Are they true ways to know God? How can I know?

ANSWER:
In the end, those who seek after the truth will have to answer this question for themselves. Many people, of course, say that religions other than Christianity are "different paths to the same end." This is a very attractive philosophy, but this idea disagrees with logic, reason and common sense. Why is this? The different world religions contain beliefs and claims which are absolutely incompatible with one another. For example:

1. Hinduism has many gods (is polytheistic), while Christianity has only one God (is monotheistic). Hinduism teaches that the physical world is essentially evil, while the Bible teaches that the physical creation is "very good."

2. Buddhism includes a belief that "God" (if there is a God, because Buddha was agnostic about God) and nature are basically coexistent—that humans are a manifestation of divinity (this is

known as pantheism), while Christianity teaches that humans are individual and separate creations of a personal God.

3. Islam claims that Jesus is not God—that he is more or less on par with the other prophets such as Muhammad and Moses, and that he definitely did not die on a cross for the salvation of souls. It is absolutely impossible to take the deity of Jesus out of true Christianity. If Muhammad is right and the death of Jesus does not provide salvation for sin, then Christianity is a lie. Islam and Christianity are definitely not two legitimate paths to the same thing, as their claims about God are diametrically opposed to one another.

4. Buddhists, Hindus and others claim that our destiny after death is to come back to experience another life (reincarnation), while the Bible claims that *"man is destined to die once, and after that to face judgment"* (Hebrews 9:27).

Dozens more examples such as these can be given. The bottom line is that two religious systems which have fundamentally opposed views on such basic ideas as who God is and what the nature of the relationship between man and God is cannot be "two parallel paths to the same end." Logically, opposite viewpoints cannot both be correct. To bury this obvious truth under a deceptive ecumenical plea is to agree to an obvious lie.

Therefore, those who seek the truth must investigate Christianity as well as Buddhism, Sikhism, Judaism, Islam, Confucianism, Mormonism, Hinduism or whatever "ism" carefully to decide which, if any, is true. The history of mankind tells us that we cannot find the truth using human reasoning alone. Therefore, the truth, if it is to be found at all, can only be discovered through authoritative teachers or writings. Whether or not a religious claim is true can only be established by evaluating the accepted scriptures of that religion and their associated historical events. Let me suggest a few questions which one can ask when looking at the scriptures of various religions. A reasonable list of marks of inspiration include the following:

1. Is the teaching consistent within itself?

2. Does the teaching work in the lives of those who actually follow it?

3. Are there internal marks of inspiration, such as fulfilled prophecy and the like?

4. Is what is contained in the scripture accurate when compared to what we know from other disciplines such as science and history?

5. Is the revelation confirmed by supernatural events which occurred in concordance with the giving of the revelation?

I believe that if you study the scriptures of the world's major religions, I feel you will find that Christianity and Judaism pass all five tests with flying colors, but no other religion meets any of these criteria sufficiently to create confidence.

I am including an essay I wrote on the Christian world view which may provide a more detailed analysis of the relative merits of various religious and philosophical points of view.

Apologetics and the Christian World View

A number of years ago I wrote and published a book which I thought at the time covered all of the important basic topics relating to Christian Evidence for those trying to build up the faith of young Christians and non-believers. The book is titled, *Reasons for Belief: A Handbook of Christian Evidence*. It brings together evidence in support of Christian belief from the claims of Jesus, miracles, the resurrection, messianic and other prophecies, archaeology, history and the Bible, support for the documentary reliability of the Bible, science and the Bible, and it discusses supposed inconsistencies in the Bible. In the past three years I have come to the conclusion that there is one major topic which is essential in any basic but comprehensive Christian evidences discussion which is not included in my book. This is the subject of world view.

What is a world view and why is a discussion of world view essential to even the most basic attempts to create and sustain Christian belief? Quite simply, one's world view is the perspective one uses to process and interpret information received about the world. James W. Sire put it this way, "A world view is a set of presuppositions (ie. assumptions) which we hold about the basic makeup of our world." We live in a world in which the Christian world view is not only not the norm, to the vast majority-even to many who attend church regularly-it seems about as strange as belief in lepruchans or the tooth fairy. Our intellectual institutions are dominated by postmodern philosophy and scientific materialism. Many believe that all religions are more or less the same. The very existence of truth is denied, both in the halls of our universities and in popular media. It will be very difficult to plant the seed of rational evidence in such unfertile ground. We must explore and explain the major world views and demonstrate carefully why that proposed by the Bible is superior, because it is logically most consistent with the world as it really is, because it answers most successfully the fundamental questions all human beings ask, and because it comports best with what the human conscience knows is good and right.

In this essay I will be analyzing the most influential world views in modern culture; contrasting these to the Christian world view, explaining why we feel that the Bible offers a view of the world which is superior, both in its consistency with the world as it is and in the way it solves the fundamental human questions. For those who want to dig a little deeper into the topic, let me suggest a good primer on the subject. It is *The Universe Next Door*, by James W. Sire[4] (several copies available as I write at Amazon for less than 1$!). For those who want to dig really deep, there is the tome produced by J. P. Moreland and William Lane Craig, *Philosophical Foundations for a Christian Worldview*. A note of caution, this book is not easy reading and it is not cheap to buy!

In the first part of this essay, I will be describing briefly the Christian world view. It is tempting to assume that a Christian, almost by definition, understands the Christian world view, and of course there is a grain of truth in this. However, it is my own experience that many believers in Jesus Christ have an insufficient understanding of how he viewed the world in which humans exist. For this reason, this introduction will be used both to more carefully define the world view to which Christians ought to hold, and as a point of comparison when we discuss the world view of postmodernism, naturalism, new ageism and the major world religions.

First, let us ask what a "good" world view ought to look like? Is a "good" world view, by definition, one that we like—that we find ourselves naturally agreeing with? Is it one which creates good physical or emotional health? Is it the one which creates the greatest amount of human happiness? Perhaps it is the one which results in the creation of the greatest amount of economic growth and movement away from poverty and political upheaval. In fact, according to one world view, that of naturalism, there is no such thing as a "good" world view, as all such value judgments are meaningless. There is a sense in which this question of what constitutes a good world view is a personal decision for all of us. Each of us reading this article must, in the end, decide what constitutes a good and legitimate world view. Let us put this out there as a starting thesis. It is not possible to have no world view at all (please forgive the double negative). We will have one by default if we do not choose to think about it. Given that our world view in large measure defines who we are and determines how we live our lives, surely it is worth the time and intellectual effort to examine, evaluate and perhaps even change our world view toward one which more accurately reflects reality and makes us a better citizen of the universe in which we live and move and have our being.

A "Good" World View

What makes for a good world view? It has already been said that this has to be a personal decision, but let me propose a few qualities for us to consider when looking at the major world views.

The first quality which one might want to consider that makes a world view "good" is that it is true. To hold to an idea which is false is surely not to be preferred to holding to an idea which is true. There is no virtue and there is very rarely an advantage in being wrong. What makes something true? This is a question for philosophy, but let us try to keep this relatively simple. Something is "true" if it is consistent with reality. This is sometimes called the Correspondence Theory of Truth. If a belief is in clear contradiction with well-established facts about the world, then it is not true. This may seem a truism, but we will see that the Postmodern does not accept the Correspondence Theory of Truth. If one holds to the belief that gravity does not operate to attract masses toward one another, that view will be disproved by letting go of a heavy object. If one holds to the idea that refusal to communicate leads to peace, that too will be shown by reality not to be true. The sticking point, of course, comes with defining how one decides what is reality and what is true. One perspective, that of the empiricist, is that truth is determined solely by what we can observe with our senses and what we can measure with our instruments. Another perspective, that of rationalists such as DesCartes, is that which is true is that which my mind and clear reasoning tells me is true. What is true must be logical. The one who said, "We hold these truths to be self-evident" was speaking as a rationalist. Most of us who do not occupy the rarified regions of philosophy can be more practical in our definition. We can combine the two ideas. Those things we hold to be true must be consistent with what we can observe-with our own "history" and hopefully that of others, and they must be rational-logically consistent. It must not be supported by circular or patently poor reasoning or require us to believe what we know not to be true.

The second quality which makes for a "good" world view is that it successfully answers the important questions humans ask. What these important questions are and how one is to define success in answering them is, of course, subjective to some extent. However, there are a number of questions for which people everywhere seek the answers. Below is the list of such questions from *The Universe Next Door*, slightly reworded:

1. What is prime reality? (or What is the ultimate cause? or What is the nature of God?)
2. What is the nature of external reality-the world around us?
3. What is a human being?
4. What happens to a person at death?
5. Why is it possible for us to know anything at all?
6. How do we know what is right and wrong?
7. What is the meaning of human history?

To these let me add:

8. What is my purpose?
9. What is the nature of my relationship, with the "prime reality?"

The third quality which makes for a "good" world view is that those who ascribe to it are better human beings for having taken this as their world view. Again, of course, "better" is going to be subjective, but there are a few measures to which nearly all people can agree. If one's world view results on balance in an increased likelihood of genocide, racial or any other kind of hatred, poverty, anarchy, physical and emotional suffering or war, then such a world view is easily identified an deficient. We will be subjecting the important world views to scrutiny based on these three definitions of what make for a good world view. Is it true? Does it successfully answer the important questions? and Does it make those who hold to it "better" people?

The Christian World View

Clearly, a lot of things can be included under the heading of the Christian world view. My intent here is to keep it very simple and not necessarily provide a lot of scriptural support at this point. We will add to these ideas as we go along, as well as giving them flesh. In order to provide a useful basis as we proceed to analyze, compare and contrast the biblical with other world views, the points will be outlined and numbered.

1. The physical world is:
    a. real
    b. created and
    c. essentially good.

These points are established before we get out of the first chapter in the Bible. The reader should be aware that these presuppositions are definitely NOT held to by many of the influential world views. Many believe that the physical world is an illusion. Many believe that the universe(s) have existed forever. Even more hold to the belief as part of their view of the world that physical reality is corrupted and evil. To summarize, consider Genesis 1:31 (NIV) *"God saw all that he had made, and it was very good. And there was evening, and there was morning-the sixth day."*

2. There exists a parallel unseen spiritual reality which is not limited to or defined by the physical reality.

A scripture which supports both this presupposition and the first is Hebrews 11:3 (HCSB), *"By faith we understand that the universe was created by the word of God, so that what is seen has been made from things that are not visible."* This verse also can be used to support our third point of the Christian world view.

3. The creator of both the physical and spiritual realm is the God who is revealed and who reveals himself in the Bible.

4. Although the physical world is good, evil does exist. Such evil is the result of freedom of will given to created beings and their subsequent decision to use that freedom to "sin" (defined as transgressing the will of God).

5. Human beings have both a physical and a spiritual nature, but the spiritual nature is more essential as it is eternal.

6. There is a definite right and wrong for human behavior which is determined by God.

It is interesting to note that all of these are stated or implied in the first three chapters of Genesis. It is apparent that God wanted to establish right up front how he wants his people to view the world.

My intention here is to analyze how "good" (good being defined above) the Christian world view is principally by comparing and contrasting it with other world views. In other words, the idea that the created physical world is good will be supported when I contrast it with the Hindu idea that the physical world is an illusion or the Greek idea that it is essentially evil, or the naturalist view that it is not created. In the last section of the essay, I will come back to the Christian world view, explaining why I believe it is that Jesus Christ provided us with what is far and away the "best" view of the world which has even been presented to mankind. It is my hope that in the process some of my readers will have had their view of the world changed- that it will more perfectly reflect the perspective of Jesus of Nazareth.

Scientific Materialism/Naturalism

We have already looked at why people ought to think carefully about their view of the world, and at the importance of forming and holding to a consistent world view. We have considered a reasonable set of criteria for what might make for a "good" view of the world. In addition, we have given a bare bones description of the Christian world view. The first alternative world view we will contrast with that of Christianity is Naturalism; also known as Scientific Materialism. This is probably the simplest to understand of all the world views we will cover in this series. Let us consider several statements defining Naturalism:

The only reliable or valid instrument to deciding the truth or even the value of any proposition is the scientific method.

The only reality is that which is observable by physical means. There is no spiritual reality, no moral truth, no God, no life after death, no soul, no spirit, no consciousness, except perhaps as an epiphenomenon.

Consider that of Richard Lewontin:

"We exist as material beings in a material world, all of whose phenomena are the consequences of material relations among material entities. In a word, the public needs to accept materialism, which means that they must put God in the trash can of history where such myths belong."

The following are not definitions of Scientific Materialism, but represent obvious implications of this philosophy.

A statement of Naturalism from Richard Dawkins; world-famous atheist and evolutionist:

In the universe of blind physical forces and genetic replication, some people are going to get hurt and other people are going to get lucky: and you won't find any rhyme or reason to it, nor any justice. The universe we observe has precisely the properties we should expect if there is at the bottom, no design, no purpose, no evil and no good. Nothing but blind, pitiless indifference. DNA neither knows nor cares. DNA just is, and we dance to its music.

From Thomas Huxley, known as "Darwin's bulldog":

We are as much the product of blind forces as is the falling of a stone to earth, or the ebb and flow of the tides. We have just happened, and man was made flesh by a long series of singularly beneficial accidents.

Consider for a moment the implications of this rather depressing world view. If it is true then my personal concept of "I" is a delusion. My perception of consciousness is simply the accidental result of neurons firing and chemicals moving around in my brain (ie consciousness is an epiphenomenon). When I say to my wife or my children "I love you," what this means in reality is that when I think about them my neural pathways light up in a particular way and certain neurotransmitters change their level of activity. Love is not a thing in itself (and of course the biblical statement that God is love is sheer nonsense). If the naturalist is correct then there is no purpose to life whatsoever, except perhaps the evolutionary "purpose" to procreate and create as many copies of my particular genetic material as possible. If the naturalist is right than my personal belief that murder, lying and stealing are wrong has no basis whatever in absolute truth, but is simply one person's particular opinion-one dictated not by truth but, if anything, by a genetic predisposition toward thinking that way, created by a kind of cultural natural selection.

My personal experience tells me that virtually no one can accept this world view with all its implications. Despite this fact, in many intellectual circles it is the publically accepted world view and those who do not hold to it are laughed at. Educated people who believe that there is a spiritual reality which supersedes the physical reality are treated derisively as holding to an immature, outmoded and silly idea about the world. In fact, materialists such as Richard Dawkins and Christopher Hitchens publicly declare religionists to be the enemy of human progress and directly or indirectly the cause of all evil in the world (this despite the fact that they do not believe that evil exists).

What is the genesis of this world view? To discover the source of Naturalism, one must turn the clock back to the Scientific Revolution. The fact is that the creators of the Scientific Revolution—Roger Bacon, Copernicus, Galileo and others—were all believers in the Christian world view. In fact, their belief in science followed directly from the Christian world view. Belief in the God of the Bible led Bacon and others to conclude that there must be a single, unchanging set of laws governing the physical universe. These theologians also concluded from their biblical world view that a personal God of love must have made the physical universe to be intelligible to human reason and analyzable by mathematical analysis. All of these "Christian" assumptions turned out to be true (as far as we can tell) and thus science was invented.

However, in the process of discovering how nature worked, scientists such as Isaac Newton discovered that the universe works according to what seem to be entirely mechanical laws; laws which are so regular and predictable that it seemed God could be removed from the equation. In fact, French mathematician and physicist Pierre-Simone La Place, when asked by Napolean, "Where is God?" in his theory of mechanics replied, "I have no need of that hypothesis." Scottish philosopher David Hume questioned whether we can know anything absolutely and especially whether belief in God had any empirical validity. The rise of deism in the late eighteenth century led to scientific materialism/naturalism by the nineteenth century. Although Darwin himself was not a strict materialist, his work certainly provided fodder for scientism. Only in the twentieth century did we begin to see aggressive scientific materialists such as Bertrand Russel and Carl Sagan beginning to publicly attack all other world views as infantile and foolish.

A Response to Scientific Materialism

Any claim that Scientific Materialism is a superior world view to that of Christianity ought to be analyzed according to specific criteria. Let me begin by quoting a comment on materialism as a world view. (I apologize that I can no longer find the source of this quote.) "The theorist who maintains that science is the be-all and the end-all—that what is not in science textbooks is not worth knowing—is an ideologist with a peculiar and distorted doctrine of his own. For him, science is no longer a sector of the cognitive enterprise, but an all-inclusive world view. This is the doctrine not of science but of scientism. To take this stance is not to celebrate science but to distort it." I have already proposed a set of criteria for a "good" world view we can use for consideration. A superior world view will be one which:

   1. Is true (in other words consistent with reality on various levels)
   2. Answers the questions and solves the problems human beings really care about.
and
   3. Causes the person who holds to this world view to be a "better" person.

I reject Naturalism because it is patently false, it does not answer any of the problems and questions human beings as a whole care about and it does not tend to help its believers to be better people than they would have been if holding to alternative world views.

Naturalism is self-defeating. It is based on circular reasoning and for many reasons it produces assumptions which are simply not in agreement with common human experience. Therefore it is not "true" (criterion #1 above). The scientific world-view presupposes that the universe is ordered and essentially unchanging. It assumes that the laws which govern the universe are inviolable and that the universe is observable and understandable to human beings; that the human mind has a one-to-one correspondence with the way reality is. The naturalist then proceeds to apply these assumptions to rule out all other world views. The spiritual or supernatural are, by definition, not real. This is circular reasoning. None of the assumptions made as the foundation of science can be proved by experiment or by observation. In this sense, at its most foundational level, science itself is not scientific. It is not that the discoveries of science are wrong. Not at all. Clearly science has given us access to reliable knowledge about how the physical world works. If limited to its proper sphere, science works. It is the belief that science is the only valid view of the world and the only legitimate means to acquire knowledge about reality which is based on circular reasoning. At a recent forum held in the UK a famous chemist/naturalist was asked how he knows that ALL phenomena can be explained by physical laws. After being re-asked a number of times and attempting to get around the question, in the end, this naturalist was forced to confess; to quote "I simply believe it is true." In other words, the reason the scientific materialist knows that "We exist as material beings in a material world, all of whose phenomena are the consequences of material relations among material entities." is because he or she assumes the conclusion before the investigation. This is a very slim basis on which to build a world view.

There are a number of reasons I simply have to reject naturalism as patently false. I will supply a brief list here without taking the time to provide my evidence for such reasons. I will leave to reader to decide the truth of these claims—each of which, if true, make naturalism patently and demonstrably false.

1. Morality is real. Some activities are inherently wrong.
2. The existence of good and evil is not just an epiphenomenon. Evil is real.
3. Justice is not just a concept. Some behaviors are just and some are not just.
4. A human life is inherently more valuable than that of a cockroach.
5. God exists.
6. The universe was created.
7. Life was created.
8. Beauty is real and not discoverable by any scientific means.

9. The Bible is inspired by God.
10. Jesus of Nazareth was raised from the dead.

This list can be made much longer. In the final analysis the concepts of right and wrong are not just a human invention. I have found that even those who claim that there is no right or wrong—no evil or good—are not consistent with their own belief. It is ironic to me that I have witnessed atheists expressing moral outrage over the things done by "religionists." The naturalist may protest it is not true, but I say that "I" exist. I am not just a sack of chemicals moving around, with nerve synapses firing off according to patterns guided by my genetic makeup; determined by my environment. I am a person with a reality apart from my chemicals. I have a brain. I am not merely a brain. Naturalism is just plain not true.

Point number two of the argument for why naturalism is not a "good" world view: It does not answer any of the questions or solve any of the problems human beings really care about. Science is good at answering questions such as When? How much? Where? How long? It can answer provisional questions of why, such as why does it rain or why do stars form, but it cannot answer any of the fundamental/ontological/teleological why questions; even about the natural world. For example, science is not helpful at all for answering such basic questions as "Why is gravity as strong as it is," or "Why does the electromagnetic force exist,?" or "Why does the universe exist?" If science cannot answer these questions, it certainly cannot even hint at an answer to a single one of the questions people really care about (as listed above) such as: "Why am I here?" "What is my purpose?" "Does God exist?" "What happens to me when I die?" "How should I act?" "How should I treat other people?" "Why is it possible for humans to understand how the universe works?" "Why is there evil in the world?" Bottom line, scientific materialism does not even give wrong answers, it gives no answer at all to these questions (There is one exception. Science provides an answer to the question What happens when I die? The "scientific" answer is that life simply ends and entropy takes over.) It says that these are nonsense questions. My experience tells me that ignoring important questions and pretending that difficult problems do not exist is a bad way of dealing with such questions and problems. I do not mean to imply that Naturalists do not ask these questions or that they do not on an individual basis try to help solve some of the important human problems. It is just that their world view is not at all helpful for these things.

The third criterion from my personal list of qualities which make for a "good" world view is that holding to this view of the world must cause a person to be "better" than he or she would otherwise have been if not holding to this world view or if holding to alternative world views. Admittedly, this criterion is fairly subjective, but there are a number of measurements of goodness to which virtually all humans would subscribe. I believe that Naturalism is not a good world view if judged by this criterion. Let me state before entering this area that I have a number of friends who are naturalists. This is only "natural" because I am a scientist by profession. Some of my scientific materialist acquaintances are rather arrogant and hold to ethical and moral ideas with which I cannot agree. However, others have strong ethics and are some of the nicest people I know. No world view has a corner on the goodness market, including the one I hold to.

With this qualification in mind (and please do not forget it!), let us consider the motivation for doing "good" under the Naturalist world view. In theory, the Naturalist believes that there is no purpose to life and no inherently correct morality. Even ethics is extremely difficult or impossible to derive from this world view. Like I already said, some materialists do good deeds. If so, it is probably not because they are motivated out of their world view. Something else must be operating here. As my good friend Robert Kurka has said the materialists "hijacks" his or her morality and ethics from the Christian world view.

At the risk of offending some, I will make a bold statement here. I believe that scientific materialism is potentially a dangerous world view. According to this view, human beings have no definable value, except as a source of genetic material for subsequent generations. Of course, the vast majority of atheists are not violent people and value human life, but there is no moral imperative against murder or rape or robbery or any other of activities that the Christian and other world views hold to be morally wrong. Where does one find the moral compass? Any category of sexual behavior is acceptable as long as no one is hurt. Lying may be advantageous to survival and therefore "good."

A lot of evil has been done in the name of religion. Anyone who denies this is not looking at history or is altogether denying the existence of evil. The difference with the Christian world view compared to that of Naturalism, however, is that a Christian who is prejudiced or who lies or who wages war on another for reasons of greed or power is violating his or her world view and is subject to being shown to be doing wrong. There is accountability and justice under the Christian world view. To the Christian there is an imperative to help our fellow mankind. Jesus commanded that those who follow him must *"Do to others what you would want them to do to you."* Such altruism flies is the face of Naturalism as a philosophy. In the Christian world view, as exemplified by its creator Jesus Christ and as taught by its scriptures, there is a strong imperative to love others, to be honest, to serve others, to shun violence, greed, arrogance and so forth. Many Naturalists follow a strong and admirable personal ethic, but what is the imperative toward these "good" behaviors under the Scientific Materialist world view?

If there is one, I have not yet seen one, although some materialists have made the attempt.

Having admitted that much evil has been done by believers, let us consider the small but significant number of societies which have publicly avowed an atheist or an anti-God world view. Examples of this sort which come to mind are France immediately after the French Revolution, Communist Russia, Communist China, Cambodia under Pol Pot and North Korea[5]. Inspection of this list of regimes speaks for itself. In each of these societies individual souls were treated as if they had little value, with tragic results. The empirical fact that a societal commitment to belief in no God has such a poor record in producing human good is not proof that it will never do so. However, the track record is something we should not ignore.

What about justice and human rights? In the United States, many subscribe to the idea that "We hold these truths to be self-evident, that all men were created equal." Does this idea come from scientific inquiry? Based on their DNA, some are more fit than others. The Christian ought to believe that all humans are infinitely valuable as they are created in the image of God. I am happy to report that almost none of the Naturalists I have met are racially prejudiced. Hopefully the scientifically-inspired Eugenics movement in the early twentieth century will remain an anomaly, but what is the inherent source of human dignity and value if, as Huxley said, "man was made flesh by a long series of singularly beneficial accidents."?

To summarize, the committed Naturalist believes that the only truth in the universe is that which can be discovered by the scientific method, through experiment and rational analysis of the information derived from empirical evidence. This world view fails miserably at the three criteria proposed in this paper for deciding what world view is best. Its support is circular and its conclusions are patently false. It cannot answer the most important questions or solve the fundamental problems that human beings care about. It does not, in and of itself, tend to cause those who hold to it to be "good." I believe that the Christian world view is vastly superior to Materialism on all these counts and, for that matter, on any other reasonable measure I have seen of what makes for a good world view.

New Age and Eastern Religion/Philosophy

We have already considered the definition of world view and why the consideration of world view is important for the believer, and for the non-believer for that matter. We also considered the world view of Naturalism or Scientific Materialism, the implications for humanity and whether it is a "good" world view. In this section we will look at the view of the world which is held more or less in common by peoples in the East (generally cultures in Asia) and their close cousin, the New Age Movement.

It may seem presumptuous to describe in fairly simple terms the world view of nearly half the world's people. If we include the population of India and China alone, this accounts for about 2.6 billion of the roughly 7 billion people in the world. Obviously, we will be painting the world view held to by the world's Hindus, Buddhists, Sikkhs, Jainas, Taoists and Confuscianists with a broad brush. To include the modern-day New Age movement in this group is to make the brush stroke even broader. Yet, the world view held by the followers of these religious ideas is so radically different from that of the Christian, that even such a broad description will tell us a lot about how people from the East think about the world.

The Eastern world view is essentially pantheistic. This is a gross simplification and the nuances will be discussed below. Nevertheless, this description will be very helpful. The pantheist sees God as being coextensive with the universe. Pan means all and pantheists believe that God is all and everywhere. This is not a personal god at all. If the pantheist is right, then we human beings are part of God. We cannot have a relationship with God because we are God. The goal of the pantheist is to be swallowed up into the ineffable, all-pervading god-essence of the universe. The pantheist believes that the physical world around us is an illusion. The word used for this concept in both Hinduism and Buddhism is maya. The physical reality is a shell to contain the cosmic oneness. Buddhists, Jaina, Sikks and Hindus have a rather complicated cosmology. They believe that reality exists on many levels or planes, and we are on one of the lower of these planes. This is the common Eastern cosmology. Our goal is to get to a higher level of reality where the spiritual is more real and the physical reality is less pervasive. Ultimately, the goal is to lose self and to be swallowed up into the all-pervading goodness.

If the Eastern idea is right, then our goal is not to know and have a personal relationship with God outside of us, but to discover the God-nature inside of us. The search for God is essentially a search within ourselves. It is literally a selfish journey. We find Brahman, the ineffable expression of God, and a state of bliss known to the Hindu as nirvana by finding atman (soul) within ourselves. I have been using the Hindu way of describing things as this is the most common of the Eastern religions, and because it is the essence of New Age religion.

The Buddhist idea has much in common with Hinduism, but of course much is different as well. The Buddha gave his followers a philosophy; the eight fold path for right living. The four "noble truths" of Buddha are 1. Suffering is not getting what one wants. 2. The cause of suffering is desire which leads to rebirth. 3. The way to end suffering is to end desire, and 4. The way to the end of desire and of suffering is the eight-fold path. Buddha taught dispassion rather than compassion.

Gautama refused to address the God question with his believers because he felt this was not particularly relevant. One gets the sense that the Buddha was not an atheist and that his concept of God was pantheistic. His religion included the concepts of maya and reincarnation.

The Jain and Sikh religions can be thought of as flavors of Hinduism. In fact, Sikhs tended to consider themselves a sect of Hinduism until fairly recent persecution in India and Pakistan, as well as the British tendency to define things from a Western perspective, painted them as a separate religion. Both religions retain the multiple level cosmology, but reject the highly structured priestly caste system. Jainism is thoroughly pantheistic. Sikhism and Jaina include the belief that physical reality is an illusion (*maya*), as well as holding to reincarnation and a karmic thinking about "sin."

As for Taoism, this Chinese-born Eastern religion, founded by Lao Tzu, retains a strong pantheistic view of the world. Enlightenment is gained by contemplating self and nature. Like Buddhism, we come into contact with our cosmic nature through non-involvement in the world. Dispassion rather than compassion is the key to enlightenment.

So, what is New Age religion? Is it palm reading? Channeling? Seances? Meditation? Reincarnation? Occultism? Gurus? Paganism? Gnosticism? Mother Goddess worship? Yes, all the above, but in its essence, it is Western pantheism. The common thread in the rather eclectic beliefs of New Agers is that you are God, I am God, we all are God! It is monism. God is everything and we are God. To quote a well-known New Age author, "Once we begin to see that we are all God, then I think the whole purpose of life is to re-own the God-likeness within us."

Let us analyze this world view. Is it a "good" world view? Let us apply our three criteria. Is the Eastern/New Age world view true? It will be very hard to give a fully satisfactory answer to this question in a short essay. Put it this way, the cosmology of the Eastern religions, with its endless repeating cycle of creations and destructions, and with its multiple levels of reality is not true. Material evidence for the big bang seems to preclude this cosmology. The second law of thermodynamics does not allow for a cyclical repeat of cosmic history. The eastern mind believes that this universe is not real. Some have tried to tie the twentieth century discovery of quantum mechanics, with its probabilistic view of physical reality and its discovery of the uncertainty principle as evidence that the Buddhist cosmology is valid. The problem is that science definitely assumes that the universe is real. In fact, the scientific materialist believes that the physical universe is the ONLY reality. Unlike the situation between science and Christian theology, there is an inherent and unresolvable conflict between science and Eastern cosmology. The physical world is very real. We will not help solve the problems in this world by pretending that it is not real (and that the problems themselves are therefore not real).

It is debatable whether science can help settle the question of whether "God" is pantheistic and impersonal or theistic and personal. Nevertheless, we can ask what is the evidence supporting the central claims of Christianity and those of various Eastern religions. Christian belief has the advantage of scripture with fulfilled prophecy, verifiable historical accuracy and much more. The scripture of Eastern religions is entirely lacking in such logical/rational evidential support. In fact, one cannot even find apologists for these religions as a rule. Rational "evidence" seems to be nearly immaterial to these beliefs.

Does Eastern religion answer the important human questions? The answer is yes and no. It certainly does better here than scientific materialism. Eastern religion provides possible answers (whether right or wrong) to questions such as "What is ultimate reality?" "How did I get here and where am I going?" With other questions it is less successful. What is the nature of external reality—the world around us? The eastern believer says that it is not real. This is not helpful. What is the solution to the problem of evil? How do I become righteous? Eastern religion provides unhelpful answers. Suffering is not real, sin does not exist (unless one allows for the idea of karma which has as much or more to do with the actions from supposed past lives as with our own life).

Are the practitioners of Eastern religion or philosophy better people for holding to these beliefs? If we compare to atheism or agnosticism, the answer surely is yes. With their idea of karma and ideal of becoming one with the pantheistic universal soul, surely the devoted Buddhist or Hindu is more likely to be peaceful, patient and possessed of a sense of responsibility for the consequences of his or her actions than the average non-believer. However, there are some weaknesses here. The New Age philosophy tells its believers, sin, if it exists at all, is the lack of personal understanding that you are God. Hindu thought does include a measure of personal responsibility for sinful acts, but it also includes the possibility of "atoning" for sin in this life in some still future life. It also carries the responsibility for unknown past lives into the current incarnation. Surely this weakens the sense of personal responsibility for our own actions in this life, at least for the average believer.

The Eastern world view has one looking inward, not outward. It inspires dispassion rather than compassion and disinvolvement in the world rather than involvement. I am not saying that Sikhs are completely unloving. Obviously there are many loving and giving Taoists. However, these religions teach that suffering is not real. I have traveled to India as well as Buddhist countries such as Cambodia and Thailand. It is not an accident that a majority of the organized benevolent programs in Hindu and Buddhist countries is done by Christian groups. This is not just an accident and it cannot be fully explained by the wealth in Western countries. The pattern of "Christian" benevolence is repeated in the small Christian communities in these countries. The native Christian groups do more than their share of meeting the needs and creating social justice in these countries. Julian "the Apostate," the pagan grandson of Constantine noted of the Christian in the Roman Empire, "Atheism (i.e. Christian faith) has been specially advanced through the loving service rendered to strangers, and through their care for the burial of the dead. It is a scandal that there is not a single Jew who is a beggar, and that the godless Galileans care not only for their own poor but for ours as well; while those who belong to us look in vain for the help that we should render them." This criticism of Julian's own pagan religion and compliment of the Christians of his day apply quite well to the situation in countries where Eastern religion predominates. Why? Because these are bad people? No. To a great extent it is because of their world view.

On a personal note, when I came to a belief in God while in college, I was initially strongly attracted to Eastern religion. I became involved in a Western-style eastern mysticism, read Hindu scripture, became a vegetarian and tried to find God in this way. In the end, I was attracted to Christianity because of the love I saw in devoted Christian lives and because of the evidence which so strongly supported Jesus being the one and only Son of God.

To summarize, the essence of the Eastern world view, and that of its many Western incarnations such as New Age believers is pantheism. It is a belief that the universe is filled with an impersonal god-force, a spark of which is in us. The physical world is an illusion, sin is not real, and the goal of humanity is to escape from the passions which trap us in these physical bodies. The reader will have to decide whether this world view is attractive, but from my perspective, this is a defective world view. It is defective, first of all, because it is not true. The evidential support for this view is not strong. In addition, I am not attracted to this world view because its essence is selfish. I am attracted to a view of the world which calls its adherents to seek social justice and to show compassion for those less fortunate than them.

The Christian World View

Thus far we have looked at Naturalism, Eastern religion/philosophy and its cousin, the New Age philosophy/religion. Having defined these world views, I attempted to evaluate them with respect to the proposed criteria for a "good" world view. Obviously, this treatment is not comprehensive. We have not evaluated the world view of the Postmodernist (which is, in essence, that no world view is "true"), Nihilist (which is somewhat closely related to that of the naturalist), or the Existentialist, the Stoic, dualist, neo-

Platonist or of the Muslim. All of these, with the exception of the postmodern world view and Islam, can be seen as more or less closely related to one of these we have considered. Time and space are not sufficient for us to cover all of these in detail.

I will now return to Christianity. We will consider in much more careful detail what the Christian world view really is. We will also analyze this world view with respect to the three criteria I have been using throughout. Many Christian believers may think that the Christian world view is fairly obvious and for the seasoned follower of Jesus relatively little need be said about it. By way of response, let me say that one point of this series of essays is that it is essential for those of us who seek to influence our neighbors to have a solid and deep understanding of both our own and of competing world views. I will make the claim that many Christians do NOT have a sufficiently deep understanding of the world view which they ought to have if they accept, by faith, the biblical view of the world. I make this statement because as I have traveled around the world to visit more than one hundred churches in dozens of countries, when I ask some rather basic questions about things such as predestination, natural and special revelation, salvation, the cause of suffering and so forth, the answers show a rather disturbing lack of understanding of who the God of the Bible is.

Of course, some will ask "Which biblical world view?" In other words, some claim that there is more than one world view found in the Bible—that one has to choose which of these competing views one will take to be the actual biblical/Christian world view. This is another question which deserves careful and systematic response. Let me say for the sake of this essay that I personally completely reject this view. Although I will not take the time to support the claim at this point, it is my conviction from careful study of the biblical scriptures over thirty years that there is a single, consistent, non-contradictory world view and picture of who God is. The God of Genesis is the God of Isaiah is the God of John and of James and Paul. So, what is the Christian world view? I will attempt to describe it by a series of propositions, each of which will be expanded somewhat, using biblical passages by way of support.

1. The physical world is: a. real b. created out of nothing (ex nihilo) and c. essentially good.

Genesis chapters 1-3 is in my opinion the most brilliant little piece of philosophy I have ever read. "In the beginning God created the heavens and the earth." (Genesis 1:1). As the Hebrew writer put it, *"By faith we understand that the universe was formed at God's command, so that what is seen was not made out of what was visible."* If this statement is true, then animism, polytheism, pantheism, dualism, naturalism, nihilism, and postmodernism are all proved untrue. Just as significant to the Christian world view is this: not only did God create the physical universe, but this creation was essentially good. The way God puts it in Genesis 1:31, *"God saw all that he had made, and it was very good."* Eastern philosophy has the physical world to be an ephemeral illusion. Greek philosophy agrees, adding that the physical world is decaying and essentially evil. Naturalism agrees that it is real, but denies that there is a supernatural reality which created it. It certainly is not "good," as such a description in meaningless in a random accidental universe. When God says his creation was good in its entirety, this does not deny the existence of evil. The question of evil will be addressed below.

2. There exists a parallel unseen spiritual reality which is not limited to or defined by the physical reality. Human beings have a spiritual aspect to their nature.

The fact that God, one who is "invisible," created the universe establishes that there is a non-physical reality which is at least in some sense greater than the physical. The physical universe is real, but it is not all there is. Jesus confirmed this idea. *"God is spirit, and his worshipers must worship in spirit and in truth."* (John 4:24) Acknowledging that there is a spiritual reality is not the same as dualism. Dualism has the world being governed by more or less evenly matched forces of good and evil. It is also not naturalistic monism, which denies the existence of spiritual reality entirely. We have a soul and a spirit. That we are created "in the image of God" (Genesis 1:27) is a spiritual rather than a physical claim. It is not a statement of our equality with God, but rather a description of our spiritual nature. I have a body, but I am not a body. "I" exist, and "I" am not defined by the chemicals which compose my body. Consciousness is not a mere epiphenomenon as naturalism requires. Our God-likeness has to do with our spiritual nature, our possession of a soul, our inherent understanding of good and evil, our ability to create and to love.

3. The creator of both the physical and spiritual realm is the God who is revealed and who reveals himself in the Bible.

Not only did God create the physical universe (Genesis 1), he also created the spiritual—the heavenly realms. In Colossians 1:15-16 Paul says of Jesus, *"He is the image of the invisible God, the firstborn over all creation. For by him all things were created: things in heaven and on earth, visible and invisible, whether thrones or powers of rulers or authorities; all things were created by him and for him. God has made himself known to his people "from what has been made."* (Romans 1:20), but he has also revealed himself and his will in the Hebrew and Greek scripture. Most particularly, he has revealed himself through his Son, Jesus Christ; the image of God. *"In the past God spoke to our forefathers through the prophets at many times and in various ways, but in these last days he has spoken to us by his Son." (Hebrews 1:1-2). *"No one has ever seen God, but God the only Son who is at the Father's side, has made him know."* (John 1:18) God has revealed himself to us through creation, through the Old and New Testaments and through the person Jesus Christ.

4. Human beings have both a physical and a spiritual nature, but the spiritual nature is more essential as it is eternal.

Our physical nature is obviously more apparent to us than our spiritual nature, but this fact is deceptive when compared to our ultimate reality. Like Jesus said, *"Do not be afraid of those who kill the body and after that can do no more. But I will show you whom you should fear: Fear him who, after the killing of the body, has power to throw you into hell."* (Luke 12:4-5) As Paul put it, *"We fix our eyes not on what is seen, but on what is unseen. For what is seen is temporary, but what is unseen is eternal."* (2 Corinthians 4:18)

5. God cannot be easily defined but he can be characterized by certain qualities. God is love, God is just, God is holy, God is omniscient, omnipotent and omnipresent.

What God is he is fully and infinitely. God is not merely loving: he is love. Love defines and determines all his actions toward us. From a human perspective, this seems to conflict with his justice and his holiness. God is not merely just: he is justice. He is incapable of an unjust act, even if we feel his love and his justice are in apparent conflict. God is holy, in him there is no darkness at all (1 John 1:5). These are facts about God. How does this affect our world view? In every way. Every act in our life and in the lives of our neighbors is subject to the justice of God. This has a profound effect of how we view our own lives and how we should respond to injustice. *"Do not take revenge,… 'It is mine to avenge; I will repay,' says the Lord."* If God really is love, then this has an unfathomable effect on how we understand the events which surround our lives. All of them are either caused or permitted by an omniscient, omnipotent, omnipresent God who acts toward all out of love.

6. Although all God's creation, including the physical world is good, evil does exist. Such evil is the result of freedom of will given to created beings and their subsequent decision to use that freedom to "sin" (defined as transgressing the will of God).

This brings us back to Genesis. The story of Adam and Eve is the story of us. God gave us everything for our pleasure and enjoyment. Why? Because he loves us and because he wants us to love him. But what did we all do? We rebelled and chose to do things which are unholy. As Augustine put it, evil is not a thing in and of itself. If it were, that would be dualism. Rather evil is good which has been corrupted by free moral agents. Something which was created for good purposes is turned for evil. Nothing God created is evil, but some of what God created is capable of doing evil. God gave us a choice. He asks us to *"choose life"* (Deuteronomy 30:19), but many of us choose rebellion. The physical laws which are discoverable by science are not the only "natural laws." There are moral laws as well, and they are as inescapable as the law of gravity. Rebellion against God's holiness produces suffering in this world (Exodus 20:5-6), both on those who sin and on those around them. This is the answer to the "problem" of pain, suffering and evil.

7. Because of God's justice and his holiness, those who choose to rebel against him will ultimately be judged and separated from God for eternity.

Not only does our choice to rebel and to sin bring on temporary physical and emotional suffering in this life, it also brings judgment in the world to come. *"For we will all stand before God's judgment seat."* (Romans 14:10) *"'The Lord will judge his people.'" It is a dreadful thing to fall into the hands of the living God."* (Hebrews 10:30-31). God cannot be mocked. He is patient and kind, and he wants all men to be saved and to come to a knowledge of the truth (1 Timothy 2:4), but *"the wages of sin is death."* Again, as with all the qualities of God, this fact is unavoidable. God does not change or compromise his holiness. It has been said that God does not send people to hell, but he accepts their choice to rebel and be eternally separated from him.

8. The solution to evil and its eternal consequences is provided by God through the atoning substitutionary sacrifice of Jesus Christ.

This is the essence of the gospel. As was prophesied, *"the Lord laid on him the iniquity of us all."* (Isaiah 53:6) *"By his wounds we are healed."* (Isaiah 53:5). *"But God demonstrates his own love for us in this: While we were still sinners, Christ died for us."* (Romans 5:8). God's holiness and justice were not superseded or violated in this substitutionary death. *"He did it to demonstrate his justice at the present time, so as to be just and the one who justifies the man who has faith in Jesus."* (Romans 3:26). Biblically, this is a theological fact. How does this affect one's world view? If this is true, then everything is different. Suffering makes sense. The existence of evil makes sense. Our innate and universal sense of justice makes sense as well. Yet, we can live as free men and women, not using our freedom as an excuse to do evil, but using this gift of freedom to love and serve others (paraphrasing Galatians 5:13-15) without living in constant fear of judgment when we fall short, as we inevitably will do.

Is This a "Good" World View?

In describing the Christian world view, some might choose to emphasize certain points more and others less than I have, but this seems to reasonably well summarize how the Bible describes the world. Having done this, we will now proceed to do the somewhat subjective job of asking whether, by the criteria described above, this is a "good" world view.

Is it True?

First, is it "true?" By this I mean: Is this world view consistent with what we know? I am not asking whether we can provide a mathematically precise, scientific, logical "proof" of the truth of the biblical world view. This is obviously not possible.

Is the physical world real? I will challenge the post-modernist or the practitioner of Eastern religion on this question. I say it is real. A wise Christian philosopher once challenged his Hindu friend to prove his own confidence that physical reality is not real by allowing him to strike him with a club. The guru politely declined the opportunity to show confidence in his own philosophy. Science has shown that this "illusion" is surprisingly, uncannily consistent and predictable. Fantasies and illusions are rarely so predictable. Our naturalist friends may be out on a limb when they say there is no evil and no justice, but surely they have it right in this. The physical world is real.

Is the physical creation good, as claimed by the Bible? Given the existence of disease and natural disasters it certainly is reasonable to question the claim that physical creation is "very good" as God says in Genesis. My response is that creation is very, very good. Physicists tell us that the universe we live in is absolutely, spectacularly fine-tuned so that advanced life forms can exist. If any of more than two dozen parameters which define how the universe functions were changed by even a small fraction, we would not be here. To avoid the obvious implications, naturalists have speculatively proposed there are an infinite number of universes, and we are lucky to live in the right one. Lucky indeed! Suffering brought on by earthquakes may be troubling, but without plate tectonics (and their associated earthquakes) the earth would be sterile and we would have virtually no atmosphere. Bacteria cause disease, but without this marvelous creation we would have no nitrogen in the soil and no oxygen in the air. God's creation is spectacularly wise and good. To those who do not agree, I challenge them to conceive of a better set of working physical laws and then to bring their conception into existence.

Is the physical reality the only one, or is the Biblical world view correct when it describes a co-existent spiritual reality? This is harder to prove. Yet there are a number of things which are true which point in this direction. We are self-aware. We are "conscious." We are able to understand the universe. Humans have a seemingly universal sense of what is right and moral. The universe itself exists and was created. All of these and many more point toward a non-physical creator and a non-physical nature for humans beings. Naturalists may choose to dismiss the reality of beauty, of love, of natural human rights, of conscience (not to be confused with consciousness), of good and evil and many other things, but very few people can really accept that these things are not real. Their existence implies there is a spiritual reality. Perhaps it is true that the majority does not determine truth, but very few believe they are a body (rather than they have a body) and the vast majority of all who have ever lived agree that there is a spiritual reality. The biblical view that there is a spiritual reality which supersedes the physical agrees with what we know.

Is it true that evil exists? And if so, what is the cause of this evil? Whether or not North Korea, Iran and Iraq were, in fact, an axis of evil as George Bush claimed is debatable, but the existence of evil is hard to deny. Sexual abuse of children, murder, genocide, warfare for selfish ends, corruption, greed—all of us recognize that evil is very real indeed. Ignoring this fact is a poor way to make it go away. Even arrogant atheists such as Christopher Hitchens and Richard Dawkins, while denying the existence of evil wax poetical in complaining about the evil done in the name of religion. The Bible claims that God did not create evil. Like it says in James chapter one, those who sin should not claim that God is tempting them because God does not tempt us to do evil. Evil is the result of those who choose to rebel against God's laws. Until someone can legitimately show to me that anything God has done is evil, I will stand by the claim that creation is good and that evil in this world results from the corruption of what is good by morally free agents.

The reality of God's judgment on evil and his grace and mercy for those who repent is proved by the history of Israel. The support of this claim would require much reference to history, quoting from biblical prophecy and description of historical foreshadows in the Old Testament. I have published a book on this subject for those interested in pursuing it further (**FSTR**). God told his people in Deuteronomy 28 that if they did not obey the Lord and carefully follow his commands, he would drive them to a nation unknown to them—that they would suffer at the hands of their enemies, and would be scattered among the nations. They did and He did. God judged his people at the hands of Assyria and Babylon. He also told them that if they were to repent, even if driven to the farthest part of the world, he would bring them back and bless them in the land he gave them. They did and He did as he had promised. He provided Cyrus to set his people free and send them back to build Jerusalem. The story of Israel is the story of rebellion and judgment, followed by repentance and salvation. Rebellion produced slavery, but when God's people cried out for mercy, God always sent a savior to save them—whether the savior was Joseph, Moses, David or Cyrus. Jonah's rebellion brought on the sentence of death, while his repentance led to salvation. God prophesied that salvation will come through one who will be pierced (Isaiah 53:5) and through one who will be crucified (Psalms 22:16). He even predicted that a savior would come to Jerusalem to atone for wickedness in about AD 30 (Daniel 9:24-25 and see Daniel). That God will judge his creation for wickedness and that he will provide salvation through the death of Jesus Christ is difficult to prove mathematically, but the history of Israel and fulfilled prophecy makes the reality of this claim a reasonable conclusion.

Is the Christian world view true? What I can say with confidence is that it agrees with what we know to a degree which is demonstrably much greater than any competing world view.

Does it Answer the Questions People Care About?

Second, does the Christian world view answer the questions people really care about? How did I get here? (God created us) Where am I going? (to eternal honor or shame) What is my purpose in life? (to know God and be known by him) What is my value? (Jesus gave his life for us) What is my relationship with the ultimate reality? What is the right thing to do? Why is there evil and suffering in the world? Why is it that we exist? Why is it that we can understand the universe? All of the great questions of life are answered in the Christian scripture. The Biblical world view addresses the problem of sin (Romans 7:24-25). Not only does it tell us why there is suffering, it also tells us what to do about it (Matthew 9:35-36). The Biblical world view even makes sense of death. *"Where, O death is your victory? Where, O death is your sting?"* (1 Corinthians 15:54-56) The objective truth of all these biblical answers is something which can be debated. Some might call all this wishful thinking. What cannot be denied is that the Christian world view provides reasonable and satisfactory answers to every one of the important questions common to man. No other world view, be it human philosophy, Eastern religion or any other comes close.

Does Acceptance of This World View Make Us Better People?

Previously I addressed the question of whether alternative world views make one a better person. Each world view has at least some things which commend it. However, in every case, we were left with serious questions. Naturalism denies the existence of absolute moral truth. Like postmodernism it leaves us without a standard for how we should treat one another. Eastern and Greek philosophy deny the goodness of the physical creation and teach dispassion rather than compassion. Muslim theology, with its emphasis on fate and predestination removes human responsibility for our fellow humans to some extent. Let me state my conclusion on this question right at the start. I can say with great confidence that both in theory and in practice, the Christian (and the Jewish) world view is superior to all others in its effect both on humanity as a whole and on individual people.

In the Christian world view every single human being has an unlimited value. The Son of God died to redeem us individually. All people are of equal value and importance in the eyes of their Creator, even if we are given different roles and gifts. *"You are all sons of God through faith in Christ Jesus, for all of you who were baptized into Christ have been clothed with Christ. There is neither Jew nor Greek, slave nor free, male nor female, for you are all one in Christ Jesus."* (Galatians 3:26-28) Looking from our Western perspective in the 21st century, it is difficult to grasp how radical a statement this was in the 1st century. If one investigates history, one will discover that it was Christian ethics which led to the idea of individual human dignity and human rights. Where did the idea that "all men were created equal" come from? Of course the Bible was way ahead of the framers of the US constitution on this one, as full and equal rights were not given to slaves until 1863, and to women until well into the twentieth century. Slavery had been an ever present institution from the dawn of human history. It was men and women, acting out the Christian world view, who turned this upside down. William Wilberforce was not alone in pushing the abolition of slavery because of his Christian convictions. Jesus Christ was a revolutionary in the way he treated women, the poor, the diseased, the deformed and those not of his nationality.

Of course, Christians are not the only good people in the world, but it is worth asking where humanists, atheists and others got their ideas of what is "good." Is it possible that they hijacked it from Christian ideas? History certainly hints at this conclusion. Jesus said that the entire Law is summed up in the command to love God and to love one another as oneself. This idea of the centrality of our need to love and be loved comes from the Christian world view. Why? The reason we were created is because of love and for love. According to the Christian world view, we are valuable beyond comparison. Jesus implied that a single soul is more valuable than the entire world (Luke 9:25). This world view gives the individual person unimaginable dignity, and calls its believers to pour their life out in love to others. It is the best of all the competing pictures offered by religion and human philosophy in the positive effect it has on those who accept it.

The Christian world view tells us that suffering is not inherently evil. In fact, suffering is good for many reasons. It makes us stronger, it helps us to understand and experience joy. When we suffer because of our own sin, it trains us to change, it helps us to know Jesus, and when we respond to suffering in a godly way, it allows us to glorify God. So suffering is not evil, but the Christian world view nevertheless impels believers to respond to suffering with compassion. Why? Because of love, of course. James tells us that *"Religion that God our Father accepts as pure and faultless is this: to look after orphans and widows in their distress and to keep oneself from being polluted by the world."* (James 1:27). *"Does it make you a king* to have more and more cedar? Did not your father have food and drink? He did what was right and just, so all went well with him. He defended the cause of the poor and needy, and so all went well. Is that not what it means to know me? Declares the Lord." (Jeremiah 22:15-16)

Jesus was perhaps the most compassionate man who ever lived. "Jesus wept." (John 35) Why? Because Lazarus had died? No, as he was about to raise him from death. He wept because Mary and Martha wept. "When Jesus saw the crowds, he had compassion on them." (Matthew 9:36). Like I already said, Christians are not the only loving people in the world, but when they are selfish, greedy or arrogant they are violating the direct command and example of the founder of their movement. I have visited Hindu, Buddhist and Muslim countries. In most of these countries, the Christian groups, even though a small minority, do most of the benevolent work in these societies. Why? They act this way because of the Christian world view and the personal example of Jesus of Nazareth. Besides, those who accept the Christian world view believe that they will be held accountable for putting its tenets into practice. Accountability can be powerful motivation. Other religions either tell us that suffering is an illusion or that it is God's will. Does accepting the Christian world view cause one to be better for it? The answer is that if it does not have that effect, then we can be sure the Christian world view was in fact not accepted by the person. I do not want to disrespect any world religion or philosophy and I know that many who accept these as their world view are sincere and want to do right. Besides, there is at least something to be commended in all these philosophies, but the example of Jesus, the teaching of Christianity, the world view of the Christian and the facts of history lead me inexorably to the conclusion that of all the well-known world views, the Christian one is by far the best at making its believer a better person by almost any accepted measure. Why? Because the basic ethic of this world view combines great personal dignity with love, unselfishness, and unstinting service for others.

Have Christian believers ever violated the ethic implied in their world view? That is an easy question. Yes. Has evil been done in the name of Christianity? Yes, but such acts are certainly not inspired by the life or teaching of Jesus. Those who divide, hate, steal and abuse the poor and needy are by that very action rejecting the Christian world view.

The Christian world view is superior to all others on many grounds. First, more than any other, it is consistent with human reality. Second, it provides rational, reasonable and helpful answers to the important human questions, and third, those who take this world view not only as a philosophy but as a way of life are made to be the best possible human beings that they can be. Let us accept, embrace and teach the Christian world view with the authority of its creator and greatest example, Jesus Christ.

—John M. Oakes

QUESTION:

If Christianity is the only true religion, how do you explain Islam and other religions? Don't other religions just have different names for the same God?

ANSWER:

One of the most popular ideas about religion is that "all religions are more or less the same and lead to the same place." This is a very shallow belief. It is impossible to defend if one looks carefully at world religions.

One of the reasons that this philosophy has gained acceptance is the somewhat deceptive fact that the "morality" of all world religions has much in common. All world religions, at least on the surface, have a similar list of acts which are evil, including lying, stealing, anger, adultery, murder and so forth. In addition, the list of positive things to do from most religions bears some similarities. Such good acts include loving people, being unselfish, seeking the good of others and helping the needy. If religion is viewed as a list of right and wrong things to do, there is some truth in the claim that all religions are similar.

This being granted as true (if one looks in detail, even this similarity begins to fall apart, but never mind that), there is a very important reason that the claim that all religions are more or less the same falls completely flat. Religion is not about a list of rights and wrong, but it is about theology and world view. Religion makes authoritative claims about the nature of spiritual reality, of deity, and of the fundamental nature of human beings. If one looks at Islam, or at Hinduism, Buddhism, Jainism, Ba'hai or other world religions, one will find that it is absolutely impossible to see these as alternative forms of what is known as Christianity. Their theology is incompatible with that of the Bible. If the Christian religion is true, then there is one God and only one way to come into a relationship with that God—through faith in the saving power of the blood of Jesus (Romans 3:23-26, for example). If the Bible is inspired, then a relationship with God is to be found in faith and repentance on our part and grace on God's part. No other religion has a theology remotely like this (other than Judaism, of course). If we come into a relationship with the Creator through the blood of Jesus shed on the cross, then we definitely do not come to know God through the eight-fold path of Buddha, through canceling out bad karma (Hinduism), through submitting the will to Allah (Islam) or through any other system of religion. If the New Testament is the Word of God, then Hinduism, Jaina, Taoism and the other "isms" are false religions—they are a deception. No amount of comparative religion will change this fact.

Bottom line, though some would call this a close-minded statement, in the words of Peter in Acts 4 concerning Jesus: *"There is no other name under heaven given to men by which we must be saved."* Shallow similarities do not cover over the fact that the claims of Jesus Christ preclude all other religions. That is the end of the story.

QUESTION:

What about those who have not heard of Jesus? Does God choose who is saved? What about other "Christian" groups who claim to teach the truth but directly contradict one another?

ANSWER:

First, you ask about all the "Christian" denominations which are out there...all of which claim to have the right way to God, some of which directly contradict one another. My response is to throw the question back in your lap. You must begin by asking what is taught in the Bible. Many of the teachings of the religious movements you name are the result of human invention. Jesus was very strong in his condemnation of teaching human tradition that is taught as if it is from God (Matthew 15:1-10). In the context of Matthew, Jesus is critiquing the tradition-encrusted Judaism of his day. However, I believe that, if he came to us today, he would have similar scathing (but loving) comments for some of our brands of Christianity because their *"teachings are but rules taught by men"* (Matthew 15:9).

The best way to evaluate a "Christian" group's claim to be "the way" is to become thoroughly familiarized with the Bible, especially the New Testament (as it is the source of authority for Christian practice). In Acts 17:10-12, a group of people are commended by God because they were not just open to learning; they were also checking out Paul's teaching against their Jewish Bibles. In 2 Timothy 4:1-5, Paul commands Timothy to preach the Word of God. Timothy was to stick to those things which were revealed to him in the Bible and to avoid the temptation to turn to human logic and philosophy. God gave us a pattern to follow. Of course, all Christian groups claim to be following the Bible, but asking a few simple questions will reveal the truth or untruth of this claim fairly easily in the case of many Christian groups. I prefer not to get into proving why one denomination or another is or is not following the Bible at this point. Instead, I will leave it to your own research.

Then there is the question of whether the members of a religious group are saved. Ephesians 4:4 says that there is one church. This seems to be belied by the plethora of churches out there. The true church of God is composed of the saved believers in Jesus, whatever group they fellowship with. The church is not co-extensive with any single religious group. However, some "Christian" groups are far from teaching the basic truths of the Bible. Why has God allowed there to be so great a number of "churches," many of which teach blatantly false doctrine, some of which are not even helping people to get to heaven? That is a good question. It appears that God allows men to do what they choose with what he has given them. God allows us "free will," even if we abuse it. God is not proud of or happy with Mormonism or Jehovah's Witness. Do not blame God for these heretical groups, unless you want to criticize him for giving us the freedom to do or not do what is commanded in the Bible. I will challenge you, in love, to pursue the truth found in the Bible, whether it ends up agreeing with your own pre-conceived ideas about the truth or not. Pursue the truth of the Bible with great courage and stubbornness.

Next, you ask another of those "hard" questions. What about all those people who never had a chance to hear the gospel message about Jesus? Are they all condemned to hell? Isn't it unfair that these people will be judged by a standard to which they were never even exposed? The Bible does not provide a simple, unambiguous answer to your question. Romans 2:12-16 seems to imply that those who never even hear about Jesus are judged according to their consciences. But who is not guilty of abusing their own conscience at some time? In the final analysis, God will accept into heaven whomever he chooses. This is not our business. Jesus stated that the way to eternal life with God is narrow and difficult, while the way to hell and eternal separation from God is broad and easy (Matthew 7:13-14).

Given this fact, it is our job to make sure we are on that narrow road and to call as many as possible to be with us on the narrow road. It is not my job to "judge" who is and who is not on that road, but if I see someone who appears to me to be on the wide road which leads to destruction, I am compelled to warn, encourage, teach or do whatever I can to help them get on the road which leads to life.

QUESTION:
How do you explain Christianity to a Black Muslim?

ANSWER:

The simple answer is that I would explain it to this person pretty much the same way I would anyone else. I have studied the Bible with a few Muslims, but not with a Black Muslim. However, if I were to have the opportunity to share my faith with a follower of the Nation of Islam, I would present the true Jesus—Son of God, fulfiller of prophecy, worker of miracles, sacrificial lamb to take away the sins of the world and so forth. Of course, this list of basics may very well be too simple to answer your question. You may want some advice specific to the Black Muslim. The apostle Paul adapted some of the content of his message, depending on the cultural and religious background of his hearers, as evidenced by Acts 17 when he was in Athens.

In order to explain Christianity to a Muslim, or more particularly to a Black Muslim, I suggest you first try to understand his or her basic line of reasoning and assumptions about God. In other words, you need to understand his or her theology. Let me suggest a couple of books which will help you acquire a background in Islam and the Koran. The first is *Jesus and Islam*, by Douglas Jacoby (available at www.ipibooks.com). The second is *Answering Islam: The Crescent in the Light of the Cross*, by Norman Geisler and Abdul Saleeb (2nd edition, Baker Books, 2006). In addition, you will find a helpful outline and power point, as well as an audio lesson on Islam at my web site (**EFC**). Most importantly, I strongly encourage you to read the Koran for yourself. It is only about two thirds as long as the New Testament. You can read it in a few hours. There is nothing like knowing what you are talking about when discussing Islam with a Muslim.

Having given you some references, let me give you an extremely brief outline of the approach I personally would use. I suggest you focus on what makes Christianity unique. Your Muslim friend has been taught that Islam is a newer and better revelation than Christianity, but that Judaism, Christianity and Islam come from the same root and have similar teachings. This is not a complete distortion of the truth, but the basic premise of Islam about God is absolutely and diametrically opposed to that of Christianity. It is these distinctions which I would show to my friend, using the Bible.

Specifically, Islam is a religion which teaches our life is the result of predestination and fate. Christianity is a religion of choice. I would point my friend to passages in the Bible which show that being saved is a matter of a personal decision to have a relationship with a loving God who is concerned about us. This is very different from Islam, with its aloof, impersonal God. Salvation in Islam is a matter of works. If one follows certain rules, then one essentially buys their way into heaven. In Christianity, salvation is not by human effort but by the sacrificial gift of God. You should be aware that the whole idea of a savior dying on a cross to save mankind is anathema to Muslims. They absolutely deny that Jesus died on the cross for our sins. This brings me back to my original statement. I suggest you present to this person the loving, personal God who wants to adopt your Black Muslim friend into his family, to offer forgiveness of sins, not based on human effort, but based on grace and the love of God.

In addition, it will be helpful to point your Black Muslim friend to the Bible itself as the inspired Word of God. You can assume that he or she has been told that there are many mistakes and inconsistencies in the Bible, as this is standard fare among Muslims. They are told that the Bible is corrupted. You will need to patiently point out that this claim simply does not hold up to careful study. If you can convince your friend to read a Christian apologetic book such as mine (**RFB**), then that may make a big difference. You can challenge your friend's pride on this one: "If you are so sure the Bible is full of errors, why not be open-minded and read a book which presents an opposing view?" The idea here is to use the evidence to overcome the preconceived (false) idea that the Koran has greater evidence for inspiration than the Bible.

Let me say what I would *not* do. I would not try to convert my friend by laying out the dirt on Islam. I would not start by pointing out the fact that Muhammad was responsible for the unjustified execution of several hundred Jewish men for purely political reasons, or that he had at least twelve wives (violating the limit of three in the Koran itself!). I would not point out the obvious science errors in the Koran or the blatant mistakes of Jewish history found in the book. I would not confront him or her on the fact that the Koran glorifies cruelty and killing in the name of Allah. I believe it is more fruitful to present the truth than to cut down the lie. If you attack Islam or Muhammad directly, you will produce defensiveness, not open-mindedness. You want to expose your friend to the love of Jesus. If he or she is feeling attacked, this will not be helpful toward that end.

To summarize, I believe that a Muslim can (and will) come to Christ, but only because God, through the Holy Spirit, has prepared their heart. Because most Muslims are carefully indoctrinated, you need to be patient and loving, giving God time to work, waiting for the right moment to move to the next step. Patience and prayer will be a requirement. May God be with you in your efforts.

[Note: in the comments above, I have assumed that one would treat a Black Muslim as any other Muslim. Despite the racist overtones of the Black Muslim movement, I believe that beginning with the presupposition that a Black Muslim is in fact a Muslim is the place to start.]

QUESTION:

How is it possible for people who are holding on to another religion to come to salvation in Jesus? I have a lot of friends who are zealous Muslims. How can I help them? Does Romans 2:14-15 also refer to them?

ANSWER:

Call it narrow-minded, call it bigoted, call it whatever you will, but when one reads the Bible and the sayings of Jesus, it is clear that the only way you can help your Muslim friends is to introduce them to Jesus Christ and for them to accept him as Lord. Jesus said, *"I am the way, the truth and the life, no one comes to the Father except through me"* (John 14:6). Peter said, *"Salvation is found in no one else, for there is no other name under heaven given to men by which we must be saved"* (Acts 4:12). It does not take a theologian to interpret these passages. Absolutely no one is saved and no one goes to heaven or gains a relationship with God through Muhammad. It may be hard to accept that your seemingly sincere and extremely devout Muslim friends are not saved, but the plain truth, at least according to the Bible, is that they are lost.

Sincerity does not equal truth. If a person had cancer and was offered two medicines, one which was likely to bring about a cure and the other which had absolutely no value to cure his or her cancer, it would do that person a disservice to keep him or her in the dark about the true situation. A sincere belief that the bogus medicine will work will not help. Having a nice, politically correct attitude and refusing to take a stand that only one of the medicines will work definitely will not help either. The fact is that the teachings about salvation in the Bible and in the Koran are not compatible. The Bible teaches that salvation is through the grace of God and through the blood of Jesus. The response of faith, repentance and baptism are required for salvation. The Koran teaches that salvation is through obedience and submission to a set of rules—to the "will" of Allah. Salvation cannot be both by grace and by works. There is only one cure for the cancer of sin. It may seem harsh to be close-minded on the subject, but it is the only way you will be able to help your friends.

You bring up the subject of Romans 2:14-15. I believe it is difficult to be absolutely sure how to apply this passage. It suggests that, for the person who is completely unaware of the Christian teachings of God with regard to Jesus, there is at least a possibility that, if they strictly obey the truth as they know it in their conscience, they just might somehow make it into heaven. Although it is difficult to know exactly what Romans 2:14-15 means, we can be confident of one thing—it almost certainly does not apply to the case of your sincere Muslim friends. Surely they know about Jesus. Surely they have access to the Bible, and more specifically, to the New Testament. It would be a grave mistake on your part for you to give in to sentimentality and hold out hope, either in your heart or in your discussions with your Muslim friends, that they can be saved as practitioners of Islam.

So, what are you to do? Introduce them lovingly and patiently to Jesus and to the New Testament. Let them see your life and your love. In the words of 1 Peter 3:16, do this with gentleness and respect, but in the words of Ephesians 4:15, speak the truth in love.

QUESTION:

A Muslim friend made a claim to me that Deuteronomy 18:15-19 is speaking of Muhammad and not Jesus. This does not make sense to me because Muhammad was an Arab, not a Jew (Genesis 22:18). He is not of the house of David (Jeremiah 21:5). He also claimed to me that biblical prophecy is not perfect. I believe it is perfect if it is used to describe Christ. What do you think of this?

ANSWER:

It is a standard apologetic claim of Muslims that Muhammad is the fulfillment of the prophecy in Deuteronomy 18:15-19. Muslims are given this information uncritically in a way which takes the passage out of its context. I agree with you that this is completely unjustified and a misuse of the scripture. As you imply, the phrase "I will raise up for them a prophet like you from among their brothers" surely implies that the future prophet will be a Jew. It is a huge stretch to say that this scripture implies that a member of an Arab tribe is one of the "brothers" of Moses.

Perhaps a more appropriate use of this passage is to apply Deuteronomy 18:20 to Muhammad in a negative way: *"But a prophet who presumes to speak in my name anything I have not commanded him to say, or a prophet who speaks in the names of other gods, must be put to death."* Muhammad has falsely claimed to speak for God. I know this to be true, because Muhammad denied both the death of Jesus on the cross and his resurrection. 1 John 2:22 labels any such person as "the antichrist." If we allow that the Old Testament is from God, then unquestionably Muhammad is a false prophet. It is extremely presumptuous for Muslims to try to apply this passage to the false prophet Muhammad.

You are also right that the Bible says the Messiah will be from the house of David (Isaiah 11:1, 10, Isaiah 16:6 and many others), but to be fair, the passage in Deuteronomy 18 does not mention this. If Muslims claimed Muhammad fulfilled these passages—that he was of the house of David, that would be even more blatantly false, but I have never heard that claimed.

As you point out, Muslims often will claim that the Bible is full of errors. They try to point out inconsistencies as well as contradictions with teachings in the Koran. I have looked at several Islamic websites which purport to show all the "mistakes" in the Bible. I have found that the great majority of these use very simplistic arguments which are very easily explained by anyone with even rudimentary knowledge of the Bible. One gets the feeling that many Islamic critics of the Bible have never read the Bible, but only quote from other Islamic critics. To be fair, not all Islamic apologists fit this description, but most do. You will find a fairly thorough article on the Muslim apologists at my website www.EvidenceForChristianity.org. The title of the article is *The Koran: Inspiration or Human Creation?* I suggest you find this article, which is a response to many of the common criticisms of the Bible from Islamic apologists.

QUESTION:
Is it right that the religion of Islam came from Ishmael's descendants?

ANSWER:
Yes, this is essentially correct if you take the Bible at face value. It is also taught in the Koran. The Bible describes the peoples who came to be known as the Arabs as having been descended from Ishmael as well as from the descendants of Keturah, Abraham's concubine. The relevant material is in 1 Chronicles 1:29-33, in which specific Arab tribes are identified. As Muhammad (the founder and

chief prophet of Islam) is Arab, he would be a direct descendent of Ishmael (or possibly of one of Keturah's sons). This is why historians of religion claim that Judaism, Christianity and Islam all trace their roots to Abraham. Bear in mind that approximately 2,500 years separate the birth of Ishmael and Muhammad, so the relationship is extremely distant! It is also worth noting that the Koran falsely implies that Abraham's promised heir was Ishmael, not Isaac, which is in obvious conflict with the Bible (Sura 37:102). In addition the Koran has Abraham and Ishmael traveling to Mecca to worship at the Kabah! (the black meteor which Muslims bow toward in their annual pilgrimage). It is illogical to believe that Muhammad correctly identified the son of promise; whereas the Jews, who lived over 1,500 years before Muhammad, were confused about Abraham's descendents.

QUESTION:
Who is Muhammad and why does he play such an important role in Islam?

ANSWER:
Muhammad was an Arab trader who became the chief prophet and founder of the Muslim religion, also known as Islam. He lived in the sixth and seventh centuries AD. At the age of 40, while living in Mecca, he claimed to have received a vision of the angel Gabriel. In subsequent "visions," he claimed to receive the various suras (the equivalent of the "books" of the Bible) which were combined to make the Koran, the scripture of Islam. Muslims claim that Muhammed produced the Koran, despite being illiterate. After a number of years in Mecca with very little success at making converts, Muhammad moved to Medina, where he eventually converted hundreds and gained political power in that city. Muhammad was infamously responsible for the massacre of several hundred Jews while living in Medina. Later, after several piratical raids on caravans from Mecca, he eventually conquered his home town, which became the base from which he established the Muslim empire and spread his new religion throughout the Arabian Peninsula. The Muslim religion is avowedly monotheistic. It has many elements of Judaism, at least in its historical context. The religion is based on works salvation, with a very strong emphasis on predestination. It would be fair to say that Muhammad is one of the four or five most influential religious

leaders in the history of humanity. The religion he founded claims roughly one billion adherents today across North Africa, the Middle East and South Asia, as well as scatterings in almost every country in the world.

There is more information about Muhammad and Islam at my website (**EFC**), including extensive notes and a Power-Point presentation.

QUESTIONS:

I have a friend who is a Muslim. They believe in only one God. My friend asked me if I thought that Jesus was God and said that the Bible does not talk about the trinity. He also claimed that Jesus never referred to himself as God. He asked that if Jesus was God, why would he pray to himself in Gethsemane or say to himself, "Father why have you forsaken me." My friend also makes the point that if we worship Jesus and God, that would not be considered monotheism. Here are my questions. Is Jesus God? And why do we pray "In Jesus name?"

ANSWER:

It is understandable that Muslims could be confused with Christianity's claim to be monotheistic, given the Bible's doctrines of Jesus and the Holy Spirit. John 1:1 says that the Word (i.e. Jesus in the context of the passage) was God and at the same time he was with God in the beginning. From a human perspective, it is impossible to both be with God and to be God. This teaching is difficult to comprehend and to explain. Yet, it is what the Bible teaches. The Bible teaches that the one God, Creator of the universe, is formed of three "persons" who make one God. We will have to admit that this is a difficult teaching, and should not be surprised that our Muslim friends find this hard to accept at first.

Your critical friend is correct is saying that the "trinity" is not taught in the Bible per se. What I mean is that there is no passage in the Bible which uses a word which can be translated as trinity. Nevertheless, what is very clear is that the Bible claims deity for Jesus, the son of God. Consider some of the passages which claim deity for Jesus. For example, we have the parallel passages Colossians 1:16 and Hebrews 1:2. Here we have it stated about Jesus that *"all things were created by him and for him."* It says that *"all things hold together in Christ."* It says that the universe was made through Christ.

The Old Testament says that God is the Creator. The New Testament says that Jesus is the Creator. Both are true. Jesus is God.

Your friend says that Jesus never claimed deity. This is a false statement. Jesus said this in John 8:58: *"Before Abraham was born, I AM."* In this and other situations, they picked up stones to stone him because he claimed to be God. Notice, Jesus never corrected their conclusion that he claimed to be God. God's name in Exodus is I AM. Jesus said I AM. This is the clearest possible claim of deity. Colossians 2:9 says that *"in Christ, the fullness of deity lives in bodily form."* This is a very clear statement of deity for Christ. In John 20:28, Thomas says to Jesus, *"My Lord and my God."* Notice that Jesus did not correct him! In Titus 2:13, Paul says of Jesus, *"Our great God and savior, Jesus Christ."* To say that the New Testament does not impute deity for Christ is to make a false claim. The Old Testament also views Jesus as God. In Zechariah 12:10, God says, *"They will look on me, the one they have pierced...."* In this prophecy of the Messiah, God refers to Jesus as "me."

So, if your friend finds it uncomfortable to allow God to be both Father and Son, then he has a problem with the Bible. I believe you should admit that this teaching is difficult to understand in human terms. The question we should ask is not if we find it easy to accept the idea of one God being expressed in three persons. The question we should ask is whether or not it is true. The evidence of Jesus' life without committing sin, his miracles, his fulfillment of Old Testament prophecy and his resurrection from the dead speaks for themselves. Even if our Muslim friends find it hard to accept, it is true. Jesus is God. Jesus is the Son of God. Jesus is deity. As Jesus said, *"I and the father are one"* (John 10:30).

You ask one other question, which is why do we pray to or through Jesus? Your friend claims that a jealous God would not tolerate us praying to Jesus. Let me point out that God said of Jesus on the mount of transfiguration, *"This is my son, of whom I am well pleased."* The Father is proud of the Son. He is not jealous. Given that Jesus is deity, as proven above, I would imagine that the Father does not mind at all that we pray to Jesus or through Jesus. As it says in 1 Timothy 2:5, there is one mediator between man and God, Jesus Christ. The fact that Jesus is mediator for us with the Father may be one reason many pray to God in Jesus' name. As far as I know, there is no requirement for us to pray in Jesus' name. This is a tradition. It is not necessarily a bad tradition, but it is a tradition. The pattern we find in the New Testament is praying to God or praying to the Father.

We do not have examples of praying to Jesus in the Bible. However, I find it hard to criticize praying to Jesus, as Jesus is God. As for praying "in Jesus' name," again, this practice is not found in the New Testament, but 1 Timothy 2:5 calls Jesus a mediator between God and men. Given that Jesus is our mediator, I can see nothing wrong with praying "in Jesus' name," as long as we remember that this is a tradition, not a commandment.

QUESTION:
Is heaven a worldly place as described in the Koran? Isn't Muhammad appealing to people's darkest desires?

ANSWER:
Your characterization of the Koran that it gives a rather "worldly" view of heaven is accurate. Heaven is described as a place of fountains and feasts and being waited on by beautiful virgins with big, brown eyes (Sura 2:25, Sura 4:57, Sura 13:35, Sura 22:14, Sura 44:43-55). I would not necessarily say that this pleasure-oriented picture of heaven plays toward people's "darkest desires." The desire to have comfort and pleasure is something given to us by God, not Satan. Even the sexual desire is given to us by God. The desires fulfilled by the Koran's description of heaven are only evil if overindulged or sought for selfish purposes, to the exclusion of helping others. God gave us good-tasting food to eat and a desire for pleasant climate and an appreciation of beauty. The "darkest desires," in my opinion, are those to abuse others or to take advantage of them, or to exercise power over them for our own advantage.

Personally, I advise caution about criticizing the Koran for its picture of heaven, even though I agree with your basic thesis. Let me be the "devil's advocate" and defend the Koran for just a second. I can imagine a Muslim apologist defending the passages in question by saying, "Obviously, this is just a metaphorical description in our scripture. The prophet Muhammad is telling us that heaven is a wonderful place to be, and he is describing this in a way that an Arabic person in the seventh-century AD would understand it. It is a place of great reward, very much like the heaven described in the Bible." So I agree with you to some extent, but I would be careful not to state things too strongly. We should, in the words of Jesus, treat others as we would want to be treated. We should treat the "scriptures" of other people by giving them the benefit of the doubt, even if we are convinced in the end that they are not from God at all.

In summary, I agree that the description of heaven in the Koran is uncomfortably worldly from my perspective. Trying to be fair to Muslims and the Koran one could interpret the relevant passages in the Koran metaphorically without doing too much damage to the text. I agree with you that the description of heaven in the Koran could be described as a way to get converts, but then again, we could say the same thing about the description of heaven in the Bible!

In the end, what it comes down to is that the Bible shows every sign of being inspired by God, but the Koran does not. [Note: the next question is relevant to this.]

QUESTIONS:

1. Are there any clear errors in the Koran?
2. I found online some obvious errors in the Koran. It says that Alexander the Great was given his power from Allah and was a prophet, but the way I see it, he was a sinner and an idolater. It also said he built a huge wall to keep an army out, which has no historical basis (Sura 18:83-30). What is your view on this?
3. What is your opinion on errors in the Koran? My Muslim friends say that the Koran is without error. They try to attack the credibility of the Bible by saying it is full of errors. Can give you an example of an error in the Koran? I have heard one example which is in Suras 16:15, 21:13, 31:10, and 78:6-7, which say Allah threw down mountains to stabilize the Earth. What is your view on this, and what is your opinion on the Koran itself?

ANSWER:

You ask whether the Koran is "perfect" as its supporters claim, or whether it has blatant errors—ones which cannot be logically explained away by a reasonable person. Your comments imply categories of possible errors, such as:

1. Internal inconsistencies
2. Historical errors
3. Errors of fact relating to scientific claims in the Muslim scripture.

My response is that, despite the claims of Muslim apologists, yes, there are absolutely clear examples of mistakes in the Koran. The only way those who argue that the Koran is perfect can deal with these is by ignoring the questions. I have considered this matter carefully and done quite a bit of study of the Koran myself to test these claims.

First, let me say that it is important for anyone who criticizes the Muslim scripture to be both careful and fair. I am very sensitive to this because I have seen innumerable examples of such unfair and unreasonable attacks on the validity of the Bible as an inspired text. Many have made unfounded claims about the Bible in all three of the categories listed above. Numbers have claimed that the Bible is loaded with blatant scientific errors, historical inaccuracies and obvious inconsistencies with itself. I have considered many dozens of these criticisms and found all of them to be false. Some of them come from people who have no care for accuracy and fairness, but are simply looking for mud to sling around. Such people find supposed "inconsistencies" in the Bible which are so easily explained by anyone who understands the Bible as to be irresponsible. Others have looked with a more careful eye and still discovered what they feel to be mistakes in the Bible. I have found that these do not hold up well to careful analysis either.

  The point is this—in the spirit of the Golden Rule, which was given to us by Jesus, we should be very careful in pointing out "errors" in the Koran. Many Christian groups have not done a good job here. There is a tendency to pass along all charges against the Koran, whether they are substantiated by careful scholarship or not. Even when we discover blatant signs of human wisdom in the Muslim scripture, we should not resort to childish behavior when pointing out the mistakes. Let me suggest a more fair way to develop Christian comparative apologetics as they relate to Islam. For those Christians who explain and compare the Koran to the Bible, what should be done first and foremost is to read and study the Koran itself. The second priority should be to read the works of Islamic apologists. How do they explain and defend the Koran? Dead-last priority should be given to reading the "dirt" on Islam to be found in the works of Christian apologists who are not sufficiently careful to be fair.

  One way to come to the realization that this is a wise path is to read the typical criticisms of the Bible which come from the pens of Islamic critics. If one reads the books or peruses the websites of Islamic apologists, one will discover immediately that most of these criticisms are very shallow. The accusations against biblical science and the supposed inconsistencies and historical errors one can find at most anti-Christian websites—especially at Islamic-oriented ones representing almost uniformly poor scholarship. Most come from people who have not tested their statements by carefully reading the Bible or by simply asking a Christian scholar whether their arguments will stand up to reasoned analysis. It becomes obvious that the majority of such critics get their material from trolling the other anti-Bible groups for "dirt" on the Bible.

  If we find such behavior to be offensive, then the Golden Rule would dictate that Christian apologists ought to be far more fair and considerate in their analysis of other religions and their scripture. I have read material at quite a few websites devoted to "disproving" the Koran. The average quality of the material used at these sites may be somewhat over that of their opposite foes, but not by much. As intimated above, I find that most of the dirt one finds on the Koran is recycled material from others sources, which shows little, if any, sign of coming from someone who has actually read the Koran, and even more importantly, from an understanding of current Islamic theology or Koranic interpretation. I will admit that careful analysis of the Koran and a commitment to listen to Islamic scholars is a lofty goal which may require a considerable amount of work, but as the old saying goes—anything worth doing is worth doing well.

You ask a general question about the Koran, but you also ask specific questions about criticisms you have read. This is a good way to approach the subject. First, let me consider the example you raise about Sura 18:83-100. Is this a legitimate example of a blatant error in the Koran? First of all, the person you quote assumes that this passage in the Koran definitely refers to Alexander the Great. I did a bit of research and found that it is true that many Islamic scholars have interpreted this as a reference to Alexander. It would appear, though, that this is not universally the case. To quote from Islamic scholar Abdullah Yusef Ali: "Literally, 'the Two-horned one,' or the king with two horns: Who was he? In what age, and where did he live? The Koran gives us no material on which we can base a positive answer. Nor is it necessary to find an answer, as the story is treated as a parable. Popular opinion identifies Dhu al Quarayn (the ruler in Sura 18:83-100) with Alexander the Great. An alternative suggestion is an ancient Persian King, or a prehistoric Himyarite King." As I read it (in English translation, of course), it is not obvious to me at all that this passage has to be a reference to Alexander. In fact, Alexander is best described as a one-horned one rather than a two-horned ruler. Persia is better described as a two-horned kingdom (see **Daniel** ch. 10). Without doing a thorough treatment of this example, let me give a preliminary conclusion. If we were to assume that the Koran is inspired by God, and if we can also assume that Sura 18:83-100 is indeed intended to be a literal description of the work of Alexander the Great, then you would indeed have a possible example of an error in the Koran. There is no way to understand Alexander as a man of faith according to Islam! However, if I were trying to develop a clear and fair case against the inspiration of the Koran, I would not use this example for the simple reason that it is debatable. I would prefer to use examples which would hold up to scrutiny even in the face of open discussion with Islamic apologists.

You give a second example. This involves what the Koran appears to say about the nature of Earth's mountains and their purpose. Examples, as you mention, include Suras 16:15, 21:31, 31:10, 78:6-7. Sura 16:15 says, "And He has cast great mountains in the earth lest it might be convulsed with you, and rivers and roads that you may go aright." Sura 21:31 says, "And We have made great mountains in the earth lest it might be convulsed with them, and We have made in it wide ways that they may follow a right direction." Sura 31:10 says, "He created the heavens without pillars as you see them, and put mountains upon the earth lest it might convulse with you." I am not a scholar in Arabic, to say the least, but would agree that this does appear to be a good example of bad science in the Koran. These passages definitely do seem to be saying that Allah created mountains in order to prevent earthquakes, whereas we know that mountains definitely do not prevent earthquakes. In fact, they are the *result* of earthquakes. I have found a number of other examples of statements in the Koran which represent obvious scientific errors, some of which are listed below.

Let me move to your question about my opinion of the Koran in general. I would say that, on the whole, it is an impressive book. If one considers its literary and even its moral value, coming as it does from a pagan who was born into a violent, polytheistic society, the Koran is an impressive accomplishment. However, to consider it as inspired by God in the sense that the Bible clearly is, there is no way that it even comes close to passing this test. The obvious scientific error you mention above is one example. Let me supply just a couple of others.

First, right in the context of the Sura you mention above, there is a scientific blunder of the obvious sort. Consider Sura 18:86: "He journeyed on a certain road until he reached the West and saw the sun setting in a pool of black mud. Hard by (i.e. near the pool of mud into which the sun set) he found a certain people. 'Dhu al Qarnayn,' We said, 'You must either punish them or show them kindness.'" Muhammad is not the first to spread around the false idea that the sun sets into a body of water. This rather obvious error is the result of human thinking on the motion of the sun.

Another clear scientific misconception in the Koran is found in Sura 21:33: "It is He who created the night and the day, and the sun and the moon: all (the celestial bodies) swim along, each in its rounded course." The idea that the sun goes in a circular course around the earth was discredited with the work of Copernicus and Galileo. Geocentrism was the false concept of the heavens, common in the time of the writing of the Koran. Unfortunately for the claim of inerrancy of the Muslim scripture, this false idea slipped into the Koran. When I read Sura 21:33, I see no other way to interpret this passage!

Or consider Sura 34:9: "If We will, We can cause the earth to cave in beneath their feet or let fragments of the sky fall upon them." The idea that the heavens were composed of solid crystal spheres has long since disappeared, but it was the common conception of the ancients, which would explain this odd statement being in the Koran. As I read Islamic commentators, I see no answer to this fact. One makes the shard of sky be a metaphorical challenge in people's life, which is a pretty questionable interpretation of this passage.

Sura 18:9-26 has a fable of three boys and a dog entering a cave, falling asleep, and waking 309 years later, as if they had never fallen asleep. It is hard to take this fable seriously.

There are many rather obvious historical errors in the Koran as well. For example, one can find it stated that King David wore an iron coat chain mail in Sura 34:9. The problem with this claim is that iron-chain armor was not invented until many centuries after David lived. The Koranic commentators I have read on this gloss over this error.

As a second example, consider the story of Abraham as described in Sura 21:51-71. Here, Muhammad has Abraham confronting his father and family because of the many family idols which they worship. Abraham smashes all their idols except the largest one. When confronted, he tells his family that the large idol smashed the smaller ones. 'It was their chief (idol) who smote them. Ask them (i.e. the idols) if they can speak.' The idolaters admit that the idols cannot speak, at which point Abraham chides them, 'Would you then worship that, instead of God, which can neither help nor harm you. Shame on you and on your idols! Have you no sense?' They attempt to burn Abraham to death in a fire, but God makes the fire cool so that he does not die. Where did this fable come from? Actually, Muhammad borrowed it from Jewish folklore of the second-century AD, specifically from the Midrash Rabbah, which has a virtually identical myth. Which is one to believe, the Jewish account of Abraham's life from about 1400 BC, or the Koranic account, borrowed from a Jewish folk tale of the second-century AD? The Islamic response is to claim that the account of the life of Abraham in Genesis is inaccurate—that the version found in the Koran was expunged from the original. This is a spurious argument.

Consider a third example of obvious historical inaccuracy in the Koran. In Sura 19:29-33, the writer of the Koran has the little baby Jesus talking. The infant Jesus says, "I am the servant of God. He has given me the Book and ordained me a prophet. His blessing is upon me wherever I go, and He has exhorted me to be steadfast in prayer and to give alms as long as I shall live." The baby Jesus continues with his discourse in Sura 19. Quite a vocabulary for an infant! Did Muhammad receive this information by revelation? Possibly, but it is worth noting that an apocryphal "Gospel of the Infancy of Jesus Christ" from second-century AD Egypt has a very similar account. Sura 3:49 also has Jesus taking clay, breathing on it and turning it into a bird. Is this an accurate record of an actual event? More likely, Muhammad borrowed it from one of his eleven wives, two of whom are believed to have been "Christians." This Koranic fable is borrowed from the apocryphal "Gospel" of Thomas which says of Jesus as a young child, "Then he took from the bank of the stream some soft clay, and formed out of it twelve sparrows… Then Jesus, clapping together the palms of his hands, called to the sparrows, and said to them: 'Go, fly away.'" We can see that there is no doubt that Muhammad borrowed from both Jewish and Christian myth, which makes any attempt to describe the Koran as inspired by God very difficult to support.

 Another obvious error is found in Sura 7:124, which has Pharaoh threatening to crucify those who follow Moses more than 1,000 years before crucifixion was even invented. In this case, the writer should have checked his sources.

 Other obvious historical errors in the Koran include confusing Ishmael and Isaac (Sura 37:102), Noah's fourth son drowning (Sura 20:120), Zechariah (John the Baptist's father) is silent for three days (rather than nine months) (Sura 3:41). And there are many more examples which could be mentioned. Islamic scholars typically explain the inconsistency with the Bible record by saying the Bible is wrong. This argument does not hold up to scrutiny, partly because many or most of the errors in the Koran are actually borrowed from obviously bogus apocryphal works. In the case of Zechariah, in order to believe the Koran, we have to assume that those who actually knew Jesus' mother got it wrong, while Muhammad got it right over 600 years later. This is simply not believable.

 The third category of errors in the Koran is internal inconsistencies. There are a great number of examples in which Muhammad or another author makes statements in one place in the Koran which are incontrovertibly in direct opposition to statements elsewhere. This fact is so well known, even to Islamic scholars, that they have developed a doctrine to explain away the contradictions. The means of explaining away the obvious errors in the Koran are called "abrogations." Apparently, even those who put together the Koran in its final form were aware of the blatant inconsistencies in the Suras, as is clear from Sura 2:106: "If we abrogate a verse or cause it to be forgotten, We will replace it by a better one or one similar." This is a striking statement! Can you imagine reading such an apology in the Bible? In this passage, Allah admits that some of his early statements need to be abrogated. Islamic scholar Jalalu'd Din says the number of required abrogations (i.e. corrections, mistakes) in the Koran is between five and 500. The passages which must be annulled (mansukh) are called nazikh. The idea is that more recent passages can annul older passages. One problem is that it is virtually impossible to tell which of Muhammad's writings are older than which.

Examples of inconsistencies in the Koran include Sura 2:142-144, in which the city to which Muslims must bow when praying is changed from Jerusalem to Mecca. Another abrogation is required to justify the fact that Sura 7:54 lists six days of creation, while Sura 41:9-12 lists eight days. Sura 17:103 has Pharaoh drowned with his army, while Sura 10:90-92 has him rescued as a sign to others. Sura 4:157-158 has Jesus definitely not dying, but being called to Allah, while Sura 19:33 states that Jesus died and was raised from the dead. Islamic scholars have a very difficult time with this one. An almost innumerable list of examples can be given.

In summary, the Koran is certainly an amazing book, considering the time and the circumstances under which it was written. However, the claim that it is perfect—that it is inspired by an all-powerful God—does not hold up to careful study. Unless my concept of inspiration is mistaken, divine scripture will not contain material culled from folklore and myth, obvious scientific errors or mistakes that even its supporters admit are in the text. Having said this, I believe Christians need to apply careful scholarship along with fair, reasonable and respectful treatment of the text of the Koran.

Translations of the Koran are taken from:

1. Abdullah Yusuf Ali, *"The Meaning of the Holy Koran"* (Amana Publications, Beltsville, Maryland, 2001).

2. N. J. Dawood, *"The Koran,"* (Penguin Classics, London, England, 1997).

QUESTION:

I have heard that the Mormons claim that when Jesus died he went to preach to long-dead people in the Old Testament. Any comment on this claim?

ANSWER:

There are two possibilities with regard to what you heard. One possibility is that you are misunderstanding a Mormon teaching. What the *Book of Mormon* does claim is that, immediately after his resurrection, Jesus came to the New World and preached repentance and baptism for the forgiveness of sins to native Central Americans. If you read the *Book of Mormon*, you will get the idea from the context that the place Jesus came to preach is somewhere in Central America. As strange as the claim may be to Christians, this teaching in the Book of Mormon does not involve time-travel!

Actually, it is easy to make the mistake I believe you have made (or else, whoever told you this has made) because the *Book of Mormon* has people teaching about Jesus and preaching repentance and baptism for forgiveness of sins as early as about 544 BC, and even more clearly in the second-century BC. This is one of the most obvious mistakes in the *Book of Mormon*. There is an excellent summary of the content of the *Book of Mormon* at my website (**EFC**). This summary was written by a friend named Joe Fields. It is titled, *The Book of Mormon: A Summary*. If you read this summary, you will see why your friend got confused about the time-travel idea.

A second possibility is that what you heard is a reference (not a specific Mormon teaching) to what is said in 1 Peter 3:17-18. This passage says about Jesus, *"He was put to death in the body but made alive in the Spirit, in which also he went and preached to the spirits in prison who disobeyed long ago when God waited patiently in the days of Noah while the ark was being built."* This is one of the more obscure and difficult-to-understand passages in the New Testament. I myself am not sure exactly what it means. However, almost certainly it is not about Jesus traveling back in time to preach to long-dead people!

QUESTION:

How can you disprove Mormonism? Why are there so many different versions of the Bible?

ANSWER:

One can consider the validity of this religion from two main perspectives. First of all, we can ask whether the teachings of Mormonism (as contained in the *Book of Mormon*, the *Doctrine and Covenants* and the *Pearl of Great Price*) are consistent with the inspired word of God—the Old and New Testaments? Second, do the character and life of Joseph Smith show evidence of him being a prophet of God as he claims? I believe the evidence in both cases very strongly leads to the answer "no."

Let me supply a very succinct outline which will give information about both the person Joseph Smith and the teachings of the religion he founded.

Mormonism (The Church of Jesus Christ of the Latter Day Saints)

Founder: Joseph Smith (1805-1844)

HISTORY:
Joseph Smith: Born in Vermont, 1805, raised in rural New York State. Joseph was not known for holding a regular job. He turned to scamming people, including divining, dousing and treasure hunting. He was arrested and convicted of scamming people out of money from a treasure-hunt scheme in Palmyra, New York. He used "magic stones" to find buried treasure. He married a daughter of one of the farmers whom he had bilked of his money. When he could not make sufficient money from treasure hunting, he turned to a religious pseudo-Christian scam.

Joseph Smith said he was visited by an angel named Moroni in 1823, who told him of an ancient record containing God's dealings with the former inhabitants of the American continent. He claimed to have seen a vision and to have received a direct commission from the Father and the Son, Jesus Christ. He told his followers he found golden tablets buried under ground in 1827 on which was inscribed the Book of Mormon in a kind of Egyptian writing which historians agree has never existed. He translated the tablets by putting his head inside a hat and holding magic rocks which he called the Urim and the Thummim. To assure skeptics that the plates did, indeed, exist, he showed them to several trusted witnesses, who signed statements affirming that they had beheld the plates. In preparation for viewing the plates, the chosen witnesses prayed for several hours. After lengthy praying, one witness reported that he saw only an empty box. Joseph sent him out for additional prayer, after which the golden plates were visible to the witness. Joseph later announced that he had returned the plates to the angel who had first led him to them. The angel took them off to eternity.

The Mormon movement grew rapidly. Because it inspired persecution wherever it went, the followers of Smith moved to Kirtland, Ohio, Independence, Missouri and Far-West, Missouri. Finally, the Mormons found a refuge in Nauvoo, Illinois between 1839 and 1844. Joseph Smith became mayor of the town. He took on a number of other wives, including stealing wives from some other leaders in the movement. Persecution at Nauvoo became intense, and Smith was arrested and later killed in a shootout at a jail in nearby Carthage, Illinois. The movement scattered—many moved to Independence while others followed Brigham Young to Salt Lake City, Utah.

MORMON SCRIPTURES

A. THE BOOK OF MORMON

The Book of Mormon was supposedly translated from "Reformed Egyptian" (Mormon 9:32). Mormon 8:18 says, "Don't demand to see the plates or you will be killed." The book was originally published in 1830. It went through several early editions. The original contained thousands of obvious spelling and grammar errors, revealing the very poor level of education of its author, Joseph Smith. The first edition is not generally available. The book is a grade B religious fantasy about a group of Jews who crossed the Atlantic Ocean in a cubic-shaped boat with one hole in the bottom, one in the top and no windows! Another "lost tribe" of Jews migrated as well to the New World around 600 BC. The apparent scene of the book of Mormon is Central America. The Mormon scripture describes many wars in which over two million soldiers were killed and large cities were destroyed. No archaeological discovery supports any of the claims in the Book of Mormon. The Book of Mormon has cows and horses in Central America when there were none (Enos 1:21). It also has silk in the New World in 600 BC (Ether 7:9). It even has elephants in pre-Columbian America (Eth 9:19). Baptism in the name of Jesus for forgiveness of sins is taught in 600 BC! Jesus came and preached to these people after being resurrected (3 Nephi 9).

B. PEARL OF GREAT PRICE

I. Articles of Faith (Smith)
II. The Doctrine and the Covenants (Smith, Brigham Young and others)

Mormons believe in progressive revelation. They still add new revelation to the *Pearl of Great Price*. Most of the bizarre teachings of Mormonism are found in the *Pearl of Great Price*, rather than the *Book of Mormon*.

C. THE BIBLE (so long as it is properly interpreted by the Mormon priesthood)

TEACHINGS OF MORMONISM

1. The original church completely fell away with the death of the original apostles. There was no legitimate church for about 1,700 years.
2. Joseph Smith is a prophet of God.

The Father, Jesus Christ and the Holy Spirit are three separate gods. Mormonism is a polytheistic religion. Joseph Smith declared, "I will preach on the plurality of Gods. I have always declared God to be a distinct personage, Jesus Christ a separate and distinct personage from God the Father, and the Holy Ghost was a distinct personage and a Spirit: and these three constitute three distinct personages and three Gods" (Teachings of the Prophet Joseph Smith, p. 370).

4. Truly spiritual people can become gods as well, eventually having their own world to be the god of. As Lorenzo Snow, fifth prophet of the LDS Church exclaimed, "As man now is, God once was; as God now is, man may be" (Ensign, February 1982, pp. 39-40). Joseph Smith preached this in perhaps his most famous sermon: "God himself was once as we are now, and is an exalted man, and sits enthroned in yonder heavens...I am going to tell you how God came to be God. We have imagined and supposed that God was God from all eternity. I will refute that idea, and take away the veil so that you may see...He was once a man like us" (Teachings of the Prophet Joseph Smith, pp. 345-46).

5. Faith, repentance, water immersion baptism for salvation, along with Holy Spirit baptism. Baptism of living people for already-dead family members and others for their salvation is also taught.

6. Polygamy. This practice was openly taught and practiced by Smith and other Latter Day Saint leaders. Smith even took married women. Polygamy was officially denounced in a new revelation by the Utah Mormons in 1890 in order to be given statehood.

7. Blacks, and especially Indians, are degenerate humans. Mormon 5:15 says, "Indians are dark, filthy and loathsome." 1 Nephi 11:13 says, "Dark people are sinful." 2 Nephi 5:21 says, "Dark skin is loathsome." The doctrine of racism was officially renounced in the 1980s.

8. A group of 12 "apostles" receive modern-day revelation.

This short list is obviously not complete, but it can give the reader an idea of whether the scripture of Mormonism is indeed the inspired word of God.

Note: The second question about versions of the Bible is answered later in this book.

QUESTION:

What is deism? Is it considered atheist? Could one go to hell for belief in deism?

ANSWER:

You will find a wide range of groups and individual religious beliefs which could be labeled as deist. It is wise to take any definition of deism with a grain of salt. However, let me give a basic definition. A deist is a person who believes in the existence of God, but does not accept any particular definition of God according to any of the major world religions. The deist believes in God as a creator, but (in general; there may be exceptions to this) do not accept any particular scripture as inspired by that God. It is interesting to take note of some of the very famous personages in history who were deists. This list includes George Washington, Thomas Jefferson, James Madison, Isaac Newton, Joseph Priestley, Benjamin Franklin and many more. The Freemasons were deists. The Unitarian Church is deist.

Bottom line, deists do not accept the divinity of Jesus Christ or the inspiration of the Bible. Therefore, by any definition, they are not Christian. It may surprise you to hear that Washington, Jefferson and others were deists, not "Christian," even by the most generic definition. These guys quoted the Bible often. They are the ones whom religious conservatives give credit to for making the United States a "Christian" nation. You should be aware that our founding fathers were not Christian, and they were trying to protect their ability to be deists in a culture which was predominantly Christian, at least on paper.

Is a deist an atheist? No, they are not. The deist definitely acknowledges that there is a force which created the universe and set it in motion. Most deists believe that once the universe was created, the Creator has kept his hands pretty much out of things, allowing the universe to go along according to natural laws.

Can a Christian be a deist and are deists going to hell? You should judge for yourself, but if one takes the Bible seriously, the answer is clear. Consider 1 John 2:22-23: *"Who is the liar? It is the man who denies that Jesus is the Christ. Such a man is the antichrist—he denies the Father and the Son. No one who denies the Son has the Father; whoever acknowledges the Son has the Father also."* Deists, by definition, do not acknowledge the deity of Jesus Christ, making the answer to your question from a Christian perspective obvious.

QUESTIONS:

Are Jehovah's Witnesses part of a cult? How did this religion come to be and what is it they believe?

I was wondering how to refute the teachings of the Jehovah Witnesses? I have a sister who is very involved in this religion and I don't know how to reach her without her getting defensive.

ANSWER:

Whether or not the Jehovah's Witness are a cult depends on your definition of the word. For me, personally, the word "cult" has come to have a very negative connotation. The working definition which I believe our culture uses for a cult is a group which is dominated by an individual who exercises a very dominating influence on the members of the group. By this definition, the Jehovah's Witness group may have been a cult back in the 1880s-1930s, under the cult-like leadership of Charles Russel and "Judge" Rutherford. Again, it is a matter of definition, but in my opinion, the Witnesses are not a cult in the most common negative sense of the word as it is used today.

There is a fairly extensive outline of the history of the Jehovah's Witness religion and their doctrine, as well as a Power-Point presentation at my website (**EFC**). I also recommend a book by Ron Rhodes, *Reasoning from the Scriptures with the Jehovah's Witnesses* (Harvest House Publishers, 1993). I have found members of this group to be particularly difficult to engage in useful discussions about the Bible. This is true because the group does an excellent job of indoctrinating their members. You will find a level of devotion amongst the Witnesses which would put to shame most modern Christian groups. Their devotion is based on an intellectual commitment to the teachings of the Watchtower Society. It is very difficult to "convert" Jehovah's Witnesses to correct biblical teaching because their commitment to the group is not based on open-minded analysis of the biblical text, but on a logical, but deeply unbiblical line of reasoning inherited from the Watchtower Society. I would not suggest studying with members of this group unless they are by themselves and are already disaffected from their religion. Typically, they will engage in arguments, but not in real discussions or matters of the heart. My suggestion, if you have a close friend or family member who is in this group, is to love the person, to pray for them and to make them feel safe to talk around you. Most Witnesses are used to thinking of other Christian groups as apostate and uncommitted to God. You need to set a great personal example of commitment to Christ. Hopefully, through your example, God will create an opportunity when your friend or relative is asking real questions. It is at that time that you need to be aware of what this group teaches. I will supply a very brief outline below.

The group was begun by Charles Taze Russel in the late 1870s. He was from an Adventist background; a movement started by William Miller in the 1830s. This line of Christian thought included Ellen G. White and the Seventh Day Adventists. Russel veered into a radically non-Christian doctrine. He rejected belief that Jesus and the Holy Spirit are deity. This is the Arian heresy which the early church dealt with in the third and fourth centuries. Thanks to Russel, the Jehovah's Witnesses believe that Jesus is the Archangel Michael—that he was created by God. ["Michael the great prince is none other than Jesus Christ Himself." (*The Watchtower*, Dec, 1984, p. 29)] They believe that the Holy Spirit is not a person or deity, but only a spiritual force. The Jehovah's Witness do not believe in hell as a place of torment or punishment. They teach that Jesus Christ already came back in 1914. They teach that the only correct name for God is Jehovah, and that the New Testament was changed by apostate Christians to remove the name Jehovah from the Bible. They believe that Christianity became completely apostate soon after the apostles died, and that members of their group are the only true Christians.

The Witnesses have many other shockingly non-Biblical beliefs. This group is so far from accepting the teaching of Jesus Christ, that I believe they are not even marginally Christian. John wrote of such groups: *"Who is the liar? It is the man who denies that Jesus is the Christ. Such a man is the antichrist—he denies the Father and the Son."* Their false theology is maintained by the dictatorial control of the Watchtower Society which carefully controls all the teachings and the finances of the group. The Watchtower Society is a shadowy organization of very old men who control virtually every aspect of the governance of the worldwide organization. To lend credence to their publishing empire, they claim that the Watchtower Society is the "faithful and discrete servant" prophesied in Matthew 24:45-47. The fact that they have the gall to claim that their own publishing house and its governing board were prophesied by Jesus shows how irrational their beliefs are.

One difficulty you will have is that the Witnesses use their own translation of the Bible—the *New World Translation* (NWT). This version includes obviously incorrect translation of many of the passages which prove Jesus is deity. Famously, the NWT has this for John 1:1: "In the beginning was the word. The word was with God. The word was a god." Of course, the original Greek for this passage does not even have a word for **"a."** Many examples could be listed. Where the NIV has God saying, *"They will look on me, the one they* *have pierced."* the NWT has "They will look on the one they have pierced." They simply remove the word "me" because of the obvious implication about Jesus. This is a very cynical effort to support the lie that the Bible teaches that Jesus was created.

In summary, the Jehovah's Witness group is not Christian because it does not accept Jesus Christ to be who the Bible clearly says he is. Because of the careful indoctrination and the use of intimidation of its members, it is normally very difficult to have useful discussions with people in this group. Being well-prepared, setting a great example, praying and waiting for God to work are required. I pray God blesses your efforts.

QUESTION:

I have heard people say that Islam is a religion of war. How can I explain that the God of the Bible is a God of peace, given some of the things that happened in the Old Testament?

ANSWER:

You ask a question which is on a lot of people's mind with the events of 9/11. Muslims claim that their religion is akin to Judaism and Christianity. In fact, they claim Moses, Abraham, David and Jesus as prophets of Islam. The question you ask, however, is whether Islam is a religion of war or, more carefully, if the Koran supports the doctrine of killing for Allah. Let us look at this issue by looking at both the Bible and the Koran.

First, you should note that most Muslims claim that Islam is a religion of peace, not war. Of course, the idea of jihad is in the Koran, but the majority of Muslims who are moderates will tell you that the word jihad means struggle, and that it does not necessarily imply that good Muslims will fight and kill for Allah. Most claim that jihad for Allah in a modern context means contending and struggling for righteousness through personal struggle using peaceful means. We can only hope that all members of Islam take this view. The question to be considered here is which is the correct interpretation of the Koran? Or perhaps more importantly, is the interpretation of the Koran that it sanctions killing for Allah a reasonable one?

Let us consider a few passages taken from the Koran. Surah 4:95 encourages those who fight wars for Allah with rewards in heaven. Verse 104 of the same Surah encourages the Muslim to follow those enemies who retreat and kill them. Surah 8:12 commands Muslim soldiers to cut off the finger-tips of their enemies and stab them in the head. Surah 8:16 implies that those who retreat in Jihad will go to hell. Surah 8:16 implores Muslims to not take prisoners, but instead to kill all the enemies. Surah 11:3 promises salvation to martyrs and killers for Allah. Surah 47:4 commands Muslims to kill ruthlessly in Jihad and to go for the neck. There are a number of other passages of this sort in the Koran.

What about Muhammad? The founder of Islam was a ruthless military leader. When a group of Jews in Medina proved unwilling to convert and began to undermine his leadership, he had all 700 male Jews massacred. This is mentioned in Surah 33:26-27. Muhammad brought in income for his early movement by raiding desert caravans, killing the people and stealing their possessions. So, judge for yourself whether Muhammad was a man of peace and whether the Koran is a book of peace.

It is worth noting that the great majority of Muslims are peace-loving and are certainly not terrorists or even supportive of terrorists. Many of the laws laid down in the Koran promote justice and fair treatment of people. To be fair, there are a number of positive teachings in the Koran. However, to claim, as some Muslims do, that the concept of jihad in the Koran does not sanction killing people for Allah is to ignore many clear statements in the book itself. It also requires us to ignore the history of the early spread of Islam. When radical Islamic terrorists seek justification for their attacks, they need look no farther than the pages of the Koran to justify their actions. In fact, that is exactly what they do. Let me add that it is extremely unlikely that Muhammad himself, if he were alive today, would sanction the murderous deeds of today's terrorists.

You ask an important but difficult corollary question about Christianity. More precisely, you are asking about Judaism and the Old Testament, not about the teachings of Christ. There is absolutely no question that Jesus Christ was a man of peace. He said, *"If anyone strikes you on the right cheek, turn to him the other also"* (Matthew 5:39). Isaiah prophesied about Jesus, *"A bruised reed he will not break, and a smoldering wick he will not snuff out"* (Isaiah 42:3). There is no conceivable justification for a Christian to go around killing people for God based on the teaching and life of their Lord, Jesus Christ. The crusades of the Middle Ages were an abomination to God. Jesus would not have authorized killing people in his name in warfare, nor popes standing at the head of armies. Nothing could be clearer than that. The Roman Inquisition, which was responsible for killing untold thousands because of real or perceived heresy, was an abomination as well.

The New Testament teaching is clear, but you raise an important and, to be honest, a difficult question with regard to warfare and the Old Testament. In Joshua one can find God's people ordered to destroy very sinful peoples who occupied the Promised Land. This can be a troubling fact to think about for the reader of the New Testament, given Jesus' teaching on anger and violence. Apparently, God allowed the Jews, under his authority, limited sanction to pursue warfare and even to kill pagans without mercy in order to allow them to occupy the Promised Land. Bear in mind, however, that the Jews were not authorized to pursue world conquest or to attack any foreign power in God's name—only to occupy the Promised Land. God gave them only a very limited license to pursue war.

Having said that, God did charge the army of Israel to remove the Amelekites and others from Canaan. It is worth bearing in mind that the Amelekites had such disgusting religious practices as sexual prostitution in their temples and sacrificing babies in the fire in order to appease their gods. Can anyone blame God for refusing to tolerate such behavior and for judging these people? The nation of Israel was a theocracy. In the violent environment of the world at that time, it was impossible to maintain an independent political entity without being willing to defend one's territory. God's plan to send his Son Jesus to provide salvation included choosing a people and a nation. Such a nation had to have an army and to defend its territory. The New Testament does not foresee a Christian theocracy. Jesus said, *"My kingdom is not of this world"* (John 18:36). Although God allowed a limited warfare in the Old Testament, no such thing is conceivable for those in the kingdom of God under the law of Christ.

In conclusion, both the scriptures and the history of Islam support the claim that this religion sanctions using violence to advance its cause. The New Testament is absolutely and radically in opposition to this. It is true that the Jews had a very limited sanction to use violence against some incredibly sinful pagan groups in order to occupy the Promised Land. They were also authorized by God to defend themselves from their enemies. However, this was a very limited thing and was in no way at all a general permission to use violence to spread Judaism to neighboring lands.

Chapter Twelve

General Apologetics

QUESTION:
How should I balance investigating evidence of things such as the alleged contradictions in the Bible with putting faith in the Bible being true? Should I be cautious about what I read and study?

ANSWER:
I respect your desire to ask the hard questions about the evidence for Christianity. I have spent over 30 years studying the evidence for (and against) Christianity. My experience is that belief in Jesus as the Messiah and in the Bible as the inspired Word of God holds up extremely well indeed to any kind of rational investigation. You seem to have a sense that it may be wise to have some control on the kind and amount of evidence you look at. I believe that some people take this way too far—practically banning study of any works which are critical of Christianity. They call any literature which teaches another religion or undermines Christianity "spiritual pornography." I believe it is not a healthy practice to isolate ourselves from our critics. However, a certain amount of wisdom about the kinds of material we spend time studying is a good idea.

Let me cite a scripture which is relevant. Psalms 1:1-3 says, *"Blessed is the man who does not walk in the counsel of the wicked or sit in the way of sinners or sit in the seat of mockers. But his delight is in the law of the Lord, and on his law he meditates day and night. He is like a tree planted by streams of water, which yields its fruit in season and whose leaf does not wither. Whatever he does prospers."* This passage advises us to be careful what we expose ourselves to. It does not outlaw all exposure to thoughts contrary to God. The principle is that we need to keep a wise balance which favors reading the Bible and literature which honors God and supports belief in biblical inspiration. There is more than enough evidence for us to believe Jesus is the Son of God and the Bible is inspired by God. This includes messianic prophecy, the resurrection of Jesus, the historical accuracy of the Bible, consistency of science with the Bible and so forth. The evidence is strong enough that it is reasonable to give the Bible the benefit of the doubt when we are exposed to claims which oppose what we believe in. It is our conviction about this benefit of the doubt which will protect us when we study the writings of those who attack the Bible.

Having given these admonitions, I believe it is good and even helpful to consider the claims and evidence of the critics of Christianity. Peter admonished us to be prepared to give an answer to those who ask us to explain our faith (1 Peter 3:15). We will not be able to answer people's doubts if we do not understand their arguments. We cannot understand the arguments of our critics if we do not study them and think about them. If we want to deepen our faith and be able to answer those who have questions, we cannot afford to ignore the "evidence" of the critics of faith. It is not a good idea to simply ignore those with whom we do not agree. This is not intellectually honest. It is my experience that, when I read materials by Bible critics, it actually has the effect of increasing my faith when I see how obviously wrong those who attack Christianity are. So, I say it is a good idea for you to devote some time to reading what the critics have to say. However, I urge you to spend the great majority of your mental time and energy studying the Bible and the writings of those who respect God and the Bible. You already have more than enough reason to believe in God and in Jesus. Do not give the benefit of the doubt to the enemies of Christianity. Listen to them, but remember that these people are rejecting what you already know to be true. Jesus Christ was raised from the dead on the third day. Surely this fact alone will tell you to take with a massive grain of salt the writings of those who seek to destroy faith in Jesus and in the Bible. Should you be cautious? Yes, but do not be so overly cautious that you remain ignorant of the arguments of those with whom you do not agree.

General Apologetics

QUESTION:
If the Bible/Christianity is so obviously the truth and the correct religion, why isn't the whole world Christian by now? Why don't we see more things in the media about the evidence which supports Christianity?

ANSWER:
There are reasons that not everyone is a follower of Jesus, and these reasons have nothing to do with the sufficiency of the evidence. The reasons people do not come to believe in Christ tend to fall in one of three categories:

1. They do not know of him

2. They do not understand him

3. They are not willing to accept his message

The first reason has become rare in the modern world. There are very few people left who have not at least heard of Jesus and are not aware that he is an important religious leader.

The second cause of lack of belief in Jesus is that many are not aware of the true Jesus presented in the Bible and of the evidence for his claims. It may seem obvious to us that Jesus is who he claimed to be, based on the evidence of his miracles, fulfilled prophecies and so forth. However, a majority of people have either not been informed at all or have been seriously misinformed about Jesus. Many do not even realize that he claimed to be God or that he claimed to be the only way to God (John 14:6). A lot of people have been exposed to lies and distortions concerning Jesus.

Another difficulty is many understand Jesus mainly through the examples of those who claim to be his followers. The great number of very poor examples from people who ought to represent Jesus to the world creates confusion in people. The "disconnect" between the life and example of Jesus and hypocritical supposed followers can prevent many from believing in Christ. Bottom line, a great number of people have not been exposed to the real Jesus and the evidence for him. If something is true but people, in general, are not aware of the evidence that it is true, it should not be surprising that many do not believe it. There is a lot of misinformation about Jesus out there in the media. Who is the real Jesus? Is he the good teacher who accepts everyone? Is he just a man? Those who do not understand that he is God cannot believe in him. Many who profess other religions fall into this category. The vast majority of Muslims, Hindus and others have been presented with a distorted picture of Jesus. No wonder they don't believe in him.

There is a third reason many do not accept faith in Jesus. This explains the majority of those who do not believe in him in Western countries, in my opinion. There are many people who are well aware of, or at least sufficiently well aware of who Jesus is. They know enough of the evidence for the Bible and for the deity of Christ to believe, but are unwilling to accept the personal implications. If Jesus is Lord and master, then I am his servant. If Jesus is God, then I am not. If what Jesus said is true, then I am in trouble over my sin and I need to repent of that sin. For a great number of people, the requirement of Jesus that we repent of our sins and turn our life over to him is sufficient reason to not be a Christian. What many people do about this fact is that they choose not to believe, or they choose to believe only that about Jesus which is comfortable to them. To believe is to necessitate change. We rationalize our unbelief. The way Paul puts it in Romans 1:18-19—many, because of their unrighteousness, *"suppress the truth, since what can be known about God is evident..."*

Jesus put it this way: *"This, then, is the judgment: the light has come into the world, and people loved darkness rather than the light because their deeds were evil."* The people in Jesus' day had plenty of reason to believe his claim to be the Son of God. The resurrection of Lazarus spoke for itself. Yet, many refused to come into the light.

What many who are not willing to accept the message of Jesus end up doing is they find a way to rationalize away belief in Jesus. They manufacture logical arguments, or they twist or ignore data to justify not believing in Jesus. I have read a number of books by skeptics and critics of Christianity. Most of their arguments are obviously false, yet these writers find a way to convince themselves of their reasoning. It is my experience that what people believe has more to do with emotion than evidence. When belief in something challenges our security, our pride or our desire to seek pleasure, we are more than willing to conveniently ignore the evidence and to construct a belief in something that is not true.

There are a variety of reasons people do not believe. One thing for sure, it is not for lack of evidence. In most cases it is not due to lack of time for the evidence to have gotten around. Our job as believers is to try to help all three groups of non-believers come into the light through our personal example and careful instruction.

A comment on your last question: The reason you do not see the evidence for Christ on TV or in the media in general is that non-believers have control of the media. The reason information about DNA has spread whereas the gospel has not is that people, in general, do not have an emotional reason to reject belief in DNA. Newsweek magazine does not make money selling magazines with articles about why the Bible is accurate, but there is much profit to be made from titillating articles such as those which imply the Gospel of Judas is legitimate history.

QUESTION:

I'm doing my senior project in high school on the topic of whether Jesus was actually the Son of God, and thus everything he said was actually true. I have a few questions: Is it possible that the Bible lasted for so many years just because no one questioned it? For example, Aristotle's theories lasted until they were questioned in the Enlightenment period. Since the four main Gospels of the New Testament were written way before the scientific method was created, isn't it possible that people just didn't question things? Then by the time of the Enlightenment, all that evidence about how there were so many copies of the Bible and they were all similar could be used to justify the Bible. By the way, I'm reading *History of God* by Karen Armstrong, *The Case for Christ* by Lee Strobel and *Holy Blood, Holy Grail* by Michael Baigent, Richard Leigh and Henry Lincoln. Would you say those are good books? What books would you recommend?

ANSWER:

I am proud of you for being willing to defend Jesus in your school. Many believers shy away from doing this. I am also proud that you ask perceptive questions, rather than accept simple answers.

To answer your question, there is some truth to the issue you raise concerning the fact that, through most of the history of Christianity, the validity of the scripture was not questioned by believers much at all. To be more specific, the Bible was intensely questioned by both believers and opponents in the 2nd-4th centuries AD. A number of Greek and Roman philosophers attacked the Bible, both on religious and philosophical grounds. Such pagan philosophers as Porphyry and Celsus examined the Bible and Christianity vigorously and sought to undermine faith in Jesus. Biblical Christianity was defended during this time by Christian teachers/philosophers such as Justin Martyr; quite successfully, I might add. You can tell from Justin's common name the result of his efforts (His last name was not Martyr!).

All this changed beginning a generation or two after the edict of toleration under Constantine in AD 312. Once Christianity became the dominant political power, the scenario you describe of the central claims of Christianity not being significantly challenged became true and remained so for well over 1,000 years. During the time of the ascendancy of the Roman and Greek Catholic churches, it was almost unheard of for anyone to publicly question the authority of the Bible. To do so was to court death. Besides, questioning religious authority was not part of the tenor of the times.

All this changed around 1450 with the Resnaissance and even more so in about 1680 with the Age of Enlightenment. The Renaissance changed the intellectual climate in Europe greatly, allowing scholars to think more for themselves. Believers began to apply human reasoning, especially that of Aristotle, to understand Christian theology. Initially, intellectuals questioned what the correct form of Christianity was. This led to the Reformation and to Protestantism. Only later did many begin to examine the authority of the Bible itself, beginning roughly 1680. The career of the French philosopher Voltaire made critiquing the Bible a possible job description. This brings us to the Enlightenment, as mentioned in your question. During the Enlightenment, skepticism became not only possible—it became fashionable. For the past 350 years, many people have tried to attack the accuracy and the truth of the Bible. I believe that the Bible has stood up very well to these criticisms, but the attacks on the biblical world view has been vigorous!

The situation with the ideas of Aristotle has a little bit in common, as you mention. The philosophy and teachings of Aristotle went relatively untested for almost 2,000 years (this is a bit of a simplification, as other Greek philosophies such as those of Plato, Plotinus, the Stoics and the Epicureans competed with Aristotle). Christian theologians such as Augustine and Thomas Aquinas accepted the logical approach to knowledge of Aristotle, along with his faulty ideas about the laws of nature, almost without question. That having been said, there is a big difference between Aristotle and the Bible with regard to how well they withstand scrutiny. When people such as Roger Bacon, Copernicus, Galileo and Robert Boyle began to test Aristotle's theories concerning the laws of nature, he was repeatedly proven wrong. Aristotle's theory of elements, his theory of geo-centrism and his laws of motion were all shown to be false. The difference between Aristotle's natural philosophy and the Bible is that, with the Bible, many have tried to prove it is inaccurate history, that its prophecies are not real, that it has scientific errors, that the text is unreliable, that Christianity is philosophically bogus, etc. All these efforts to prove the Bible unreliable have failed miserably.

Even today, many try to disparage the scripture, but these arguments fail to disprove the inspiration of the Bible.

I am glad you are reading those books. I like Strobel's book, but I have not read the other two. I will recommend two other books. One is *Mere Christianity*, by C. S. Lewis. Another is *Compelling Evidence for God and the Bible*, by Douglas Jacoby (www.ipibooks.com). Both of these show how Christianity and belief in Jesus are reasonable. As for more fact-oriented apologetics, I will have to say that my favorite is my own **Reasons For Belief**. There are many good books on apologetics, but this one covers all the key areas of evidence.

QUESTION:

I now believe in God as a creator due to the complexity of the creation. Why should I believe in Christianity rather than Judaism or Islam?

ANSWER:

Thanks for your question. It is a bad assumption that one can simply leap from belief in God based on the scientific evidence to belief in Christianity. I believe there are two reasons a believer in God might choose Christianity rather than a generic deism or belief in another religion. One is the empirical evidence that the Bible is inspired. The other is the evidence seen in the life and character of those who have been transformed by a relationship with God through Jesus.

Before I say a little about these two, let me give you a couple of bad reasons that you should believe in Christianity. I am saying "bad" somewhat tongue-in-cheek because any reason a person comes to saving faith in Jesus is ultimately good.

One "bad" reason to believe in Christianity is because you happen to live in a country where it is the principle religion. I could list dozens of examples of things which have been believed by the majority which we now know to have been patently false. The fact that all the ancients believed the Earth was the center of the universe did not make it so.

Another "bad" reason to believe in Christianity is that this is the religion in which you were raised. There are hundreds of millions of believers in Hinduism, Islam and other religions who accept these teachings simply because it is the belief of their family. For them, this strategy will have tragic eternal consequences. If you accept Christianity, it should be because it is true, not because it is the religion of your birth. Paul said (1 Corinthians 15:19) that if our faith in Christianity is a false hope, we are to be pitied above all men. Please, if Christianity is not true, do not give your life to it.

Another inadvisable reason to believe in Christianity is because it appeals to you. That which is appealing is not necessarily true. If we get a diagnosis of cancer from a doctor, the appealing thing is to assume it will go away. This assumption can prove fatal. We should accept faith in what is true, not that which strokes our ego or which seems like a good idea to our human way of thinking.

Returning to your question, I said there are two reasons to believe in Christianity. One is the evidence which proves the divine inspiration, and therefore the authority of the Bible. Fulfilled messianic prophecy, scientific and historical accuracy, internal consistency, the confirming miracles and many other empirical sorts of evidence make belief in Christianity reasonable. I would go so far as to say such evidence makes unbelief in Christ to be unreasonable. Let me make a suggestion. You should read an apologetics book such as **RFB**, but you should also spend some effort learning about other world religions. I advise you to put some time into reading the Koran, the scripture of Islam. You might want to expose yourself to the Vedas, the Upanishads, the Puranas or other scriptures of Hinduism. I suggest that you will find the quality of the Bible to be head and shoulders above the rest.

The second reason to believe in Christianity is the dramatic effect saving faith in Jesus has on the lives of his true followers. Jesus put it this way: *"If anyone chooses to do God's will, he will find out whether my teaching comes from God or whether I speak on my own"* (John 7:17). He said that those who put his principles into practice will see for themselves that he speaks for God. Jesus said that the lives of his followers will be able to convince many that they were seeing the real thing: *"By this all men will know you are my disciples, by your love for one another"* (John 13:35). As a scientist, I tend to be skeptical of experiential reasons for belief, but Jesus did not see it that way. He said that the way the world will know that God sent him was the miraculous unity and relationships of the believers (John 17:23).

A word of caution is appropriate here. Not everyone who takes the name of Jesus is a true follower of the Master. You should balance looking for examples of Jesus lived out in the lives of his followers with reading about what Jesus commanded of those who follow him.

Bottom line, if Christianity is of God, then Taoism, Buddhism and any other religion for that matter is not. This is because the theology (definition of God) of all other religions is diametrically opposed to that of the Bible. Jesus said, *"No one comes to the Father except through me"* (John 14:6). If Christianity is not the "right" religion, then Jesus is a false witness. God has given you freedom of mind and of will, so it is up to you to search for him. I believe that if you do, you will discover that Jesus is the way to God.

Let me give you one more suggestion. In order to begin your search for what religion is from God, you can use an outline at my website **EFC**. There is an article there titled "Other Religions." This is an outline which will give you a very brief introduction to the history, teachings, theology and scriptures of all of the major world religions. The website also has outlines and power points on Islam, Eastern Religions and many more.

QUESTION:

If you discovered a truth which was truer than the Bible, would you go for it? In other words, if you were to discover there to be a higher truth than the Bible, do you love truth enough to put aside your convictions to adhere to this greater truth?

ANSWER:

My first response to this interesting question was that it sounds a bit like one of those "if a person was convinced of Jesus in the middle of the desert and wanted to be baptized, but there was no water, and he died, would he go to heaven?" kind of questions. I assume you know what I mean. Then I thought about it for a bit longer, and I think that this is actually a deep and significant question. Please forgive my first reaction!

Actually, Augustine of Hippo faced a similar question at one time in his life. He had formerly been convinced of the truthfulness of Manichaeism, but had a nagging question which none of the leaders in his religion could answer. It was a question about a Manichean teaching concerning the heavens which seemed to him to be in contradiction to clear evidence from all observation of the heavens. Eventually the most influential teacher of Manichaeism in his day came to the city where Augustine was living. When Augustine confronted him, this respected leader blew off the question rather than explain the apparent inconsistency Augustine had found in Manichaean cosmology. When his questions went unanswered, Augustine was forced to reject the entire premise of his religion. It was not long after that that he was drawn to the religion of his mother—Christianity.

I would have to say that, yes, in principle, if I could find a set of truths which fundamentally were more in line with what I know and with how things work—if I was shown a truth-claim which had deeper and more convincing evidence (although it is hard for me to imagine what form such evidence would take), I would have to say that I would absolutely have to reject what I have believed and accept the new "truth." There is an interesting analogy in the way science works. Historians of science have discovered that it progresses by revolutions rather than by slow, steady growth. Thomas Kuhn was the first to apply the word paradigm to the completely new, out-of-the-box change in model which has happened at times in the history of science. Examples are plate tectonics, germ theory, relativity and so forth. In every case, there was a former paradigm which seemed, for the time, to explain all phenomena in that field, but eventually, evidence arose which was unexplainable by the current "truth" (paradigm). Such inconsistencies eventually led to new models—new paradigms with broader and more consistent explanatory power. Classical Mechanics led to Quantum Mechanics. The Effluvia Theory led to Germ Theory.

Having said all that, I struggle to understand what truth could overthrow the resurrection of Jesus. The evidence for inspiration of the Bible and the evidence that Jesus was not a liar seem absolutely overwhelming to me. However, a truth which is not examined is a shallow one, and I would have to say that, at least in principle, one must be honest with oneself and hold out the possibility of having been mistaken in one's interpretation of the evidence.

Let me turn it around on you. What kind of evidence might you imagine which could overthrow the resurrection of Jesus? I do not say this to ridicule the question, but to arouse your thinking. It seems that this new truth would have to either contain Jesus or overthrow Jesus. To contain Jesus means that there is a sense in which it cannot be greater than Jesus. To overthrow Jesus is to prove him mistaken about being God.

So, in summary, I have to say "yes" to your question in general grounds, but I struggle to see what form this higher truth might take. One of my favorite quotes seems to address this question. It is from Michael Faraday; a renowned scientist and a man of deep convictions about the Bible. He said, regarding the search for truth, "The man who is certain he is right is almost sure to be wrong; and he has the additional misfortune of inevitably remaining so." I believe this truism even applies to belief in the God of the Bible.

QUESTION:
How do we keep the faith despite the many challenges of life?

ANSWER:
I assume you are asking about keeping up your own faith, rather than the faith of others. This is the key to the problem in any case. I do not have any easy answer to this question, but I do have a couple of suggestions to offer. There are a number of ways to maintain our faith in troubled times, but I will suggest ones which relate mainly to Christian evidence.

First, you need to continually remind yourself of the things you already know are true and the reason you are confident they are true. There are a few things I am absolutely convinced of which cement my faith. I tend to come back to these things. One of these things is the resurrection of Jesus from the dead. Do you believe Jesus was raised from the dead? Why do you believe that? If you believe that Jesus was raised from the dead, does that not validate Christianity in general? If so, then why are you doubting right now? If so, what does that mean about your life?

Another absolutely solid and thoroughly established fact for me is the inspiration of the Bible. Do you believe the Bible is inspired by God—that it is, without comparison, the greatest book ever written? Why do you believe this? What is implied about your life if the Bible is definitely from God? If you believe God determined what is in the Bible, then why are you doubting your faith right now?

A third point of assurance which underlies my faith when I am tempted to doubt is my salvation. If point one and two above are true, then salvation is real, and I can have assurance of my salvation. The book of 1 John was written *"that you might know (be confident) that you have eternal life"* (1 John 5:13). Are you saved and going to heaven? If so, does that make the current problem you are experiencing seem a bit smaller? If you are saved, then is the thing which is causing you to doubt God right now of fundamental importance?

A passage I think of in this connection is Philippians 3:15: *"All of us who are mature should take such a view of things. And if on some point you think differently, that too God will make clear to you. Only let us live up to what we have already attained."* The point is that it is easy to forget the basics of faith and truth in the business of everyday life. You have so much reason to be encouraged about your life if you really think about the things you are totally sure about already, never mind the things you have not yet figured out. Paul expressed the importance of remembering what we are sure of when thinking of less important things about which we are in doubt. Paul reminds the Philippians (and us) that, when we are confused about lesser things, we should not forget what we are already sure about, and live by these things. This helps me to keep the faith despite the many challenges of life.

Another suggestion I have is that you keep a running, written list of questions which you are unable to answer about Christianity and about the Bible. All of us have them, but most of us shove them under the rug. Rather than ignoring these questions, I suggest you write them down. At first, this list will grow, but as you earnestly seek answers to the questions, the ones which you check off as answered will eventually far outweigh the ones you still have not answered. This will provide visual evidence that what you believe is true and reasonable.

Of course, there will still be unresolved questions and issues in your life. Remember Paul's word in Philippians: *"Only let us live up to what we have already attained."* In other words, do not ignore the hard questions, but trust that God will make them clear to you eventually. The main thing is to focus on trusting in God and doing the things you know are true already. I am sure that if you focus in on doing what you know is right already, you will have more than enough to keep you busy. You will avoid the "paralysis of analysis." Your faith will be challenged, of course, but you will be able to plot a steadier course.

QUESTION:

Why is it so hard to keep my faith? I have been a Christian for the last five years, and for the last three, I have served as a minister. I believe my problem is my relationship with God, or maybe my lack of relationship with God! I just would like to ask why it is so hard to have faith? I want to just believe, but I can't! And thus I feel that every day I'm going farther and farther away from God, whom I cannot see or feel! I just would like to know what I can do to end the pain that is in my heart.

ANSWER:

[The answer to this question originally contained much in common with the one above. It has been edited; only keeping what is new in this answer.] Believe me—you are not alone in your struggles. At times when we are struggling with sin and personal issues, it is very common for fundamental faith issues, which we thought were settled a long time ago, to surface at what would seem the worst possible times. This can be very discouraging. It can lead to guilt, and even thoughts of giving up. I am sure this is especially true for a person who works as a minister for a church!

The simple answer to your question as to why it is so hard to believe is that Satan is trying to get you to not believe. Satan is crafty (2 Corinthians 11:14). We need to be aware of his schemes (2 Corinthians 2:11). All of us have doubts. That is part of the human condition. The question is what will you do with those doubts? Let me give you just a couple of suggestions to get you started.

First, I suggest you spend a good amount of time in the book of John. Like John said, *"These are written that you may believe that Jesus is the Christ, the Son of God, and that by believing you may have life in his name"* (John 20:31). All of the Bible can help support your faith, of course, but we have one book about which the author himself said it was specifically written to create and uphold faith. In reading John, I suggest you focus on the amazing claims of Jesus and on the miracles which support Jesus' right to make these claims. If you truly believe these claims, and if you can hold onto the evidence which supports them, this may help your faith in the long run.

A second suggestion is to read the book of Hebrews. This book was written specifically for followers of Jesus who have been in the faith for a while but who find themselves considering turning back to the world. Hebrews will point you back to the basics and to the reason you became a follower of Jesus in the first place: *"So do not throw away your confidence; it will be richly rewarded. You need to persevere so that when you have done the will of God, you will receive what he has promised"* (Hebrews 10:35-36).

When we go through struggles in our faith (and that certainly describes your life right now), the weak points in our devotion to Jesus become obvious. Satan always goes for the weak points. At a time like this, you should be asking yourself some fundamental questions. What do I really believe? Why have I been doing what I have been doing? The writer of Hebrews does not pretend this is easy. Faith is being assured of things which we cannot see (paraphrasing Hebrews 11:1). This is never easy. It requires time and energy. I suggest that perhaps you have not put in sufficient time over the long run laying a solid foundation for your faith. If problems in your church are causing you to doubt your faith, it is a good indication that you have focused your "faith" more on human relationships than on God. Now is a good time to fix this problem!

I suggest you ask yourself what, in the final analysis, you really believe. What are you really sure of? I imagine that you are confident that God exists. I am assuming that you already have sufficient evidence to conclude that Jesus Christ really did live, that he was crucified and that he rose from the dead. The evidence for the resurrection of Jesus is very convincing. I believe that if we accept and truly believe that Jesus was raised from the dead, then this answers a lot of questions. If Jesus was raised from the dead, then we know for sure that God loves us and that he wants to have a relationship with us through Jesus Christ. This truth can outweigh any struggles that the local church you are part of is going through if you will remember these things. Another fundamental truth which stands on its own, despite whatever emotions you are feeling right now, is that Jesus is the Messiah, sent by God to save mankind from their sin. I strongly suggest that you take some time in the next few days and weeks to step back and consider what you really believe. You should strip away some of the baggage—mistakes made toward you, problems and failures in your life, persecution from family and friends, worries about jobs and money, etc.—and ask yourself whether God truly loves you, whether you want to go to heaven and whether the Bible is the inspired Word of God. I really believe that if you do this, you will find a bed-rock of faith to begin rebuilding your spiritual life upon: *"Let us fix our eyes on Jesus, the author and perfecter of our faith, who for the joy set before him endured the cross, scorning its shame, and sat down at the right hand of the throne of God. Consider him who endured such opposition from sinful men, so that you will not grow weary and lose heart"* (Hebrews 12:2-3).

Chapter Thirteen

Philosophical/Theological Questions

QUESTION:
If the Bible is a book written by humans, using it to explain or prove God is invalid, correct? There is little or no evidence that the things in the Bible happened. Also, there is no one like Moses doing miracles today. And what about all the evidence and proof against the existence of God?

ANSWER:
I believe that there is an inconsistency in your line of thinking. I hope I can say this with a spirit of humility. Your question implies you make the assumption that the Bible is the product of human wisdom and knowledge. If you start with the belief that the Bible is a "human-written book," then you assume the answer before you ask the question. I believe that the internal evidence for the inspiration of the Bible by God is overwhelming. Simply stating by fiat that it is not inspired by God does not prove your conclusion that it is not inspired. That is false reasoning. The question of whether or not the Bible is inspired by God will stand or fall on the evidence.

To state that there is little or no evidence that the events in the Bible occurred proves to me that you have not studied out the subject carefully. There is extensive external evidence of the validity of many of the historical references in the Bible. I will give a short list below:

1. The fact of David being king of Israel, as well as several of his descendants, as proved by the Tel Dan inscription.
2. The defeat of Israel by the Assyrians and the tribute paid by Jehu to Shalmanezer (2 Kings 17:3-6) is proved by the Black Obelisk of Shalmanezer III.
3. The attack of Sennacherib on Jerusalem in 691 BC, as well as his inability to overcome the city, is supported by an inscription on the Sennacherib Prism.
4. The attack on and eventual defeat of Jerusalem by Nebuchadnezzar in 597 BC (2 Kings 24:10-17), as proved by the Babylonian Chronicles.
5. The statement that Cyrus decreed that the Jews could return to Jerusalem to rebuild the Temple (Ezra 1) is confirmed by the Cyrus Cylinder.
6. The fact that Pontius Pilate was procurator of Judea at the time of the crucifixion of Jesus, as proved by the Pilate inscription found in Caesarea.
7. The fact that Jesus was crucified in Jerusalem and that it was claimed that he rose from the dead at that time, as proved by the writings of Josephus and Tacitus.

I could go on with dozens of facts which are recorded in the Bible and which are confirmed by archaeological discovery. A more comprehensive list is available in **RFB** ch. 7. Of course, it is true that there are more details in the Old Testament which are not directly confirmed by external sources than those which are, but the general pattern of confirmation of the historical accuracy of the Old Testament makes it reasonable to assume that, in general, the OT is a reliable historical document—at least as reliable as the histories of Herodotus and Thucydides.

You ask "what about all the evidence against God?" There is literally not a single piece of evidence that God does not exist. What is the evidence that he does not exist? What physical evidence, or any other sort of evidence for that matter, can you show which provides evidence that God does not exist? To be honest, I believe that the burden of proof for the existence of God lies with the believer, not with the atheist. It is not the job of the atheist to prove that God does not exist. Having said this, it remains a fact that there is literally not a single piece of evidence that God does not exist. I have read many books by non-believers, and their principal line of argument is to attempt to discredit the evidence for God. But they have no positive proof that there is no God. [Author's note: The argument from pain and suffering may be the only exception to this statement. I discuss this in an article at **EFC** which is too long to include here. The reader may want to go to my website to read this article.]

I agree that the miraculous events recorded in the Bible do not have their equivalent occurrences happening today, at least as far as I know. At first glance, it would appear that you have a good point here. Actually, if one looks at the history of the Jews, there are only a few brief periods of time when God was working miracles, with long periods in between when there is no record of the miraculous occurring. Hebrews 2:4 provides a logical explanation of the fact that God has caused dramatic public miracles only at certain times. When God brought new revelation to mankind, such as at the time of Moses, or the time of the prophets or during the ministry of Jesus Christ, there was a burst of miraculous activity which God caused in order to confirm the message was from him. Based on the Biblical record, we should not be surprised that God is not causing dramatic public miracles at this time, because God is not adding to his inspired revelation at this time.

QUESTIONS:
Where did God come from?
If God made me...then who made God?

ANSWER:
You ask a question that is really more for the philosopher than the scientist. This is something which people have pondered from the time belief in God, or even in "gods," has existed. Although I am a scientist, not a philosopher, I will give a philosophical answer to this question.

Philosophers of religion say that God is, by definition, the uncaused cause. In other words, our universe clearly exists. One almost universally accepted law which governs the universe we live in is that everything which happens has a cause. This is called the law of causality. Yet, clearly at some point, there was a first cause which, by definition, was uncaused. That uncaused cause is God. What I am saying is that God simply is. In fact, this is exactly what he said to Moses in Exodus. When asked to say who had sent him to the Israelites, God told Moses to say that I AM had sent him. God's first property is that he exists. He was not created. God is, by definition, that which exists outside of being caused.

This is a bit tough to take in, but it is who God is. The real question is not where God came from, but whether God, as defined by the Bible, is the uncaused cause. In other words, the universe exists and it was caused by the uncaused cause. Is the God as described in the Bible that God? That is a question for you to answer based on your own careful study of the evidence.

The Catholic theologian, Thomas Aquinas, addressed this question back in the 13th century. He was dealing with the concept of causality. He noted that everything which happens in the natural universe has a cause. He also noted that there had to be an initial cause of the first things. He defined God as the initial causer of all things. God is "the uncaused cause," according to Thomas Aquinas. Although this is clearly a very abstract definition and proof of God, I believe Aquinas' argument is still valid.

Philosophers of science come up against the ultimate cause problem as well. For example, a scientist might ask why objects fall. Isaac Newton's answer is that all objects with mass exert a force called gravity on each other. The answer to the first question raises another question. Why do objects with mass produce gravitational force? Physicists have proposed an answer, which is that objects with mass emit particles called gravitons. The interaction of gravitons creates the force. Of course, this raises another question. Why do objects with mass emit gravitons? Scientists might answer this question with a more fundamental theory such as String Theory. But this only raises a new question. Why do strings have the properties they have (assuming they exist)? The point is that, at some point, inevitably, the scientist must throw up their hands. At some point, the question "why" becomes theological, not scientific. Science cannot answer the ultimate "Why?" questions. The answer of the atheist to the ultimate "Why?" is that there is no answer. The answer for the agnostic is "I don't know." The answer for the believer is "because God made it that way."

I apologize for giving you an answer which probably raises more questions than it solves, but that is the nature of the universe we live in. God is, by definition, the uncaused cause. God is that thing which stands outside our own universe and reality as the ultimate Creator. God, by definition, was not created, at least by the definition of creation or cause/effect as it works in our reality. Bottom line, God exists. We have more than sufficient evidence of God in nature, in the Bible and so forth, but in the end, God is who he is. To use his own words: "I AM."

COMMENT: To take as given that spiritual reality exists is to commit to a path that is self-validating and circular. To believe in the "ghost in the machine" is to add a superfluous hypothesis which adds nothing to the explanation of the observed phenomena; in fact, it confuses it unnecessarily, as Ockham's Razor would point out.

RESPONSE: I do not take spiritual reality as given at all. I believe in a spiritual reality because of the evidence. There is voluminous evidence which compels me to believe in a spiritual reality.

I am well aware of Ockham's Razor and the specific argument you use. It is not at all compelling in my opinion (for the reader, Ockham's Razor goes something like this: with two competing explanations of a particular phenomenon, the simpler explanation is to be favored over the more complex explanation). Actually, Ockham's Razor was never intended to prove anything, but only to help choose the more reasonable path when all else fails. Ockham's Razor prefers heliocentrism over geocentrism, and in this case, it is correct, but not because of the logical argument. It is correct because of the evidence for heliocentrism. Ockham's Razor prefers classical mechanics over quantum mechanics, but in this case, Ockham's Razor makes the wrong choice. Again, the evidence decides, not Ockham. Ockham's Razor no more disproves the existence of spiritual reality than it proves or disproves anything else.

My confidence in the reality of a spiritual aspect of existence is based on the evidence, not on a logical quandary. If there is no spiritual reality, then Jesus Christ is a liar (but I know he is not a liar). If there is no spiritual reality, then Jesus did not work miracles (but the evidence says that he did). If there is no spiritual reality, then the hundreds of types, foreshadows and prefigures in the Old Testament which are fulfilled in the New Testament (see FSTR) are all coincidence. If there is no spiritual reality, then the fact that the Bible is the only consistently reliable historical record of the ancient world is just plain luck. If there is no spiritual reality, then the dozens of incontrovertible messianic prophecy fulfillments are impossibly lucky. I can go on if you like. The examples just listed make what may seem like a logical argument based on Ockham's Razor into an weak argument against the spiritual dimension of the world.

QUESTION:

I am skeptical of the existence of the human soul. What are the properties of a soul?

ANSWER:

As a scientist I cannot define the word soul. As far as I know, the soul has no physical reality. Rather, it has a spiritual reality; not subject to experiment. It is ontological, metaphysical. I will freely admit that my belief in a soul rests principally (though not totally) on the authority of the Bible, so I will answer your question by quoting the Bible.

1. It is something with which we can love God and our neighbor (Deuteronomy 4:29, 10:12, Mark 12:30, etc.).
2. It is a center of human emotion (1 Samuel 1:10, Job 3:10—bitterness; Job 30:25—grief; Psalms 35:9—joy; Isaiah 29:6—yearning)
3. It is the seat of human affection (1 Sam 14:7).
4. It is a part of us which takes part in worship (Psalms 23:4 of an idol; Psalms 42:2 of God).
5. It can be "lost" or "saved." In other words, it is in some sense eternal, although it was created (Psalm 49:15, Psalm 86:13, Proverbs 23:14, Proverbs 11:30, Matthew 16:26, Mark 8:37, 1 Peter 1:9).
6. It can be blamed for the wrong it motivates us to do (Ezekiel 18:20, Micah 6:7, 1 Thessalonians 5:23).
7. It can be healthy or sick, at least in some sense (3 John 2).
8. It belongs to God (Ezekiel 18:4).

Many more verses can be cited in each category. To summarize, the human soul is created. It is "eternal" (but the exact meaning of this word is not absolutely clear). It is the seat of desire and emotion. God will hold our soul responsible for the actions which its desires cause us to do or to not do.

QUESTION:
What is the definition of spirit?

ANSWER:

It is easier to biblically define soul than spirit for the simple reason that the word "soul" in the Bible almost always refers to a human soul, whereas the word "spirit" (pneuma in Greek) has reference to the spirit of a person, to the Spirit of God and to spirit in a metaphorical sense. The word can be metaphorical because spirit can mean essence in a more general connotation.

First, there is the passage in Hebrews 4:12 which states that the Word of God is so sharp that it can even separate soul from spirit.

Philosophical/Theological Questions

This implies two things—soul and spirit are definitely different, and it is very difficult to completely separate the two by mere definition.

Second, I do not believe that spirit is a physical thing in any sense of the word. For this reason, we probably will never be able to prove the existence of spirit by any conceivable scientific experiment. At least I assume it cannot be done, the work of ghost-busters not withstanding. My belief in, and definition of, spirit is based on the inspiration and authority of the Bible alone. I believe that the existence of a spiritual reality is obvious outside of scripture, but the definition I will give here is to be found solely in scripture. It is not my opinion—based on my own religious/spiritual experiences.

1. My first definition of spirit is that it is that part of human beings which is made "in the image of God." Obviously, if we are made in the image of God, our God-likeness certainly is not defined by our physical bodies. Any implication that God has physical attributes is clearly ridiculous. All such references (God's hand supported me and so forth) are clearly intentional anthropomorphisms. It is in our spiritual nature that we are like God. For example, consider John 4:24: "God is spirit, and his worshippers must worship in spirit and in truth."

2. A spirit is identified as somehow associated with a person, but not all spirits are human. The Bible often calls a person a spirit. In that sense, the spirit of a person is the essence of that person: 1 Samuel 16:23— "and the evil spirit left him..."; 1 Kings 22:21—"Finally, a spirit came forward..."; Mark 9:20—"When the spirit saw Jesus, it..."; 1 Peter 3:19— "preached to the spirits in prison who disobeyed God."

3. While a human being is alive, their spirit is somehow constrained or localized (in a way I am powerless to define) to a body, but the spirit lives on after the body dies. At that time, the spirit is no longer tied to the body (1 Peter 3:19 again. I assume that these are human spirits who are no longer physically embodied). Ecclesiastes 12:7—"the spirit returns to the God who gave it..."; Acts 7:59—"Lord Jesus, receive my spirit..."; Luke 8:55—"Her spirit returned..."

4. From God's perspective, a human body without its spirit is dead (James 2:26). I will admit that I do not fully understand the implications of this statement.

5. One's spirit is affected by emotions (but it is not the emotions themselves. Unless I am mistaken, one's emotions are associated with the soul). John 13:21—"Jesus was troubled in spirit..."; John 11:33—"he was deeply moved in spirit..."; Daniel 7:15—"I, Daniel, was troubled in spirit.." ; Psalm 51:12,17—"a willing spirit... a broken spirit..."

6. The human spirit is in some ways similar to, and responds to, the Holy Spirit and to God in general (because God is spirit). Romans 8:16—"The Spirit himself testifies with our spirit..."

7. The human spirit is eternal. Unlike God, the human spirit was created, but like God, it is eternal. I will admit that the literal meaning of the Greek word for eternal (aionios) can be debated, so the exact meaning of this claim is not as obvious as some might think. Nevertheless, the spirit is eternal. Zech 12:1—"who forms the spirit of man within him..."

More can be said, but this is a good beginning to a biblical definition of the human spirit.

QUESTION:

What do you think of human reasoning? Would you say that using reason is the wrong way to approach religion? Is human reasoning reliable for discerning what is true? The way I understand it, the use of human reasoning to decide what is true was invented in the Enlightenment and that people are taught how to think. So, maybe reason isn't as pure/accurate/scientific as we think? What do you think about this?

ANSWER:

The Greeks were the first to develop a carefully defined system of reasoning and logic. It may be true that the Enlightenment in Western Europe was a time when the power of human reason to determine what is true was emphasized—almost worshipped by some. However, it definitely is not true that reason was not invented until the Enlightenment. The Greeks philosophers Pythagorus, Socrates, Plato, Aristotle, Plotinus, Epicurus and many others developed entire philosophical systems and even religions (in the case of Pythagorus and Plotinus) based on reason. The early Christian church was very strongly influenced by Greek reasoning. Justin Martyr defended the truth of the gospel in one of the first published Christian apologetics in around AD 150 using Greek methods of reasoning. The Gnostics were a heretical "Christian" group which based their false understanding of Jesus on Greek notions of what is reasonable.

Reasoning in and of itself is neither good nor bad. The ability to reason is a gift given to us by God. Like almost any gift from God, it can be used either for good or for evil. As a scientist, I know that human reasoning can be used to decide which is to be preferred between two proposed explanations of a phenomenon.

However, human reasoning cannot tell us what is true. That is why the Enlightenment ultimately failed. Aristotle tried to determine the "truth" about natural laws using pure reason. He decided that the Earth was the center of the universe (wrong: the Earth goes around the sun and the sun moves), that there were four elements—air, earth, fire and water (wrong: there are over 100 elements), that it is impossible to make a vacuum (wrong: a vacuum exists in space) and that the natural state of motion is at rest (wrong: the natural state of motion is with constant velocity). This tells me that reasoning alone is not a reliable instrument to determine truth.

Nevertheless, reason is a tool which followers of Jesus ought to use. Although we cannot use reason to determine "truth," it remains that when something is true, it ought to be reasonable. This was the claim of 13th-century theologian, Thomas Aquinas, who tried to show that Christianity is reasonable (it is). We can use reason to defeat illogical arguments. Many false attacks on Christianity can be defeated by using reason. Although we cannot use reasoning to determine truth, we can use reasoning to help decide what the best way is to apply truth to particular situations.

Is reasoning accurate? The word accurate does not really apply to reasoning. The word "accuracy" is relevant to numbers and measurements, not truth. I would say that if one begins with true assumptions, then reasoning provides reliable predictions. The problem with reasoning is that it is only as good as the assumptions used. This is why reasoning alone is a poor instrument to determine ultimate truths such as the origin of life, the meaning and purpose of human existence, morality, ethics and so forth.

My conclusion is that human reasoning cannot reveal the truth about God. In fact, over-reliance on reasoning tends to create human pride, not humility, and can work against spiritual growth. Nevertheless, our ability to reason is a gift of God which can and should be used to God's glory.

QUESTION:

What is the difference between choice and fate, and how does that affect our thinking about the Christian life? I would appreciate it if you dealt with Adam and Judas in this respect.

ANSWER:

This is one of the most significant theological/doctrinal debates in the history of Christianity—indeed in all religions. Given that God is all-knowing and all-powerful, and given that he exists outside of time, it seems logical that he already knows what we will do before we even do it. Does God pre-determine our fate in some way, or does he, despite his power, give us "free will" to make our decisions? To put it even more simply, does God foreknow or does he predetermine? You might be surprised that the Bible does not answer this question directly. The phrase "free will" is not in the Bible. The honest truth is that there is at least some evidence in the Bible for both points of view. However, in the big picture, I believe that the overwhelming truth is that God does allow us to make our own ultimate choice to serve him or to reject him.

Let me start by giving some biblical evidence for "predestination." A good place to start is Romans chapter nine. In this chapter, God, through Paul, says to his people, *"But who are you, O man, to talk back to God? Does not the potter have the right to make out of the same lump of clay some pottery for noble purposes and some for common use"* (Romans 9:19-21)? Paul specifically uses the example of Pharaoh, whose heart God hardened in order that he could bring about the miraculous release of Israel from bondage. One can say that, at the very least, this passage shows that in order to see his overarching will accomplished, God is willing to step into history to affect the lives of certain people. We could call this fate. Israel was predestined to be released from slavery as a foreshadowing of our spiritual release from bondage to sin. Pharaoh's free will was partially limited by God in order to accomplish his sovereign will. On the other hand, I believe that, in the end, Pharaoh had every opportunity to repent and to turn to God. My conclusion from the biblical evidence is that God intervenes and provisionally trumps our free will with his sovereign choice quite rarely and only when things which relate to the coming of Jesus to die for our sins are at stake. The hardening of Pharaoh's heart and the events surrounding the betrayal of Judas are good examples of this principle.

If it is established that God will, in certain cases, step in to influence the course of human events, is one right to extrapolate to say that all of our lives and all of our decisions are pre-determined by God—in other words to say that there is no free will and that our lives are fated from birth? Are we just puppets on strings? My answer to that is a definite "no"! If we do not have a choice, then why would Moses have said to God's people, *"Now choose life that you and your children may live, and that you may love the Lord your God, listen to his voice, and hold fast to him"* (Deuteronomy 30:19-20). As another clear example of God giving ultimate choice to humans in their relationship with him, consider Joshua 24:15: *"But if serving the Lord seems undesirable to you, then choose for yourselves this day whom you will serve, whether the gods your forefathers served beyond the River, or the gods of the Amorites..."* We certainly see free will here. Jesus clearly believed in "free will," even if he did not use that philosophical term. "If anyone would come after me, he must deny himself and take up his cross daily and follow me" (Luke 9:24). And consider John 7:17: *"If anyone chooses to do God's will, he will find out whether my teaching comes from God or whether I speak on my own."* Evidently, God has a particular will for our lives, but evidently, he also allows us to choose to accept that will or to reject it. Dozens of passages which clearly teach the idea of free will can be mentioned.

Given all this, how did theologians such as John Calvin reach a radical doctrine of predestination? That is a good question. John Calvin (and therefore most Presbyterians and Baptists, to mention two denominations strongly influenced by Calvin) taught that we were all born predestined to either salvation or condemnation and that there is nothing we can do to resist God's will in that regard. Calvin used Romans 8:29 to support his opinion: *"For those God foreknew he also predestined to be conformed to the likeness of his Son, that he might be the firstborn among many brothers. And those he predestined, he also called; those he called he also justified; those he justified he also glorified."* On the face of it, this passage does at least seem to justify the radical predestination doctrine. However, a rule of biblical interpretation is to allow the entire Bible to speak, especially to such a large question. We cannot use a single passage to disprove a great number of passages which appear to contradict it. We must reach a reasonable conclusion on such important matters by considering in balance all the passages which relate to the issue.

Let me explain how I understand Romans 8:29. I believe that God has predestined all of us to be saved, but because God gives us "free will," not all of us inherit this destiny. In that sense, all of us are predestined to conform to his Son. Therefore, all of us are predestined in that sense, but not all of us are called, as not all hear the message. And not all who hear the message respond and are justified. And not all who are justified (saved) remain faithful and ultimately make it to heaven (are glorified). Based on this, Paul is giving a descending list. All are predestined, less are called, less are justified, still less are glorified. I will admit that this is not the immediately obvious interpretation of Romans 8:29, but it is the only interpretation which makes sense if I consider books such as Hebrews, which so very clearly warns against falling away and losing our justification. There is no way to support a radical doctrine of predestination in view of the hundreds of statements in the Bible which prove beyond a reasonable doubt that God gives us a choice to serve him or not.

You specifically mention Adam and Judas. God predestined Adam to have a relationship with him. Adam, like the rest of us, chose to reject that relationship by sinning. In so doing, he set the pattern for all of us who followed. Choice (free will) is one of the themes of Genesis three. All of us sin and fall short of the glory of God (Romans 3). Yet we all have open to us the choice to turn our back on our sins, to respond to God, to repent and to be made new in Christ.

I believe that Judas is an example of a person into whose life God stepped in order to bring about his larger will in having Jesus killed for our sins. In that sense, he is like Pharaoh. This is an example of a limited kind of "predestination." In certain situations, God's sovereign will trumps our personal free will. Nevertheless, I believe that Judas still had open to him the opportunity for repentance and renewal. He chose suicide and eternal separation rather than to repent of what he had done to Jesus. Even in this case, although God did, to use my words, "step in," I do not believe he violated Judas' ultimate free will.

To summarize, I believe a limited sort of predestination is biblical. For one, God has predestined all of us to be with him in heaven, although not all of us choose to accept that destiny. Also, in order to bring about the saving sacrifice of Jesus Christ on the Cross, and also in order to create the many foreshadows and prefigures of the events of Jesus' life (**FSTR**), God has, on occasion, stepped directly into certain individual's lives. In that sense, he took away their free choice and directed some aspect of their life. In every case, he did this because of the greater goal of bringing about the possibility of salvation for all people. However, even when God does this, I believe he has always left open the possibility for the person so affected to choose to believe in him in the end.

QUESTION:
What was the Holy Spirit doing in the beginning? Was it already in existence during the Old Testament?

ANSWER:
The Holy Spirit, being God, existed before the creation of the world. He was not created, but has always existed, just like the Father and the Son. As proof of this, one can look all the way back to

Genesis 1:1: *"and the Spirit of God was hovering over the waters."* Although the Old Testament does not go into detail about the Father, the Son and the Holy Spirit, there are hints of all three aspects of the godhead scattered throughout the Old Testament. You ask what the Holy Spirit was doing at the beginning. Genesis 1:1 gives one hint. Apparently the Holy Spirit was involved in creating the world. John 16:8 shows that part of the work of the Holy Spirit is *"to convict the world of guilt in regard to sin and righteousness and judgment: in regard to sin, because men do not believe in me; in regard to righteousness, because I am going to the Father..."* I assume that since mankind has existed on the Earth, the Holy Spirit has been working in this way. There are a number of instances in which one can see the Holy Spirit working directly in the Old Testament. Examples of this would include Psalms 51:11, in which David asked God not to remove his Holy Spirit from him, and 1 Samuel 19:19-24, in which the Spirit is even poured out on King Saul.

In summary, there is no other way to view the Bible's picture of the Holy Spirit except to conclude that he is an eternal part of God. Although the Holy Spirit is given to those who are in Christ in a special way, he has always worked to bring people to God.

Chapter Fourteen

Da Vinci Code and Related Topics

QUESTION:
I read Dan Brown's, *The Da Vinci Code*. He makes a convincing claim of the possibility that Jesus was married to Mary Magdalene. Is there any possibility of truth in this?

ANSWER:
Brown labels his book as fiction, but anyone reading it knows immediately that he expects us to take his proposals seriously. To quote from one of Brown's characters, "As I said earlier, the marriage of Jesus and Mary Magdalene is part of the historical record." Having read a number of Brown's arguments, I find them to be totally unconvincing. Which historical record is he referring to? He argues according to a closed logic which will break down immediately upon very simple questioning by anyone who has a general awareness of the biblical or the extra-biblical background to Jesus. Proposing the idea that Jesus was married and that the early church covered up this fact is a really interesting idea and it certainly has earned Mr. Brown a lot of money. What the idea is missing is a single shred of evidence which will support it. All Mr. Brown can offer is some interesting speculative interpretation of some passages which lend themselves

far more easily to a less sensational (and therefore less profitable) interpretation. Clearly, if Jesus had been married, the apostles would have been aware of it. It seems beyond the possibility of belief that they would not have noticed that Jesus was married. Therefore, if Brown is correct, then the apostles and their close associates were conspirators and liars. This is absolutely inconsistent with the character of the apostles, all of whom were willing to die for their faith in Jesus. Brown has absolutely no external evidence that Jesus was married to Mary Magdalene, other than his own speculations and quotes from other modern writers with similar speculations.

Actually, Brown does have one piece of "evidence" that Jesus was married to Mary Magdalene. He pulls a quote from the Gnostic "Gospel" of Phillip. This book was definitely not written by Phillip. It was produced in the late second century by people who had no interest in the historical Jesus. There is a passage in this apocryphal book which has Jesus kissing Mary Magdalene. First of all, this gospel is simply not credible as a historical record. Second, even if Jesus did kiss Mary Magdalene, this is not evidence that they were married. We know from New Testament documents, such as 1 Corinthians 16:20, that the holy kiss was common practice among the followers of Jesus. This is the totality of Brown's "historical record."

There are a great number of reasons why it would not make sense to believe Jesus was married. The Bible describes the Church as the bride of Christ. This would be a strange metaphor if Jesus was actually married to Mary Magdalene. Jesus certainly never seems to have acted as a husband if one looks at his lifestyle during his three years of ministry. It is hard to believe the Son of God would have been anything less than a stellar husband. The idea of Jesus having sexual intercourse is pretty hard to imagine, given his ministry and the suffering and death which God knew were in store for him. It is fairly easy to "prove" almost anything one wants to if one takes a few references out of context and quotes from others who already agree with you. This is a familiar bogus method of research which has led to all kinds of interesting, titillating and profitable conclusions, but one would do well to hold to a healthy skepticism and to ask for information from primary sources before accepting such ideas.

In conclusion, the answer is a definite "no." The proposal that Jesus was married to Mary Magdalene and that he had children by her is insupportable, either from logic or from the evidence.

QUESTIONS:

How do I answer some specific questions regarding Dan

Brown's, *The Da Vinci Code?* A friend told me that Jesus is a myth and that the myth of Jesus came from the religion Mithraism. Here are some examples my friend used about the Persian god Mithras. How do you explain these?

1. Mithra was born of a virgin on December 25th in a cave, and his birth was attended by shepherds.

2. He was considered a great traveling teacher and master.

3. He had 12 companions or disciples.

4. Mithra's followers were promised immortality.

5. He performed miracles.

6. As the "great bull of the Sun," Mithra sacrificed himself for world peace.

7. He was buried in a tomb and after three days rose again.

8. His resurrection was celebrated every year.

9. He was called "the Good Shepherd" and identified with both the Lamb and the Lion.

10. He was considered the "Way, the Truth and the Light" and the "Logos," "Redeemer," "Savior" and "Messiah."

11. His sacred day was Sunday, the "Lord's Day," hundreds of years before the appearance of Christ.

12. Mithra had his principal festival at what was later to become Easter.

13. His religion had a eucharist or "Lord's Supper," at which Mithra said, "He who shall not eat of my body nor drink of my blood so that he may be one with me and I with him, shall not be saved."

14. His annual sacrifice is the passover of the Magi, a symbolical atonement or pledge of moral and physical regeneration.

15. Shmuel Golding is quoted as saying that 1 Corinthians 10:4 has "identical words to those found in the Mithraic scriptures, except that the name Mithra is used instead of Christ."

16. The Catholic Encyclopedia is quoted as saying that Mithraic services were conduced by "fathers" and that the "chief of the fathers, a sort of pope, who always lived at Rome, was called 'Pater Patratus.'" These points were raised by a person called Acharya S. I am wondering if any of this is substantiated by recognized scholars.

ANSWER:

I am extremely skeptical of the claims of Acharya S. I have read some of her material and she impresses me as the type who will bend, mold and even make up information out of nothing in order to create a sensational scandal. I am sorry if I am coming across harshly, but I believe that she is a publicity hound with financial gain as a motive. This reminds me of Dan Brown, author of Da Vinci Code. My advice to you as you read her material is to begin by assuming that everything she says is either not true or is taken out of context in a very biased way. That is not to say that you should automatically reject everything she says. I am going on the assumption that there is at least a grain of truth in much of what she writes. However, unless I can find original sources who, upon a reasonable reading by a reasonable person, agree with her conclusions, I will be very skeptical of this person. I believe that if you went to the original sources, you would find yourself saying, "Where did she get that from?"

Let me be specific about the claims you list. "Acharya" (which, by the way, is not this person's name—it is a pseudonym) is very clever. She uses a variety of logical fallacies to make her point. Some of her examples are actual elements found in Mithraism, but which were added to the religion because of Christianity. In other words, in the second and third century in the Roman Empire, Christianity began to have a great number of converts. The evidence is that the priests of Mithraism inserted Christian elements into their religion. Mithraism was always quite syncretistic (bringing together elements of many religions). The evidence is clear. The date of December 25 was taken from Christianity into Mithraism (December 25th is not in the Bible anyway, of course), as was the idea of twelve disciples, the burial and resurrection on the third day and others on your list. We know this for two reasons. First, because these elements appeared in Mithraism after they were found in Christianity. Second, and perhaps even more importantly, because Jesus was a historical figure who really lived and did the things recorded in the New Testament. Mithras was a mythical figure. There is no evidence extant that he was a real person. How can the events which actually happened to a real person be borrowed from the events in the life of a myth? This is completely illogical.

Here is why, to be honest, I am quite annoyed at Acharya S. It is very unlikely that she is unaware that Mithraism included resurrection on the third day, birth from a virgin on the 25th of December and so forth after Christianity. Surely she is aware that the evidence implies Mithraism borrowed from Christianity and not vice-versa. Yet, she still uses this "evidence."

Some of Acharya's examples fall into a second category. They are supposed parallels between Jesus and Mithra which don't really prove anything. For example, "Both were considered a great teacher and master," "Mithra's followers were promised immortality" and "He performed miracles." These are claimed for most cult/religious leaders. They certainly do not show that Christianity borrowed from Mithraism.

A third kind of poor example from the list above is when she uses a questionable claim by a second party. The last two on the list above fall into this category. For example, Acharya tells us that Shmuel Golding says that 1 Corinthians 10:4 has "identical words to those found in the Mithraic scriptures, except that the name Mithra is used instead of Christ." Who is Shmuel Golding? Why does she not give us the reference? Would anyone like to bet if we read both 1 Corinthians 10:4 and the Mithraic scripture that they would be virtually identical as Acharya claims? Also, Acharya tells us that the Catholic Encyclopedia says Mithraic services are conducted by "fathers" and that Mithraism has a kind of a pope. First, biblical Christianity does not include "fathers." In fact, Jesus commanded that his followers not be called father (Matthew 23:7). Biblical Christianity definitely does not include a pope-like figure. I doubt the Catholics borrowed either practice from Mithraism, but Christianity certainly did not.

In summary, Acharya's claim that Christianity borrowed the Jesus myth from Mithraism is completely bogus. There is plenty of evidence that mythical Mithraism in the third and fourth century borrowed from historical Christianity, but there is no significant evidence that the New Testament writers borrowed from Persian Mithraism. Acharya is not just guilty of bad scholarship. She is guilty of deceitfulness.

QUESTION:

A woman by the name of Acharya S. tries to support atheism by claiming that Christianity took many ideas from other religions that, as she claims, are very similar to Christ. In her website article, http://www.truthbeknown.com/origins.htm, she gives specific similarities between Jesus and different "holy men" like Mithra, Horus and Krishna. So far, I have not found any solid support for these people as much as I have for Jesus. I just want to know the truth behind these people and whether or not she is lying.

ANSWER:

I have spent some time at this website. It is interesting reading.

The author makes some of the most outrageous and unfounded statements about Jesus Christ that I have ever heard. Despite the fact that she is a pretty good writer and does a fair amount of research, her lack of clear thinking is so blatant as to be almost comical. I do not mean to come off mean-spirited, but that is my honest response to what I read at this website. Let me cut and paste a couple of statements at the site and discuss them briefly.

> *In other words, it has been demonstrated continually for centuries that this character, Jesus Christ, was invented and did not depict a real person who was either the "son of God" or was made into a superhuman by enthusiastic followers.*

I am sorry, but this statement is completely illogical and unsupportable, based on the evidence. Even in her own statement, this author is making an illogical conclusion. She mentions the "enthusiastic followers" of Jesus. Who were these enthusiastic followers in the first century following? Krishna never had followers, as he was not a real person. It is difficult to follow a myth. The enemies of Jesus during and immediately after his lifetime did not struggle with the question of whether he existed. Josephus (Flavius Josephus, *Antiquities of the Jews* and *The Jewish Wars*), a Jewish historian, mentions Jesus, where he lived and how he was crucified by the Romans. Why would Josephus invent Jesus Christ? It is a historical fact that there were tens of thousands of believers alive within one generation of the life of Jesus Christ who were willing to suffer to the point of death for their belief in Jesus Christ. Is it possible that they were convinced to believe in a person who did not even exist? Josephus was not the only non-Christian historian to mention Jesus Christ. Tacitus (Cornelius Tacitus, *Annals, XV, 44*), a Roman historian of around AD 100, mentions Jesus Christ and his followers. The Jews, the greatest enemies of Jesus Christ's claims to be the Messiah, never questioned his existence. Jesus is mentioned in Jewish writings of the first and second centuries such as the Talmud. We have the writings of many other non-believers who lived at the time of Jesus or in the next few generations who accepted as a given that he was a real person. It is impossible for a reasonable person to conclude that Jesus Christ was a myth. Based on the statement quoted above alone, I believe you can probably safely ignore most or all of the conclusions of Ms. Acharya.

Let us look at another claim I found at Acharya's website.

> *The gospels are all priestly forgeries over a century after*

> *their pretended dates. Turning to the gospels themselves, which were composed between 170-180 C.E.*

No serious scholar can make this spurious claim. Acharya, like Dan Brown, author of The Da Vinci Code, make these claims, not because of the evidence, but because of an agenda. They are trying to create room for their otherwise unsupportable claims such as Christianity borrowing from Mithraism or the Gnostic writings being equal to the canonical Gospels. Even the most vigorous enemies of Christianity who study out the facts would not make so unfounded a claim in a public forum. In fact, archaeologists have found partial manuscripts of the New Testament which have been dated to the early second century. For example, the Rylands Papyrus, a fragment of the Gospel of John, has been dated to AD 125. More examples can be found in **RFB** ch. 6. In addition, passages from every book in the New Testament were quoted from early Christian authors of the late first and early second centuries. One can reconstruct nearly the entire New Testament from quotes made before the AD 170-180 date mentioned above. What were these authors quoting from if the New Testament was not yet even written as this author claims? Ms. Acharya loves to refute Christianity using Justin Martyr, but she fails to notice that Justin was killed before the date she mentions above, and Justin quoted freely from the books she claims were not written until after he died.

Let's look at one more statement at this website.

> *The Krishna tale as told in the Hindu Vedas has been dated to at least as far back as 1400 B.C.E. The same can be said of the well-woven Horus myths, which also is practically identical, in detail, to the Jesus story, but which predates the Christian version by thousands of years.*

Acharya mentions many supposed parallels between the "lives" of Krishna or Horus and Jesus. There is a problem here. The first two did not have lives—they are mythological characters. No one would argue in a scholarly setting that these were real people. There is no acceptable date or location for their birth, as there is absolutely no evidence whatsoever that they lived. These are not historical figures at all. Besides, you should be extremely suspicious of the supposed claims that the parallels she lists are real. If you go to primary sources, you will find that these parallels are more a matter of imagination than reality.

Chapter Fifteen

The History of Christianity

QUESTION:
Where did Christianity originate?

ANSWER:
Christianity originated in the city of Jerusalem in present-day Israel. The founder of Christianity, Jesus Christ, was born in the small town of Bethlehem, just a few miles southwest of Jerusalem. He was raised in the town of Nazareth in the region of Galilee, about 100 miles north of Jerusalem. However, prophecy demanded that the Messiah come to Jerusalem, *"riding on a donkey, on a colt, the foal of a donkey"* (Zechariah 9:9). The New Testament records Jesus riding into Jerusalem on a donkey and only a few days later being crucified there. Two days later, Jesus was raised from the dead. Jesus told his apostles to wait in Jerusalem for the sending of the Holy Spirit. Forty-nine days after his resurrection—on the day of Pentecost—the Holy Spirit fell on the apostles as they stood in the temple and Peter preached the first public gospel sermon. All this is recorded in Acts chapter two. From its birth, with 3,000 baptisms on the first day, the church rapidly grew in Jerusalem, later spreading to Judea, Samaria and Galilee in the first few years. Once the first

non-Jews were baptized (Acts 10), the church rapidly spread outside what were traditionally Jewish lands into all the Roman Empire and beyond during the next three or four centuries.

A question which arises is whether we can be confident from sources outside the New Testament that the accounts in the New Testament are accurate history. This is a broad question, but the general consensus of historians is that the history described above is on the whole accurate. Both the Jewish historian Josephus (late first century) and the religious Jews who wrote the Talmud (second through fourth centuries) agreed that Jesus was a real person who did indeed die in Jerusalem. All the evidence we have points toward the conclusion that the earliest preaching of the gospel of Jesus Christ included the central teaching of his resurrection. The proclamation of his resurrection began in Jerusalem almost immediately after his death. Therefore, it can be stated with confidence that the church of Jesus Christ, and therefore Christianity itself, began in Jerusalem.

QUESTION:
Did Christianity originate in Ethiopia?

ANSWER:
No it did not. I am not sure where you might have gotten the idea that Christianity originated in Ethiopia. That is a new one for me. It is true that Christianity spread to Ethiopia at a very early date. Acts 8:25-39 records the conversion of a high Ethiopian official who then (presumably) went back to Ethiopia where he shared his newfound faith in Jesus Christ. This happened some time around AD 40; probably 10 years or less after the church had begun in Jerusalem. Some believe the conversion of the Ethiopian official marked the historical beginnings of the church in Abyssinia (Ethiopia), although it cannot be proven. What we do know from historical records is that Christianity had been established in Ethiopia by about AD 300, and probably much earlier. The first recorded Ethiopian "bishop," Frumentius, was consecrated some time around AD 325. Even today, the national church in Ethiopia is the Coptic Church, which can trace its roots all the way back to the earliest history of Christianity. The first country to become officially "Christian" was Armenia, under Tiridates III (AD 238-314), who was the first ruler to Christianize his people, but Ethiopia was not far behind Armenia.

QUESTION:
When did Christianity begin?

ANSWER:
The church began on the day of Pentecost, as described in Acts Chapter two. One can debate this date. For example, one can say that Christianity began the day Jesus rose from the dead, or that it began the day Jesus was born, or the day he began his public ministry. Since "Christianity" is not defined precisely in the New Testament, one can always debate the day it started.

The reason I pick this date is two-fold. First, the events in Acts chapter two are the first recorded example of the public preaching of salvation in the name of Jesus Christ. In Acts 2, we find the first example of repentance and baptism for forgiveness of sins being taught to the people. It is debatable whether anyone was saved through repentance and baptism in the name of Jesus before this time, as the Bible is silent on the issue.

Another reason to point to Pentecost as the date Christianity began is that Jesus pointed to it as a beginning of a new age—some would say the beginning of the Christian age. The day of Pentecost was when the Holy Spirit was poured out with power on the apostles in a miraculous way. God was definitely calling attention to the event! We see tongues of fire, people preaching and being understood in more than ten languages, a great rushing wind and so forth. In Acts 2, we see the fulfillment of the great prophecy of the coming of the Kingdom in Joel 2:28-32. Peter declared that the events on Pentecost were a direct fulfillment of this prophecy (Acts 2:16). Jesus clearly predicted the great pouring out of the Spirit more than once as a starting point (Acts 1:4-7, Matthew 16:19) for the kingdom, as did John the Baptist (Matthew 3:11).

If we accept Pentecost as the beginning of Christianity, there remains the question of the year this happened. From Luke's comment, saying that Jesus was born during the reign of Herod the Great (who died in 4 or possibly 3 BC), we know that Jesus was born in about 6-5 BC. Given that the crucifixion had to occur in a year when the pre-Passover Seder feast occurred on a Friday, possible years for the crucifixion are AD 29 or AD 33. The day of Pentecost occurred 50 days after the Passover (and thus the name Pentecost) and 49 days after the Feast of First-fruits (and thus the other common name for Pentecost, which is the Feast of Weeks). Therefore, taking the day of Pentecost as the day the Christianity began, it would be 50 days after the Passover (15th of Nisan) in the year AD 29 or AD 30.

QUESTION:
Do you have information on the changing of the Sabbath Day by Constantine?

ANSWER:
I have no information on this because it never happened. One of the most persistent false claims about the early history of the church is that somehow Constantine was able to change Christian doctrine or even the scriptures of the New Testament. Such rumors center on the council of Nicea which was called together by Constantine in AD 325 in order to settle the Arian controversy.

It is true that Constantine was the first Roman emperor to accept and to encourage Christianity. It is also true that he called together the bishops of the entire Christian world to the first official church council in the city of Nicea in Asia Minor (although it was mostly bishops from the Eastern church rather than Western bishops who attended). This council, under Constantine's encouragement, dealt successfully with the Arian heresy, with its doctrine that Jesus was a created being. This council produced the first officially accepted Christian statement of faith outside the Bible—the Nicene Creed, although the creed was not officially sanctioned until the second church council. One should bear in mind that Constantine was almost certainly not a Christian at this time. There is some question about whether or not he became a convert at the very end of his life. Constantine continued to oversee pagan ceremonies, remaining Pontifex Maximus, the high priest of Roman pagan worship, throughout his time as emperor.

Bottom line, there is not a shred of evidence that Constantine changed Christian doctrine in any way or that he was able to somehow convince the council of bishops to change the Bible. This is true with regard to the day of Christian worship as well. Every piece of evidence we have available to us, including biblical passages and hundreds of references by dozens of early church fathers, proves beyond a doubt that, from its very earliest days, the disciples of Jesus met on the first day of the week—in other words, on Sunday. Some have referred to examples of Paul meeting with Jews in the synagogues in Acts as proof that the early church met on the Jewish Sabbath, or Saturday. In fact, these references prove the exact opposite. The accounts in Acts prove that Paul was in the habit of visiting the Jewish synagogues on the Sabbath because that is when the Jews came together. However, Paul always met with the disciples on Sunday. The testimony of the church fathers, from the end of the first century onwards, is unanimous in testifying that the church came together to share the Lord's Supper on Sunday, not Saturday.

Add to this the fact that Christianity does not have a Sabbath day. Colossians 2:11-19 teaches that the law was nailed to the cross with Jesus, so that those who are in Christ are no longer bound by law. Verse 16 states that followers of Jesus should not judge or be judged by observance of a Sabbath. Sunday was never a Sabbath for the early church, but was a celebration of the death, burial and resurrection of Jesus. Constantine could not have changed the Christian Sabbath because there was none.

Those who claim that Constantine changed the Sabbath will often imply that he also changed the content of New Testament. Again, there is not a single reliable piece of evidence in support of the charge. We have dozens of manuscripts of the New Testament from this time and before. The church would not have tolerated Constantine changing the scripture, but even if he had, we would know it because we have manuscripts from before that time. These would provide "smoking gun" evidence. Such evidence does not exist. The idea that Constantine changed Christian doctrine was born out of wishful thinking by certain groups who want to be able to claim that their particular false teaching has ancient roots in scripture. Believers in reincarnation, Gnosticism, Islam, mother-goddess worship and many obviously non-Christian ideas have tried to make the spurious claim that the Bible was changed by the Council of Nicea to excise the passages which supposedly supported their doctrine. The problem with such a theory is that it is only of value when actual evidence supporting it is brought forth.

QUESTIONS:

The Emperor Constantine converted to Christianity and is credited (by some) as being responsible for Christianity flourishing. But Constantine chose one form of Christianity and killed anyone who practiced any of the other forms. What about these other forms? Combine this with the Crusades and we get the classic line "history is written by the victors." How can this be a valid religion when it has thrived by butchering anyone who dared speak against it? Note: I was raised a Christian and was faithful well into my college years. But as I started asking the hard questions, no one had answers. Even now, I want to believe, but it would be a lie to blindly say I believe.

ANSWER:

You have a lot of questions here. Let me attempt to address them one at a time. To begin, your information on Constantine has some truth, but it includes some important misconceptions. It is debatable whether Constantine ever became a Christian. It is commonly believed that he was only baptized on his deathbed. He very wisely played the religion card to his best political advantage. His mother was a very passionate believer in Christ, but his attitude was ambivalent, despite politically supporting the church. He was not against forming alliances with pagan rulers and did not fully reject the pagan influence in the empire.

Second, it is true that he supported the orthodox bishops against the Arians in the doctrinal disputes of his time. In fact, he called the council of Nicea in order to force a decision on Arianism. However, Constantine himself did not actively persecute the Arians to the point of death. Constantine was relatively tolerant of all religions, including non-Orthodox forms of Christianity. I know of no example recorded in history of Constantine having anyone put to death for their religious beliefs, although he may have looked the other way a few times when others did such things. Your statement that Constantine killed anyone who practiced different forms of Christianity is simply not true.

Whether Constantine's efforts led to the flourishing of Christianity is debatable. It will depend on your perspective. Because of his edict of toleration and political support for orthodox Christianity, millions of the unconverted poured into the church. At the same time, the standard of morality and conviction of the church took a huge turn in the wrong direction. One can make a strong case that, despite efforts on his part, sincere or otherwise, Constantine's actions did more to destroy the church than the persecutions of his predecessors. Again, this is a debatable statement, but it is my opinion.

What about the "other forms" of Christianity? I intend to bring out a new book on Church History later this year. This book will address the claim that there were a lot of competing versions of Christianity and that no one form was to be preferred over another. In the early church, there were the Docetists, Gnostics, Ebionites and so forth. The heresy of greatest concern in the time of Constantine was Arianism. Arius held that Jesus was not co-equal with God, but that he was actually the first creation of God. This is the view of the Jehovah's Witness sect. You will have to decide for yourself, but I believe Constantine was on the right side in the controversy over Arianism.

In my opinion, it does not really matter all that much what Constantine's or anyone else's opinion of the day was. What is important is what is written in the Bible, as this is the inspired word of God. Bottom line, whether Constantine was right or wrong does not affect me, except as a means to understand the history of Christianity. What is important is that we seek the truth in the Bible and obey it.

Switching subjects, it is my perspective that the Crusades have little to do with Christianity. They were called by popes who I believe had no right to speak for followers of Christ. The history of the papal hierarchy and the Roman church in the Middle Ages is a litany of greed, sexual immorality, power politics and every form of worldliness which disqualified its leaders from authority over followers of Jesus. The atrocities committed in Jesus' name during the Crusades and the Inquisition were not carried out by true Christians. These actions certainly would not have been supported by Jesus. I am ashamed that people have performed such acts in the name of Jesus Christ, and as far as I am concerned, the "Christian" leaders of the Middle Ages will have to give account to God for their actions. Again, what we need to do is to look to Jesus and ask how it is that we should live. In doing so, you will discover that those who called for the Crusades were not doing the will of God.

By the way, it is worth noting that the "Christians" lost the Crusades. Within 150 years of the First Crusade, the Arabs completely recovered the territory won by the Crusaders, except for the island of Cyprus. In this case, history was written by the losers, not the winners!

You are certainly asking valid questions. When one looks at history, it is impossible to ignore the shameful acts committed in the name of Jesus. I suggest you try to put these acts aside, as difficult as that may be, and judge Christianity by the scriptures and by the life of the founder of Christianity—Jesus Christ. Christians, like anyone else, ought to be held accountable for their actions, but you should judge for yourself, based on the Bible, if the perpetrators of the Crusades were Christians.

QUESTION:

Do Good Friday and Easter Sunday represent the actual date that Jesus was crucified? What is the significance of church on Sundays?

ANSWER:

Jesus was crucified on a Friday—on the eve of the Passover. He was raised on the day after the Passover, which was a Sunday. The original meaning of Good Friday was as a remembrance of the crucifixion, while the intent of Easter was as a celebration of the resurrection of Jesus from the dead. The early church began to commemorate the day of the resurrection fairly early—certainly by the first half of the second-century AD. By the third century, the celebration of what we now call Easter became common in all of the churches. Therefore, the answer to your question is "yes," these holidays fall on the actual dates of the events. You should be aware that the date of Easter moves around on the Gregorian calendar (the one we use) because the Jews use a lunar calendar. Their calendar is based on the timing of the new moon, so the date of Easter and Good Friday changes dates on our calendar from year to year. This is why Easter falls anywhere from late March to late April. There was some debate about the correct date for celebrating Easter in the first few centuries. The Western (Roman) churches celebrate Easter on a different date from the Eastern (Orthodox) churches. It would be fair to say that the argument is over a disputable matter which is not important in the big scheme of things.

The celebration of Good Friday and of Easter is not commanded or even suggested in the Bible. Some would argue that these are therefore not "Christian" holidays. Whether it is a good idea or not to celebrate Easter as a Christian holiday is debatable.

As for the church meeting on Sundays, this tradition goes all the way back to the time of the apostles. The Bible does not command that Christians meet specifically on Sunday, but it is worth noting that this is what the churches established by the apostles did. Some say that, because the tradition was begun by the apostles, it is binding on all Christians. This may be going a bit too far, but for churches today to follow the example of the apostles seems like a really good idea to me. The early church called Sunday "The Lord's Day" (Revelation 1:10). The Lord's Day fell on the day after the Jewish Sabbath, prompting the early church to call Sunday the eighth day. An example of the church celebrating together and sharing the Lord's Supper on Sunday is found in Acts 20:7.

In conclusion, we know that Sunday worship was the practice of the churches established by the apostles everywhere they went. The history of Easter and Good Friday probably do not go back to apostolic times, but we cannot rule out the possibility that even as early as apostolic times the resurrection of Jesus was celebrated on a special day. Easter is debatable as a Christian holidays, but it is celebrated on the correct Jewish date.

QUESTION:

Was Jesus born on December 25th or is that only an approximation? How did we come to this date? I would especially appreciate if you had relevant scriptures.

ANSWER:

I will answer this question by including an article I published at the website **EFC** on the topic.

Is Christmas a Christian Holiday

Christmas sure has taken a beating lately, seemingly from all sides. The secularists demand that we say "Happy Holidays" instead of Merry Christmas, while some believers have threatened to boycott a certain large retail corporation for caving in to political correctness and no longer mentioning Christmas. When my checkout person said "Happy Holidays" to me the other day, I was tempted to retort, "and a Merry Christmas to you, too." Some Christian groups celebrate Christmas as the highlight of their religious year, while other more conservative sects claim that Christmas is a pagan holiday which should be shunned by all believers. Who is right? What is the correct doctrine of Christmas?

The answer is that there is no "correct" answer to this question. Obviously, Christmas is not mentioned in the Bible, but this fact can be used by either side. Some argue that since the Bible does not prohibit the celebration of the birth of Jesus, we are free to celebrate it. Others say that since the celebration of Christmas is not authorized by the Bible, to do so is to add to God's word and is therefore not biblical. True, it is not biblical, but then neither are church buildings or Sunday school or ushers or nearly any of the specific things we do when we gather to worship God. Such traditions are harmless unless we let them rise to the level of doctrine (Matthew 15:9). Arguably, some have done exactly that with Christmas. The apostle Paul seems to answer the question once and for all in Colossians 2:16f, in which he declares that no one should judge anyone else with regard to a religious festival, a New Moon celebration or a Sabbath. The judging should not occur in either direction, pro or con.

So, we are free to celebrate the birth of Jesus if we like, but is it a good idea to do so? Let us look for just a moment at the history of this Christian holiday. First of all, there is the issue of the date of the birth of Jesus. The fact is that we do not know for sure even the general time of the year of Jesus' birth, never mind the exact day. Scholars have argued for a late spring or early fall date, based on the fact that the shepherds were out in the fields with their sheep. Bottom line, no one knows when Jesus was born.

If we are to celebrate the birthday of the Son of God, someone had to choose a date. Why was December 25th chosen by the Western churches (by the way, the Eastern Orthodox churches celebrate Christmas on January 7th)? The evidence is that, in the third century AD or possibly earlier, the leaders of the Christian churches set the date of December 25th to celebrate the birth of Jesus because this coincided with the Roman holiday of Saturnalia. Saturnalia is named after the Roman god Saturn. This holiday was timed to coincide with the turning of the days at the winter solstice. The birth of a new year was celebrated not just by the Romans, but by most of the ancient cultures as the point when the amount of daylight began to increase. It represented a new beginning—new hope for everyone. Because the Roman holiday Saturnalia was chosen as the time for the celebration of the birth of Jesus, opponents have claimed that it is a pagan holiday. This is a spurious argument. Yes, it is true that the church leaders chose a pagan holiday as the date, but what kinds of holidays were there to co-opt other than pagan ones? Obviously, the early church had absolutely no intention of making this a pagan holiday! Given that they had no idea of the actual date of Jesus' birth, and given that the Christians already had a holiday from work scheduled at this, the slowest time of the year, what better date could they have chosen?

So we have a traditional date which is neither better nor worse than any other. One thing we can be sure of is that we are stuck with this date. For those of us in the Northern Hemisphere, it just so happens to come at a time when we really need a celebration of new birth and new hope. What better time to celebrate the birth of Jesus (assuming that the idea is a good one in the first place)?

This brings us to the meaning of Christmas. The word is a compound of the words "Christ" and "mass." "Christ" comes from the Greek for anointed one. The Hebrew equivalent word is "Messiah." The word "mass" in the English evolved from the Anglo-Saxon word maesse, which derived in turn from the Latin missa, which is a form of the verb mittere, which means "to send." So, the meaning of the word Christmas is the sending of the Messiah. If we celebrate Christmas according to the original intent of the Christian church, we are celebrating the coming of the Messiah. If we can put aside the crass commercialization and all the associated "stuff" which comes with the Western celebration of Christmas, the heart of the holiday seems like a pretty good idea, at least to this observer.

What, then, about all the "stuff" that comes with Christmas? What about the trees, the wreaths, ornaments, Yule logs and holly. What about the mistletoe, Santa Claus, Rudolph and Frosty the Snowman? Some of these have an interesting history. Yes, it is true that many, if not most of these traditions were borrowed from pagan celebrations. What else is new? What else would we expect? The custom of bringing branches from evergreen trees into the home during the dark days of winter predates Christianity and was a reminder that the sun would return, the snow would melt and the vegetation cycle would begin again. Some argue against Christmas trees using Jeremiah 10:2-4: *"Do not learn the ways of the nations or be terrified by the signs in the sky...For the customs of the peoples are worthless; they cut a tree out of the forest, and a craftsman shapes it with his chisel. They adorn it with silver and gold; they fasten it with hammer and nails so it will not totter."* I certainly am not here to defend the religious significance of the Christmas tree. The best I can tell, there is none! However, unless we are actually worshipping it as an idol, we are not guilty of violating the command in Jeremiah 10:2-4.

What about Santa Claus, otherwise known as Saint Nick? Many ancient cultures had a myth of a magical figure that came once a year to spread around gifts for the poor and the children. The Christian church adapted this idea quite early to serve its purposes. The story of "Saint" Nicholas is interesting. Nicholas was a bishop in Asia (present-day Turkey). He was born in the mid to late third century, coming from a wealthy family. Traditions differ, some saying he gave up his social position, others saying he was orphaned. Either way, he dedicated himself to preaching, teaching and the spread of the gospel. He defended the Christian faith against the heresy of Arias of Alexandria, and eventually was martyred for his faith. Nicholas was known throughout the churches for his sacrifice and charity for the sake of others. As the early church began to make Saints (with a capital S) out of well-known saints, they began to celebrate a day devoted to Nicholas. Because of his charitable spirit, and because his day fell in December, he began to be associated with gift-giving on Christmas. Santa Claus comes from the Dutch Sinter Klaas, which comes from Saint Nicholas. The jolly fat man dressed in red is an invention of 19th-century British writers, but that is another story.

What is the "Christian" response to all this? Despite the fact that most of the traditions which have grown up around the celebration of Christmas have their roots in pagan traditions, there is nothing inherently sinful in putting up a wreath or stringing lights or hanging ornaments. Nothing wrong, that is, unless we are also worshipping the pagan deities with which these were once associated. The Santa Claus thing is more troubling from a religious point of view, but I would prefer to leave Santa alone. The blatant materialism, commercialization and outright greed which is associated with the holiday is another thing altogether. How are Christian families to emphasize the celebration of the coming of Jesus without caving in to the selfishness associated with the holiday? Perhaps those who say the whole thing is from Satan (after all, Santa is Satan respelled) and that Christmas is sinful have a point. Perhaps, given the fact that celebrating the birth of Jesus is not biblical, the holiday does more harm than good.

For me, I am not prepared to take that step. I still find "Joy to the

> World" to be one of the most inspiring of Christian songs. Yes, Christmas can do more harm than good, but if the followers of Christ will make the effort to bring Christ back into Christmas, to emphasize giving rather than receiving, to celebrate the coming of the Savior into the world, then maybe we can still save Christmas. The proper response of the Christian is a matter of opinion, but to accept the status quo without response is not a wise path. So let us celebrate the season, and let us "Remember Jesus Christ, descended from David" (2 Timothy 2:8).
>
> Merry Christmas, —John Oakes

QUESTION:
Why did celibacy become mandatory for priests?

ANSWER:
How celibacy became common and *why* it became required are two very different questions. In the third and fourth centuries, it became a common practice for men (and, to a lesser extent at that time, for women) to choose asceticism as a way of expressing their devotion to God. Asceticism is a general term to describe the philosophy that one becomes close to God through radically denying oneself the pleasures of life. Historically, Christian asceticism has included celibacy, ritualistic fasting, cloistering (removal from all outside human contact in monasteries), willful injury of oneself (walking on knees many miles, cutting oneself in places where Jesus was wounded, etc.), becoming a hermit, wearing only very simple clothes, complete renunciation of worldly possessions and many similar practices. Celibacy has certainly not been limited to Christianity. The Essenes were an ascetic Jewish sect active at the time of Jesus Christ. Hinduism, Buddhism and notably Jainism are world religions which have inspired many to turn to asceticism.

Getting back to Christianity, there was a strong movement in Christianity toward asceticism by the third-century AD. This was especially dominant in the North African churches. Many, in their misguided but perhaps sincere desire to become godly chose to become hermits, to practice celibacy and so forth. From the time of the edict of toleration by Constantine in the early fourth century, the Christian churches, as a whole, became very worldly. Many sincere believers felt they needed to escape the worldly church to practice true Christianity, so they fled into the desert! In the early years of the practice, the ascetics were mostly individuals with little or no organization. By the fourth and fifth centuries, organized orders of monks became common. Anthony began the first monastery in

Egypt about AD 300. The Benedictines were organized in the West about AD 500. Members of these orders took vows of celibacy.

During this time, one might be surprised to know that celibacy amongst priests was not all that common. Of course by this time, the Christian role of presbyter or overseer, who was required to be married and to have faithful children had been radically changed into a separate class of ordained "priests." It was more common in the early centuries for "lay" Christians to choose celibacy. In fact, in the eighth, ninth and tenth centuries AD, polygamy and concubinage was common in the Roman priesthood. Eventually, Rome even sanctioned Catholic priests taking a second wife if their first became sick. However, this clear violation of biblical teaching led to a problem. With so many children of priests around, inheritance and nepotism became a huge problem. In an effort to protect church property, Pelagius I (AD 556-561) required all priests to sign an agreement not to allow any of their children to inherit church property. In AD 1022, Pope Benedict VIII officially declared that priests were banned from taking on wives or mistresses in order to protect church property rights, although those who were married before entering the priesthood were allowed to keep their wives. Finally, in AD 1139, Pope Innocent II declared all priest marriages annulled, establishing celibacy as the rule for all Catholic priests from that day forward. To be fair to Innocent II, his reforms were at least as much directed toward eliminating the blatant sin in the priesthood as toward protecting church property. There were a number of attempts from within the Catholic priesthood to reinstate marriage as a possibility right up until the 16th century.

To summarize, asceticism in general, and celibacy in particular, were begun as a sincere but misguided attempt by some early Christians to express their spirituality. When celibacy was finally enforced for the priesthood, it was principally as a rather cynical means of protecting church property from inheritance by the children of priests.

Consider two passages from the New Testament which have bearing on the lack of wisdom of using asceticism as a means of spirituality. Colossians 2:20-23 teaches that asceticism—the enforced denial of normal (but not sinful) human pleasure—has absolutely no value in protecting us from real temptation. Also, 1 Timothy 4:1-5 teaches that those who seek to enforce asceticism as spiritual requirement (specifically, celibacy, fasting from certain foods and so forth) are hypocritical liars and that their teachings come from *"deceitful spirits and doctrines of demons."* Let us not fall into this temptation.

Let me add a comment on the New Testament teaching on

priesthood. The idea of a separate priesthood in Christianity whose function is to act as a representative and go-between for "normal" Christians to come to God is completely foreign to the Bible. 1 Peter 2:4-10 describes all Christians as a royal priesthood. This doctrine is sometimes called the priesthood of all believers. The idea of a disciple of Jesus coming to God through the mediation of a human being is unknown to biblical teaching, as seen from 1 Timothy 2:5: *"For there is one God and one mediator between God and men, the man Jesus Christ, who gave himself as a ransom for all men."*

QUESTION:
What happened in early Christianity from AD 180-311?

ANSWER:
I am going to assume that you did not choose these dates arbitrarily. Probably you found the starting and ending date for your question in a book you read. Possibly, the start date of your question is the publication of Irenaeus' book, Against Heresies, which some think of as the first published systematic theology. Most likely, the end date for your question, AD 311, is a reference to the edict of Toleration which was issued by Emperor Constantine, which allowed for the free expression of religion throughout the Roman Empire. Of course, this decree was principally designed by Constantine to officially legalize Christianity. It is fairly natural to divide Christian history between that which occurred before and after the legalization of Christianity in the Roman Empire. By the way, this edict was actually issued in AD 313, not 311.

During the period AD 180-313, a lot of things were happening in the church. Most prominent among them, at least judging by the writings of the early church fathers, was a fight to prevent the influence of heretical teachings about Jesus. Among the heresies strongly opposed by the mainstream church in this time were Montanism, Gnosticism, Arianism and others. I will let you do your own research into these topics, but all of these groups tended to deny some aspect of either the deity or the humanity of Jesus Christ.

Another significant development in the church during this period was the move toward a stronger hierarchical structure. What had been a group of elders in many churches became a head bishop with elders under him. Not only that, but the larger churches had "metropolitans" who had control over the churches in larger regions. There were several levels of such hierarchy. During this time, the head bishop in Rome began to claim a greater authority over all the other bishops, although few others acknowledged such authority.

There was another trend worth noting during this time. This was the tendency to systematize and ritualize Christian practice, including a move toward what Roman Catholics today would call sacraments (priesthood, last rites, baptism and so forth). During this time, baptism of very young children, and even infants, was begun. The worship service became ritualized, with standard prayers, readings and so forth. In addition, the church calendar, including Easter and Christmas, began to take shape.

Another major trend during this time was toward the practice of asceticism. Beginning especially in North Africa, many followers of Jesus chose to express their faith by removing themselves from society, practicing extreme poverty and denying themselves many seemingly normal pleasures, including marriage and family. This eventually led to orders of monks and nuns.

I would be remiss to not mention the persecutions which followers of Jesus went through during this period. Contrary to popular opinion, there was more intense persecution between AD 180 and the edict of Toleration in AD 313 than in the earlier period of the church. The persecution under Decius (AD 249-251) and that under Diocletian and Galerius (AD 303-310) were particularly horrendous.

Many say that the edict of Toleration under Constantine led to the downfall of Christianity, as it led to the acceptance of millions of people into the church who had no concept of discipleship or sacrifice for Jesus. Those who say this have a good point. The acceptance into membership of many who were only nominally believers in Jesus certainly was a major factor in the move toward a worldly church. However, the examples given above show that many of the trends which led to an apostate Roman Catholic Church were begun before AD 313.

QUESTION:

I have heard the claim that the early church fathers were from pagan backgrounds and their basis for explaining the godhead came from Plato and Aristotle and that they therefore cannot be trusted in terms of their view of God. Is this true?

ANSWER:

First of all, the statement that the early church fathers were from a pagan background is true to a great extent. The only writer of the New Testament who may have had a pagan background is Luke. For this reason, the statement you have heard would not apply to the New Testament writers. However, it would be relevant to most of the writings of the early church fathers such as Irenaeus, Polycarp, Clement of Rome, Origin, Tertullian and so forth. Many of these early church fathers wrote extensively on Christianity and were of pagan (mainly Greek) background. Because we are talking about non-biblical writers, this issue is not of great relevance to most Christians. A majority do not even read the early church fathers. If one restricts oneself to the New Testament, the answer is that this claim does not hold up.

However, let us get back to the early church fathers. Like I already stated, it is true that many of them were from pagan backgrounds. As time passed, some of them did allow themselves to be influenced to a significant extent by their pagan backgrounds. Platonic or neo-Platonic philosophy had a noticeable (and sometimes even profound) influence on some writers. Justin Martyr was thoroughly trained in Platonic thought. He used many of the ideas of Platonism to explain Christianity to his intellectual readers. Justin is a hero to many, being the first important Christian apologist. What is less well known is his willingness to concede some validity to the teachings of Aristotle, Plato and others. Many of the early Christian authors freely borrowed in this way from the pagan philosophers. They called it "borrowing from the Egyptians" (using an analogy to what Israel did when they took riches from the Egyptians at the time of their escape from Egypt). Justin considered Plato something like a pre-Christian philosopher; seeming to imply that his teachings were almost inspired by God.

Origin and his disciples in Alexandria went even farther in this direction than Justin. Origin's principle mode of interpreting the scripture was by allegory. To allegorize is to look for hidden, non-literal meaning behind the obvious literal meaning of the text. Such interpretation is rarely justified. He learned allegorical interpretation from the pagan philosophers. Origin was a leading theologian in the orthodox church of his day. He was greatly concerned with explaining and rationalizing Christian theology to intellectuals of a Greek mindset. His philosophical speculations, seemingly borrowing much from pagan philosophy, eventually led to him being declared a heretic after his death.

The examples already given are of mainstream Christians who borrowed from pagan philosophy. Of course, the Gnostics also borrowed from pagan ideas. In fact, one can make a strong case that they were principally pagan in their thinking, and only had a veneer of true Christianity in their theology. They borrowed from neo-Platonism, dualistic religion and the Mystery Cults, teaching that Jesus was a spiritual but not a physical being, and that Jehovah, the God of the Old Testament, was an evil, earthly God. Scholars believe that the book of 1 John was written in part to counteract Gnostic influence.

There may be an underlying motivation to the claim you have heard. I am thinking that the one who made this claim may be trying to insinuate that Greek/pagan ideas made their way into the New Testament itself. This claim is much harder to prove. I am not sure that I can absolutely and categorically deny that any pagan ideas had any influence at all on the writers of the New Testament. However, the biblical idea of the one God of the universe coming to Earth as a physical being and taking on the sin of all humanity as a sacrifice for sin is fundamentally opposed to any idea of Aristotle, Plato or the other pagan philosophers. Add to this the fact that the Old Testament is filled with foreshadows, prophecies, prefigures and types which anticipated exactly this idea. There are not many scholars who would be brazen enough to claim that Isaiah was influenced by pagan philosophy. For information on the Old Testament foreshadows of the gospel message, you can read my book, **FSTR**.

Getting back to your original question, the claim of the writers you mention is true to some extent. Although you can surely trust the New Testament for good theology (ideas about God), you should read the writings of the early church fathers with a grain of salt, knowing that even though most of them were sincere and were believers in Jesus, they may have been influenced by their pagan backgrounds in ways which influenced their theology to some extent.

QUESTION:

I've heard many people claim that the apostles would not have let themselves be put to death for a lie, and this should be taken into consideration when studying the evidence for Jesus. But what evidence outside of the scriptures do we have that the apostles were actually put to death?

ANSWER:

I respect your desire to be sure that when you make a point about the early church the claim is historically verifiable. It is tempting to use "common knowledge" or preacher's examples which are not verified by evidence.

It is "common knowledge" that all the apostles were killed for their faith, with the likely exception of the apostle John. According to tradition, the Romans attempted to execute John, but he survived the attempt, living to a very old age. The careful person will ask where this tradition comes from and how reliable the resources for such tradition are.

The only apostle whose martyrdom is recorded in scripture is James, the son of Zebedee. His execution by Herod Agrippa in AD 44 is described in Acts 12:1-2. Although pagan authors do not mention the death of the apostle James, the Jewish historian Josephus does describe the death of Herod Agrippa (Antiquities of the Jews, XIX, 8), including details in good agreement with Luke's description in Acts 12:21-23. Josephus is considered a relatively reliable historian. This agreement in detail between Luke and Josephus lends indirect extra-biblical support to the martyrdom of the apostle James.

The only companion of Jesus whose martyrdom is specifically described by non-Christian sources is James "the Just," the brother of Jesus and the assumed author of the book of James. His execution in AD 62 by stoning under Ananus the high priest is described by Josephus (Antiquities of the Jews, XX, 9). James was the principal leader of the church in Jerusalem at that time.

For information concerning the persecution and execution of the other apostles, one must turn to Christian historians. The most important of these is Eusebius. Eusebius was bishop of Caesarea in the early 300s AD. His book *Ecclesiastical History* includes accounts of the executions of Peter and Paul under the emperor Nero in Rome, as well as stories of the persecution and execution of most of the other apostles. There is no reason to assume that Eusebius made up his accounts. However it would be fair to say that Eusebius is not an extremely reliable historian. Besides, he wrote over 200 years after the events. The number of witnesses to the death of Paul and Peter in Rome, including several before Eusebius is sufficient that we can say with quite a bit of confidence that these two were martyred for their faith. You will do well to be cautious about stating that we know how the other apostles died.

I believe you may, with clear conscience, continue to share with people that the apostles maintained their faith and their claim that Jesus was raised from the dead to their deaths. They did so in spite of the fact that certainly some, and probably most, of them were martyred for their faith. After the execution of James, a death sentence was hanging over the heads of all the apostles, either as an immediate threat or at least as a likely eventuality for the rest of their lives. This provides very strong evidence that these men were absolutely convinced that Jesus Christ was raised from the dead.

Chapter Sixteen

General Biblical Questions

QUESTION:
    Christians say that the Old Testament is inspired, and that the Jews were the chosen people. What changed this? The Torah states 23 times "this is an eternal law for all generations" (to name a few, Exodus 12:14, 12:17, 12:43, 27:21, 28:43). If the Torah was at one point true, then this statement implies that all of the laws in the Torah must be kept and not "replaced" for eternity. Likewise, concerning Jesus Christ, many times the Torah warns against false prophets—what makes Jesus a "true prophet," not antithetical to Torah's warnings?

ANSWER:
    I just had a student leave my office less than five minutes ago who was asking the exact same question! This is an interesting one. The key is the meaning of the Hebrew. The Hebrew word which is translated forever is also translated "until the end of the age." In that sense, the covenant with Moses did indeed last forever. It lasted until the end of the age. A new age began along with the New Covenant. The Old Testament gives clear testimony that God was planning on giving a new covenant. Jeremiah 31:31-34 says, *"The time is coming,*

declares the Lord, when I will make a new covenant with the house of Israel and with the house of Judah...I will put my law in their minds and write it on their hearts...For I will forgive their wickedness and will remember their sins no more." In the Hebrew sense, "forever" ended when a new covenant was put into place.

    Jesus said that he did not come to abolish the law (of Moses), but to fulfill the law (Matthew 5:17). That is exactly what he did. Jesus brought the requirements of the Mosaic Law to completion through his life and his death on the cross. The book of Hebrews does a wonderful job of explaining this. Hebrews 10:9 says, *"He sets aside the first to establish the second."* Hebrews 9:13-14 adds, *"The blood of goats and bulls and the ashes of a heifer sprinkled on those who are ceremonially unclean sanctify them so that they are outwardly clean. How much more, then, will the blood of Christ, who through the eternal Spirit offered himself unblemished to God, cleanse our consciences from acts that lead to death...For this reason, Christ is the mediator of a new covenant..."* Colossians 2:16 calls the New Moons, Sabbaths and so forth shadows of the New Covenant reality. To summarize, the Torah always has been and still is true. However, the covenant established at Sinai has been replaced by a new and greater covenant.

    Jesus is a true prophet for many reasons. First of all, in Deuteronomy 13:1-3, it says that if a prophet predicts something and it does not happen, then that person is not a prophet. Jesus predicted the destruction of Jerusalem in AD 70 with great accuracy (Luke 21:20). His predictive prophecy came true. Based on his correct prediction of future history, he is qualified as a prophet. Second, God told Moses that he would raise up a prophet "like him" from among the Jews (Deut 18:18-19). Moses gave the first covenant, Jesus gave the second covenant. In many ways, Jesus was like Moses. Both set God's people free. Both left a position at the right hand of a king to serve God's people. Both went out into the desert to prepare for their ministry (Jesus for 40 days, Moses for 40 years). Moses gave the people bread from heaven, Jesus is the bread which came down from heaven (John 6:32-33). Both were under a death penalty as infants due to the jealousy of a king. The list of ways in which Jesus was like Moses is truly amazing (more in **FSTR** ch. 2). Given all these things, we can be assured that Jesus was the prophet God told Moses would come after him.

    Jesus fulfilled every one of the prophecies of the Messiah. He was born in Bethlehem (Micah 5:2). He was sold for 30 pieces of silver (Zechariah 11:12-13). He was crucified (Psalms 22:16) and so forth. Jesus said he fulfilled all the prophecies (Luke 24:44). History lends credence to this claim. For this and many other reasons, we can be assured that Jesus is the true prophet, priest and king—the Messiah.

QUESTION:

The "correct" religion should not only have an outstanding code of ethics, but those who follow this religion should have the highest level of morality. How does Christianity explain the recent indictments of the priests and the high percentage of immorality among people who profess Christianity?

ANSWER:

It certainly is true that the sex-abuse scandals of the past few years are hard to justify, given that these priests claimed to represent Jesus Christ to the world. I do not believe that the Roman Catholic priesthood and its hierarchy should in any way be taken to represent true Christianity. The Roman church became apostate from true biblical Christianity a long time ago. Some of the evidence for this is the behavior of the priesthood over the centuries—especially during the Middle Ages. I believe the Roman hierarchy lost its right to claim to be "the church" a long time ago. Nevertheless, they profess Christianity and they clearly have a major morality scandal on their hands.

Human beings are not perfect, and one cannot expect perfection, even of true disciples of Jesus. However, the corrupt priesthood system, the papacy and many other traditions of Catholicism are not part of true Christianity. It is not reasonable to judge Christianity based on people who profess the religion but are not part of it.

Jesus said that *"you will know that they are my disciples by their love for one another"* (John 13:35). It is not my right to judge individual members of any Christian group, but Jesus said, *"By their fruit you will recognize them"* (Matthew 7:20). Jesus commanded us to take up our cross daily, deny self and follow him. I am deeply saddened that some priests did these things. Whether or not they are true Christians, they give Christianity a bad name.

What should we do about this? We cannot undo the grossly hypocritical acts of certain people. What we can do is watch our life and doctrine closely (paraphrasing 1 Timothy 4:16). As individual followers of Jesus, we need to join in with a fellowship of believers. This group will not be perfect, but their fellowship will be marked by an uncommon love. They will not be perfect, but you will find a heartfelt commitment to righteousness in the people. You will find a group dedicated to putting the teachings of the Bible into practice on a daily basis. You will find a group something like the model in Acts 2:42-47. It is disturbing that a small but significant percentage of leaders in a particular group have been guilty of outrageous behavior. It is frustrating that several hypocritical and greedy televangelists have set a horrible moral example as well. We cannot change this, but we can repudiate such behavior and join with a group who are devoted to walking as Jesus did.

QUESTION:

Mark 16:16 says that signs would accompany those who believe, and John says that we can do greater work than Jesus Christ. What are these greater works?

ANSWER:

Although I can see how one might make the connection, I would be cautious about using Mark 16:16 to interpret John 14:12. Let me start with the John passage. It seems that, in this context, Jesus is making the point that the Kingdom of God is about to arrive in a special way, and that those who are part of this new revelation of the Kingdom will, almost by definition, be doing greater things. Various words can be used to describe the change which Jesus revealed was about to come about. It is described as a new covenant (Jeremiah 31:31). Some theologians call it a new dispensation. Some call it a new Kingdom, although that terminology may be questionable. It is probably more accurate to say that the Kingdom of God came in a new and special way at the day of Pentecost, when the Spirit was poured out on the apostles. A citizen of a greater and more special Kingdom is in a sense greater than any citizen of the former kingdom (i.e. Israel). A passage which supports this interpretation is Matthew 11:11, which says that anyone in the "Kingdom" is greater than John the Baptist. Who among us would claim to be greater than John the Baptist? Yet, Jesus says we are greater than John. Why is that? We are greater than John, not because of any great work we have done, but because we are part of the spiritual Kingdom of God.

The next question regarding John 14:12 is whether there is any actual, specific "thing" which those in the Kingdom of God (i.e. those who are saved by Jesus) will be doing? I believe that Jesus is not talking about specific acts (such as miraculous exploits) in John 14:12. However, it is worth mentioning that after Jesus died and was raised, those in the Kingdom of God have the privilege of ushering people into salvation through the blood of Jesus. Helping to save souls for eternity is an act greater than anything done by people before Jesus died on the cross. When the Spirit was poured out on the day of Pentecost (Acts 2), this ushered in a new manifestation of the Kingdom. Under the New Covenant, people can be guaranteed their salvation, they can be washed by the blood of Jesus and they can be given the Holy Spirit as a deposit (Ephesians 1:13-14). In that sense, a lowly Christian can do things even greater than Jesus had done up to that time.

It is extremely unlikely that Jesus is referring to miraculous works in John 14:12. First of all, that is not the point of the passage. Second, it is doubtful that any of us will surpass Jesus as a worker of miracles. Even if we were to do the acts implied in Mark 16:16, we would not surpass Jesus as a worker of miracles.

Lastly, this brings me to Mark 16:16. I have already shown that Jesus is probably not referring to working miracles in John 14:12. This means that Mark 16:16 will probably not help us to understand John 14. Nevertheless, there are some Christians who definitely see a connection between the two passages. Let us consider this possibility. First of all, it is worth bearing in mind that there is a significant amount of doubt about whether Mark 16:9-16 was in the original book of Mark. The earliest manuscripts did not include this passage, and many doubt its authenticity. This may make interpretation of the passage a moot point. In any case, Jesus appears to be saying in Mark 16:16 that miracles will accompany those who believe. I believe that if we allow the entire New Testament to give this passage context, the most reasonable conclusion is that Jesus is talking about the miraculous gifts which were made available in the first century church by the laying on of hands by apostles. This passage is not about the church in modern times, but about the early church, when gifts were necessary in order to confirm the message (Hebrews 2:4) because the New Testament was not complete. What I am saying is that, in Mark 16:16, Jesus is giving the apostles a list of "signs" which will accompany the believers in the first-century church which validated that their message was from God.

To summarize, to make a connection between John 14:12 and Mark 16:16 is probably not helpful. In the John passage, Jesus is talking about a spiritual greatness for those in the Kingdom of God which no one before—not even Jesus—had. Those in the Kingdom of God have the Spirit, they have salvation, they have forgiveness of sins and they are in Christ. Based on this consideration, Jesus is probably not talking about the miraculous, and Mark 16:16 will not help us to understand John 14:12.

QUESTION:
Please help me understand the prophecy about 666. Is it literal? Will some people really get forehead markings?

ANSWER:
The only biblical use of the number 666 is in Revelation 13:18. Almost without question, this number is to be taken symbolically, not literally. Of course, many have used the literal number 666 to reach all kinds of conclusion, but this is not justified. A few years ago, many pointed out that Ronald Reagan's first, middle and last names all had six letters in them. Coincidence, these people asked? Ronald Reagan was the Beast? I assume they have since moved on to other unjustified literal applications of the apocalyptic literature in Revelation.

In order to understand the meaning and application of the number 666, it is important to bear in mind that the visions in Revelation are written in what is known as apocalyptic language. This was a common mode of writing for the Jews, especially in the two or three centuries before and after the time of Jesus. Old Testament books written in apocalyptic style include all of Zechariah and Joel, as well as parts of Ezekiel and Daniel. In most biblical writing, statements should be taken literally unless the context demands otherwise. With apocalyptic writing, the opposite applies. The descriptions should be taken symbolically unless the context demands otherwise. To illustrate this, in Acts 2:16-21, Peter says that the description in Joel 2:28-32 was being fulfilled before their eyes. Joel described an event including *"signs on the earth below, blood and fire and billows of smoke. The sun will be turned to darkness and the moon to blood before the coming of the great and glorious day of the Lord."* Peter says this (i.e. the coming of the Holy Spirit at Pentecost) is the fulfillment of the prophecy in Joel. The sun did not literally turn to darkness that day in Jerusalem. Neither did the moon turn to blood. Here is the point with apocalyptic language—the meaning is symbolic.

The book of Revelation is perhaps the most clear-cut example of apocalyptic writing in the Bible. We are not to take the description of "the Beast out of the earth" literally. Neither are we to take the numbers in the book literally. In Hebrew literature, the number seven represents perfection, while the number six is the number of man, or the number of wordliness, or of Satan. It is the number of mankind in rebellion to God. The passage in Revelation 13:18 confirms this interpretation: *"for it is man's number."* When God states that the number of the beast is 666, he is saying that this represents a great power which is aligned against God and the spiritual forces in heaven.

Let me share my opinion about who this "Beast" is. I believe that, in the context of Revelation, the Beast is Rome and its power over humanity. It almost certainly is not an individual person some time in the indefinite future, as many popular Christian teachers claim. Rome was the great enemy of the saints. Rome tried to destroy the church. I believe that all the descriptions in Revelation 13 apply well to Rome, its power, and its opposition to the Lord's church. John was told that his vision concerned events which would soon take place (Revelation 1:1). This causes me to assume that most of the prophecies and visions in the book applied to the situation of the church in the first centuries under the persecution of Rome. Those who look for some sort of beast with a literal number 666, or for people to have that number branded on them, are most likely chasing a fantasy.

With any prophecy, a good piece of advice is to say "time will tell." Perhaps time will show that my interpretation is not correct. Humility is called for. Perhaps the visions in Revelation describe the persecutions of Rome against the church, but also have a second fulfillment in the future. It is my opinion that this is not the case, but we will see.

QUESTION:

Who is Melchizedek, the person mentioned in Hebrews Chapter 11?

ANSWER:

Melchizedek is an interesting and enigmatic figure in the Bible. He is the person Abraham met after defeating a coalition of forces which had earlier defeated Sodom and captured Lot. What is intriguing here is that Melchizedek is called a priest of Jehovah even though he lived hundreds of years before the Levitical priesthood was established during the time of Moses. In Genesis 14, Abraham acknowledges the spiritual authority of Melchizedek, giving him an offering of 10% of all he had gained in the war. A messianic prophecy in Psalm 110:4 gives another enigmatic hint about this character Melchizedek. It says that the future Messiah will be a priest, not from the order of Aaron, but from the order of Melchizedek.

The writer of Hebrews picks up on this, declaring Jesus as a priest, not by physical descent from Levi, but by spiritual descent from Melchizedek, the priest of the High God to whom Abraham gave tribute. The difference between Melchizedek and priests from the order of Aaron is that he was chosen directly by God as priest, and was not born into his position. Like Melchizedek, Jesus is priest on his own merits, not by birth. Similarly, we become priests of God when we are baptized into Christ, not by physical birth, but by spiritual rebirth. The point of the Hebrew writer is that Jesus, as high priest, is far above the Jewish high priests.

QUESTION:
What needs were answered by Christianity?

ANSWER:
Rather than state my own ideas, I will simply list a few (hundreds could be listed) Bible verses in answer to your question.

Romans 3:23-25: *"There is no difference, for all have sinned and fall short of the glory of God, and are justified freely by his grace through the redemption that came by Jesus. God presented him as a sacrifice of atonement, through faith in his blood."*

Romans 5:1: *"Therefore, since we have been justified through faith, we have peace with God through our Lord Jesus Christ, through whom we have gained access by faith into this grace in which we now stand."*

Romans 5:9-10: *"Since we have now been justified by his blood, how much more shall we be saved from God's wrath through him! For if, when we were God's enemies, we were reconciled to him through the death of his Son, how much more, having been reconciled, shall we be saved through his life!"*

Ephesians 2:1-8: *"As for you, you were dead in your transgressions and sins, in which you used to live when you followed the ways of this world and of the ruler of the kingdom of the air, the spirit who is now at work in those who are disobedient. All of us also lived among them at one time, gratifying the cravings of our sinful nature and following its desires and thoughts. Like the rest, we were by nature objects of wrath. But because of his great love for us, God, who is rich in mercy, made us alive with Christ even when we were dead in transgressions—it is by grace you have been saved. And God raised us up with Christ and seated us with him in the heavenly realms in Christ Jesus, in order that in the coming ages he might show the incomparable riches of his grace, expressed in his kindness to us in Christ Jesus. For it is by grace you have been saved, through faith—and not from yourselves, it is the gift of God."*

Romans 6:23: *"For the wages of sin is death, but the gift of God is eternal life in Christ Jesus our Lord."*

Christianity does not necessarily fulfill all our desires, but all of our needs are fulfilled in abundance, both in this life and in eternity. Those who are in Christ have forgiveness of sins, they have a relationship with God, they have the hope of eternal life and they have abundant life in the here and now. Through Christ, our need for forgiveness, for love and for purpose is fulfilled.

QUESTION:

Does Hebrews 6:4-7 teach that those who fall away cannot repent? Does God prevent them from being restored to the faith? Also, in Matthew 24:12, what does it mean when it says that the love of most will grow cold?

ANSWER:

Hebrews 6:4-7 says: *"It is impossible for those who have once been enlightened, who have tasted the heavenly gift, who have shared in the Holy Spirit, who have tasted the goodness of the word of God and the powers of the coming age, if they fall away, to be brought back to repentance, because, to their loss they are crucifying the Son of God all over again and subjecting him to public disgrace."* If one simply reads this passage in isolation, two possible interpretations come to mind. It could mean that for a person who falls away, their heart must be so hard that it becomes impossible for them to repent again. Another possible interpretation is that once a person falls away, God will not accept them once again to renew their salvation—he prevents them from being saved again. In order to decide which interpretation is the correct one, let us go elsewhere in Hebrews and then look throughout the New Testament. The first passage that comes to mind which helps me to decide which interpretation is correct is Hebrews 10:26-30. This passage says, *"If we deliberately keep on sinning after we have received the knowledge of the truth no sacrifice for sins is left...Anyone who rejected Moses died without mercy on the testimony of two or three witnesses. How much more severely do you think a man deserves to be punished who has trampled the Son of God under foot...who has insulted the Spirit of grace?...It is a dreadful thing to fall into the hands of the living God."*

Based on this passage, I am convinced that when a person "falls away," the Holy Spirit (the deposit guaranteeing our salvation Eph 1:14) is taken away from that person. We become liable to spiritual death again. Hebrews 6:4-6 states emphatically that this position is impossible to escape. As it says in 2 Peter 2:19-20, *"we are worse off than we were at first"* if we are saved but *"again entangled and overcome."* Falling away is irreversible. Once we insult the Spirit and God removes the Holy Spirit from us, we are lost for eternity.

This conclusion has important implications about the doctrine of falling away. Many refer to people who no longer attend their church as a fall-away. I believe we should be reticent to make such a judgment. Many have talked about trying to bring a fall-away back to repentance, when this is not possible. Instead, I believe we should say something like, "this brother or sister is not being faithful now." Who am I to judge someone as fallen away? Only God can decide and it is a dreadful thing to fall into the hands of the living God.

So, to answer your question, it is God who makes it impossible for us to be saved once we have committed the unforgivable sin, have insulted the Spirit, have trampled on the blood of Jesus and have committed blasphemy against the Holy Spirit. I suppose one can argue that such a person would be unable to repent anyway, but I do not want to speculate on such a thing. If we reject the grace of God in such a blatant way that he takes away the Holy Spirit, then this is a final judgment of God. This is a hard teaching, but I believe it is the best way to interpret passages on this subject.

On Matthew 24:12, the "most" is us (assuming that we are saved). Just like the Hebrews in the wilderness (Hebrews 3:14-4:7), most of whom did not make it, the sad fact is that many of those who are saved will not prove faithful. I believe that Matthew 24:12 is referring to a particular situation; perhaps the destruction of Jerusalem, or more likely at the very end of days. At this time, most will not prove faithful, but the gospel will be preached to all nations, then the end will come. Matthew 24 is a fairly difficult passage to interpret because Jesus bounces back and forth between talking about the destruction of Jerusalem (ex. 24:15-21) and about his return at the end of time (ex. 24:30-31). For this reason, I would not want to make very confident statements about which 24:12 refers to, but I believe it is about the end of days. However, Matthew 24:12 has an application to all Christians as a warning that we must stand firm. Either way, for us it is a warning to strive to remain faithful.

QUESTION:

Could the Greek for "he" and "him" in John 1:1 be better translated "it"? If so, the Word (logos) might not be a person, and in a sense, not God.

ANSWER:

Let me begin by saying that I am not an expert in Greek. Please take whatever I say with a grain of salt and plan on doing some of your own research. I assume you are referring, not to John 1:1, but to

John 1:2, where the verse reads, *"He was with God in the beginning."* The word translated as "He" here is the Greek houtos, which most literally would be translated as "This one." The word does refer back to logos. So the passage could read, "This one (i.e. the *logos*) was with God in the beginning. If I am not mistaken, it could have been translated as either he or it, depending on the context.

Why, then, is it translated as "he" rather than "it"? Could this be some sort of conspiracy to push a particular theological agenda? I already said that the context determines the translation. If one moves down just a few verses, one comes to John 1:14, which reads, *"The Word became flesh and lived for a while among us. We have seen his glory, the glory of the one and only Son, who came from the Father, full of grace and truth."* This passage inescapably identifies the logos of John 1:1 as Jesus Christ, the Son of God. In John 1:14, the Word (logos) is definitely male in gender, which determines the context for John 1:2, demanding the word "he" not "it."

I am sure that you could get a more thorough and scholarly treatment of the Greek from another source, but I suspect that this is more or less what you will get from anyone who knows the Greek well, is fair-minded and does not have a particular theological axe to grind. In conclusion, I suspect that the person whose work you read is trying to use Greek grammar to push a particular theological agenda. The claim that the word translated as "he" could in some cases be translated as "it" is true, but to say that it demands "it" or even to say that the context implies "it" is not supported by the passage.

QUESTION:

Can you help me understand the nature of the trinity? I have heard a scholar say that there are three Gods having different personalities. Another says that there is one God who is three persons. What is the truth about this?

ANSWER:

Thousands of volumes and, believe it or not, more than one war has been fought over this question. I would not be so arrogant as to think that I can add a lot to this discussion. The question of the nature of God is broad and deep. Let me mention one interpretation which is definitely not correct and give at least a foundation on which you can base your own study and thinking.

First, there are not three Gods: *"Hear, O Israel: The Lord our God the Lord is one"* (Deuteronomy 6:4). The New Testament does not introduce polytheism. Jesus said, *"I and the Father are one"* (John

10:30). Jesus was not created by the Father, but existed with him from the beginning: *"Before Abraham was born, I AM"* (John 8:58). The same could be said of the Holy Spirit. In Genesis 1:2, the Holy Spirit is described as being an agent in the creation of the world. Jesus, the Son is also described as an agent in the creation and the one who holds together the world. Colossians 1:16 says of Jesus, *"For by him all things were created: things in heaven and on earth, visible and invisible, whether thrones or powers or rulers or authorities; all things were created by him and for him."* Colossians also says of Jesus that *"He is before all things"* (Colossians 1:17).

What about the "trinity?" It is worth bearing in mind that nothing like the word trinity is found in the Bible. The word was coined by theologians in the early church to explain the nature of God. The first to use this word was Tertullian at the end of the second century. There is nothing wrong with the word trinity, but it comes with some theological baggage within Roman Christianity with which I am personally not comfortable. I tend not to use this word to describe God because of the theological implications within Catholicism with which it tends to be associated.

Nevertheless, the implication of the word trinity is that God is somehow three and one at the same time. This much is true. It is extremely difficult to put the Bible's description of God into simple terms, but this comes about as close as any. In John 1:1, Jesus is described in the following well-known statement: *"In the beginning was the Word, and the Word was with God, and the Word was God. He was with God in the beginning."* Verse 14 continues, *"The Word became flesh and lived for a while among us. We have seen his glory, the glory of the one and only Son..."* John describes Jesus as the Son who is with God and who at the same time is God. In human terms, this description is not logical. Nevertheless, this is how God describes himself. There are several phrases which describe the nature of the trinity in a helpful way. One can think of the Son, the Spirit and the Father as three aspects of God, or perhaps three emanations of the godhead. I believe the description you quote from a scholar that God has three personalities is not appropriate. I see no difference in personality between the Father, the Son or the Spirit, although there is a difference of role. Some have tried to describe the three-in-one nature of God using the analogy of the three forms of water: ice, liquid water and steam, but as a chemist, I believe that this analogy is not particularly helpful.

Theologians will write their treatises, scholars will accumulate sources claiming to explain the three-fold nature of God and skeptics will scoff at this doctrine, but in the end, the believer is left to ponder the awesome and inscrutable nature of God. It would take a lifetime to take it all in. Fortunately, we do not have to have a completely understandable and logical description of God to know that he loves us, that he died for us and that we must come to him and repent of our sins to be saved and to avoid separation from God forever. I suggest you spend most of your energy sticking to the basics of obeying your Creator, but continue at times to step back and consider the awesome nature of our God.

QUESTION:

Why does the Bible talk about slavery, and why did God allow slavery in the Old Testament?

ANSWER:

One reason the Bible talks about the practice is that slavery was a very common phenomenon in both Old Testament and New Testament times. It is only natural that the topic would come up, both from a legal stand point and simply as a common part of the history recorded in both Testaments.

Your second question is more challenging. The fact is that God does not condemn slavery in the Old Testament. This may seem odd to us, as slavery is such a clear violation of basic human justice. It is true that the owning of slaves is not outlawed in the Old Testament, but neither is it encouraged. You will not find a single passage of scripture which in any way encourages any follower of God to own slaves. However, in the Old Covenant, God did allow for slavery. We should bear in mind that God allowed a number of practices under the Old Covenant which he nevertheless did not want his people to participate in. God made concessions under the Old Covenant for divorce, although he never wanted divorce to happen: *"Moses [and presumably God] permitted you to divorce because your hearts were hard. But it was not this way from the beginning"* (Matthew 19:8). I assume God's attitude toward slavery in the Old Testament falls into the same category. Slavery was a fact of life in the ancient world. Victory in battle produced slaves. Therefore, for reasons we cannot know for sure, God chose to regulate the cruelty of slavery rather than to ban it outright for the Jews under the Law of Moses. He commanded that slaves be set free automatically after a certain amount of time. He forbade excessive cruelty to slaves. He commanded that they be allowed a certain level of access to the ceremonies of Judaism and so forth. See Deuteronomy 23:15, Leviticus 25:44-46 and Leviticus 19:20 for some of the regulations on slavery. The regulations in the

Old Testament, if obeyed, made slavery in Israel more tolerable and humane than any of their neighbors.

What about the New Testament? Slavery is neither specifically allowed nor specifically condemned in the New Testament. At first, knowing Jesus' teaching, this may seem a bit surprising. Clearly, Jesus would never own slaves! Nevertheless, slavery was a pervasive institution under Greek/Roman civilization—as many as half of all people were slaves. If Jesus had declared all slaves free under the New Covenant, it would have brought unnecessary persecution down on the early church. Perhaps this is why God chose not to specifically condemn slavery. Paul encouraged Philemon to free his slave, Onesimus. Yet, in general, he encouraged new disciples, even slaves, to be willing to stay in the situation they were in when converted. As far as God is concerned, whether one is a slave or free here on Earth is not the main issue. The chief concern is whether one is a slave to sin. God, through Paul, encouraged Christian slaves to be the best possible workers for their masters in order that they might come to Christ. He also encouraged them to seek freedom if they could. He did not incite slaves to revolt from their masters. I am sure that a slave who was owned by a Christian in Rome would have lived under fair conditions, if he or she was not freed outright.

It is worth noting that, in the end, it was Christianity and the teachings of the Bible which led to the worldwide ban on slavery. William Wilberforce, the British parliamentarian used a more than thirty year campaign based on Christian principles to finally shame the British into banning slavery throughout the British empire. History tells us that it was the teachings of Jesus which caused the downfall of one of the cruelest institutions mankind ever invented.

QUESTION:

How can Jesus sit at the right hand of God when God is a spiritual, not a physical being? The Bible also talks about us singing in heaven, but that is physical. How can you explain this?

ANSWER:

The writers of the Bible, especially the writers of the Old Testament, often use metaphorical language when referring to God. This is especially true in poetic writing such as Psalms and Job. The Bible never portrays God as a physical being with physical attributes. He is always portrayed as spiritual. However, it should not be surprising to us that those who write about him use physical analogies to describe God. There is a technical term for this. When one uses physical, human attributes to describe something which is not physical or not human-like, it is called anthropomorphism. When the Bible says that God looks down on us, we do not infer that God literally has eyes. When David says that God's hand lifts him up, he is using metaphorical language to describe how God helps him in times of trouble. Isaiah 40:22 says that God sits above the circle of the Earth. God does not literally sit. Neither is he "above" the Earth. Isaiah assumes that the reader understands his references to be metaphorical. In Psalms 23:4, David says of God that *"your rod and staff comfort me."* Again, David obviously does not mean that God literally has a rod and a staff, but that, metaphorically, as a shepherd takes care of his sheep, God takes care of his people.

In the same way, when the Bible describes Jesus sitting at the right hand of God, this is metaphorical. God does not have hands. Presumably, he neither sits nor stands. What the Bible is saying is that, in heaven, the Son takes second place in authority to the Father. Jesus said, *"For I did not speak of my own accord, but the Father who sent me commanded me what to say and how to say it. I know that his command leads to eternal life. So whatever I say is just what the Father has told me to say"* (John 12:49-50). Jesus is God. He is equal to the Father, yet he takes a submissive role to the Father. The Bible describes this as sitting at the Father's right hand.

As for singing in heaven, I am not sure what to say about that. We do not know enough about what our bodies will be like. Will they be physical? Probably not! (1 Corinthians 15:50-54) Will we sing literally, or will we sing metaphorically? I am not sure, but I do know that it will be a joyous thing.

QUESTION:

I was fielding some good questions from co-workers today. "If the 'all roads lead to heaven' philosophy is not true, then how do we know which one is right? I know many people from different religions that seem very happy and fulfilled from their faith. It's not fair that God will send people to hell if they're wrong on some doctrine but are very sincere about knowing him." A co-worker who believes in Judaism asked me straight out if I thought he would go to hell right now if he died. I told him God will judge, but he would not let me off the hook. How would you respond to such a question?

ANSWER:

First of all, good job for being out there, getting into such conversations! On the first question, I will challenge people with what may seem obvious to us, but not to much of the world, especially in a postmodern age. Two diametrically opposed claims cannot both be simultaneously true. If Venezuela is in South America, then it cannot also be in Asia. One person may claim that Venezuela is in South America, another may claim that it is in Asia. At least one of them, or perhaps both of them, must be wrong. Now, let us consider the theology of Hinduism, Buddhism, Islam or any other proposed "way to God." If Buddha was right, then Jesus is a liar and a hoax. The "god" of Buddhism (if there is one, as this religion is not really clear on God) cannot be reconciled with the God of the Bible. If Jesus was who he said he was, then Muhammad cannot be a true prophet of God, because his picture of God is absolutely incompatible with that of the Bible. Besides, Muhammad denied Jesus' deity and his death on the cross. If Jesus is not God, then Christianity is a lie. You cannot have it both ways. In general, it is difficult to convince those who are of the "all roads lead to heaven" philosophy of this obvious truth, but I believe with patience and careful instruction, at the right moment, you may be able to help your friends see this point.

The key is to point people to Jesus—to get them to read the Bible. A good place to start is the book of John. I was having a conversation the other day with a Muslim friend who made a lot of false claims about the Bible. I asked him if he had ever read the Bible, and, of course, he had not. I asked him politely to stop making false claims about the Bible until he reads the book. Of course, it is important that I have read the Koran. Giving your friend a copy of a good book on apologetics might be helpful as well. Those who say "all roads lead to God" clearly do not believe in any of the roads. They do not have faith. Your job is to help them to come to faith.

About your second question, I have been in the exact situation you describe a couple of times (although the religion of the person confronting me and demanding an opinion was different). I agree with your strategy of attempting not to personally judge people. However, if someone confronts you face to face, I believe you are required to be honest and let God do the work. When in this situation, I have simply said that, "based on my understanding of what the Bible says, I would be forced to conclude that you are lost. However, I urge you to check it out for yourself in the Bible so that you can reach your own conclusion." What else can you do?

On the third question, you hit the nail on the head. The key to belief in heaven or hell is not grandma's opinion. It is not some preacher or anyone else. The only legitimate reason I know of to believe in heaven or hell is because they are promised in the Bible. Your role is to encouragingly challenge your friends to be open minded enough to read the Bible.

For more information about the ministry of Dr. Oakes go to
www.EvidenceForChristianity.org

To purchase Dr. Oakes books and audio/video teaching sets go to
www.ipibooks.com

Illumination Publishers International

Toney Mulhollan has been in Christian publishing for over 30 years. He has served as the Production Manager for Crossroads Publications, Discipleship Magazine/UpsideDown Magazine, Discipleship Publications International (DPI) and on the production teams of Campus Journal, Biblical Discipleship Quarterly, Bible Illustrator and others. Toney presently serves as the Editor of Illumination Publishers International. He is happily married to the love of his life, Denise Leonard Mulhollan, M.D. They make their home in Houston, Texas along with their daughters, Audra Joan and Cali Owen.

For the best in Christian writing and audio instruction, go to the Illumination Publishers International website. We're commited to producing in-depth teaching that will inform, inspire and encourage Christians to a deeper and more committed walk with God. You can reach Toney Mulhollan by email at toneyipibooks@mac.com or at his office number, (832) 559-3658.

www.ipibooks.com